ELSEVIER'S DICTIONARY OF POLICE AND CRIMINAL LAW

ELSEVIER'S DICTIONARY OF POLICE AND CRIMINAL LAW

English - French and French - English

compiled by

ROY INGLETON
Legal Translator
Maidstone, Kent, Great Britain

ELSEVIER
Amsterdam – London – New York – Tokyo 1992

ELSEVIER SCIENCE PUBLISHERS B.V.
Sara Burgerhartstraat 25
P.O. Box 211, 1000 AE Amsterdam
The Netherlands

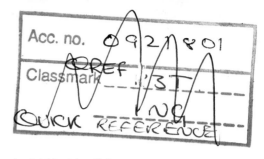

Library of Congress Cataloging-in-Publication Data

Ingleton, Roy D.
    Elsevier's dictionary of police and criminal law : English-French
  and French-English / compiled by Roy Ingleton.
      p.   cm.
    Includes bibliographical references.
    ISBN 0-444-89102-1
      1. Criminal law--Great Britain--Dictionaries. 2. Police--Great
  Britain--Dictionaries. 3. Criminal law--France--Dictionaries.
  4. Police--France--Dictionaries. 5. Criminal law--Great Britain-
  -Dictionaries--French. 6. Police--Great Britain--Dictionaries-
  -French. 7. Criminal law--France--Dictionaries--French. 8. Police-
  -France--Dictionaries--French. 9. English language--Dictionaries-
  -French. 10. French language--Dictionaries--English. I. Title.
  KJC7974.6.I54 1992
  345.41'003--dc20
  [344.10503]   92-19125
                                                                CIP

ISBN: 0-444-89102-1

This book is printed on acid-free paper.

Printed in The Netherlands

Preface

The increased interaction between the police forces in the UK and those in France, resulting from the removal of the restrictions on the movement of persons between the EC countries and manifested in a rapidly-growing professional involvement in criminal matters on either side of the Channel, together with an increasing academic interest in the organisation and work of the police of these two great nations, has prompted the compilation of this work.

Police officers, lawyers, writers of detective novels, professional linguists and others concerned in this rapidly growing field have increasingly expressed their concern at the lack of a single reliable work of reference and term bank to assist them in the translation of the various specialised words and phrases they encounter in the course of their work.

Now, for the first time in a single dictionary, it is possible to find definitive equivalents for, and explanations of, many of the terms used to describe the criminal law and rules of evidence, police organisation and functions (traffic control, drugs, terrorism, accidents and disasters), together with some of the more entrenched slang and jargon terms in common use by both the police and the criminal fraternity. This is supplemented by an extensive list of the relevant acronyms employed in the two languages.

The entries are deliberately designed and reflect the police and criminal justice systems in France and in England and Wales; occasional references are made to those applying in other anglophone (Scotland, USA) and francophone (Belgium, Switzerland) countries, but no attempt has been made to provide a comprehensive record of all the terms used in the Anglo-Saxon and Roman Law legal and policing systems as a whole.

My thanks are due to Liliane Cohen for her invaluable advice, editorial assistance and proof reading and for bringing to my notice many imperfections and omissions which had escaped my attention. I should also like to acknowledge the considerable assistance afforded by the following works:

An English Reader's Guide to the French Legal System. M. Weston, Berg
Collins Robert French Dictionary. B. Atkins et al., Harper Collins
Dictionary of Modern Colloquial French. R.J. Herail & E.A. Lovatt, Routledge
Dictionnaire Economique et Juridique. J. Baleyte et al., Navarre
Dictionnaire Juridique. Lemeunier, La Maison du Dictionnaire
Droit Pénal. C. Penhoat, Aengde-Clet
Droit Pénal et Procédure Pénale. G. Levasseur & A. Chavanne, Sirey

Droit Pénal Général et Procédure Pénale. J. Larguier, Dalloz
European Communities Glossary. EC Terminology Service
Harrap's Standard French & English Dictionary. J.E. Mansion, Harrap
Les Institutions de la France. B. de Gunten et al., Nathan
Lexique de Termes Juridiques. R. Guillien et al., Dalloz
Petit Robert Dictionnaire de la Langue Française

Other bibliographical assistance was obtained from the following periodicals:

The Police Review
Police
La Revue de la Police Nationale
La Revue de la Gendarmerie Française
Revue de la Gendarmerie (Belgium)

Roy Ingleton
April 1992

Abbreviations and Symbols

Abréviations et Symboles

indicates that the expression should be handled with extreme care by the non-native speaker as it may cause offence	*	marque les expressions très familières qui sont à employer avec la plus grande prudence, car l'emploi risque d'être ressenti
indicates a near-equivalent in the target language	=	introduit une équivalence culturelle dans la langue d'arrivée
masculine gender	(m)	genre masculin
feminine gender	(f)	genre féminin
masculine plural	(mpl)	genre masculin pluriel
feminine plural	(fpl)	genre féminin pluriel
both masculine and feminine	(m & f)	genre féminin ou masculin
alternative meanings	(1),(2)	traductions alternatives

Contents

Table des Matières

ENGLISH - FRENCH

ANGLAIS - FRANÇAIS

A

abandon : abandonner, renoncer, se désister, délaisser

    ~ prosecution : renoncer aux poursuites

    ~ed vehicle : véhicule *(m)* abandonné, épave *(f)*, ventouse *(f)*

abandonment : délaissement *(m)*

    ~ of prosecution : délaissement de poursuites

    ~ of child : abandon *(m)* d'enfant

abate : abolir, annuler, diminuer

abatement : annulation *(f)* d'un acte judiciaire, arrêt *(m)* de la procédure

abduction : enlèvement *(m)*, rapt *(m)*

    ~ by consent : rapt par séduction

    ~ of minors : détournement *(m)* de mineurs

abductor : ravisseur *(m)*

abet : provoquer, encourager, soutenir

abetment : incitation *(f)* au crime ou délit

abeyance (law fallen into ~) : (loi tombée en) désuétude *(f)*

abide : demeurer, rester en suspens, se conformer, s'incliner, se soumettre

    ~ by a decision : se soumettre à un jugement

    law-abiding citizen : citoyen *(m)* respectueux des lois

ability : capacité *(f)*, pouvoir *(m)*, compétence *(f)*, aptitude *(f)*

    ~ to pay : capacité de payer

able : capable

abnormal load : convoi *(m)* exceptionnel

abode : demeure *(f)*, habitation *(f)*, résidence *(f)*

    place of ~ : domicile *(m)*, résidence

    of no fixed ~ : sans domicile fixe

    at his usual place of ~ : au lieu ordinaire de son domicile

abolish : abolir, annuler, abroger

abolition : abolition *(f)*, suppression *(f)*

abominal crime : crime *(m)* abominable (sodomie et bestialité)

abortion : avortement *(m)* provoqué

      procuring of ˜ : manoeuvres *(fpl)* abortives

abortionist : faiseuse *(f)* d'anges*

abortive : manqué, avorté

    ˜ offence : infraction *(f)* manquée

above-named : susnommé *(m)*

abroad : à l'étranger

abrogation : abrogation *(f)*

abscond : se soustraire à la justice, fuir, s'évader

absconder : accusé *(m)* défaillant, fugitif *(m)*, évadé *(m)*

absconding : évasion *(f)*

absence : absence *(f)*, défaut *(m)*

    ˜ without pay : congé *(m)* sans solde

    in the ˜ of evidence to the contrary : jusqu'à preuve du contraire

    leave of ˜ : congé *(m)*

    sentence in ˜ : condamnation *(f)* par défaut, par contumace

absentee : insoumis *(m)*

absolute : sans conditions

    ˜ discharge : dispense *(f)* de peine

absolve : absoudre, acquitter

    ˜ from a penalty : remettre une peine

abstract (1) : résumé *(m)*, abrégé *(m)*, sommaire *(m)*, précis *(m)*, extrait *(m)*

    ˜ case : cas *(m)* hypothétique

abstract (2) : distraire, soustraire, détourner

    ˜ funds : détourner des fonds

abuse : (1) abus *(m)*; (2) violenter, souiller, abuser

    ~ of authority : détournement *(m)* de pouvoir

    ~ of process : abus de droit

    child ~ : maltraitance *(f)*

accelerate : accélérer, appuyer sur le champignon

accept : agréer

acceptance (by the court) : qualification *(f)* (judiciaire)

access : accès *(m)*

    right of ~ : droit *(m)* d'accès

accessory : complice *(m&f)*, comparse *(m&f)*
Celui qui aide ou qui pousse une autre personne à commettre une infraction même sans être lui-même présent.

    ~ after the fact : complice après coup, complice par assistance

    ~ before the fact : complice par instigation

accosting : raccrochage *(m)*

accident : accident *(m)*, cas *(m)* fortuit

    ~ report : constat *(m)* d'accident

    failure to stop after an ~ : délit *(m)* de fuite

    fatal ~ : accident mortel

    personal injury ~ : accident corporel, accident de personne

    road traffic ~ : accident de la circulation

accidental : accidentel, par hazard, casuel

accomplice : coauteur *(m)*, équipier *(m)*, complice *(m)*, comparse *(m&f)*

    to be an ~ to a crime : tremper dans un crime

accomplished fact : fait *(m)* accompli

accordance (in ~ with) : conformément à

according (to) : conformément (à), suivant, en fonction (de), selon

accordingly : en conséquence

---

account : (1) compte *(m)*; (2) exposé *(m)*

    falsification of ˜s : faux *(m)* en écritures *(fpl)* comptables

accountability : responsabilité *(f)*

accounting : comptabilité *(f)*

    falŝɛ ˜ : faux *(m)* en écritures *(fpl)*, falsification *(f)* de documents *(mpl)*

accuracy : exactitude *(f)*

accusation : accusation *(f)*, dénonciation *(f)*, fargue *(f)*, inculpation *(f)*

    false ˜ : dénonciation calomnieuse

accusatorial procedure : procédure *(f)* accusatoire (cf. procédure inquisitoire)
*Procédure menée dans certains droits archaïques devant des hommes
libres, et présentant un caractère oral, public et contradictoire, les
preuves étant légales et formelles. Ce type de procédure a été conservé
par certains systèmes juridiques, par ex. l'Angleterre.*

accuse : accuser, incriminer, farguer, inculper

accused : prévenu(e), inculpé(e), accusé(e)

accuser : accusateur *(m)*

achievement : exploit *(m)*

acid * : acide *(m)*, LSD *(m)*

acquit : acquitter

acquittal : acquit *(m)*, acquittement *(m)*, décharge *(f)*

acronym : sigle *(m)*

act : (1) loi *(f)*; (2) acte *(m)*, action *(f)*; (3) agir

    ˜ against the interests of someone : porter atteinte *(f)* aux intérêts de qn.

    ˜ for : faire fonction de, remplacer, suppléer, agir à titre de

    ˜ of God : force *(f)* majeure

    ˜ of Parliament : loi

    ˜ of preparation : acte préparatoire

    ˜ under duress : agir sous contrainte

    criminal ˜ : acte délicteux, acte criminel

acting : par intérim, intérimaire, provisoire

action : action *(f)*, cause *(f)*, instance *(f)*

> **civil ~** : action civile

> **disciplinary ~** : poursuites *(fpl)* disciplinaires

> **penal ~** : poursuite *(f)*

> **~ ultra vires** : excès *(m)* de pouvoir

activity : activité (f), occupation *(f)*

> **fraudulent activities** : agissements *(mpl)* frauduleux

actual : réel, véritable, effectif

> **~ bodily harm** : violence et voies de fait, coups et blessures

> **~ case** : cas concret

> **~ knowledge** : connaissance directe

> **~ possession** : possession effective, possession de fait

> **~ residence** : résidence effective

> **~ strength** : effectif réel

actually : réellement, véritablement, effectivement, au fait

actus reus : corps *(m)* du délit, élément *(m)* légal, faute *(f)*

addicted : accroché (à la drogue)

addiction : assuétude *(f)*

address : adresse *(f)*

> **~ for service** : domicile *(m)* élu

> **~ to the court** : plaidoirie *(f)*, plaidoyer *(m)*

> **counsel's opening ~** : exposé *(m)* des faits, requête *(f)* introductive d'instance

> **full ~** : adresse complète

addressee : destinataire *(m&f)*

adduce : apporter, offrir, alléguer

> **~ evidence** : fournir une preuve

adjective law : procédure

adjourn : ajourner, différer, remettre, renvoyer, suspendre

    ~ a hearing : ajourner/suspendre une audience, remettre une affaire

adjournment : ajournement *(m)*, interruption *(f)*, renvoi *(m)*, remise *(f)*, suspension *(f)*

adjudicate : juger, décider judiciairement, rendre un arrêt, statuer

adjudication : jugement *(m)*, décision *(f)*, prononcé *(m)* d'un jugement

adjutant : adjudant-majeur *(m)*

administer (the oath) : déférer (le serment)

administration : administration *(f)*, direction *(f)*, gestion *(f)*

    ~ of noxious substances : administration de substances nuisibles

    ~ of oaths : assermentation *(f)*

    ~ of regulations : application *(f)* des règlements

administrative : administratif

    ~ charges : frais de dossier

    ~ law : droit administratif

admissibility : recevabilité *(f)*

admissible : recevable

    ~ evidence : preuve *(f)* recevable

admission : admission *(f)*, acceptation *(f)*, confession *(f)*, aveu *(m)*

admit : reconnaître, avouer

    to ~ one's guilt : se reconnaître coupable

admonishment : admonestation *(f)*, blâme *(m)*, réprimande *(f)*

adult : adulte *(m&f)*, majeur *(m)*

adulteration : fraude *(f)* alimentaire, falsification *(f)* d'aliments, frelatage *(m)* (des vins et des alcools)

adulterate : trafiquer

adultery : adultère *(m)*

advanced training course : stage *(m)* de perfectionnement

advantage (to take ~) : profiter, tirer parti

adversarial procedure : voir **accusatorial procedure**

adverse : défavorable

~ **witness** : voir **hostile witness**

advertisement : réclame *(f)*

advice : conseil *(m)*, avis *(m)*

advise : conseiller, recommander, avertir, instruire

adviser : conseiller *(m)*, conseil *(m)*

legal ~ : conseil juridique

advocate : avocat *(m)*

judge-~ general : chef de la justice militaire

aerodrome : aérodrome *(m)*

aeroplane : aéronef *(m)*, avion *(m)*

affidavit : attestation *(f)* par écrit et sous serment

affirmation : affirmation *(f)* solennelle tenant lieu de serment

affix : apposer

to ~ **a seal** : apposer les scellés

affray : menaces *(fpl)*, violence *(f)* et voies de fait, bagarre *(f)*

aforegoing : précédent

aforementioned : susmentionné

aforenamed : susnommé(e)

aforesaid : susdit, susmentionné. précité

aforethought : préméditation *(f)*

with malice ~ : avec intention *(f)* criminelle

age : âge *(m)*

~ **of consent** : nubilité *(f)*

~ **of majority** : majorité *(f)*

old ~ : vieillesse *(f)*

under ~ : minorité *(f)*

agency : agence *(f)*

      travel ~ : agence de voyage

agenda : ordre (m) du jour

agent : agent *(m)*, représentant *(m)*, préposé *(m)*, intermédiaire *(m&f)*

      law enforcement ~ : agent de police

      secret ~ : agent du service des renseignements

aggravate : aggraver, accroître, qualifier

      ~d assault : voie de fait

      ~d theft : vol qualifié, vol aggravé

      ~d burglary : cambriolage qualifié

      aggravating circumstances : circonstances aggravantes

aggressor : agresseur *(m)*

agree : s'entendre

agreement : contrat *(m)*, accord *(m)*

aggrieved party : victime *(f)*, partie *(f)* lésée

aid : (1) aide *(f)*, assistance *(f)*, secours *(m)*; (2) secourir

      legal ~ : aide judiciaire

aiding and abetting : complicité *(f)*, aide et assistance *(f)*

aim : but *(m)*, point *(m)* de mire

      to ~ a weapon : braquer une arme

aimless : sans objet *(m)*

air : air *(m)*

      ~ navigation : navigation *(f)* aérienne

      ~ transport : trafic *(m)* aérien

      ~ weapon : arme *(f)* à air comprimé

aircraft : aéronef *(m)*

airfield : aérodrome *(m)*

airplane : avion *(m)*, aéronef *(m)*

airport : port *(m)* aérien, aéroport *(m)*

    ~ **tax** : taxe d'aéroport

alarm : (1) alarme *(f)*; (2) donner l'alarme

    ~ **system** : système d'alarme

    bandit ~ : bouton *(m)* rouge, alarme clandestine

alcohol : alcool *(m)*

    ~ **level** : taux *(m)* d'alcoolémie

alcoholic liquor : alcool *(m)*

alcotest : alcotest *(m)*

A-level : examen qui correspond au baccalauréat

alias : alias *(m)*, faux nom *(m)*

alibi : alibi *(m)*

    to establish an ~ : prouver son alibi

    to produce an ~ : produire/fournir un alibi

alien : étranger *(m)*

alienate : céder, transférer, concéder

alive : vif, vivant

allegation : (1) allégation *(f)*, articulation *(f)* des faits; (2) chef d'accusation, moyen *(m)* de défense

allege : alléguer, exciper de, prétendre

alleged : présumé, allégué

    ~ **offence** : infraction imputée

alley(way) : allée *(f)*, passage *(m)*, ruelle *(f)*, traboule *(f)*

all fours (on ~ **)** : pareil, semblable

allocate : affecter, attribuer, assigner

allow : accorder

allowable : admissible, permis, déductible

allowance : pension *(f)*, rente *(f)*, indemnité *(f)*

> **expense** ~ : allocation *(f)* pour frais professionnels

> **family** ~ : indemnité familiale

> **rent** ~ : prime *(f)* de logement

allowed : permis

all risks : tous risques

alter : fausser

alteration : altération *(f)*, falsification *(f)*

alternative route : itinéraire *(m)* de délestage

amalgamation : fusion *(f)*

ambulance : ambulance *(f)*

ambush : embuscade *(f)*

amenable : relevant de, justiciable de, ressortissant à

> ~ **to a fine** : passible d'une amende

> ~ **to law** : soumis à la loi

amend (a bill) : amender (un projet de loi)

amendment : modification *(f)*, amendement *(m)*, correction *(f)*, rectification *(f)*

amount (to) : s'élever (à)

ammunition : munition *(f)*
Explosifs et projectiles pour le chargement des armes à feu, comprennant balles, cartouches, fusées, obus et bombes.

amnesty : amnistie *(f)*

analysis : analyse *(f)*

angling permit : permis *(m)* de pêche

animal : animal *(m)*
Dans la plupart des textes légaux, ceci comprend tous les mammifères à l'exception de l'homme.

> **cruelty to** ~**s** : acte de cruauté envers les animaux

> **wild** ~ : animal sauvage
> *Tout animal (à l'exception des oiseaux) qui était à l'état sauvage avant qu'il soit tué ou apprivoisé.*

anonymous : anonyme

another : autrui

annals : annales *(fpl)*

annotate : annoter

annual leave : congé *(m)* annuel

annuity : rente *(f)*

annulment : abrogation *(f)*, cassation *(f)*

answer : répondre

antecedents : antécédents, histoire et caractère personnels

antedate : antidate *(f)*
> *Erreur ou fraude consistant à donner à un écrit juridique une date antérieure à celle de sa signature.*

anticipate : prévoir

anti–lock (brakes) : antiblocage *(m)*

anti–spin (wheels) : antipatinage *(m)*

apology : excuses *(fpl)*

apparent : apparent, manifeste

    ˜ death : mort *(f)* apparente

appeal : (1) appel *(m)*, pourvoi *(m)* en cassation; (2) se porter en appel
> *Tout recours à une instance supérieure*

    ˜ on a point of law : appel incident, appel joint

    court of ˜ : cour *(m)* d'appel

    late ˜ : appel tardif

    notice of ˜ : avis *(m)* d'appel

    to hear an ˜ : juger en appel

    to lodge an ˜ : faire appel, interjeter appel

    unfounded ˜ : fol appel

    without ˜ : en dernier ressort *(m)*

appear : paraître, apparaître, comparaître

> **summons to ~** : citation à comparaître

> **to ~ in court** : ester en justice

> **to fail to ~** : faire défaut

appearance : air *(m)*

appellant : appelant *(m)*, appelante *(f)*

appertain : appartenir à, relever de

applicant : demandeur *(m)*, demanderesse *(f)*, postulant *(m)*

application : (1) administration *(f)*; (2) demande *(f)*

apply : appliquer, mettre en pratique, postuler

appoint : désigner, nommer, constituer, établir

appointment : (1) nomination *(f)*, désignation *(f)*; (2) poste *(m)*, emploi *(m)*; (3) rendez-vous *(m)*, rencard *(m)*

appraisal : estimation *(f)*, évaluation *(f)*, appréciation *(f)*, expertise *(f)*

> **~ interview** : entretien *(m)* d'aptitude

> **official ~** : expertise *(f)*

apprehend : appréhender, arrêter

apprehension : arrestation *(f)*, prise *(f)* de corps

apprentice : apprenti *(m)*

approaches : voies *(fpl)* d'accès

approbation : approbation *(f)*, sanction *(f)*

appropriate : approprier

appropriation : appropriation *(f)*

> **~ of funds** : détournement *(m)* de fonds

approval : approbation *(f)*, agrément *(m)*, assentiment *(m)*, ratification *(f)*

approve : agréer

aptitude : aptitude *(f)*

> **~ test** : épreuve de vérification des aptitudes

arbitration : arbitrage *(m)*

area : zone *(f)*

    ~ **beat officer** : îlotier *(m)*

    ~ **car** : voiture *(f)* "police secours"
        Voiture de patrouille dans un secteur délimité

arguable : discutable

argument : discussion *(f)*, dispute *(f)*, débat *(m)*, argument *(m)*, plaidoirie *(f)*

    conclusive ~ : argument concluant, argument probant

    counsel's ~ : plaidoyer *(m)*

    fallacious/specious ~ : argument faux

    legal ~ : discussion juridique

arise : survenir, se produire, se poser, provenir de, se rapporter à

armed : armé

    ~ **forces** : forces *(fpl)* armées
        En Angleterre, ce sont l'Army, la Royal Air Force et la Royal Navy.
        Elles ne comprennent ni gendarmerie ni d'autres forces de police.

    ~ **robber** : braqueur *(m)*, holdopeur *(m)*, voleur *(m)* à main armé

    ~ **robbery** : braquage *(m)*, hold-up *(m)*, vol *(m)* à main armée

arms : armes *(fpl)*

    ~ **smuggling** : contrebande *(f)* d'armes, trafic *(m)* d'armes

arraign : traduire en justice, mettre en accusation

arraignment : mise *(f)* en accusation
    *Le juge donne lecture à l'inculpé de l'acte d'accusation (**indictment**) et lui*
    demande s'il se reconnaît coupable.

arrangement : disposition *(f)*

    to make ~**s** : prendre des dispositions

array (the jury) : faire l'appel nominal, dresser le tableau (des jurés)

arrest : (1) arrestation *(f)*, arrêts *(mpl)*;   (2) arrêter, mettre en état
    d'arrestation, appréhender

    citizen's ~ : arrestation par un citoyen (voir **arrestable offence**)

    close ~ : arrêts de rigueur

false ~ : arrestation arbitraire

open ~ : arrêts simples

power of ~ : droit *(m)* d'arrestation

to effect an ~ : opérer une arrestation

under ~ : en état d'arrestation

warrant of ~ : mandat *(m)* d'amener, ordre *(m)* d'arrestation

arrestable offence : délit *(m)*, crime *(m)*
Toute infraction pour laquelle la peine est au moins de cinq ans de prison ferme. L'auteur peut étre arrêté en flagrant délit par n'importe quel citoyen

serious ~ : crime *(m)*

arson : incendie *(m)* volontaire

art theft : vol *(m)* d'oeuvres et d'objets d'art

artic : voir **articulated vehicle**

articulated vehicle : semi-remorque *(m)*

artifice : artifice *(m)*, déception *(f)*

as : en qualité de, à titre de.   **~ of right** : de droit

ascertain : constater, vérifier, déterminer, établir, s'assurer

ascribe : imputer

asportation : enlèvement *(m)* de biens

assailant : agresseur *(m)*

assault : (1) agression *(f)*, (tentative de) voies *(fpl)* de fait; (2) agresser

~ and battery : menaces *(fpl)* et voies de fait

~ occasioning actual bodily harm : coups *(mpl)* et blessures *(fpl)*

common ~ : voie *(f)* de fait simple

indecent ~ : attentat *(m)* à la pudeur, outrage *(m)* aux moeurs

assembly : assemblée *(f)*, rassemblement *(m)*, réunion *(f)*

right of ~ : droit/liberté de réunion

unlawful ~ : rassemblement illicite

assent : sanction *(f)*

assert : alléguer

assertion : dire *(m)*

assessment : évaluation *(f)*

assign : assigner

assignment : délégation *(f)*, emploi *(m)*, mission *(f)*

assistance : aide *(f)*, assistance *(f)*, concours *(m)*

> **National** ~ : assistance publique

assistant : aide *(m&f)*, adjoint *(m)*

> ~ **chief constable** : directeur *(m)* adjoint de police
> *Comme l'un des adjoints d'un **chief constable**, il a un grade à peu
> près égal à un contrôleur-général dans la police française.*

> ~ **commissioner** : directeur *(m)* de police
> *Un grade qui n'existe pas à l'extérieur de Londres, il est
> l'équivalent d'un **chief constable** en province, et donc équivaut à un
> directeur dans la police française.*

assizes : cour *(f)* d'assises
*Anciennes sessions des juges-délégués de la **High Court** dans les
différents comtés d'Angleterre. Remplacées en 1971 par les **Crown Courts**.*

associate : associé *(m)*

> ~ **in crime** : co-délinquant *(m)*

association : association *(f)*, société *(f)*

> **in** ~ **with** : en société avec

assurance : voir **insurance**

attachment : saisie *(f)*

attack : atteinte (f)

attainder : condamnation *(f)* pour crime (terme désuet)

attainment : obtention *(f)*

attempt : (1) tenter;   (2) tentative *(f)*

> ~ **to commit an impossible crime** : tentative de délit *(m)* impossible

attend : assister, étre présent, s'occuper de

    ~ **a meeting** : assister à une réunion

    ~ **a trial** : assister aux débats

    ~ **to someone/something** : s'occuper de quelqu'un/quelque chose

    to be summoned to ~ **as a witness** : être appelé à témoigner

attendance centre : centre *(m)* d'éducation surveillée

attention : garde *(m)* à vous (ordre militaire)

attenuating (circumstances) : (circonstances) atténuantes

attorney : mandataire *(m&f)*, fondé *(m)* de pouvoir

    ~ **-général** : + Procureur *(m)* Général, Ministre *(m)* de la Justice
        Membre du parlement britannique, chef officier judiciaire et président du barreau national

    power of ~ : procuration *(f)*

attributable : imputable

auction : (vente *(f)* aux) enchères *(fpl)*

    ~ **room** : salle *(f)* des ventes

    Dutch ~ : enchères au rabais (illégal en Angleterre)

    sale by public ~ : vente publique

audible warning instrument : avertisseur *(m)*
    Instrument obligatoire pour indiquer la présence d'une automobile (par exemple, klaxon). L'usage de sirènes est interdit sauf pour les véhicules de police, pompiers, ambulances, etc.

audience (right of ~ **)** : (droit d'~) audience *(f)*

auditing of accounts : vérification *(f)* des comptes

authentic : authentique

    ~ **copy** : copie authentique, copie conforme

    ~ **deed** : document authentique

    ~ **text** : texte qui fait foi

authenticate : légaliser

authorisation : autorisation *(f)*, mandat *(m)*

authorised : autorisé

authority : autorité *(f)*, pouvoir *(m)*, mandat *(m)*, compétence *(f)*, puissance *(f)*

    abuse of ~ : abus de pouvoir

    police ~ : direction *(f)* de la police
        *A l'exception de la **Metropolitan Police**, pour laquelle **the Home Secretary** est **the police authority**, les forces de police sont dirigées par un comité mixte, formé des conseillers du comté et des **magistrates.***

    police complaints ~ : commission *(f)* des plaintes contre la police
        *Commission gouvernementale, chargée de veiller à la constatation, l'enquête et l'audience des plaintes déposées par les tiers contre un ou plusieurs policiers. Se compose de gens nommés par **the Home Secretary** qui ne sont pas eux-mêmes des policiers.*

    public ~ : les pouvoirs publics

    to exceed one's ~ : outrepasser ses pouvoirs

automatic pistol : pistolet *(m)* automatique

automatism : automatisme *(m)*

automobile : automobile *(f)*, voiture *(f)*

    ~ Association : club d'automobilistes (semblable au Touring Club de France)

autopsy : autopsie *(f)*

autotheft : vol *(m)* d'une voiture

autrefois acquit, autrefois convict : de par l'autorité de la chose jugée (acquittement ou condamnation antérieur pour la même infraction).

auxiliary : auxiliaire *(m&f)*

available : disponible

avenue : avenue *(f)*

    ~ of appeal : voie *(f)* de recours

award : adjuger, octroyer, attribuer

    ~ of costs : jugement sur frais

    to ~ damages : accorder des dommages-intérêt

awkward customer : hérisson *(m)*

axle : essieu *(m)*

B

bachelor : célibataire *(m)*

    ~ pad : garçonnière *(f)*

back-bear : emporter (les biens d'autrui)

back-berand : voir **back-bear**

backdate : antidater

backed for bail : endossé pour remise en liberté sous caution
Un mandat d'arrêt peut être endossé avec mention par le juge que la personne peut être remise en liberté sous caution, pourvu qu'elle remplisse certaines conditions.

background : historique *(f)*, antécédents *(mpl)*

    ~ information : documentation *(f)* de base

backhander : bakshich *(m)* (paiement illicite)

backlash : contre-coup *(m)*, répercussion *(f)*

back pay : rappel *(m)* de traitement

backsight : hausse *(f)*

bad : mauvais, faux

    ~ debt : créance irrécouvrable

badge of rank : insigne *(m)* de grade

badger : blaireau *(m)*
Les blaireaux sont protégés par la loi britannique.

bag : sac

    ~ snatcher : arracheur *(m)* de sacs

baggage handler : soutier *(m)*

bail : caution *(f)*, cautionnement *(m)* judiciaire

    on ~ : en liberté *(f)* provisoire

    remand on ~ : contrôle *(m)* judiciaire

    to grant ~ : admettre une caution

    to jump ~ : se dérober à la justice

    to release on ~ : mettre en liberté sous caution, relâcher sous caution to stand ~ : se porter caution, cautionner, garantir, intercéder

bailee : dépositaire *(m)*

bailiff : huissier *(m)* de justice, bailli *(m)*

balance sheet : bilan *(m)*

ban : interdiction *(f)*

bandit : bandit *(m)*

~ **alarm** : bouton *(m)* rouge, alarme *(f)* clandestine

one-armed ~ : bandit-manchot *(m)*

banged-up * : mise en cellule

banger (old ~ **)** : bagnole *(f)*, brouette *(f)*

bang to rights * : incapable de nier culpabilité

banishment : bannissement *(m)*

bank : banque *(f)*

~ **account** : compte *(m)* en banque

~ **book** : livret *(m)* de banque, carnet *(m)* de banque

~ **holiday** : jour *(m)* de fête, jour *(m)* férié

~ **note** : billet *(m)* de banque

~ **statement** : bordereau *(m)* de situation, relevé *(m)* de compte

data ~ : banque de données *(fpl)*

merchant ~ : banque d'affaires *(fpl)*

Post Office savings ~ : Caisse *(f)* d'Epargne postale

banker's draft : chèque *(m)* bancaire, traite *(f)* bancaire

bankruptcy : banqueroute *(f)*, faillite *(f)*

banish : exiler

baptism : baptême *(m)*

bar : (1) bar *(m)*, café *(m)*, bistro *(m)*; (2) barre *(f)* (de cour); (3) barreau *(m)* (association des avocats), (4) galon *(m)* (insigne de grade) (5) prescription *(f)*, empêchement *(m)*, (6) exclure, empêcher, opposer, prescrire

~ **chart** : diagramme comparatif sous forme de colonnes parallèles

prisoner at the ~ : l'accusé *(m&f)*

to ~ **by statute of limitations** : prescrire

barbed wire : barbelouses *(fpl)*

baronet : dignité personnelle ou héréditaire mais non titre de noblesse

barracks : caserne *(f)*

barred : irrecevable

barrel : (1) fût *(m)*; (2) canon *(m)*

sawn–off ~ : canon scié

barricade : barricade *(f)*

barrier : barrière *(f)*, entrave *(f)*

barrister : avocat *(m)*

barrow boy : marchand *(m)* des quatr' saisons

base : base *(f)*

data ~ : base de données

naval ~ : base navale de guerre

basis : pied *(m)*, base *(f)*

bastard : bâtard *(m)*, enfant *(m&f)* naturel(le)

Bath star : étoile *(f)*
*Insigne de grade, porté par les **chief/inspectors** et par les officiers militaires.*

baton : bâton *(m)*, verge *(f)*

battalion : groupement

battered : cabossé

~ **wife** : femme battue
Epouse qui a été assujettie aux coups et blessures de son mari.

battery : blessure *(f)*, violence *(f)* et voies *(fpl)* de fait
*L'emploi de la force corporelle et illicite contre autrui. Dans la pratique, le terme "assault" est souvent employé comme synonyme de **battery** mais, en droit, les deux termes sont distincts.*

assault and ~ : menaces *(fpl)* et voies *(fpl)* de fait

bawdy house : tripot *(m)*, lupanar *(m)*

bawl : gueuler

bayonet : baïonnette *(f)*

beadle : bedeau *(m)*

beak * : gerbier *(m)*, juge *(m)*

beam : faisceau *(m)*

      main/dipped ~ : feu *(m)* de route/de croisement

beard : barbe *(f)*

beat : battre

      ~ **up** : rosser, bourrer, accommoder, amocher, assaisonner, astiquer, sonner, tabasser

beat : îlot *(m)*, zone *(f)* de patrouille

      ~ **officer** : îlotier *(m)*

beating : raclée *(f)*

bed-sitter : studio *(m)*

beetle (VW car) : coccinelle *(f)*

beg : mangaver, pilonner

beggar : mendigot *(m)*

begging : mendicité *(f)*

behead : décapiter

behind closed doors : à huis clos

being : être *(m)*

belly : ventre *(m)*, bide *(m)*, bidon *(m)*

belong : appartenir

belongings : affaires *(fpl)*

below-mentioned : sous-dit *(m)*

Bench : la magistrature *(f)* assise, la judicature *(f)*

      ~ **warrant** : mandat d'arrêt lancé par un tribunal

bench : banc *(m)*, siège *(m)*

beneficiary : ayant droit

benefit : (1) allocation *(f)*, bénéfice *(m)*, indemnité *(f)*, prestation *(f)*; (2) bénéficier

    ~s office : caisse *(f)* de sécurité sociale

bent * : (1) corruptible; (2) ayant des tendances homosexuelles

    ~ copper : ripou *(m)*

bequeath : léguer

bequest : legs *(m)*

bestiality : bestialité *(f)*, relations *(fpl)* avec un animal

bet : (1) pari *(m)*, (2) parier

betray : arnaquer

betrayal : trahison *(f)*

betting : paris *(mpl)*

    ~ levy : impôt *(m)* des jeux

bias : inimitié *(f)*

bicycle : bicyclette *(f)*, bécane *(f)*, vélo *(m)*

    ~ -mounted policeman : hirondelle, raper

big : grand, gros

    ~ shot : huile *(m)*

    ~ -wig : gros bonnet *(m)*, grosse légume *(f)*

    Mr. ~ : gros Léon *(m)*

bigamy : bigamie *(f)*

biker : motard *(m)*

bill : (1) facture *(f)*; (2) projet *(m)* de loi, proposition *(f)* de loi; (3) affiche *(f)*

    ~ of indictment : acte *(m)* d'accusation

    ~ sticking : affichage *(m)*

    Old ~ * : les flics *(mpl)*, la bigorne *(f)*, la police *(f)*

bind over : mettre en liberté conditionnelle

    ~ **to keep the peace** : relaxer quelqu'un sous condition qu'il ne trouble pas l'ordre public.

birth : naissance *(f)*

    ~ **certificate** : extrait *(m)*/acte *(m)* de naissance

blackleg : briseur *(m)* de grève, jaune *(m)*

blacklist : mettre à l'index

blackmail : (1) chantage *(m)*, gouale *(m)*; (2) exercer un chantage

blackmailer : maître-chanteur *(m)*

Black Maria : panier *(m)* à salade, carrosse *(m)*, voiture *(f)* cellulaire

black market : marché *(m)* noir, trafic *(m)* clandestin

blackout (news ~) : blackout *(m)*

blade : lame *(f)*, lingue *(m)* *

blag * : hold-up *(m)*, vol *(m)* à main armé

blagger : holdopeur *(m)*

blind : aveugle

    ~ **drunk** : rétamé

    ~ **spot** : angle mort

    colour ~ : daltonien

block : bloquer

    road ~ : barrage *(m)*

blockage : blocus *(m)*

bloke : gars *(m)*

blood : sang *(m)*

    ~ **-hound** : limier *(m)*

blow : coup *(m)*, atteinte *(f)*, beigne *(f)*

blower * : bignou *(m)*, bigophone *(m)*, téléphone *(m)*

bludgeon : casse-tête *(m)*

blunt instrument : arme *(f)* contondante

board : table *(f)* et, par extension, tout ce qui se réunit autour d'une table, commission *(f)*, comité *(f)*, conseil *(m)*, administration *(f)*

    ~ and lodging : pension *(f)* complète, logement *(m)*

    ~ of directors : conseil d'administration

    ~ of enquiry : commission d'enquête

    promotion ~ : conseil d'avancement

boarding school : internat *(m)*

boat : bateau *(f)*

    pleasure ~ : bateau de plaisance

    speed ~ : vedette *(f)*

bodily : corporel

    ~ injury : dommage corporel, préjudice corporel

body : (1) corps *(m)* humain, cadavre *(m)*; (2) arsenal *(m)*, corps *(m)*

    ~ corporate : personne *(f)* morale

    ~ of evidence : corps de preuves

    ~ of the law : l'arsenal législatif, corps des lois

    ~ search : fouille *(f)* à corps, visite *(f)* de personnes

    dead ~ : cadavre *(m)*

bodyguard : garde *(m)* du corps, gorille *(m)*

bodywork : carrosserie *(f)*, tôlerie *(f)*

bogus : faux, frauduleux, simulé

    ~ company : société *(f)* fantôme

boiler suit : bleus *(mpl)* de travail

bollard : balise *(f)*

bollocking * : abattage *(m)*, engueulade *(f)*

bolt : (1) boulon *(m)*, verrou *(m)*; (2) fermeture de culasse *(f)*

    ~ croppers : charlotte *(f)*

bomb : bombe *(f)*

    ~ **disposal expert** : artificier *(m)*

    ~ **hoax** : avertissement malicieux de l'existence d'une bombe

    to ~ **along** * : bomber *

bomber jacket : blouson *(m)*

bonded goods : marchandises *(fpl)* en douane

bona fide : de bonne foi

bone-shaker : bagnole *(f)*, guimbarde *(f)*, tacot *(m)*

bonnet : capot *(m)*

bonus : gratification *(f)*, prime *(f)*, sursalaire *(m)*, allocation *(f)* spéciale

    no-claims ~ : prime de non-casse

booby trap : traquenard *(m)*, objet *(m)* piégé

book : livre *(m)*, livret *(m)*

    account ~ : livre des comptes

    bank ~ : livret de banque

    by the ~ : au pied de la lettre, régul-régul

    cheque ~ : livret/carnet *(m)* de chèques

    to ~ **someone** : dresser un procès verbal, porter mention d'une arrestation
        au registre de la police

book-keeper : comptable *(m&f)*

book-keeping : comptabilité *(f)*

booklet : livret *(m)*, carnet *(m)*

bookmaker : book *(m)*

boot : (1) botte; (2) (auto) coffre *(f)*

booth : cabine *(f)*

booty : butin *(m)*, barbotin *(m)*

booze-up * : arrosage *(m)*

border : frontière *(f)*, limite *(f)* du territoire

~ **pass** : carte frontière

~ **police** : police de l'air et des frontières

borderline case : cas *(m)* limite

borough (terme désuet) : commune *(f)*, municipalité *(f)*

~ **council** : conseil *(m)* municipal

~ **police force** : police *(f)* municipale, police *(f)* communale (Belgium)

borstal institution : centre *(m)* d'éducation surveillée
Depuis 1982, remplacé par **youth custody.**

boss : patron *(m)*

bottle * : courage *(m)*, atout *(m)*

bottleneck : embouteillage *(m)*, goulot *(m)* d'étranglement

bouncer : barreur *(m)*, videur *(m)*

boundary stone : borne *(f)*

bowl over : assabouir

box : caisse *(f)*

jury ~ : banc *(m)* des jurés

witness ~ : banc *(m)*/barre *(f)* des témoins

boys in blue : flicaille *(f)*, police *(f)*

bracelets * : cabriolets *(mpl)*, cadennes *(fpl)*, canelles *(fpl)*, chapelets *(mpl)*, fichets *(mpl)*, menottes *(fpl)*

braid : broderie *(f)*, soutache *(f)*

gold ~ : broderie d'or

brake : frein *(m)*

~ **lever** : levier *(m)* de frein

disk ~ : frein à disque

drum ~ : frein à tambour

foot ~ : pédale *(f)* de frein

branch : branche *(f)*, unité *(f)*, service *(m)*

brass (1) : laiton *(m)*

brass (2) * : artiche *(f)* *, aspine *(f)* *, douille *(f)* *, galette *(f)* *, grisbi *(m)* *, joncaille *(f)* *

brawl : bagarre *(f)*, barrabille *(f)*, baston *(m)*, castagne *(f)*, rixe *(f)*

breach : (1) rompre, entamer; (2) bris *(m)*, violation *(f)*

    ~ **of copyright** : contrefaçon *(f)*

    ~ **of duty** : manquement *(m)* au devoir

    ~ **of the law** : violation de la loi

    ~ **of the rules** : infraction *(f)* au règlement

    ~ **of seals** : bris de scellés

    ~ **of the peace** : atteinte *(f)* à la paix publique, délit *(m)* contre l'ordre publique, trouble *(m)*, bruit *(m)* et tapage *(m)*

    ~ **of trust** : abus *(m)* de confiance

bread (1) : pain *(m)*

bread (2) * : artiche *(f)* *, aspine *(f)* *, blé *(m)* *, douille *(f)* *, galette *(f)* *, grisbi *(m)* *, joncaille *(f)* *

breadwinner : soutien *(m)* de famille

break : (1) effraction *(f)*; (2) bris *(m)*; (3) pause-café *(f)*; (4) enfreindre

    ~ **in** : casse *(f)*, cassement *(m)*, effraction

    prison ~ : bris de prison

    to ~ **in** : caroubler, forcer une entrée, s'introduire par effraction

    to ~ **open** : forcer

    to ~ **seals** : lever les scellés

    to ~ **the law** : transgresser la loi

breakdown : (1) panne *(f)*;   (2) tomber en panne

    ~ **truck** : camion-grue *(m)*, dépanneuse *(f)*

breaker * : casseur *(m)*, cambrioleur *(m)*

    car ~ : épaviste *(m)*

breathalyser : alcotest *(m)*

breath test : vérification *(f)* du niveau d'alcool dans l'haleine

breech : culasse *(f)*

    ~ **block** : boîte *(f)* de culasse

Bren gun : fusil-mitrailleur *(m)*

Brewster sessions : séance d'un tribunal pour décerner les autorisations aux débits de boissons

bribe : (1) pot-de-vin *(m)*, bakshich *(m)*; (2) corrompre, graisser la patte, soudoyer

bribery : corruption *(f)*

    ~ **fund** : caisse *(f)* noire

bridewell : cachot *(m)*

bridleway : chemin *(m)* équestre

brief : (1) cause *(f)*, dossier *(m)* d'une procédure; (2) bavard *(m)* *, bavocheux *(m)* *, avocat *(m)*; (3) donner des instructions

briefcase : serviette *(f)*

briefing : instruction *(f)*

bring : (1) apporter; (2) intenter

    ~ **an action** : intenter un procès

    ~ **in a verdict** : rendre un verdict

British : britannique, anglais

    ~ **possession** : territoire d'outre-mer britannique

    ~ **protected person** : ressortissant d'un territoire protégé par la Reine

Broadmoor : hôpital fermé pour les aliénés aux tendances criminelles, violentes ou dangereuses

broke : fauché

brothel : bordel *(m)*, maison *(f)* close, maison *(f)* d'abattage

    ~**-keeper** : taulière *(f)*, sous-mac *(m)*

bug * : écoute *(f)*

buggery : accouplement *(m)* anal
    *Antérieurement strictement proscrite, **buggery** n'est plus criminalisée si les parties sont d'accord, ont au moins 21 ans et si l'acte est accompli dans un lieu privé.*

bugging : surveillance *(f)* électronique

build : (1) taille *(f)*; (2) construire, bâtir

builder : entrepreneur *(m)* en bâtiment

building : immeuble *(m)*

    ~ **contractor** : entrepreneur *(m)* de bâtiment

    ~ **plot** : lotissement *(m)*

    ~ **trade** : le bâtiment *(m)*

    tenement ~ : immeuble de rapport

built-up area : agglomération *(f)*

bullet : balle *(f)*

bullet-proof : pare-balles

    ~ **glass** : verre pare-balles

    ~ **waistcoat** : gilet pare-balles

bully : fier-à-bras *(m)*

bumper : pare-chocs *(m)*

bump off * : mettre en l'air *, allonger *, apaiser *, décoller *, ébouser *

bundle : liasse *(f)*, balandrin *(m)*, baluchon *(m)*

bungle : louper

buoy : balise *(f)*

burden : charge *(f)*

    ~ **of proof** : charge de la preuve, fardeau *(m)* de preuve

bureaucracy : bureaucratie *(f)*, chinoiseries *(fpl)*, paperasse *(f)*

burglar : cambrioleur *(m)*, lourdeur *(m)*, marcheur *(m)*

    ~ **alarm** : signalisateur *(m)* anti-vol

    ~ **-proof** : anti-effraction, incrochetable

burglary : cambriolage *(m)*, vol *(m)* avec effraction

    aggravated ~ : cambriolage qualifié
       Cambriolage à main armé.

~ **artifice** : entrée *(f)* par ruse

burgle : cambrioler

burn : brûler

burst : (1) éclater; (2) rafale *(f)*

bury : enterrer

bus : autobus *(m)*

    double-decker ~ : autobus à impérial

    late night ~ : noctambus *(m)*

bush telegraph : téléphone *(m)* arabe

business : affaires *(fpl)*, commerce *(m)*, activité *(f)*

    ~ **centre** : centre *(m)* d'affaires

    ~ **concern** : entreprise *(f)* commerciale

    ~ **premises** : immeuble *(m)* à usage commercial

businessman : brasseur *(m)* d'affaires, homme *(m)* d'affaires

busted * : arrêté, appréhendé (surtout pour possession des drogues)

butt : (1) coup *(m)* de boule; (2) crosse *(f)* d'appui

buy : acheter

    ~ **a witness** : suborner un témoin

bye-law : arrêté *(m)* municipal, loi *(f)* municipale, règlements *(mpl)* administratifs
statut *(m)* local

    county ~ : arrêté préfectoral

by pass : périphérique *(m)*, tangentielle *(f)*

C

cab : (1) cabine *(f)* (d'un camion); (2) taxi *(m)*

cabby : loche *(m)*, conducteur *(m)* de taxi

cadet : policier *(m)* auxiliaire

calculated : prémédité, délibéré

calendar : calendrier *(m)*

    ~ year : année *(f)* civile

    prison ~ : livre *(m)* d'écrou

call : (1) appeler, citer à comparaître, assigner; (2) appel *(m)*, coup *(m)* de fil

    on ~ : de permanence

    roll- ~ : appel nominal

    to ~ as a witness : appeler en témoignage

    to ~ into question : mettre en cause

calumny : calomnie *(f)*
Fausse accusation, dans l'intention de nuire.

camera : appareil *(m)* photographique

    in ~ : à huis *(m)* clos

Camic (breath) analyser : marque d'éthylomètre ou alcootest

cancel : annuler, infirmer, résilier, révoquer

cancellation : biffure *(f)*

cane : canne *(f)*

cannabis : chanvre *(m)* indien, banga *(m)*, bhang *(m)*, kif *(m)*

canteen : cantine *(f)*

    ~ culture : subculture des gardiens de la paix ou gendarmes

canvas cover : bâche *(f)*

cap : casquette *(f)*, bonnet *(m)*

    flat ~ : crêpe *(f)*

capable : capable, habile (à)

capacity : capacité *(f)*, qualité *(f)*

capital : capital

~ **offence** : crime capital

~ **punishment** : peine capitale
N'existe plus à l'exception de la haute trahison et de la piraterie qualifiée.

capture : prise *(f)*

car : automobile *(f)*, voiture *(f)*

~ **breaker** : casseur *(m)*, épaviste *(m)*

~ **breaker's yard** : cimetière *(m)* à bagnoles

Panda ~ : voiture pie

caravan : caravane *(f)*, roulotte *(f)*

carbine : carabine *(f)*

card : fiche *(f)*, carte *(f)*

~ **index** : fichier *(m)*

credit ~ : carte de crédit

green ~ : carte verte
Carte d'assurance automobile internationale.

smart ~ : carte à mémoire, carte à puce

care : (1) diligence *(f)*;   (2) garde *(f)*, soin *(m)*, souci *(m)*

~ **and control** : garde *(f)*, soin *(m)*, gestion *(f)*

~ **proceedings** : poursuites en vue de la tutelle d'un mineur

in ~ : pupille *(m&f)* de l'état

career : carrière *(f)*

careless : négligent

~ **driving** : conduite négligente

carelessness : négligence *(f)*

care of ... : aux bons soins de .....

caretaker : concièrge *(m&f)*, gardien *(m)*, cloporte *(m)*, lourdière *(f)*

cargo : cargaison *(f)*

carnal knowledge : rapports *(mpl)* sexuels

carriage : (1) voiture *(f)*, wagon *(m)*; (2) transport *(m)*, port *(m)*

carriageway : chaussée *(f)*
> *Une route à l'usage du public, qui a le droit de passer dessus à pied, à cheval, ou en voiture.*

carrier : voiturier *(m)*, transporteur *(m)*, entrepreneur *(m)* de transports

    common ~ : voiturier public

carry out : accomplir, appliquer, mettre en oeuvre, s'acquitter (de)

cartage : camionnage *(m)*

carter : voiturier *(m)*

cartridge : cartouche *(f)*

    ~ case : douille *(f)*

case : procès *(m)*, affaire *(f)*, cas *(m)*, cause *(f)*, instance *(f)* judiciaire

    ~ before the court : affaire en cause

    ~ for/against : arguments *(mpl)* pour/contre

    ~ for the prosecution : accusation *(f)*, réquisition *(f)*

    ~ law : jurisprudence *(f)*, droit *(m)* jurisprudentiel

    ~ paper : pièce *(f)* de la procédure

    closed ~ : chose *(f)* jugée

    famous ~s : causes célèbres

    in ~ of necessity : en tant que de besoin

    test ~ : cause décisoire

    to try a ~ : faire juger une affaire

    to withdraw a ~ : se désister

cash : espèces *(fpl)*, liquide *(m)*

cash-and-carry : payer-prendre *(m)*

casualty : accidenté *(m)*, victime *(f)*

catalogue : répertoire *(m)*

catalytic converter : pot *(m)* catalytique

catastrophe : sinistre *(m)*

cat-burglar : acrobate *(m)*, bijoutier *(m)* du clair de lune, monte-en-l'air *(m&f)*

catch : saisir, attraper

cat-house * : maison *(f)* d'abattage

cattle : bétail *(m)*

caught in the act : pris en flagrant délit

caution : avertissement *(m)*, réprimande *(f)*
> *Il en existe deux types : (1) une réprimande, émise en général par la police, à quelqu'un au lieu de le faire passer devant le tribunal. Utilisée surtout pour les jeunes délinquants. (2) La formule orale informant un suspect en état de prévention, de ses droits. Cette formule et les conditions pour son application sont imposées par le* **Police and Criminal Evidence Act.**

cavalry : cavalerie *(f)*

cell : cellule *(f)*

cemetery : cimetière *(m)*

censure : réprimande *(f)*

central planning unit : unité centrale d'examens et de formation des moniteurs

centre : centre *(m)*

    business ~ : centre d'affaires

    shopping ~ : centre commercial

certificate : certificat *(m)*, acte *(m)*, attestation *(f)*

    birth/death/marriage ~ : acte de naissance/décès/mariage

    ~ of competence : brevet *(m)*/certificat d'aptitude

    ~ of good character : attestation de bonne vie et moeurs

    ~ of insurance : attestation d'assurance

certified : certifié

    ~ date : date authentique

    " ~ a true copy" : "pour copie conforme"

certify : attester, authentifier, certifier, déclarer, légaliser

certiorari (order of ~) : ordre de renvoi à un tribunal supérieur

chain of command : hiérarchie *(f)*

chair : présider

chairman : président *(m)*

challenge : récusation *(f)*

chambers : étude *(f)*
     *Le bureau d'un juge ou d'un avocat **(barrister)**.*

chance : chance *(f)*, hasard *(m)*, probabilité *(f)*

chancellor : chancelier *(m)*

   ~ of the Exchequer : = ministre *(m)* des finances

   Lord (High) ~ : = ministre *(m)* de la justice

change : (1) monnaie *(f)*;   (2) changement *(m)*, mutation *(f)*

   ~ of ownership : mutation

   to ring the ~s : vol au rendez-moi

chap : bougre *(m)*, mec *(m)*, type *(m)*

character : caractère *(m)*, réputation *(f)*

   ~ enquiries : enquête *(f)* de personnalité

   ~ witness : témoin *(m)* de moralité

   good ~ : bonne vie et moeurs

characteristics : signalement *(m)*

charge : (1) accusation *(f)*, fargue *(f)*, inculpation *(f)*, acte *(m)* d'accusation, mise *(f)* en prévention, chef *(m)* d'accusation; (2) accuser, farguer, inculper, prévenir; (3) charge *(f)*, frais *(mpl)*; (4) obligation *(f)*, devoir *(m)*

   ~ card : carte *(f)* client

   ~ sheet : cahier *(m)* des délits et écrous d'un commissariat de police

   counter– ~ : contre-accusation *(f)*

   details of the ~ : réquisitoire *(m)*

   officer in ~ : officier *(m)* commandant

   on a ~ of murder : sous l'inculpation de meurtre

the ~ **is murder** : l'inculpé est accusé de meurtre

to give someone in charge : faire arrêter quelqu'un

to lay a ~ : porter plainte

to take in ~ : arrêter

chargehand : chef *(m)* d'équipe

charges : droits *(mpl)*

charity : (société de) bienfaisance *(f)*

chart : graphique *(m)*

bar ~ : graphique en forme de colonnes

pie ~ : fromage *(m)*, camembert *(m)*

chartered : qualifié, agréé

~ **accountant** : expert-comptable *(m)*

chassis : chassis *(m)*

~ **number** : numéro *(m)* de chassis

chat : causer

~ **up** : baratiner

chattels : biens *(mpl)* meubles, mobiliers *(mpl)*, possessions *(fpl)*

cheat : escroquer, estamper, flouer, friponner, gruger

cheating : tromperie *(f)*

check : (1) contrôler; (2) contrôle *(m)*, vérification *(f)*

~ **of credentials** : vérification de pouvoirs

identity ~ : contrôle d'identité

checking : vérification *(f)*

cheque : chèque *(m)*

bouncing/rubber ~ : chèque en bois

~ **card** : carte *(f)* d'identité bancaire

Giro ~ : chèque postal

to cash a ~ : toucher un chèque

chief : (1) chef *(m)*; (2) principal

    ~ **constable** : directeur *(m)* d'une des **police forces** britanniques

    ~ **inspector** : officier *(m)* de paix principal

    ~ **superintendent** : commissaire *(m)* divisionnaire

child : enfant *(m&f)*

    abandonment of ~ : abandon *(m)* d'enfant

    ~ **abuse** : maltraitance *(f)*

    ~ **destruction** : avortement *(m)* après le septième mois de grossesse

    ~ **in care** : pupille *(m&f)* de l'état

    ~ **welfare** : protection *(f)* de l'enfance

    with ~ : enceinte

chiv * : couteau *(m)*, amiral *(m)*

choke : étrangler

chopper * : hélicoptère *(m)*, battoir *(m)* d'oeufs *

chose : chose *(f)*

    ~ **in action** : droit *(m)* incorporel

    ~ **in possession** : droit *(m)* corporel

Christian name : prénom *(m)*

christening certificate : acte *(m)* de baptême

circuit : circuit *(m)*

    ~ **judge** : juge *(m)* en tournée, juge *(m)* itinérant
        *Les pays d'Angleterre et de Galles sont divisés en six circuits pour l'audience des affaires criminelles par les **Crown Courts**.*

circular : circulaire *(f)*

circulate : circuler, écouler

circumstances : circonstances *(fpl)*, état *(m)* de choses

    aggravating ~ : circonstances aggravantes

    extenuating ~ : circonstances atténuantes

circumstantial evidence : preuve *(f)* indirecte, preuve *(f)* par présomption

20

cite : citer

citizen : citoyen *(m)*, ressortissant *(m)*

    ~'s arrest : arrestation *(f)* par un citoyen
> *Des pouvoirs très limités sont accordés aux citoyens, par certaines lois et par le droit coutumier, pour certains délits et crimes, surtout en cas de flagrant délit. Le prisonnier doit être mis entre les mains de la police ou d'un juge aussitôt que possible.*

    ~s' band (CB) : bande de fréquence autorisée pour les particuliers

    law-abiding ~ : citoyen respecteux des lois

civic : civique, civil, municipal

    ~ centre : mairie *(f)*, hôtel *(m)* de ville

    ~ rights : droits civils

civil : civil

    ~ action : action civile

    ~ commotion : émeute *(f)*

    ~ court : chambre civile

    ~ defence : protection civile

    ~ engineering : travaux *(mpl)* publics

    ~ law : droit civil

    ~ liability : responsabilité civile

    ~ liberty : liberté civile

    ~ rights : droits civils

    ~ servant : fonctionnaire *(m&f)* d'état

    ~ service : corps *(m)* de la fonction publique

    ~ status : état civil

civvies * : ciblot *(m)*, tenue *(f)* de Pékin

claim : (1) prétention *(f)*; (2) prétendre, alléguer, réclamer, requérir

    ~ for damages : réclamation *(f)* en dommages-intérêts

clamour : tapage *(m)*

clamp : (1) sabot *(m)* d'Anvers; (2) poser un sabot d'Anvers

clam up * : s'écraser, se taire

clandestine : clandestin, occulte

clapped out * : déglingué

clarification : éclaircissement *(m)*

clarify : élucider

clash : conflit *(m)*

clasp knife : eustache *(f)*

class : classe *(f)*, catégorie *(f)*, qualité *(f)*

    ~ **of 1991** : promotion *(f)* de 1991

    governing ~ : classe dirigeante

    middle ~ : classe moyenne

    working ~ : classe ouvrière

classification : classement *(m)*, classification *(f)*

    ~ **of offences** : classification des infractions

    fingerprint ~ : formule *(f)* digitale

classify : classer

clause : clause *(f)*, article *(m)*

clear (of suspicion) : défarguer, laver

    to ~ **oneself** : se disculper

clemency : clémence *(f)*, indulgence *(f)*, grâce *(f)*

clerical : de commis

    ~ **assistance** : secrétariat *(m)*

    ~ **error** : erreur *(m)* de plume

    ~ **staff** : personnel *(m)* de bureau

clerk : employé *(m)* de bureau, clerc *(m)*, commis *(m)*, secrétaire *(m&f)*

    ~ **of the court** : greffier *(m)*

    confidential ~ : secrétaire particulier

    judge's ~ : aide *(m&f)* au juge

justices' ~ : greffier *(m)* (au tribunal de police)

town ~ : secrétaire de mairie

clinch : accrochage *(m)*

clink * : ratière *(f)*, cabane *(f)*, taule *(f)*, prison *(f)*, trou *(m)*

clock : contrôler la vitesse

close : (1) impasse *(f)*; (2) proche

~ **protection** : protection *(f)* rapprochée

cloverleaf : échangeur *(m)*

club : club *(m)*, cercle *(m)*

bingo ~ : club de loto (joué par les membres pour de l'argent)

~s **and vice unit** : brigade *(f)* des moeurs
Unité à Londres, responsable de la surveillance des clubs, de la prostitution, de la pornographie, des mineurs ...

gaming ~ : club de jeu privé

members' ~ : club dirigé les membres eux-mêmes
Un tel club n'est pas considéré comme un débit de boisson, bien que les alcools y soient vendus aux membres.

proprietary ~ : club dirigé par un ou plusieurs particuliers
Etant pour leurs propres bénéfices, un tel club doit être enregistré comme un débit de boisson.

clue : indice *(m)*

clutch : embrayage *(m)*

~ **lever** : levier *(m)* d'embrayage

co-accused : coaccusé *(m)*

coach : (auto)car *(m)*

coaching : entraînement *(m)*

coastguard : garde-côte *(m)*

cocaine : cocaïne *(f)*, blanc *(m)*, coco *(f)*, neige *(f)*

cock-and-bull story : galéjade *(f)*, histoire *(f)*

cock-fighting : combat *(m)* de coqs

code : code *(m)*

~ **of practice** : code de procédure
> *Le **Police and Criminal Evidence Act** fournit des **Codes of Practice** concernant l'identification, la détention, le traitement et l'interrogation des suspects, ainsi que les fouilles, etc.*

Highway ~ : code de procédure pour les usagers de la route. Il n'a pas force réglementaire.

co-defendant : coaccusé *(m)*, codéfendeur *(m)*

coercion : coaction *(f)*, coercition *(f)*, contrainte *(f)*

cogent : probant

~ **argument** : argument probant/incontestable

coil spring : ressort hélécoïdal

collar * : (1) arrêter, agricher, coffrer, coincer; (2) crâne *(m)*

collation : collation *(f)*

colleague : collaborateur *(m)*, collègue *(m)*, confrère *(m)*

collection (for charity) : quête *(f)*, collecte *(f)*

house-to-house ~ : quête porte-à-porte

street ~ : quête dans la rue

collective responsibility : responsabilité *(f)* collective

college : collège *(m)*, école *(f)*

The Police Staff College : Ecole nationale supérieure de la police
> *Ecole où sont formés les policiers qui ont été pressentis pour être les futurs dirigeants des diverses forces de police britanniques.*

collide : percuter

collision : impact *(m)*, collision *(f)*

collusion : collusion *(f)*, connivence *(f)*

colour blind : daltonien

colours : pavillon *(m)*, drapeau *(m)*

come clean * : accoucher

command : (1) ordre *(m)*; (2) commander

commandant : directeur *(m)* (d'un centre de formation)

commander : commandant *(m)*

    divisional ~ : commissaire *(m)* central

commercial : commercial, de commerce, marchand

    ~ court : tribunal *(m)* de commerce

    ~ law : droit commercial, droit des affaires

    ~ vehicle : véhicule *(m)* utilitaire

commission : (1) commission *(f)*, mandat *(m)*, délégation *(f)* des pouvoirs; (2) commission *(f)*, comité *(m)*;   (3) consommation/perpétration *(f)* (d'un crime)

    ~ for racial equality : commission pour l'égalité raciale

    Royal ~ : Commission d'enquête parlementaire

commissioner : commissaire *(m)*

    ~ of police : directeur-général de la police de Londres
    Les fonctions du **commissioner of police** *sont semblables à celles du Préfet de Police de Paris mais il est toujours un policier de carrière, plutôt qu'un fonctionnaire d'état. Pour des raisons historiques, outre le* **Commissioner of the Metropolitan Police**, *il y a un* **commissioner** *pour le tout petit corps de police de la Cité de Londres. Dans le cas des autres* **police forces**, *le plus haut policier s'appelle* **chief constable**.

commit : commettre, confier, livrer, remettre, perpétrer

    to ~ a crime : commettre un crime

    to ~ for trial : mettre en état de prévention, mettre en accusation

    to ~ to prison : écrouer

committal : remise *(f)*

    ~ for sentence : remise pour condamnation à un tribunal supérieur

    ~ for trial : mise *(f)* en accusation/prévention, renvoi

    ~ order : ordre *(m)* d'écrou, mandat *(m)* de dépôt

    ~ proceedings : instruction *(f)*

    ~ to prison : ordre *(m)* d'écrou, incarcération *(f)*

committee : comité *(m)*, conseil *(m)*, commission *(f)*

commodities : denrées *(fpl)*

common : commun

 ~ **assault** : voies *(fpl)* de fait simple

 ~ **good** : intérêt commun/général

 ~ **informer** : voir **informer**

 ~ **knowlege** : fait *(m)* notoire, preuve *(f)* par commune renommée, rumeur *(f)* publique

 ~ **land** : terrain *(m)* à usage communal (surtout comme pâturage)

 ~ **law** : droit *(m)* coutumier et jurisprudentiel
  *(1) L'ensemble des institutions de droit anglo-saxon en tant qu'entité distincte des systèmes juridiques issus du droit romain **(civil law)**. (2) Le droit historique, antérieur aux codifications modernes. Cependant, ce droit reste valable tant qu'il n'a pas été remplacé par une loi moderne **(statute)**, qui reste d'interprétation étroite.*

 ~ **Sergeant** : titre historique de l'un des **circuit judges**

 ~ **weal** : intérêt commun

commotion : insurrection *(f)*

communication : communication *(f)*, liaison *(m)*

 interception of ~s : interception d'un liaison téléphonique, mise sur table d'écoute

community : communauté *(f)*, collectivité *(f)*

 ~ **policing** : îlotage *(m)*, police *(f)* de proximité

 ~ **service** : travail *(m)* d'intérêt général

commutation : commutation *(f)* de peine

commute : commuer

commuter : navetteur *(m)*

company : société *(f)* commerciale ou industrielle

 ~ **name** : dénomination *(f)* sociale

 limited liability ~ **(Ltd)** : société à responsabilité limitée (SARL)

 public limited ~ **(PLC)** : société anonyme (SA)

compel : contraindre

compensate : dédommager, compenser, indemniser

compensation : indemnité *(f)*, récompense *(f)*, dédommagement *(m)*

    claim for ~ : action en indemnité

    entitlement to ~ : droit à une indemnité

competence : capacité *(f)*, compétence *(f)*, ressort *(m)*

    ~ of a court (as to subject matter) : compétence absolue/matérielle/quant au fond

    ~ of a court (geographically) : compétence du lieu/locale/territoriale

competent : compétent

competition : (1) concurrence *(f)*, rivalité *(f)*; (2) concours *(m)*, compétition *(f)*

    ~ for prizes : concours dans lesquels les prix sont décernés selon les résultats des compétitions sportives prévus par les participants. En général, ces concours sont interdits.

competitive examination : concours *(m)*

complain : se plaindre, réclamer, rouspéter

complainant : plaignant *(m)*

complaint : plainte *(f)*

    ~ against the police : plainte contre la police
      *Toute plainte contre un policier ou contre les activités de la police en général doit être examinée à fond par le chef de police responsable et l'action appropriée mise sur pied. Dans le cas d'une plainte grave, il doit faire passer le dossier à la **Police Complaints Authority**. Cette dernière supervise toutes les plaintes et peut, soit passer le dossier au procureur pour qu'une instruction soit ouverte, soit conseiller qu'une audience disciplinaire ait lieu, soit ordonner que l'affaire soit classée sans suite.*

    ~ s office : bureau des plaintes

complete : compléter

completed crime : délit *(m)* instantané, infraction *(f)* consommée

completion : consommation *(f)*

complicity : co-activité *(f)*, complicité *(f)*, connivence *(f)*, corréalité *(f)*

comply : se conformer, observer, obtempérer, obéir

compose : rédiger

compound : (1) fourrière *(f)*; (2) composer, pactiser

   to ~ a felony : voir **to compound an arrestable offence**

   to ~ an arrestable offence : composer/pactiser (avec un criminel)
   *Infraction introduite en 1967 pour remplacer le délit **to compound
   a felony**, et qui consiste à fermer les yeux sur un crime contre
   rémunération.*

compulsion : coaction *(f)*, contrainte *(f)*, violence *(f)*

compulsory : obligatoire, forcé

   ~ retirement : mise *(f)* à la retraite d'office

   ~ transfer : déplacement *(m)* d'office

computer : ordinateur *(m)*

   ~ fraud : fraude *(f)* télématique

   ~ hacker : pirate *(m)* informatique

   ~ peripherals : péri-informatique *(m)*

   ~ program : programme *(m)* d'ordinateur

   ~ science : informatique *(f)*

con * : dindonner, échauder, entourer, feinter, rouler

conceal : dissimuler, planquer, cacher

concealment : recel *(m)*, suppression *(f)*, dissimulation *(f)*

   ~ of birth : suppression de part

   ~ of body : recel de cadavre

   ~ of evidence : dissimulation de preuves

concerned : compétent, intéressé

   the department ~ : le service compétent

   the parties ~ : les intéressés *(mpl)*

concertina effect : effet *(m)* accordéon

conclusive : concluant, décisive, péremptoire

   ~ argument : argument concluant

   ~ evidence/proof : preuve décisive, fait concluant

~ **written evidence** : document probant

concourse : hall *(m)* d'accueil

concurrence : conflit *(m)*   ~ **of jurisdiction** : conflit de compétence

concurrent sentences : confusion *(f)* des peines, cumul *(m)* des peines

condemned : condamné   ~ **prisoner** : détenu condamné

condition : condition *(f)*, situation *(f)*, état *(m)*

> **in good/bad** ~ : en bon/mauvais état

> **prior** ~ : condition préalable

conditional : conditionnel

> ~ **discharge** : mise *(f)* à l'épreuve

condom : préservatif *(m)*, capote *(f)* anglaise

conduct : (1) comportement *(m)*; (2) mener, entamer, diriger, gérer

> ~ **money** : frais *(mpl)* de déplacement

> **safe** ~ : sauf-conduit *(m)*

> **to** ~ **an investigation** : faire une enquête

cone : balise *(f)*

confederate : complice *(m)*, comparse *(m&f)*

confess : avouer, admettre, accoucher, affaler, s'allonger, cracher

confession : aveu *(m)* judiciaire

confidence : confiance *(f)*

> ~ **trick** : escroquerie *(f)*, ramastique *(f)*, repassage *(m)*, vol *(m)* à l'américaine

> ~ **trickster** : escroc *(m)*

confidential information : coupure *(f)*

confinement : (1) détention *(f)*, emprisonnement *(m)*; (2) couches *(fpl)*

> **solitary** ~ : emprisonnement cellulaire (au secret)

confiscation : confiscation *(f)*

conflagration : incendie *(m)*

conflict : conflit *(m)*, dérogation *(f)*, contradiction *(f)*

confuse : brouiller

    ~ the scent : brouiller les pistes

connivance : connivence *(f)*

con-man : arnaqueur *(m)*, bidonneur *(m)*, filou *(m)*

consecutive (sentence) : cumul (des peines)

consent : consentement *(m)*

    age of ~ : âge *(f)* nubile (16 ans)

consideration (of the verdict) : délibéré *(m)*

consignee : destinataire *(m&f)*

consignor : expéditeur *(m)*

consistent : conforme, compatible, cohérent

conspiracy : association *(f)* de malfaiteurs, complot *(m)*, conspiration *(f)*, machination *(f)*

constable : (1) agent *(m)* de police; (2) gardien *(m)* de la paix
*Terme d'origine latine, **comes stabuli** (comte de l'étable), ayant la même racine que le mot français connétable. A l'origine un officier supérieur dans un château fort normand, le terme fut appliqué aux agents élus dans une commune pour maintenir l'ordre publique et pour faire appliquer les lois et règlements **(parish constables)**. Actuellement, tous les policiers britanniques ont la qualité de **constable**, bien que le terme soit réservé en fait aux grades les plus bas **(police constable)** et les plus hauts **(chief constable)**.*

    chief ~ : directeur *(m)* d'une des forces de police britanniques

    detective ~ : enquêteur *(m)*

    obstructing or resisting a ~ : gêner/entraver ou offrir de la résistance à un policier dans l'exercise de ses fonctions

    parish ~ : garde *(m)* champêtre, regardateur *(m)*

constabulary : police *(f)*
*Des lois de 1839 et 1856 ont obligé les autorités dans les **counties** à former leur propres forces de police, de même que dans les villes. Ces forces existent toujours dans la plupart des comtés tandis que, petit à petit, à l'exception des grandes agglomérations, les polices des villes ont été absorbées par les polices des comtés. Plus récemment, les polices de certains petits comtés se sont amalgamées pour former une police plus importante et plus efficace.*

constituency : circonscription *(f)* électorale

constraint : contrainte *(f)*, sujétion *(f)*, obligation *(f)*

construction : interprétation *(f)*

      strict ~ : interprétation littérale

constructive : établi par déduction

consultant : expert *(m)*

      legal ~ : conseil *(m)* juridique

consulting room : cabinet *(m)* de travail

consumable : chose *(f)* consomptible

contempt : mépris *(m)*

      ~ of court : atteinte *(f)* à l'autorité de la justice, mépris de la cour, contumace *(f)*, délit *(m)* d'audience

contents : (1) sommaire *(m)*, table *(f)* des matières;   (2) contenu *(m)*

contested : querellé

contiguous : limitrophe

contingency : contingence *(f)*, éventualité *(f)*, évènement *(m)* incertain

      ~ plan : plan *(m)* prévisionnel destiné à parer aux cas imprévus

continuing offence : infraction *(f)* continue

contraband : contrebande *(f)*

contract : contrat *(m)*

      ~ killing : nettoyage *(m)*

      ~ of employment : contrat d'emploi

contractor : entrepreneur *(m)*

contra-flow : circulation à deux sens sur une moitié d'autoroute (pour faciliter l'entretien, etc.)

contrary : contraire à, en opposé, à l'encontre de

      ~ to the law : contrairement aux prescriptions de la loi

      until the ~ is proved : jusqu'à preuve du contraire

contravene : contrevenir, transgresser, enfreindre

contravention : violation *(f)*

control : diriger, gouverner, avoir la maîtrise

> ~ **room** : salle *(f)* de commande

conversion (fraudulent ~) : malversation *(f)* de fonds d'autrui, détournement *(m)* de fonds

convertible (car) : décapotable *(f)*

convey : transporter

conveyance : transport *(m)*, véhicule *(f)*

convict : (1) condamné *(m)*, forçat *(m)*, bagnard *(m)*; (2) convaincre, condamner

> ~ **colony** : lieu *(m)* de transportation

> ~ **prison** : bagne *(m)*, pénitencier *(m)*

convicted : déclaré coupable

> ~ **person** : condamné *(m)*

conviction : condamnation *(f)*, balancement *(m)* *

> **record of previous ~s** : casier *(m)* spécial, dossier *(m)* du prévenu

> **summary ~** : condamnation par un juge de paix

convincing : crédible

co‑offender : codélinquant *(m&f)*

cooking the books * : cuisinage *(m)*, falsification *(f)* des comptes

cooler * : séchoir *(m)*, cellule *(f)*

cooling down * : dégrisement *(m)*

cooling off period : période de réflexion pour les adversaires dans un conflit

cooperation : concours *(m)*

cop * : (1) bordille *(f)* *, cogne *(f)* *, poulet *(m)* *, flic *(m)* *; (2) écoper *, piger *, récolter *

> ~ **culture** : subculture des gardiens de la paix ou gendarmes

> ~**-shop** * : lardu *(m)* *, Maison *(f)* pouleman *, commissariat *(m)* de police

> **to ~ a five‑year stretch** : écoper de cinq longes

copper : (1) cuivre rouge *(m)*; (2) * see **cop**

copy : ampliation *(f)*, copie *(f)*, exemplaire *(m)*, numéro *(m)*, expédition *(f)*

"**certified a true ~ "** : "pour ampliation", "pour copie conforme"

certified ~ : copie authentique

corner shop : magasin *(m)* de proximité

coroner : officier d'ordre judiciaire et administratif à la fois, chargé de faire une enquête **(inquest)** en cas de mort violente ou suspecte

corporal : (1) brigadier *(m)*; (2) corporel

~ punishment : peine corporelle, châtiment corporel

corps : corps *(m)*

~ of drums : batterie *(f)*

corpse : cadavre *(m)*, macchabée *(m)*

correct : régulier, en bonne et due forme

corroborate : corroborer, confirmer

corroboration : corroboration *(f)*, confirmation *(f)*

corroborating evidence : preuve *(f)* corroborante

corrupt : (1) corrompu, vénal; (2) corrompre, pervertir

corruption : corruption *(f)*

cosh : boudin *(m)*, casse-tête *(m)*

costermonger : marchand *(m)* de quatre saisons

cost of living : coût *(m)* de la vie

costs : dépense *(f)*, frais *(mpl)*, coût *(m)*

court ~ : frais judiciaires, frais de justice

cough * : cracher *, avouer, se mettre à table

council : conseil *(m)*, assemblée *(f)*

borough ~ : conseil municipal

~ chamber : parloir *(m)*

~ for the resettlement of offenders : comité *(f)* de probation et d'assistance   aux libérés county ~ : conseil général

district ~ : conseil communal

town ~ : conseil municipal

councillor : édile *(m)*, conseiller *(m)*
Membre élu d'un council.

counsel : conseiller *(m)*, avocat *(m)*, avocat-conseil *(m)*

~ for the defence : défenseur *(m)*

~s speech : plaidoirie *(f)*

count (of indictment) : chef *(m)* d'accusation

counter : comptoir *(m)*, guichet *(m)*

counter-espionage : contre-espionnage *(m)*

counter-evidence : contre-preuve *(f)*, preuve *(f)* contraire

counterfeit : contrefaire

~ coin : fausse monnaie

counterfeiting (coins) : falsification/fabrication *(f)* (de fausse monnaie), faux-
monnayage *(m)*

counterfoil : talon *(m)*, souche *(f)*

countermand : annuler, rappeler, révoquer

countersign : contresigner

counter-signature : contreseing *(m)*, visa *(m)*

counter-subversion : contre-ingérence *(f)*

country : pays *(m)*

county : comté *(m)*, = département *(m)*

~ council : conseil *(m)* général

~ court : tribunal *(m)* d'instance (chambre civile)

couple : couple *(m)*, binôme *(m)*

course : (1) parcours *(m)*; (2) stage *(m)*

in the ~ of duty : dans l'exécution de la fonction

training ~ : stage de formation

court : cour *(f)*, tribunal *(m)*

> **Central Criminal ˜** : cour d'assises de Londres
> *La **Crown Court** s'appelle ainsi quand elle siège à Londres. Elle est plus familièrement connue comme **The Old Bailey**.*

> **circuit ˜** : tribunal criminel itinérant

> **civil ˜** : tribunal civil, chambre civile

> **county ˜** : tribunal de première instance

> **˜ house** : siège *(m)* du tribunal de police

> **˜ list** : rôle *(m)*

> **˜ martial** : conseil *(m)* de guerre, tribunal aux armées, falot

> **˜ minutes** : feuille *(f)* d'audience

> **˜ of appeal** : cour d'appel

> **˜ of criminal appeal** : cour d'appel contre des condamnations criminelles
> *Abolie en 1966 et remplacée par la division criminelle de la cour d'appel.*

> **˜ of criminal jurisdiction** : cour de juridiction criminelle
> *Par exemple : les **magistrates' courts, crown court, Queen's Bench divisional court, court of appeal (criminal division)** et the **House of Lords**.*

> **˜ of summary jurisdiction** : expression désuète pour **magistrates' court**

> **˜ records** : archives *(fpl)* judiciaires

> **˜ room** : salle *(f)* d'audience

> **˜ sitting/hearing** : audience *(f)*

> **criminal ˜** : tribunal correctionnel, chambre *(f)* correctionnelle

> **juvenile ˜** : tribunal pour mineurs

> **Law ˜s** : palais *(m)* de justice

> **magistrates' court** : tribunal de simple police

> **open ˜** : audience *(f)* publique

> **police ˜** : tribunal de simple police

> **Queen's Bench Divisional ˜** : cour d'appel
> *Statuant sur des questions d'interprétation du droit, ses décisions forment la base du droit jurisprudentiel.*

cover : (1) pli *(m)*, (2) fausse identité *(f)*

      plain ~ : pli neutre

covering letter : lettre *(f)* annexe

covert : occulte, clandestin

create a disturbance : troubler l'ordre public

credit card : carte *(f)* de crédit

craft knife : cutter *(m)*

crafty : roublard

crash : collision *(f)*, accident *(m)*

      ~ **bar** : arceau *(m)* de protection

      ~**-landing** : atterrissage *(m)* forcé

crawler * : cafard *(m)* *, cafardeur *(m)* *

credentials : papiers *(mpl)* d'identité

crew : équipe *(f)*

crime : acte *(m)* criminel
    Tout acte ou omission illégale qui est une contravention contre le public
    (l'Etat) et qui rends le/la coupable susceptible d'une peine.

      continuing ~ : délit *(m)* continu

      ~ **complaint** : plainte *(f)*

      ~ **of passion** : crime *(m)* passionnel

      ~ **prevention** : prévention *(f)* de la criminalité

      ~ **sheet** : feuille *(f)* des accusations

      ~ **statistics** : criminalité *(f)*

      organised ~ : banditisme *(m)*

criminal : (1) pénal, criminel; (2) truand *(m)*, malfaiteur *(m)*

      ~ **act** : délit pénal, action criminelle

      ~ **attempt** : attentat *(m)*

      ~ **bankruptcy** : banqueroute *(f)*

      ~ **court** : chambre *(f)* correctionnelle

~ **damage** : dommages *(mpl)* délictueux, destruction *(f)*, dégradations *(fpl)* et dommages *(mpl)*, dommage *(m)* aux biens

~ **injuries compensation board** : commission *(f)* d'indemnisation des victimes d'infractions pénales

~ **intelligence** : renseignements criminels

~ **intent** : dol *(m)*, faute *(f)* intentionnelle, intention *(f)* délicteuse

~ **investigation** : recherche criminelle

~ **investigation department** : police *(f)* judiciaire

~ **jurisdiction** : juridiction pénale

~ **law** : droit pénal, code pénal, loi *(f)* répressive

~ **liability** : responsabilité pénale

~ **libel** : écrit *(m)* diffamatoire qui risque de troubler l'ordre publique

~ **matters** : affaires criminelles

~ **offence** : délit *(m)*

~ **procedure** : procédure pénale

~ **proceedings** : poursuites criminelles

~ **propensities** : état *(m)* dangereux

~ **recklessness** : faute *(f)* d'imprudence

~ **record** : casier *(m)* judiciaire, case *(m)*, almanach *(m)*, pédigree *(m)*

~ **record office** : casier *(m)* judiciaire

~ **responsibility** : responsabilité pénale

~ **trespass** : violation *(f)* de domicile

petty ~ : demi-sel *(m)*

criminology : criminologie *(f)*

crook : truand *(m)*, escroc *(m)*, agrincheur *(m)*, faisan *(m)*, grinche *(m)*, malfrat *(m)*, malin *(m)*

cross-border : transfrontalier

crossbow : arbalète *(f)*
  Les arbalètes ne sont pas classées comme armes à feu mais la vente et l'usage en est contrôlé par une loi particulière.

cross-examination : audition *(f)* contradictoire, interrogatoire *(m)* croisé

crossroads : carrefour *(m)*, croisement *(m)*

crowbar : pince-monseigneur *(f)*, pied-de-biche *(m)*, dingue *(f)*, peigne *(m)*

crowd : foule *(f)*, cohue *(f)*

~ **control** : contrôle *(m)* des foules

crown : la Couronne, la Reine, (= l'Etat)

~ **court** : tribunal *(m)* de grande instance

Crown Prosecution Service : le parquet *(m)*, la magistrature *(f)* debout

crude : basique

cruelty : cruauté *(f)*, sévices *(mpl)*

~ **to animals** : cruauté envers les animaux

crush : écraser, supprimer

cul-de-sac : cul-de-sac *(m)*, impasse *(f)*, voie *(f)* sans issue

culpable : coupable, blâmable

~ **negligence** : négligence coupable

culpability : faute *(f)* délictuelle

culprit : coupable *(m&f)*

cumulative offence : infraction *(f)* d'habitude

currency : monnaie *(f)*, devises *(fpl)*

current : en vigueur

curtilage : enclos *(m)* avec habitation

custodial sentence : peine *(f)* privative de liberté, peine *(f)* afflictive

custody : garde *(f)*, emprisonnement *(m)*

~ **of a child** : garde d'un enfant

~ **officer** : policier *(m)* responsable pour la réception des prisonniers

~ **record** : procès-verbal *(m)* de garde à vue
*Etat dressé par un **custody officer** pour chaque personne en état de prévention, à qui une copie doit être remise sur demande.*

in ~ : en état de prévention

surrender to ~ : se rendre aux autorités judiciaires
> *Dans le cas d'un individu remis en liberté sous caution, le fait de se rendre à la police ou au tribunal, selon les modalités de la caution.*

custom : coutume *(f)*, habitude *(f)*, usage *(m)*

customary : accoutumé, d'usage, habituel

~ residence : résidence habituelle

customs : douane *(f)*

Board of ~ : Administration *(f)* des douanes

~ duties : droits *(mpl)* de douane

~ officer : douanier *(m)*, gabelou *(m)* *

~ post : bureau *(m)* de douane

~ search/rummage : visite *(f)* de la douane

H.M. ~ : Direction *(f)* des douanes

customer : client *(m)*

awkward ~ : hérisson *(m)*

cut (1) * : fade *(m)*, taf *(m)*
> *La distribution du butin.*

cut (2) : couper

to ~ in : faire une queue de poisson

cycle : (1) bicyclette *(f)*; (2) faire de la bicyclette

motor- ~ : motocyclette

cyclist : cyclard *(m)*

cylinder : barillet *(m)* (d'un revolver)

D

dab * : arpège * *(f)*, piano *(m)*, (empreinte digitale)

dagger : poignard *(m)*

daily : quotidien, journalier, par jour

    ~ **state** : rapport journalier dressé à l'intention du commissaire central, faisant un résumé des crimes, évènements, etc. de la journée passée

damage : (1) dommage *(m)*, dégâts *(mpl)*; (2) endommager

    causing ~ **to trees** : abattage *(m)* d'arbres

    criminal ~ : destruction *(f)*, dégradations *(fpl)* et dommages, dommage aux biens, vandalisme *(m)*

    ~ **survey** : expertise *(f)* de dégâts

    ~ **to property** : dégâts matériels

damaged : sinistré

damages (award of) : dommages-intérêts *(mpl)*, intérêts *(mpl)* civils

dance : danse *(f)*, bal *(m)*

danger : danger *(m)*, péril *(m)*

dangerous : dangereux

    ~ **driver** : danger *(m)* public, chauffard *(m)*

    ~ **performance** : spectacle dangereux

    ~ **wild animal** : bête *(m)* féroce
        Le ***Dangerous Wild Animals Act, 1976*** *interdit la possession, sans autorité, des animaux féroces tels que chiens sauvages, loups, babouins, crocodiles, cobras, lions, tigres, léopards, panthères, chimpanzés.*

daredevil : casse-cou *(m)*

dark figure : chiffre *(m)* noir
    Le nombre des crimes et délits dont les autorités n'ont pas connaissance.

data : données *(fpl)*

    ~ **bank** : banque *(f)* de données

    ~ **base** : base *(f)* de données

    ~ **processing** : informatique *(f)*

date : date *(f)*

    out of ~ : périmé

    up–to– ~ : à jour, au point

dated : (1) en date du; (2) démodé, suranné

daughter : fille *(f)*

    ~ **–in–law** : belle-fille, bru *(f)*

    step– ~ : belle-fille

day : jour *(m)*

    ~ **off** : jour de congé

    ~ **of grace** : jour/délai de grâce

    ~ **training centre** : centre *(m)* de formation journalière
        Centre pour la rééducation sociale des malfaiteurs mis en liberté
        sous une telle condition.

    rest ~ : jour de repos

    working ~ : jour ouvrable

dead–end : impasse *(f)*

    ~ **job** : travail *(m)* sans débouchés, garage *(m)* *

deadline : date *(f)* limite

deadlock : impasse *(f)*

deal (in drugs) : dealer, trafiquer

dealer : marchand *(m)*

    ~ **in drugs** : dealer *(m)*, trafiquant *(m)*

dealings : agissements *(mpl)*

    fraudulent ~ : agissements frauduleux

death : mort *(f)*, décès *(m)*

    causing ~ **by dangerous/reckless driving** : homicide *(m)* par conduite
        dangereuse/imprudente

    ~ **benefit** : indemnité *(f)* en cas de décès

    ~ **certificate** : acte *(m)*/constat *(m)* de décès

~ **sentence** : arrêt *(m)* de mort, peine *(f)* capitale, condamnation *(f)* à mort

~ **warrant** : ordre *(m)* d'exécution

evidence of ~ : constatation *(f)* d'un décès

presumption of ~ : présomption *(f)* de décès

sudden ~ : mort subite

suspicious ~ : mort suspecte

debatable : discutable

debauch : débaucher, acoquiner

debauchery : débauche *(f)*

debt : dette *(f)*

debug : démicroter, dératiser

decease : décéder

deceased : défunt *(m)*, mort *(m)*

deceitful : malhonnête

deceive : abuser, baiser, blouser, doubler

decency : pudeur *(f)*

decentralisation : décentralisation *(f)*

deception : tromperie *(f)*, dol *(m)* incident

     obtaining property/services by ~ : obtention des biens/services par tromperie

decide : décider

decision : décision *(f)*, jugement *(m)*

~ **making** : prise *(f)* de décision

interlocutory ~ : décision avant dire droit

to make a ~ : prendre une décision

to make a ~ **known** : porter une décision

decisive : décisoire

declaration : (1) jugement *(m)* du tribunal; (2) affirmation *(f)*; témoinage *(m)* fait sans serment customs ~ : déclaration *(f)* en douane

~ of interest : déport *(m)*

declassify : déclasser

decline (responsibility) : décliner (responsabilité)

deconsecration : désaffection *(f)*

decoration : décoration *(f)*, médaille *(f)*

decree : arrêté *(m)*, décret *(m)*, jugement *(m)*

~ absolute : jugement irrévocable

décriminalisation : décriminalisation *(f)*

decriminalise : dépénaliser

deduction : prélèvement *(m)*

deed : (1) action *(f)*; (2) acte *(m)*, instrument *(m)*
Acte écrit, signé, scellé et signifié, concernant un marché, un contrat, une cession, etc.

deemed : supposé, jugé, estimé, considéré

deep-seated (conviction) : intime (conviction)

deface : oblitérer, effacer

defacing coin : dépréciation *(f)* de la monnaie

defamation : diffamation *(f)*
Allégation ou imputation qui porte atteinte à l'honneur ou à la considération d'une personne. Une telle action peut être opposée sur le motif de justification, vérité, privilège ou observation juste.

defamatory : infamant

defame : diffamer

default : défaut *(m)*, contumace *(f)*, manquement *(m)*

defeasible : capable d'être annulé

defect : défaut *(m)*, vice *(m)*

defective : défectueux

defence : défense *(f)*

counsel for the ~ : défenseur *(m)*

national ~ : défense nationale

self- ~ : défense de soi

defend : défendre

defendant : accusé *(m)*, prévenu *(m)*

defer : différer

defraud : frauder

defuse : désamorcer

degrade : acoquiner

degree : (1) diplôme *(m)*, licence *(f)* universitaire; (2) degré *(m)*, rang *(m)*, échelon *(m)*

~ **of accuracy** : degré de précision

delay : retard *(m)*, délai *(m)*, sursis *(m)*

delegate : délégué *(m)*, député *(m)*

~**d legislation** : règlements *(mpl)* (décrets, arrêtés, ordonnances, etc.)
Règlements issus par les ministres ou autorités administratives sous délégation de la part du Parlement.

delegation : délégation *(f)*, subrogation *(f)*

delete : radier

deletion : radiation *(f)*, suppression *(f)*

deliberate : (1) délibéré, intentionnel, prémédité; (2) délibérer, débattre

deliberately : avec préméditation

delict : délit *(m)*

delinquency : délinquence *(f)*, culpabilité *(f)*, faute *(f)*

delinquent : délinquant *(m)*, coupable *(m&f)*, fautif *(m)*

deliver : livrer, transmettre

delivery : livraison *(f)*, signification *(f)*

demanding with menaces : chantage *(m)*

"de minimis non curat lex" : "la loi ne s'occupe pas de choses peu importantes"

demise : décès *(m)*

demolish : démolir

demonstration : manifestation *(f)*

demonstrator : manifestant *(m)*

demotion : abaissement *(m)*, rétrogradation *(f)*

denial : dénégation *(f)*, déni *(m)*

> ~ of justice : déni de justice

denizen : indigène *(m&f)*, habitant *(m)*
> *Un étranger qui a reçu une autorisation du souverain, lui donnant la qualité de citoyen britannique.*

denounce : dénoncer, griller *

denouncement : délation *(f)*

denuciation : accusation *(f)* publique, dénonciation *(f)*

dented : cabossé

denunciation : délation *(f)*

Denver boot : sabot *(m)* d'Anvers

deny : désavouer, nier, contester

department : service *(m)*, sous-direction *(f)*

> ~ store : grand magasin *(m)*

dependence : assuétude *(f)*, dépendance *(f)*

> physical ~ : dépendance physique

> psychological ~ : dépendance psychique

dependant : personne *(f)* à charge, charge *(f)* de famille

deponent : déposant *(m)*

deportation : expulsion *(f)*

depose : déposer sous serment

deposit : (1) acompte *(m)*, consignation *(f)*; (2) déposer

deposition :   constat *(m)* d'audience, déclaration *(f)* sous serment

depravity : turpitude *(f)*

deprivation : privation *(f)*

    ˜ of citizenship : privation de citoyenneté (d'un citoyen naturalisé)

    ˜ de property : privation de biens, confiscation

deputize : remplacer

deputy : adjoint *(m)*, substitut *(m)*, suppléant *(m)*

    ˜ assistant commissioner : grade supérieur dans la **Metropolitan Police** (Londres), l'équivalent d'un **deputy chief constable**

    ˜ chief constable : l'adjoint à un des **chief constables.** *Ce grade correspond plus ou moins à un sous-directeur de l'un des services de police française.*

derangement : aliénation *(f)* mentale

derelict : chose *(f)* sans maître

dereliction of duty : négligence *(f)* dans le service, manquement *(m)* au devoir

description : signalement *(m)*, libellé *(m)*

descriptive form : fiche *(f)* signalétique

deserter : déserteur *(m)*, désert *(m)* *, insoumis *(m)*

desertion : désertion *(f)* délaissement *(m)*

    ˜ of the family : abandon *(m)* de famille

designate : désigner

desistance : désistement *(m)*

desk : bureau *(m)*, caisse *(f)*

destroy : démolir
Rendre quelque chose inutile pour l'usage auquel il est destiné.

detail : (1) détailler; (2) renseignement *(m)*, information *(f)*, détail *(m)*

detailed : détaillé, circonstancié

detain : détenir, retenir, garder

detainee : détenu *(m)*

detainer (writ of ˜) : mandat *(m)* de dépôt, confirmant l'incarcération d'un individu déjà détenu pour un autre motif

detection : dépistage *(m)*

detective : enquêteur *(m)*, inspecteur *(m)*

~ **chief inspector** : inspecteur divisionnaire

~ **chief superintendent** : commissaire *(m)* divisionnaire (de la police judiciaire)

~ **constable** : enquêteur

~ **inspector** : inspecteur principal

~ **novel** : roman *(m)* policier, série *(f)* noire

~ **sergeant** : inspecteur

~ **superintendent** : commissaire *(m)* principal (de la police judiciaire)

private ~ : détective *(m)*, fouille-merde *(m&f)* *

detention : détention *(f)*, incarcération *(f)*, emprisonnement *(m)*

~ **centre** : centre *(m)* de formation pour jeunes délinquants

~ **in police cells** : garde *(f)* à vue

~ **on remand** : détention provisoire

~ **on suspicion** : détention préventive

determine : constater, déterminer

detonator : détonateur *(m)*

detriment : détriment *(m)*.   **to the** ~ **of** : au détriment de

deviant : marginal *(m)*

diagram : graphique *(m)*

diary : journal *(m)*

diddle * : arnaquer *, échauder *

die : décéder

difference : différend *(m)*

differences : démêlés *(mpl)*

digest : (1) code *(m)* des lois; (2) résumé *(m)*

digs * : carrée *(f)*, piaule *(f)*

dilatory : dilatoire

dilemma : impasse *(f)*

diminished responsibility : démence *(f)*

din : vacarme *(m)*, tapage *(m)*, raffut *(m)*

diploma : diplôme *(m)*, brevet *(m)*

diplomatic : diplomatique

    ~ **bag** : valise *(f)* diplomatique

    ~ **immunity** : immunité *(f)* diplomatique, immunité *(f)* de juridiction

dipped headlights : en code

dipping * : vol *(m)* à la tire

direct : (1) diriger, ordonner, conseiller, guider;   (2) immédiat, direct

    ~ **cause** : cause immédiate

    ~ **evidence** : preuve directe

    ~ **examination** : voir **examination-in-chief**

direction : directive *(f)*, ordre *(m)*, direction *(f)*, sens *(m)*, instruction *(f)*

directive : directive *(f)*

director : administrateur *(m)*/gérant *(m)* d'une société

    board of ~s : conseil *(m)* d'administration

    ~ **of Public Prosecutions** : = Procureur *(m)* Général, chef *(m)* du parquet
        Un avocat expérimenté travaillant sous la direction générale du
        Attorney-General. *Il s'occupe du ministère public en cas*
        d'assassinat ou des affaires graves, considère des plaintes contre
        la police qui lui sont soumises, et peut représenter la Couronne à
        la cour d'appel. Son consentement doit être obtenu pour la
        poursuite de certaines infractions.

directorate : direction *(f)*

directory : répertoire *(m)*, guide *(m)*

    telephone ~ : annuaire *(m)*

    trades ~ : annuaire *(m)* du commerce, Bottin *(m)*

disability : incapacité *(f)*, infirmité *(f)*

    permanent ~ : incapacité/invalidité *(f)* permanente

disabled : incapable de travailler

~ **driver** : conducteur *(m)* handicapé
De tels conducteurs jouissent d'un régime de stationnement favorisé.

~ **person** : handicapé *(m)*, mutilé *(m)*, invalide *(m&f)*

~ **serviceman** : invalide *(m&f)* de guerre

disablement : invalidité *(f)*

disadvantaged (person) : indigent *(m)*

disaffection : désaffection *(f)*

disagreement : différend *(m)*, désaccord *(m)*

disallow : rejeter, rebuter

disarm : désarmer

disaster : calamité *(f)*, catastrophe *(f)*, sinistre *(m)*

~ **area** : zone sinistrée

~ **victim** : sinistré *(m)*

disavowal : désaveu *(m)*

disc : disque *(m)*.　　~ **brakes** : freins *(mpl)* à disques

discharge : (1) acquitter, débaucher, relâcher, relaxer, remettre en liberté, licencier;　(2) acquittement *(m)*, libération *(f)*, mise en liberté, relaxe *(f)*, licenciement *(m)*

absolute ~ : dispense *(f)* de peine

conditional ~ : mise en liberté conditionnelle

~ **from prison** : levée *(f)* d'écrou

final ~ : libération définitive

honourable ~ : mise *(f)* à la retraite

notice of ~ : préavis *(m)* de congé

disciplinary : disciplinaire

~ **action** : poursuites *(fpl)* disciplinaires

~ **body** : pouvoir *(m)* disciplinaire

~ **hearing** : audience *(f)* disciplinaire

~ **offence** : délit *(m)* disciplinaire

discipline : discipline *(m)*

disclaimer : dénégation *(f)*

discontinuance : désistement *(m)*

discovery (of documents) : communication *(f)* de pièces, édition *(f)* des pièces

discretion : discrétion *(f)*

discretionary : discrétionnaire

discrimination : discrimination *(f)*, distinction *(f)*, différence *(f)* de traitement

> ~ **on grounds of nationality** : discrimination pour raisons de nationalité
> *Défendue par le Traité de Rome.*

> **racial** : racisme, discrimination raciale
> *Défendu par le Race Relations Act, 1976.*

> **sexual** ~ : sexisme, discrimination sexuelle
> *Défendu par les Sex Discrimination Acts, 1976 & 1986.*

discriminatory : discriminatoire

discussion : discussion *(f)*, examen *(m)*, débat *(m)*, délibération *(f)*

> **under** ~ : à l'étude *(f)*

disease : maladie *(f)*

> **industrial/occupational** ~ : maladie professionnelle

disenfranchisement : incapacité *(f)* électorale

dishonest : malhonnête, de mauvaise foi

disk : disque (d'ordinateur)

dismiss : (1) congédier, renvoyer, licencier, destituer, casser;
(2) rejeter, débouter

dismissal : congé *(m)*, exclusion *(f)* définitive du service, congédiement *(m)*,
renvoir *(m)*, licenciement *(m)*; (2) rejet *(m)*, abandon *(m)*, exclusion *(f)*;
(3) relaxe *(f)*, rejet *(m)*

> **unfair** ~ : licenciement abusif

disinhibiting : désinhibant (effet de certaines drogues)

disinterested : désintéressé

dislocate : disjoncter

dismantle : désosser

dismiss : casser, destituer

dismissal : acquittement *(m)*, destitution *(f)*, révocation *(f)*

    unfair ~ : licenciement *(m)* sans justification

disobey : désobéir

disorder : désordre *(m)*, trouble *(m)*

disorderly : irrégulier, désordonné

    ~ **conduct** : atteinte *(f)* à l'ordre public

    ~ **house** : maison mal famée, maison de débauche

    drunk and ~ : en état d'ivresse publique

    ~ **behaviour** : comportement désordonné

dispatch note : bordereau *(m)* d'expédition

dispensation : délation *(f)*, relèvement *(m)*

    ~ **from taking the oath** : délation de serment

displacement : déplacement *(m)*

disposal : disposition *(f)*

disposition : disposition *(f)*

dispossess : dessaisir

dispossession : dépossession *(f)*

dispute : dispute *(f)*, litige *(m)*, conflit *(m)*, différend *(m)*

    industrial/trade ~ : conflit social, conflit de travail

disqualification : incapacité *(f)*

    ~ **from driving** : avoir son permis de conduire suspendu

disqualified : incapable

    ~ **by law** : frappé d'incapacité

    ~ **driver** : conducteur *(m)* auquel on a retiré le permis

    ~ **from making a will** : incapable de tester

disreputable : mal famé

disrupt : disjoncter

dissolute : irrégulier

distance covered : parcours *(m)*

distinguish (between) : faire la distinction *(f)* (entre)

distinguished : important, distingué

distraint : contrainte *(f)* par saisie des biens

distress : saisie en cas de non paiement de dette

    ~ **warrant** : mandat *(m)* de saisie

distribution : distribution *(f)*

district : région *(f)* (d'un pays); quartier *(m)*, arrondissement *(m)* (d'une ville),

    ~ **council** : conseil *(m)* communal

    ~ **nurse** : infirmière *(f)* visiteuse

    ~ **registrar** : juge *(m)* subordonné de la **County Court**

disturb : troubler, déranger

disturbance : agitation *(f)*, trouble *(m)*, émeute *(f)*, perturbation *(f)*

    mental ~ : aliénation *(f)* mentale

disuse : désuétude *(f)*

    law fallen into ~ : loi tombée en désuétude

dive * : (café) borgne, bouge *(m)*

diver : plongeur *(m)*

diversion : détournement *(m)*, détour *(m)*

    ~ **of documents** : diversion *(f)* de pièces

division : circonscription *(f)*, chambre *(f)*

    ~**s of the High Court** : chambres de la Haute Cour de Justice

divisional : divisionnaire

    ~ **commander** : commissaire *(m)* central

    ~ **headquarters** : commissariat *(m)* central

dock : banc *(m)* des accusés

> ~ **brief** : procédure *(f)*, largement désuète, par laquelle un accusé pouvait choisir son défenseur parmi les avocats présents dans la salle d'audience.

> ~ **statement** : déclaration *(f)*, sans serment, faite du banc par l'accusé

dockyard : chantier *(m)* naval

doctor : médecin *(m)*

> to ~ **accounts** : truquer/altérer/falsifier des comptes

document : acte *(m)*, document *(m)*, écrit *(m)*, écriture *(f)*, pièce *(f)*

> ~ **in proof** : pièce justificative

> **discovered** ~ : pièce communiquée

> **forged** ~ : faux en écritures

> **official** ~ : acte officiel, acte public

documentary evidence : instrument *(m)* de preuve, preuve *(f)* par titre

dodgy * : douteux

Doe, John : M. Un Tel *(m)*

dog : chien *(m)*

> ~ **handler** : maître *(m)* de chien

> ~ **racing** : course *(f)* de lévriers

> ~ **-section** : brigade *(f)* canine, brigade *(f)* cynophile

> **guard** ~ : chien de garde

domestic dispute : différend *(m)* entre époux

domicile : habitation *(f)*, domicile *(m)*
Alors qu'en droit français le domicile est le lieu du principal établissement et que le statut civil des personnes est régi par leur droit national, en droit anglais c'est la résidence permanente qui fournit le critère décisif de la notion de domicile.

> ~ **of choice** : domicile de choix

> ~ **of origin** : domicile de naissance

domiciliary : domiciliaire

donation : don *(m)*

door : porte *(f)*, portière *(f)* (d'une voiture)

    ~ **bell** : sonnette *(f)*

    ~ **chain** : chaîne *(f)* de sûreté

    ~ **frame** : chambranle *(m)*

    ~ **handle** : poignée *(f)* de porte/portière

    ~ **step** : seuil *(m)* de porte

door-to-door : porte à porte

    ~ **enquiries** : aller de porte en porte à la recherche des témoins

    ~ **search** : faire une perquisition systématique dans le quartier

    ~ **salesman** : démarcheur *(m)*

    ~ **selling** : démarchage *(m)*

doorkeeper : concierge *(m&f)*

double jeopardy : mise en cause de l'autorité de la chose jugée

double parked : en double file

double-cross : doubler

doubt : doute *(m)*

    benefit of the ~ : bénéfice *(m)* du doute

    reasonable ~ : doute bien fondé

doubtful : douteux

dough * : auber *(m)* *, fric *(m)* *, graisse *(f)* *, galette *(f)* *, grisbi *(m)* *, joncaille *(f)* *

down-and-out : sur le banc

downgrade : (1) déclasser; (2) dégrader

draft : avant-projet *(m)*, brouillon *(m)*

drag-net : rafle *(f)*, cueille *(f)*, filet *(m)*

draw (pistol, sword) : dégainer

    ~ **up** : dresser, établir, instrumenter, libeller, rédiger

dread : appréhender

dressing down : déshabillage *(m)*, réprimande *(f)*

drink : (1) boire; (2) boisson *(f)*

drive : conduire

driver : conducteur *(m)*, chauffeur *(m)*

    reckless ~ : chauffard *(m)*

driving : conduite *(f)*

    ~ instruction : leçon *(m)* de conduite

    ~ licence : permis *(m)* de conduire

    ~ test : examen *(m)* pour l'obtention du permis de conduire

    ~ whilst unfit : conduite en état d'intoxication ou d'ivresse

    ~ with alcohol concentration above prescribed limit : conduite avec alcoolémie au-dessus du niveau permis par la loi

    reckless ~ : conduite imprudente

drop-out : marginal *(m)*, margeo * *(m)*

drowned : noyé

drug : drogue *(f)*, stupéfiant *(m)*

    ~ addict : drogué *(m)*, toxicomane *(m&f)*

    ~ addiction : toxicomanie *(f)*

    ~ dealer : narcotrafiquant *(m)*

    ~ dependent : pharmacodépendant

    ~ trafficking : trafic *(m)* en stupéfiants

    ~ squad : brigade *(f)* des stupéfiants, antistups *

    use of ~s : usage *(m)* de stupéfiants

drum (1) : tambour *(m)*

    corps of ~s : batterie *(f)*

    ~ brake : frein *(m)* à tambour

drum (2) * : case *(f)* *, maison *(f)*

drunk : (1) ivre, intoxiqué, en état d'ivresse, givré *; (2) ivrogne *(m&f)*

~ **and disorderly** : en état d'ivresse manifeste

~ **in a public place** : en état d'ivresse publique

~ **-rolling** : vol *(m)* au poivrier

drunkenness : ivresse *(f)*, ébriété *(f)*

~ **in charge of a carriage/horse/child/firearm** : ayant la contrôle d'une voiture/cheval/enfant/arme à feu, en état d'ivresse.

due care : la prudence *(f)* exigée

dungarees : bleus *(mpl)* de travail, salopette *(f)*

duplicate : ampliation *(f)*, copie *(f)*

duplicating machine : polycopieuse *(f)*

duplicity : fraude *(f)*, tromperie *(f)*

duration : durée *(f)*

duress : contrainte *(f)*

during : durant

~ **Her Majesty's pleasure** : condamnation pour un temps indéfini *Condamnation utilisée en cas d'infraction grave par un aliéné ou pour meurtre commis par un mineur (moins de 18 ans).*

dustman : boueux *(m)*

Dutch : néerlandais

~ **auction** : enchères *(fpl)* au rabais

~ **-speaking** : néerlandophone

duties : devoirs *(mpl)*, fonctions *(fpl)*, responsabilités *(fpl)*

~ **sergeant** : brigadier *(m)* qui dresse le tableau de service d'une division

duty : (1) obligation *(f)*, fonction *(f)*, attributions *(fpl)*, devoir *(m)*, service *(m)*; (2) droit *(m)*, impôt *(m)*; (3) d'office

breach of ~ : infraction *(f)* au devoir

customs ~ : droit de douane

~ **-free** : détaxé, exempt des droits de douane

~ **officer** : agent *(m)* de service

~ **paid** : franc de douane

~ **solicitor** : avocat *(m)* d'office

excise ~ : impôts indirects, droits d'accise

export ~ : droits de sortie

off ~ : pas en service

on ~ : de permanence, en service commandé

dwelling : demeure *(f)*, domicile *(m)*, habitation *(f)*

~ **house** : maison *(f)* d'habitation

dying declaration : déclaration *(f)* faite par une personne qui croit qu'elle va bientôt mourir, concernant les événements qui ont causé sa mort.

dyke * : lesbienne *(f)*, gavousse * *(f)*, gousse * *(f)*, vrille * *(f)*

dynamite : dynamite *(f)*

E

earn : gagner

ease : assouplir

eavesdropping : atteinte *(f)* à la vie privée

edict : décret *(m)*

education : éducation *(f)*

      further ~ : formation *(f)* continue, enseignement *(m)* supérieur

effect : effet *(m)*

      concertina ~ : effet accordéon

      of no ~ : d'effet nul, nul et non avenu

      personal ~s : biens *(mpl)* personnels, effets

      to come into ~ : entrer en vigueur

      to give ~ : donner effet

      to take ~ : prendre effet

effectiveness : efficacité *(f)*

efficiency : compétence *(f)*

E-fit : portrait *(m)* robot

ejection : éviction *(f)*, expulsion *(f)*

elbow : coude *(m)*

      ~ **grease** : huile de coude

elect : élire, choisir

election : élection *(f)*

electoral roll : liste *(f)* électorale

electricity (abstraction of ~ **)** : (appropriation) d'électricité

element : élément *(m)*

eligible : apte, qualifié, admis

elimination : réduction *(f)*

elucidation : éclaircissement *(m)*

elucidate : élucider

emancipation : émancipation *(f)*

embezzlement : détournement *(m)* de fonds, abus *(m)* de confiance,
    malversation *(f)*
    Depuis 1968, ceci n'est plus une infraction distincte selon la loi anglaise.

embracery : subornation *(f)* d'un juré
    Cette infraction du droit coutumier est maintenant obsolescente.

emergency : urgence *(f)*, cas *(m)* urgent, situation *(f)* critique, cas *(m)* imprévu

    ~ **legislation** : mesures *(fpl)* d'exception, ordonnance *(f)*

    ~ **measures** : mesures *(fpl)* d'urgence, mesures *(fpl)* conservatoires

    ~ **powers** : pouvoirs *(mpl)* extraordinaires

    ~ **repairs** : réparations *(f)* d'urgence

    ~ **response unit** : police *(f)* secours

    ~ **vehicle** : voiture *(f)* de police secours

    state of ~ : état *(m)* d'urgence

emission : émission *(f)*

empanel (a jury) : dresser le tableau (des jurés)

employee : employé *(m)*

employer : employeur *(m)*, patron *(m)*

employment : emploi *(m)*, occupation *(f)*, situation *(f)*, activité *(f)*

    full-time ~ : emploi à temps plein

    part-time ~ : emploi à temps partiel

empower : habiliter, donner pouvoir

enabling order/statute : décret *(m)* ministériel, loi *(f)* d'habilitation, loi *(f)* cadre

enact : édicter, statuer, promulguer, ordonner, arrêter

enactment : texte *(m)* législatif, ordonnance *(f)*, décret *(m)*

encircle : ceinturer

enclosed : ci-inclus, joint(e)

enclosure : (1) clôture *(f)*; (2) document *(m)* annexe

encourage : encourager, atouser *

encouragement : incitation *(f)*

encroach : empiéter

    to ~ upon someone's rights : empiéter sur les droits de quelqu'un

encrypted radio : radio *(f)* chiffrée

enforce : faire exécuter, appliquer, mettre en vigueur

    ~ the law : appliquer les dispositions de la loi, faire observer la loi

    ~ obedience : se faire obéir

enforceable : exécutoire

enforcement : exécution *(f)*, mise *(f)* en vigueur

    ~ by legal process : exécution par la voie légale

    ~ of fines : recouvrement *(m)* des amendes

    ~ of the law : application *(f)* de la loi

enforcer : gorille *(m)*, terreur *(f)*

engage : engager

engine : moteur *(m)*

    ~ number : numéro *(m)* du moteur

enjoin : enjoindre

enquire : s'informer (de), se renseigner, demander, faire des recherches, enquêter

enquiry : enquête *(f)*, investigation *(f)*, instruction *(f)* (d'une affaire)

    board of enquiry : commission *(f)* d'enquête

    ~ office : bureau *(m)* de renseignements

    exhaustive ~ : enquête approfondie

    to conduct an ~ : procéder à une enquête

enrolment : enrôlement *(m)*, inscription *(f)*

enter : entrer

    ~ an appearance : comparaître

entertainment : spectacle *(m)*

enthusiast : amateur *(m)*, fêlé *(m)*

enticement : séduction *(f)*

entitlement : droit *(m)*

entrance : entrée *(f)*

entrapment : incitation *(f)* policière
  Incitation à commettre un délit qui justifiera ensuite l'arrestation de son auteur.

entrust : charger, confier

  to be ~ed with : être chargé de

entry : entrée *(f)*

  ~ fee : droit *(m)* d'inscription

  ~ into force : entrée en vigueur

  forcible ~ : effraction *(f)* (par voleur), entrée forcée (par la police)

environment : environnement *(m)*, mileu *(m)*

equipment : équipement *(m)*, matériel *(m)*

erase : radier

erasure : rature *(f)*

error : erreur *(f)*

escapade : fugue *(f)*

escape : (1) s'évader, (2) évasion *(f)*, fuite *(f)*

  ~d prisoner : évadé *(m)*, fugitif *(m)*

  ~ from custody : jouer la fille de l'air

escapee : évadé *(m)*

escort : (1) escorte *(f)*;   (2) escorter

espionage *(m)* : espionnage *(m)*

  industrial ~ : espionnage industriel

essence : essence *(f)*, fond *(m)*

  the ~ of a crime : l'élément *(m)* constitutif d'un crime

establish : établir, fonder, constater

> **to ~ a fact** : établir un fait

> **to ~ someone's identity** : établir l'identité de quelqu'un

establishment : (1) effectif *(m)*;   (2) établissment *(m)*, constatation *(f)*

> **business ~** : maison *(f)* de commerce

> **the ~** : les classes *(fpl)* dirigeantes

> **to be on the ~** : faire partie du personnel

estate : (1) domaine *(f)*; (2) biens *(mpl)*

> **~ agent** : agent *(m)* immobilier

> **real ~** : biens *(mpl)* immeubles/immobiliers

estimate : prévision *(f)*

euthanasia : euthanasie *(f)*

evade : éluder

evasion : faux-fuyant *(m)*, échappatoire *(f)*

> **~ of liability by deception** : l'échappatoire d'obligation par fraude

event : évènement *(m)*, occurrence *(f)*

> **current ~s** : l'actualité *(f)*

> **unforeseen ~** : occurrence imprévue

evict : expulser

eviction : éviction *(f)*, expulsion *(f)*, dépossession *(f)* judiciaire, rentrée *(f)* légale en possession

evidence : preuve *(f)*, raison *(f)* probante, témoignage *(m)*

> **admissible ~** : preuve recevable

> **best ~** : voir **primary evidence**

> **circumstantial ~** : preuve indirecte
> *Preuve concernant des faits indirects, à partir desquels on peut inférer un fait direct.*

> **conclusive ~** : fait *(m)*/preuve concluant

> **direct ~** : preuve directe
> *Ce qu'un témoin a vu, écouté ou éprouvé lui-même.*

documentary ~ : preuve littérale

~ a right : démontrer un droit

~ as to guilt : preuve de culpabilité

~ by witness : preuve testimoniale, témoignage

~ for the defence : preuve à décharge

~ for the prosecution : preuve à charge

~ of death : constatation *(f)* d'un décès

~ to the contrary : preuve contraire

false ~ : faux témoignage

hearsay ~ : preuve par commune renommée

inadmissible ~ : preuve irrecevable

indirect ~ : preuve indirecte
Comprend **hearsay evidence** *et* **circumstantial evidence.**

lack of ~ : insuffisance de motifs *(mpl)*

laws of ~ : théorie des preuves

new ~ : fait *(m)* nouveau

peremptory ~ : preuve libératoire

presumptive ~ : commencement *(m)* de preuve

prima facie ~ : commencement *(m)* de preuve

primary ~ : preuve qui s'impose comme la meilleure

real ~ : preuve réelle
Ce qu'on peut voir: par exemple des pièces à conviction.

secondary ~ : preuve qui laisse supposer l'existence d'une preuve meilleure (par ex. une copie d'un document)

statement of ~ : déposition *(f)*

to give ~ : déposer comme témoin

to turn Queen's ~ : témoigner contre ses complices (sous promesse de pardon ou moindre peine)

unsworn ~ : témoignage sans serment (par ex. témoignage par un enfant)

written ~ : preuve écrite

evident : apparent

examination : (1) instruction *(f)*, audition *(f)*, interrogatoire *(m)*; (2) examen *(m)*;
(3) étude *(f)*, inspection *(f)*, visite *(f)*

 competitive ~ : concours *(m)*

 cross ~ : interrogatoire contradictoire/croisé

 ~ board : jury *(m)* d'examen

 ~ of scene of crime : descente *(f)* sur les lieux

 ~ of witnesses : audition des témoins

 ~ in chief : interrogatoire par l'avocat qui a fait comparaître un témoin

 medical ~ : visite médicale

 post-mortem ~ : autopsie *(f)*

 under ~ : à l'étude *(f)*

examine : examiner

 to ~ witnesses : diligenter une enquête

examining magistrate/justice : magistrat *(m)* instructeur

exceed : dépasser, outrepasser

 to ~ one's authority : outrepasser ses pouvoirs, commettre un excès de
pouvoir

 to ~ the speed limit : dépasser la limitation de vitesse

exception to a witness : récusation *(f)* de témoin

excerpt : extrait *(m)*

excess : excès *(m)*

exchange : (1) échanger; (2) change (monnaie); (3) central *(m)* (téléphone)

excise : accise *(f)*

 Board of ~ : l'Administration des Douanes et des Contributions indirectes

 ~ duties : droits *(mpl)* d'accise, droits *(mpl)* indirectes

 ~ officer : agent de contributions indirectes

exclude : exclure

exclusion : exclusion *(f)*

~ **order** : ordre *(m)* d'interdiction
> *Interdiction d'entrée sur le territoire britannique (mesure contre-terrorisme) ou d'entrer dans certains lieux tels qu'un terrain de football (mesure de maintien de l'ordre)*

exculpation : disculpation *(f)*

excusable homicide : homicide *(m)* excusable
> *Homicide commis en défense de soi ou d'autrui, ou par accident.*

excuse : excuse *(f)*

ex-directory (telephone number) : (numéro de téléphone) sur "liste *(f)* rouge"

execute : exécuter

execution : exécution *(f)*

~ **of an order** : exécution d'une commande

in the ~ **of one's duties** : dans l'exercice *(m)* de ses fonctions

stay of ~ : opposition *(f)* à un jugement

executioner : bourreau *(m)*

executor : ayant cause *(m&f)*

exemplary damages : indemnité *(f)* pour préjudice moral

exemption : exemption *(f)*

exercise : exercer

exhaust : échappement *(m)*

~ **gas** : gaz *(m)* d'échappement

exhibit : pièce *(f)* à conviction, pièce *(f)* judiciaire

exhibition : exposition *(f)*, salon *(m)*

exhume : dépoter, déterrer

existence : existence *(f)*

ex officio : à titre d'office

exonerate : défarguer, disculper, exonérer

~ **from blame** : disculper

exonerating : déculpabilisant

exoneration : déculpabilisation *(f)*

ex parte : de la part de

expatriation : bannissement *(m)*

expel : expulser

expense(s) : frais *(mpl)*, dépenses *(fpl)*

      defray ~ : subvenir aux frais

      moving ~ : frais de déménagement

      office ~ : frais de bureau

      operating ~ : dépenses d'exploitation

      sundry ~ : frais divers

      travelling ~ : frais de déplacement

experience : expérience *(f)* professionnelle

experiment : expérience *(f)*

      ~s on animals : expériences sur les animaux

expert : expert *(m)*

      ~ opinion : avis *(m)* d'expert

      ~ assessment : expertise *(f)*

      handwriting ~ : expert en écritures, graphologue *(m&f)*

expiate : expier

expiation : repentir *(m)* actif

expired : périmé

explode : éclater

explosion : explosion *(f)*, éclatement *(m)*

explosive : explosif

export : exporter

      ~ duty : droit *(m)* de sortie

expose : exposer, dévoiler, démasquer

exposure : dénonciation *(f)*, dévoilement *(m)*

      indecent ~ : outrage *(m)* public à la pudeur

for fear of ˜ : par crainte du scandale

express : (1) exprès, formel; (2) exprimer, manifester; (3) expédier par exprès; (4) (train) rapide

expulsion : exclusion *(f)*

ex-serviceman : ancien combattant *(m)*

extended leave : rallonge *(f)*

extension (telephone ˜) : poste *(m)*

extenuating : atténuant

   ˜ **circumstances** : (1) circonstances *(fpl)* atténuantes; (2) excuses *(fpl)* atténuantes
     (1) peuvent être éventuellement admises par le tribunal; (2) doivent être admises par le tribunal selon la loi.

extinguishment : extinction *(f)*

   ˜ **of prosecution** : extinction de l'action publique

extort : extorquer

extortion : extorsion *(f)*, gouale *(m)*

extra : supplémentaire, en plus

   ˜ **costs** : frais *(mpl)* extraordinaires

   ˜ **expenses** : frais *(mpl)* accessoires

   ˜ **fare** : supplément *(m)*

   ˜ **pay** : supplément *(m)* de salaire

   ˜ **work** : travaux *(mpl)* supplémentaires

extract : extrait *(m)*

extradite : extrader

extradition : extradition *(f)*

extreme : extrême, outrancier

eyeball * : faire contact *(m)* visuel

eyepiece : oeilleton *(m)*

eye witness : témoin *(m)* oculaire

F

face : (1) figure *(f)*, gueule *(f)*;   (2) recto *(m)*

facilities : équipement *(m)*, installations *(fpl)*, moyens *(mpl)*, infrastructure *(f)*

fact : fait *(m)*, réalité *(f)*, élément *(m)*

    accessory after the ~ : complice *(m&f)* par assistance

    accessory before the : complice *(m&f)* par instigation

    ~s in issue : les faits à prouver

    primary ~s : preuve *(f)* directe
        Les faits qu'un témoin a vus ou supportés et dont il peut donner
        témoignage, ou bien la production d'un document original.

    relevant ~s: faits desquels on peut conclure les faits à prouver

factor : élément *(m)*

factory : usine *(f)*, manufacture *(f)*

    ~ worker : ouvrier *(m)* d'usine

fail : manquer, échouer, faire défaut

    ~ in one's duty : manquer à son devoir

failure : défaut *(m)*, manquement *(m)*

    ~ to appear : défaut de comparution

    ~ to report a crime : refus *(m)* de dénoncer

    ~ to stop : délit *(m)* de fuite

fair : juste

    ~ play : franc jeu *(m)*

    ~ trial : procès *(m)* équitable

    ~ wages : salaire *(m)* équitable

    ~ wear and tear : usure *(f)* normale

fairing (motorcycle) : carénage *(m)*

faith : foi *(f)*

    in good ~ : de bonne foi

fake : (1) maquiller;   (2) faux *(m)*, objet *(m)* truqué

fallacious : trompeur, erroné

   ~ **argument** : argument *(m)* faux, captieux

false : erroné, faux/fausse, trompeur, balourd

   ~ **accounting** : falsification *(f)* de documents

   ~ **accusation** : dénonciation *(f)* calomnieuse

   ~ **alarm** : fausse alerte

   ~ **arrest** : arrestation *(f)* arbitraire/illégale

   ~ **evidence** : faux témoignage

   ~ **imprisonment** : séquestration *(f)* arbitraire

   ~ **pretences** : obtention *(f)* de biens par tromperie (terme désuet)

   ~ **name** : faux nom, nom supposé

   ~ **witness** : faux témoin, faux témoignage

falsification : falsification *(f)*, faux *(m)*

   ~ **of accounts** : faux en écritures, falsification de documents, cuisinage *(m)*

falsify : falsifier, fausser
Transformer un document (par ex. par effacement) avec intention de tromper.

family : famille *(f)*.   ~ **allowance** : indemnité *(f)*/prestation *(f)* familiale

fan : fêlé *(m)*

fanatical : mordu

fancy goods : articles *(mpl)* de fantaisie

far : loin, lointain

   ~ **reaching** : d'une grande portée *(f)*, de grande envergure *(f)*

   in so ~ as : dans la mesure où

fare : prix *(m)* du transport, tarif *(m)*

farm : ferme *(f)*, entreprise *(f)* agricole

   ~ **worker** : ouvrier *(m)* agricole

fatal : mortel, fatal, inévitable

    ~ **accident** : accident *(m)* mortel

    ~ **injury** : blessures *(fpl)* ayant entraîné la mort

father : père *(m)*

    ~**-in-law** : beau-père

fatigues : corvée *(f)*, tenue *(f)* de corvée

fault : faute *(f)*, négligence *(f)*, défaut *(m)*, imperfection *(f)*, vice *(m)*

    to be at ~ : être fautif, être coupable

faulty : défectueux, erroné

fax : (1) fax *(m)*;   (2) faxer

fear : (1) appréhender; (2) appréhension *(f)*

feasibility study : étude *(f)* débouchant sur une solution techniquement possible
et applicable

feat : exploit *(m)*

feature : trait *(m)*, caractéristique *(f)*

feedback : rétroaction *(f)*, réitération *(f)*, information *(f)* en retour

fees : émoluments *(mpl)*

fellow : collègue *(m)*, compagnon *(m)*, complice *(m&f)*, mec *(m)* *

    ~**-prisoner** : codétenu *(m)*

    ~**-worker** : collaborateur *(m)*

felo de se : suicide *(m)*

felon : criminel *(m)*

felonious : criminel

felony : crime *(m)*, infraction *(f)* majeure
*Ce terme fut supprimé par la loi de 1967, qui l'a remplacé par la notion
d'**arrestable offence**.*

fence : (1) clôture *(f)*; (2) fourgat *(m)*, fourgue *(m)*, receleur *(m)*

fencing : escrime *(f)*

fiat : "Qu'il soit fait". Ordonnance délivrée par un juge de rang supérieur

fictitious name : nom *(m)* supposé

fiddle * : trictrac *(m)* *

fight : (1) bagarre *(f)*; (2) se battre, lutter

file : (1) dossier *(m)*, classeur *(m)*; (2) classer, verser au dossier

    personal ~ : dossier de personnalité

fill : remplir, exécuter

    ~ **a vacancy** : pourvoir à une vacance, nommer à un poste

filling station : station-service *(f)*

final : final, dernier, définitif, concluant

    ~ **demand** : mise *(f)* en demeure

    ~ **judgement** : jugement *(m)* définitif

financial standing : état *(m)* de fortune

find : trouver, découvrir, se rendre compte

    ~ **someone guilty** : déclarer quelqu'un coupable

finder : trouveur *(m)*, inventeur *(m)*

finding : conclusion *(f)* d'un tribunal

    ~ **of guilt** : déclaration *(f)* de culpabilité

fine : amende *(f)*, contravention *(f)*, peine *(f)* pécuniaire

fingerprint : empreinte *(f)* digitale

    ~ **classification** : formule *(f)* digitale

    ~ **identification** : dactyloscopie *(f)*

    ~ **identification form** : fiche *(f)* dactyloscopique

finish : fin *(f)*

fire : (1) feu *(m)*, incendie *(m)*; (2) tirer

    ~ **alarm** : avertisseur *(m)* d'incendie

    ~ **insurance** : assurance *(m)* incendie

firearm : arme *(f)* à feu

    ~ **licence** : permis *(m)* de porte d'arme

firecracker : pétard *(m)*

fireman : sapeur-pompier *(m)*

firework : feu *(m)* d'artifice

firing pin : percuteur *(m)*

firing range : champ *(m)* de tir

firm : entreprise *(f)*, firme *(f)*, société *(f)* de personnes

first aid : secourisme *(m)*, premier secours *(m)*

first offender : délinquant *(m)* primaire

fishery protection vessel : garde-pêche *(m)*

fishing : pêche *(f)*

fit for office : apte aux fonctions

fittings : installations *(fpl)*

fix (drugs) : (1) fixer; (2) prise *(f)*

fixed : fixe, déterminé

     ~ **penalty** : amende *(f)* forfaitaire, peine *(f)* fixe

     ~ **price** : prix *(m)* forfaitaire

fixtures and fittings : immeubles *(mpl)* par destination

flag : drapeau *(m)*, pavillon *(m)*

flagrante delicto : flagrant délit *(m)*

flash * : ridère, élégant

flasher * : exhibo *(m)*

flashing roof lamp : gyrophare *(m)*

flat cap : crêpe *(f)*

flatten : écraser

flaw : défaut *(m)*, vice *(m)* de forme

fleece : plumer

fleet : parc *(m)*

flexitime : horaire *(m)* flexible/variable

flight : fugue *(f)*, fuite *(f)*

flooding : inondation *(f)*

floor of the court : prétoire *(m)*

flout (justice) : bafouer

fly-by-night : personne *(f)* d'une moralité douteuse en affaires

Flying squad : brigade *(f)* mobile, groupe *(m)* de répression du banditisme, brigade *(f)* volante

fog : brouillard *(m)*

    ~-lamp : feu *(m)* anti-brouillard

folder : dépliant *(m)*, prospectus *(m)*

folk : gens *(mpl)*

follow : suivre, poursuivre, filer le train à quelqu'un

    ~ up a clue : suivre une piste

follower : ficelle *(f)*

foment : fomenter

foodstuffs : denrées *(fpl)* alimentaires

foot : pied *(m)*

    ~ball : foot *(m)*

    ~ passenger : piéton *(m)*

    ~path : chemin *(m)* de randonnée

    ~ patrol : patrouille *(f)* à pied

    ~ print : trace *(f)* de pas, empreinte *(f)* de pied

    ~rest : repose-pied *(m)*

    ~way : trottoir *(m)*

forbearance : indulgence *(f)*

forbid : interdire

force : (1) force *(f)*, puissance *(f)*, vigueur *(f)*, violence *(f)*; (2) forcer

    ~ majeure : force majeure

in ~ : en vigueur

police ~ : la police, la force publique

forced : forcé

forcible : violent, vigoureux, de force

~ **entry** : prise *(f)* de possession illégale d'un immeuble par violence

forcibly : par force

forecast : (1) prévision *(f)*; (2) prévoir

foregoing (the ~ **)** : ce qui précède

foreign : étranger, extérieur

~ **currency** : devises étrangères

~ **national** : ressortissant étranger

~ **Office/Secretary** : Ministère/Ministre *(m)* des Affaires Etrangères

foreigner : étranger *(m)*

foreman : contremaître *(m)*

~ **of the jury** : premier juré *(m)*

forename : prénom *(m)*, nom *(m)* de baptême

forensic : concernant des affaires juridiques

~ **medicine** : médecine *(f)* légale

~ **science** : criminalistique *(f)*

~ **scientist** : expert légiste *(m)*

~ **service** : identité *(f)* judiciaire

foresight : guidon *(m)*

forestall : prévenir

forest ranger : garde-forestier *(m)*

forfeiture : déchéance *(f)*

forge : contrefaire, falsifier, forger

forged : faux, fausse

~ **document** : pièce fausse

~ **instrument** : faux en écriture

~ **signature** : imitation *(f)* de signature

production of ~ **documents** : supposition *(f)*

forger : contrefacteur *(m)*, faussaire *(m)*, faux-monnayeur *(m)*

forgery : falsification *(f)*, faux *(m)*, imitation *(f)*, supposition *(f)*

fork : bifurcation *(f)*

form (1) : bulletin *(m)*; fiche *(f)*, imprimé *(m)*, formule *(f)*

application ~ : formulaire *(m)* de demande, de candidature

fill in a ~ : remplir une formule

form (2) : former, constituer, instituter

form (3) * : casier *(m)* judiciaire, almanach *(m)* *, case *(f)* *, pédigree *(m)* *

formal : formel.   ~ **notice** : mise *(f)* en demeure

formality : formalité *(f)*

formation : unité *(f)*

former : ancien

formula : formule *(f)*

formulate : formuler

forswear : abjurer

forthwith : sur le champ, immédiatement

fortuitous : casuel, fortuit

fortune teller : diseuse *(f)* de bonne aventure
C'est une infraction de prétendre être capable de dire la bonne aventure.

foster : (1) fomenter, stimuler; (2) élever, nourrir

~ **child** : enfant placé dans une famille

~ **home** : foyer *(m)* d'accueil

foul : malpropre, déloyal

fall ~ **of the law** : tomber sous le coup de la loi

~ **play** : scélératesse *(f)*

found : trouvé

~ **property** : objets *(mpl)* trouvés, trésor *(m)*

fourth estate : journalisme *(m)*

four–wheel drive : quatre–quatre *(m)*

fragment : pièce *(f)*, morceau *(m)*

frame : (1) cadre *(m)*; (2) monter un coup contre quelqu'un

fraud : fraude *(f)*, acte *(m)* frauduleux, coup *(m)* d'arnac, supercherie *(f)*

~ **squad** : section *(f)* des affaires économiques et financières

serious ~**s office** : bureau *(m)* des affaires économiques et financières graves

fraudsman : aigrefin *(m)*

fraudster : escroc *(m)*

fraudulent : frauduleux, dolosif

~ **conversion** : divertissment *(m)*, détournement *(m)* de fonds, malversation *(f)*

~ **misrepresentation** : fraude *(f)* pénale

~ **representation** : manoeuvres *(fpl)* frauduleuses

free : gratuit, libre, en liberté

freedom : liberté *(f)*

freight : fret *(m)*

~ **forwarder** : entrepreneur *(m)* de transports, transitaire *(m&f)*

frequenting : l'habitude de fréquenter un lieu (à des fins illégales)

fresh : frais, nouveau

~ **evidence** : de nouvelles preuves *(fpl)*

frightener * : terreur *(f)* *

frisk : arsonner, vaguer

frivolous : frivole

~ **pleading** : argument *(m)* futile, argument *(m)* non pertinent

frogman : plongeur *(m)*

front : (1) devant *(m)*, avant *(m)*; (2) couverte *(f)*, couverture *(f)*;

~ **forks** : fourche *(f)* de roue

~ **man** : homme *(f)* de paille, doublure *(f)*

~ **spoiler (auto.)** : becquet *(m)*

frontier : frontière *(f)*

~ **guard** : garde *(m)* frontière

frustrate : faire échouer

fuel tank : réservoir *(m)* d'essence

fugitive : fugitif *(m)*, prisonnier *(m)* évadé

~ **from justice** : fugitif recherché par la justice

~ **offender** : criminel *(m)* recherché dans un autre pays du Commonwealth,
vers lequel il peut être renvoyé pour être traduit en justice.

fulfil : accomplir, remplir, satisfaire à, exécuter

~ **a duty** : s'acquitter d'un devoir

full : plein, entier, complet, intégral

~ **age** : majorité *(f)*

~ **board** : pension complète

~ **disclosure** : divulgation complète

~ **name** : nom *(m)* et prénoms *(mpl)*

~ **text** : texte intégral

~ **time** : à temps plein

in ~ : en entier, intégralement

function : fonction *(f)*, office *(m)*, charge *(f)*, emploi *(m)*, rôle *(m)*

discharge one's ~**s** : s'acquitter de ses fonctions

resign one's ~**s** : se démettre de ses fonctions

functionary : fonctionnaire *(m&f)*

fund(s) : fonds *(mpl)*

funeral directors : pompes funèbres *(fpl)*

fun fair : fête *(f)* foraine, foire *(f)* foraine

furnish : fournir, pourvoir, alléguer, meubler

    ~ed accommodation : logement *(m)* garni

    ~ information : fournir des renseignements

further : supplémentaire, ultérieur, de plus, au-delà

    for ~ enquiry : pour plus ample informé

    ~ consideration : mise *(f)* en délibéré

    ~ education : formation *(f)* continue

    ~ information : renseignements *(mpl)* complémentaires

fusillade : fusillade *(f)*

fuzz * : les flics *(mpl)* *, bigorne *(f)* *

G

gag : (1) bâillon *(m)*;   (2) bâilloner

gain entrance : se faire entrer

gallows : échaufaud *(m)*, potence *(f)*

    ~-bird : gibier *(m)* de potence

gambling : jeu *(m)* de hasard

    ~ debt : dette *(f)* de jeu

    ~ den : tripot *(m)*

game (1) : gibier *(m)*

    ~-keeper : garde-chasse *(m)*

    ~ licence : permis *(m)* de chasse

game (2) : jeu *(m)*

    ~ of chance : jeu de hasard

gaming : jeu *(m)*, jeu de hasard

    ~ house : maison *(f)* de jeu

    ~ licence : concession *(f)* des jeux

gang : bande *(f)*

    ~ -bang : passage *(m)* en sérail, viol *(m)* collectif

gangland killing : règlement *(m)* de compte

gang-rape : viol *(m)* collectif

gangster : braqueur *(m)*

gantry : portique *(m)*

gaol : geôle *(f)*

    ~ fever : voir **jail fever**

garbled : inintelligible, incompréhensible

garrotting : étranglement *(m)*

gas : gaz *(m)*

gather : rassembler, recueillir, réunir, percevoir

    ~ **evidence** : recueillir des témoignages

gay : gay, homosexuel

gear : (1) équipement *(m)*, matériel *(m)*; (2) affaires *(fpl)*, vêtements *(mpl)*; (3) embrayage *(m)*, vitesse *(f)*

    change ~ : changer de vitesse

    ~ **box** : boîte *(f)* de vitesses

    ~ **lever** : sélecteur *(m)* de vitesses

    in ~ : en prise *(f)*

    neutral ~ : point *(m)* mort

general : (1) général; (2) général *(m)* d'armée

    brigadier-~ : général *(m)* de brigade

    ~ **headquarters** : direction-générale *(f)*

    ~ **office** : secrétariat *(m)*

    ~ **orders** : bulletin *(m)* de service, règlements *(mpl)* intérieurs, règles *(fpl)* de procédure

    ~ **rules/requirements** : dispositions *(fpl)* générales

    ~ **staff** : état-major *(m)*

    ~ **strike** : grève *(f)* générale

    lieutenant-~ : général *(m)* de corps d'armée

    major-~ : général *(m)* de division

genuine : authentique

gibbet : gibet *(m)*, échafaud *(m)*

gift : don *(m)*, cadeau *(m)*

gimmick : truc *(m)*

gipsy : bohémien *(m)*, gitan *(m)*, tsigane *(m&f)*, manouche *(m&f)*, rabouin *(m)* *Gens qui suivrent un mode de vie nomadique, nonobstant leur race ou origine.*

girl : fille *(f)*

Giro account : compte *(m)* courant postal (CCP)

give : donner, rendre

    ~ an order : passer un ordre

    ~ evidence : déposer

    ~ notice : donner préavis

    ~ way : céder la priorité

glasshouse : (1) serre *(f)*; (2) (mil.) caisse *(f)*

Glass's Guide : Argus *(m)*
Guide *à l'intention des garagistes et qui donne les prix des voitures d'occasion.*

glebe : terrain (m) cultivé ou qui appartient à l'église

glue-sniffing : inhalation *(f)* volontaire de colle ou solvant

goal : objectif *(m)*, but *(m)*

    ~ keeper : gardien *(m)*

goatee beard : barbichette *(f)*, bouc *(m)*

go-between : contact *(m)*, entremetteur *(m)*

god-child : filleul *(m)*, filleule *(f)*

god-father : (1) parrain *(m)*; (2) (mafia) caïd *(m)*

going equipped for stealing : en possession des outils destinés à faciliter le cambriolage, le vol ou la fraude (délit)

gold braid : broderie *(f)* d'or

gondola (supermarket) : gondole *(f)*, linéaire *(m)*

gong * : banane *(f)* *, médaille *(f)*

good : bon, bonne

    ~ faith : bonne foi *(f)*

goods : marchandise *(f)*, articles *(mpl)*

goodwill : (1) bonne volonté *(f)*, bienveillance *(f)*; (2) incorporels *(mpl)*, clientèle *(f)*

go-slow : grève *(f)* perlée

gossip : cancan *(m)*

    ~ -monger : grenouilleur *(m)*

government : gouvernement *(m)*

    ~ **employee** : fonctionnaire *(mf)* d'Etat

grace : grâce *(f)*, pardon *(m)*

grade : échelon *(m)*

graduate : diplôme *(m)*

graduation : promotion *(f)*

graffiti : graffiti *(mpl)*, graffiteur

graft * : corruption *(f)*

grand * : mille dollars, mille livres

    ~ **jury** : jury *(m)* d'accusation
        Ceci n'existe plus en Angleterre mais existe toujours aux Etats-
        Unis.

    ~ **larceny** : vol *(m)* d'une somme importante
        La distinction entre **grand larceny** *et* **petty** *(petit)* **larceny** *fut abolie*
        en Angleterre en 1827 mais elle existe toujours aux Etats-Unis.

grandeur : importance *(f)*

grant : accorder, impartir

    ~ **powers** : impartir des pouvoirs

grapevine : cancan *(m)*, téléphone *(f)* arabe

graph : graphique *(m)*

grass * : (1) arnaquer, balancer, déboutonner, donner, griller, morganer, retourner, se mettre à table, vendre; (2) balanceur *(m)*, bascule *(f)*, casserole *(f)*, chacail *(m)*, dénonciateur *(m)*, donneur *(m)*, indicateur *(m)*, informateur *(m)*, mouchard *(m)*; (3) herbe *(f)*, marijuana *(f)*

gratuitous : gratuit

gratuity : gratification *(f)*, pourboire *(m)*, pécule *(m)*

grave : fosse *(f)*

greaser : blouson *(m)* noir

green card : carte *(f)* verte

grenade : grenade *(f)*

    tear-gas ~ : grenade lacrymogène

grey figure : chiffre *(m)* noir
Le nombre de crimes qui ne sont pas portés à l'attention des autorités.

grievance : doléance *(f)*, grief *(m)*, injustice *(f)*

grievous bodily harm (GBH) : mutilation *(f)*, blessures *(fpl)* graves

grill : dépiauter, interroger

gross : gros, grossier, trop fort, brut

    ~ **indecency** : attentat *(m)* à la pudeur avec un homme ou avec un enfant

    ~ **negligence** : négligence *(f)* coupable

    ~ **weight** : poids brut

ground : (1) motif *(m)*, raison *(f)*; (2) terrain *(m)*

    ~ **for appeal** : grief *(m)* d'appel

    ~ **for complaint** : grief *(m)*

group : groupe *(m)*

    pressure ~ : groupe de pression

grown-up : grand, adult

growth : croissance *(f)*

guarantor : garant *(m)*

guard : garde *(f)*, surveillance *(f)*; (2) (corps de) garde *(m)*, piquet *(m)*;
(3) gardien *(m)*, factionnaire *(f)*

    ~ **dog** : chien *(m)* de garde, alarmiste *(m)* *

    ~ **mounting** : parade *(f)*

    ~ **of honour** : garde/piquet d'honneur

    ~ **rail** : barrière *(f)* de sécurité

    ~ **room** : corps de garde, consigne *(f)*

guardian : tuteur *(m)*, curateur *(m)*

guardianship : garde *(f)*, tutelle *(f)*

guarding : gardiennage *(m)*

guidance : direction *(f)*, conseil *(m)*, orientation *(f)*

guide : guider, diriger

guillotine : guillotine *(f)*

guilt : culpabilité *(f)*

guilty : coupable

~ **party** : auteur *(m)*, coupable *(m&f)*

gun : arme *(f)* à feu

gut-feeling : réaction *(f)* des tripes

guts * : (1) tripes *(fpl)*; (2) courage *(m)*

guv'nor : patron *(m)*

guy * : mec *(m)* *

H

habeas corpus : "que tu aies le corps (pour l'amener devant la cour)"
Formule juridique exprimant qu'un prévenu doit comparaître devant le magistrat afin qu'il soit statué sur la validité de son arrestation.

habit : habitude *(f)*, coutume *(f)*

habitation : habitation *(f)*, demeure *(f)*

habitual : habituel

~ **criminal** : repris *(m)* de justice

~ **offender** : récidiviste *(m&f)*

hacker : pirate *(m)* informatique

half : demi

~**-inch** * : voler (voir aussi **nick, pinch**)

~ **pay** : demi-salaire *(m)*

hall : salle *(f)*

hallucinatory : hallucinogène

hammer : (1) marteau *(m)*; (2) chien *(m)* de fusil, percuteur *(m)*

hand : (1) main *(f)*; (2) ouvrier *(m)*; (3) remettre, transmettre, léguer

first ~ : première main

second ~ : d'occasion

handbill : prospectus *(m)*

handcuffs, handbolts : menottes *(fpl)*, bracelets *(mpl)* *, brides *(fpl)* *, cabriolets *(mpl)* *, cadennes *(fpl)* *, canelles *(fpl)* *, chapelets *(mpl)* *, fichets *(mpl)* *, pincelles *(fpl)* *, poucettes *(fpl)* *

to handcuff someone : passer les menottes à quelqu'un

handgun : arme *(f)* de poing, artillerie *(f)* *

hand-habend : voir **hand-napping**

handicap : handicap *(m)*, déficience *(f)* physique

handle : manier, manipuler, exercer, pratiquer

~ **stolen property** : pratiquer le recel

handlebar : guidon *(m)*

    ~ **moustache** : moustache *(f)* en croc

handler of stolen goods : fourgat *(m)*, fourgue *(m)*

handling (stolen goods) : recel *(m)*

hand-napping : étant prêt à voler (terme périmé)

hand over : livrer, remettre

handwriting : écriture *(f)* à la main

    ~ **expert** : expert *(m)* en écritures

hang : pendre, suspendre, accrocher

hanging : pendaison *(f)*

    ~, **drawing and quartering** : être pendu, éventré tout vivant, et coupé en quatre morceaux (peine infligée autrefois pour haute trahison)

hangman : bourreau *(m)*

Hansard : compte rendu officiel des débats parlementaires

harassment : harcèlement *(m)*

    sexual ~ : avances sexuelles importunes

harbour : (1) port *(m)*, havre *(m)*; (2) donner asile à

    ~ **master** : capitaine *(m)* de port

harbouring a criminal : recel *(m)* de malfaiteur

harbouring prostitutes : réception *(f)* de femmes de débauche

hard : dur

    ~ **labour** : travaux *(mpl)* forcés, réclusion *(f)* avec travail disciplinaire

    ~ **pornography** : hard *(m)*

    ~ **shoulder** : bande *(f)* d'arrêt d'urgence

    ~ **work** : travail *(m)* assidu

hardboiled : dur, tenace

hardened : endurci

hardware : matériel *(m)* informatique

harm : mal *(m)*, tort *(m)*, préjudice *(m)*

    to do someone ~ : nuire à quelqu'un

harvest : (1) moisson *(f)*, récolte *(f)*; (2) récolter

hashish : hachisch *(m)*

hatch : hayon *(m)*

    ~back : bicorps *(m)*

hatchet : hachette *(f)*

haulage : camionnage *(m)*, transport *(m)*, charroi *(m)*

    ~ contractor : transitaire *(m&f)*, entrepreneur *(m)* de transports

hawker : colporteur *(m)*, marchand *(m)* ambulant

hawking : démarchage *(m)*

hazard : aléa *(m)*, hasard *(m)*, danger *(m)*

    ~ warning lights : feux *(mpl)* de détresse

head : (1) tête *(f)*; (2) chef *(m)*; (3) conduire, diriger

    ~ butt : coup *(m)* de boule

    ~lamp : projecteur *(m)*, phare *(m)*

    ~ office : siège *(m)* principal

    ~-rest : appui-tête *(m)*

heading : en-tête *(m)*, titre *(m)*, rubrique *(f)*

headquarters (HQ) : quartier-général *(m)*, service *(m)* central

    ~ staff : état-major *(m)*

health : santé *(f)*, hygiène *(f)*

    ~ and safety at work : hygiène et sécurité au travail

    ~ department : service *(m)* de santé

    ~ hazard : risque *(f)* pour la santé

    ~ officer : fonctionnaire *(m&f)* de la santé publique

    ~ service : sécurité *(f)* sociale

    public ~ : santé publique

healthy : sain

hear : entendre

hearing : audition *(f)*, comparution *(f)*, débats *(mpl)* judiciaires

hearsay : preuve *(f)* par oui-dire, rumeur *(f)* publique, commune *(f)* renommée

heavy (1) * : gorille *(m)* *

heavy (2) : lourd

     ~ goods vehicle (HGV) : poids *(m)* lourd, gros-cul *(m)*

hedonistic : hédonique

heinous : crapuleux

     ~ crime : forfait *(m)*

held : détenu, en détention

helmet : casque *(m)*

     riot ~ : casque de protection

help : (1) secourir; (2) secours *(m)*, aide *(f)*

"help!" : "au secours!"

hemp : chanvre *(m)*

     Indian ~ : chanvre indien, marijuana *(f)*

hereafter : ci-après

hereby : par les présentes

hereinafter : ci-dessous, par la suite

herewith : ci-joint

Her Majesty's Inspector of Constabulary : inspecteur-général *(m)* de police
*Les six HMIs, tous anciens **Chief Constables,** sont chargés de visiter les forces de police dans leur région pour s'assurer qu'elles sont bien gérées et efficaces, avant qu'elles reçoivent les fonds du trésor central.*

Her Majesty's Chief Inspector of Constabulary : inspecteur-général de police en chef

hick : glaiseux *(m)*

hidden : occulte

hide : planquer

hideout : planque *(f)*

hiding place : planque *(f)*

hierarchy : hiérarchie *(f)*

high : haut, élevé, supérieur

> ~ **court** : tribunal *(m)* supérieur de grande instance (civil) et
> cour *(m)* d'appel

> ~ **seas** : haute mer

> ~ **speed** : grande vitesse *(f)*

> ~ **street** : grande rue *(f)*

> ~ **treason** : haute trahison
> *Trahison contre la monarchie. La distinction entre* **petty** *(petit)*
> **treason** *et* **high treason** *n'existe plus et l'adjectif n'est plus utilisé.*

higher : supérieur

> ~ **education** : enseignement supérieur

highway : chemin *(m)* public, grande route *(f)*, ruban *(m)*

> ~ **Code** : normes *(fpl)* de conduite routière
> *A la différence du Code de la Route français, il n'a pas force de
> loi et ne comprend que des conseils.*

> ~ **patrol** : police *(f)* de la route (surtout aux Etats-Unis)

> ~ **robbery** : vol *(m)* de grand chemin

> ~**s department** : service *(m)* de la voirie

hijacking : détournement *(m)* (d'avion), piratage *(m)*, piraterie *(f)* aérienne

hinder : entraver

hindrance : empêchement *(m)*, entrave *(f)*

hire : louer, embaucher (ouvriers)

> **for** ~ **and reward** : à titre commercial

> ~ **company** : compagnie *(f)* de location, maison *(f)* de location

hired killer : tueur *(m)* à gages

hit (1) : percuter

> ~ **and run** : délit *(m)* de fuite

hit (2) * : nettoyage *(m)* *, assassinat *(m)*

> ~-**man** : rectifieur *(m)*

hitch * : accroc * *(m)*, os *(m)* *

hitch-hiker : (auto-) stoppeur *(m)*

hoax : mystification *(f)*

hold : détenir, tenir, posséder ou occuper en plein droit

> ~ **a meeting** : tenir une réunion

> ~ **an inquiry** : procéder à une enquête

holder : titulaire *(m&f)*, détenteur *(m)*, porteur *(m)*

hold-up : (1) (vol) braquage *(m)*, hold-up *(m)*; (2) (circulation) embouteillage *(m)*; (3) entraver la circulation

hole : trou *(m)*, fosse *(f)*

holiday : vacances *(fpl)*, congé *(m)*

> ~**maker** : estivant *(m)*

> ~ **resort** : villégiature *(f)*, lieu *(m)* de vacances, station *(f)* touristique

> ~ **traffic** : circulation *(f)* des départs/rentrées de vacances, rush *(m)* de vacances

HOLMES : ordinateur central pour des enquêtes importantes

holster : étui *(m)* de pistolet

home : foyer *(m)*, case *(f)*, domicile *(m)*

> ~ **address** : domicile, adresse *(f)* permanente

> **childrens'** ~ : home *(m)* d'enfants

> ~**less** : sans abri

> ~ **Office** : = Ministère de l'Intérieur

> ~ **Office crime prevention centre** : centre *(m)* national de la prévention de la criminalité

> ~ **Secretary** : = Ministre *(m)* de l'Intérieur

> **mobile** ~ : caravane *(f)*

homicide : homicide *(m)*

    ~ **squad** : brigade *(f)* criminelle

    justifiable ~ : homicide justifiable

homosexual : (1) homosexuel(le); (2) homosexuel *(m)*, homosexuelle *(f)*

honesty : moralité *(f)*

honorarium : honoraires *(mpl)*

honorary : honoraire

honour : honneur *(m)*

    ~ **guard** : garde *(m)* d'honneur

hooch * : pétrole *(m)* *

hooligan : loulou *(m)*

hooliganism : vandalisme *(m)*, comportement *(m)* troublant l'ordre public

hooter : voir **horn**

horn : klaxon *(m)*, avertisseur *(m)*

horse : cheval *(m)*

    ~**play** : chahut *(m)*

    ~ **race** : course *(f)* hippique

HO/RT/1 : ordre *(m)* écrit pour la production des papiers de conduite

hospice : centre *(m)* de soins palliatifs, hospice *(m)*

hospital : hôpital *(m)*

hostage : otage *(m)*

    ~ **taker** : preneur *(m)* d'otage

    ~ **taking** : prise *(f)* d'otage

hostel : foyer *(m)*, auberge *(f)* (de jeunesse)

    probation ~ : home *(m)* de semi-liberté

hostelry : hôtel *(m)*

hostess (club) : entraîneuse *(f)*

hostile : inamical, hostile

> **~ witness** : témoin *(m)* qui, de l'avis du tribunal, est opposé à la partie qui
> l'a convoqué

hostility : inimité *(f)*

hot goods * : lamedus *(mpl)* *

hour : heure *(f)*

> **~s of darkness** : nuit *(f)*
> *Les heures comprises entre une demi-heure après le coucher du*
> *soleil et une demi-heure avant l'aube durant lesquelles les feux des*
> *véhicules doivent être allumés.*

> office **~s** : heures de bureau

> rush **~** : heure de pointe

> working **~s** : heures ouvrables, heures de travail

house : maison *(f)*, case *(f)*

> **~breaker** : marcheur *(m)* *

> **~breaking** : cambriolage *(m)*

> **~breaking implements** : outils *(mpl)* de cambriolage

> **~hold** : ménage *(m)*, famille *(f)*

> **~keeper** : gouvernante *(f)*

> **~ of Commons** : = Assemblée *(f)* Nationale

> **~ of Lords** : = Sénat *(m)* (également la cour d'appel ultime)

house-to-house ; porte-à-porte

> **~ collections** : collecte *(f)* porte-à-porte

> **~ -enquiries** : aller de porte en porte à la recherche des témoins

> **~ search** : faire une perquisition systématique dans le quartier

housing : logement *(m)*

> **~ stock** : parc *(m)* immobilier

hub : moyeu *(m)*

hue-and-cry : clameur *(m)* publique

humane killer : pistolet *(m)* d'abattage

human rights : droits *(mpl)* de l'homme

hundred : circonscription *(f)* anglo-saxone comprennant une centaine de foyers

hung : pendu

    ~, drawn and quartered : ancienne peine selon laquelle le condamné était pendu et, pendant qu'il était toujours vivant, éventré, décapité et coupé en quatre morceaux

hunger strike : grève *(f)* de la faim

hunting : chasse *(f)*

    ~ licence : permis *(m)* de chasse

husband : époux *(m)*, mari *(m)*

    ~ and wife : les conjoints

hush money : argent donné à quelqu'un pour prix de son silence.

hypodermic syringe : shooteuse *(f)* *

I

identification : identification *(f)*, tapissage *(m)*

    ~ **by fingerprints** : dactyloscopie *(f)*

    ~ **papers** : pièces *(fpl)* d'identité, papiers *(mpl)* d'identification

    ~ **parade** : séance *(f)* d'identification, retapissage *(m)* *
      Confrontation d'un témoin avec un groupe de personnes parmi lesquelles se trouve un suspect.

identify : identifier, repérer, tapisser, retapisser

identikit picture : portrait *(m)* robot, photo–robot *(f)*

identity : identité *(f)*

    ~ **card** : carte *(f)*/pièce *(f)*/papiers *(mpl)* d'identité

    ~ **parade** : voir **identification parade**

industrial disease : maladie *(f)* professionnelle

ignition : allumage *(m)*

    ~ **key** : clé *(f)* de contact

    ~ **switch** : contact *(m)*

ignominous : infamant

illegal : illégal, illégitime, illicite

    ~ **acts** : actes illégaux

    ~ **immigrant** : immigré *(m)* clandestin

illegible : illisible, indéchiffrable

illegitimate : illégitime,

    ~ **child** : enfant *(m&f)* naturel(le), enfant illégitime

illicit : illicite

    ~ **practice** : usage *(m)* indu

illiteracy : analphabétisme *(m)*

illness : maladie *(f)*

ill-treatment : sévices *(mpl)*

ill–will : mauvaise foi *(f)*, malveillance *(f)*

imitation : (1) imitation *(f)*, (2) factice

immaterial : irrecevable, sans importance, sans rapport avec la question

    ~ **evidence** : témoignage *(m)* non pertinent

immediate : immédiat

    ~ **response unit** : unité *(f)* d'intervention immédiate

    ~ **vicinity** : voisinage immédiat

immigrant : immigrant *(m)*

immigration : immigration *(f)*

immoral : immoral

    living on ~ **earnings** : vivre de proxénétisme

immorality : immoralité *(f)*

immunity : exemption *(f)*, immunité *(f)*

    diplomatic ~ : immunité de juridiction, immunité diplomatique

    parliamentary ~ : inviolabilité *(f)* parlementaire

impact : choc *(m)*, impact *(m)*

impeachment : impeachment *(m)*, mise *(f)* en accusation

impede : entraver. empêcher

impediment : empêchement *(m)*, entrave *(f)*, obstacle *(m)*

impersonation : personnification *(f)*, supposition *(f)* de personne

implead : poursuivre en justice

implement : (1) appliquer, mettre à exécution, mettre en application, mettre en oeuvre;   (2) outil *(m)*

    ~ **a policy** : appliquer une politique

implementation : mise *(f)* en oeuvre, en application

implicate : impliquer, mêler, tremper

implied : implicite, tacite, sous–entendu

import : (1) importer;   (2) importance *(f)*

importance : importance *(f)*

important : important

importation : importation *(f)*

importune : racoler (pour prostitution)

impose : imposer, infliger

impossible offence : infraction *(f)* impossible

impotent : incapable d'engendrer

impound : saisir, confisquer

impounding (of vehicle) : immobilisation *(f)* (de véhicule)

impression : empreinte *(f)*

imprint : trace *(f)*, empreinte *(f)*

imprinter (for credit cards) : fer *(m)* à repasser

imprison : boucler, écrouer, emprisonner

imprisonment : détention *(f)*, emprisonnement *(m)*,   incarcération *(f)*

    false ~ : détention arbitraire, séquestration *(f)* illégale

    ~ for life : réclusion *(f)* perpétuelle

    ~ for non-payment of fine : contrainte *(f)* par corps

improper : abusif, impropre, incorrect, irrégulier

improve : améliorer

improvement : perfectionnement *(m)*

imprudence : imprudence *(f)*

impunity : impunité *(f)*

impute : imputer

inaccurate : inexact

inadequacy : insuffisance *(f)*

inadequate : insuffisant, disproportionné

inadmissible : inadmissible, irrecevable, non-recevable

in camera : huis *(m)* clos

incapacitated : incapable

incapacity (for work) : inaptitude *(f)* (au travail)

incendiary (device) : (engin) incendiaire

incentive : encouragement *(m)*

incest : inceste *(m)*

inchoate : en puissance, incomplet

    ~ crime : crime *(m)* non parfait

incident : incident *(m)*

incite : provoquer

incitement : excitation *(f)*, incitation *(f)*, provocation *(f)*

    ~ to commit crime : provocation au crime

income tax : impôt sur le revenu

incommunicado : au secret
    La garde d'un prisonnier au secret est interdite par la loi de 1984.

incompatibility : incompatibilité *(f)*

incompetence : impérité *(f)*, incompétence *(f)*

incompetency : incompétence *(f)*

    ~ ratione loci : incompétence territoriale

    ~ ratione materiae : incompétence matérielle

    ~ ratione personae : incompétence personnelle

    relative ~ : incompétence relative

incorrect : inexact, défectueux

incorrigible : irréformable

    ~ rogue : délinquant *(m)* invétéré
        Classification de malfaiteur maintenant en désuétude.

incorruptible : incorruptible

increase : augmentation *(f)*, majoration *(f)*, accroissement *(m)*, surcroît *(m)*

incriminate : (1) inculper; (2) impliquer dans la possibilité d'être accusé de crime

incriminating documents : pièces *(fpl)* à conviction

incumbent : titulaire *(m&f)* d'un poste

incur : encourir, subir

indecent : indécent, impudique

     ~ **assault** : attentat *(m)* à la pudeur

     ~ **display** : affichage *(m)* impudique

     ~ **exposure** : attentat *(m)* public à la pudeur, exhibition impudique

     ~ **language** : chants *(mpl)*, cris *(mpl)* ou discours *(mpl)* contraires aux bonnes moeurs

indefinite : illimité

indemnification : dédommagement *(m)*

indemnity : indemnité *(f)*

index : répertoire *(m)*

     ~-**linked** : échelle *(f)* mobile

Indian hemp : chanvre *(m)* indien

indicator: indicateur *(m)*.   ~ **lamp** : feu *(m)* clignotant

indict : accuser, farguer *

indictable offence : crime *(m)* ou délit *(m)* qui peut être jugé au **Crown Court**

indictment : accusation *(f)*, fargue *(f)* *

     bill of ~ : acte *(m)* d'accusation

indirect : indirecte

indisputable : irréfutable

individual : particulier *(m)*

induce : provoquer, persuader, inciter

inducement : pot-de-vin *(m)* *

indulgence : indulgence *(f)*

industrial : industriel

     ~ **accident** : accident *(m)* de travail

~ **concern** : entreprise industrielle

~ **dispute** : conflit *(m)* de travail

~ **estate** : centre industriel, zone *(f)* d'industrialisation (ZI)

industrialist : industriel *(m)*

inefficiency : incapacité *(f)*, inefficacité *(f)*, incompétence *(f)*

inefficient : inefficace, incompétent

ineffective : sans effet

in extremis : à l'article *(m)* de la mort, à la dernière minute *(f)*

infant : enfant *(m&f)*

infanticide : infanticide *(m)*

inferior : inférieur

infiltrate : noyauter

infiltration : noyautage *(m)*

infirmity : invalidité *(f)*

inflict : infliger

~ **injury** : porter préjudice

in force : en vigueur

inform : prévenir, retourner, dénoncer, informer, aviser

informant : déclarant *(m)*, dénonciateur *(m)*, délateur *(m)*, indicateur *(m)*, mouchard *(m)*, mouche *(f)*

information : renseignements *(mpl)*, rambours *(mpl)*, rencards *(mpl)*, acte d'accusation *(f)*, dénonciation *(f)*

confidential ~ : renseignements confidentiels

for further ~ : pour plus ample informé

~ **technology** : télématique *(f)*, informatique *(f)*

reliable ~ : renseignements sûrs

upon ~ : en vertu de renseignements

informer : agent *(m)* de renseignements, informateur *(m)*, dénonciateur *(m)*

infrastructure : infrastructure *(f)*

infringe : empiéter sur, transgresser, enfreindre, violer

infringement : infraction *(f)*, violation *(f)*

inhabitant : habitant *(m)*

inheritance : héritage *(m)*, succession *(f)*

initial : parapher, émarger

initialling : émargement *(m)*

initials : paraphe *(m)*

initiate : commencer

    ~ **proceedings** : entamer des poursuites

inject : injecter

injection : piqûre *(f)*, injection *(f)*, picouse *(f)* *

injunction : injonction *(f)*, arrêt *(m)* de suspension

injure : blesser, nuire, porter préjudice à, léser

    ~d **party** : partie *(f)* lésée

    ~d **person** : blessé *(m)*

injurious : nuisible, préjudiciable

injury : blessure *(f)*, injure *(f)*, lésion *(f)*, tort *(m)*, préjudice *(m)*, dommage *(m)*

    bodily ~ : lésion corporelle

    ~ **to property** : dommage aux biens

    ~ **to the person** : dommage à la personne

inland : intérieur, de l'intérieur

    ~ **water transport** : batellerie *(f)*

    ~ **waterways** : réseaux *(m)* intérieur de fleuves et de canaux

inn : auberge *(f)*, hôtel *(m)*

inner city : vieux quartiers *(mpl)* défavorisés au centre de grandes villes

innocence : non-culpabilité *(f)*

innocent : innocent

Inns of Court : les quatre écoles de droit à Londres, créées au XIVe siècle

in possession of : en possession *(f)* de

input : entrée *(f)*

inquest : enquête *(f)* judiciaire après mort d'homme

inquiry : enquête *(f)*, demande *(f)* de renseignements

insane person : aliéné *(m)*, aliénée *(f)*

insanity : aberration *(f)* mentale

inside job : crime *(m)* attribué à un familier de la victime

insider dealings : achat *(m)* ou vente *(f)* d'actions par des personnes qui ont eu connaissance d'un événement ignoré du public en affectant la valeur

insolvency : carence *(f)*, déconfiture *(f)*, faillite *(f)*

insolvent : insolvable

inspection : inspection *(f)*, révision *(f)*, vérification *(f)*

    ~ by judge : descente *(f)* sur les lieux

    ~ lamp : baladeuse *(f)*

    medical ~ : examen *(m)* médical

inspector : inspecteur *(m)*, contrôleur *(m)*

    chief ~ : commandant *(m)*

    detective ~ : inspecteur principal

    detective chief ~ : inspecteur divisionnaire

    Her Majesty's ~ of Constabulary : Inspecteur-Général de la Police

    police ~ : officier *(m)* de paix principal

instalment : versement *(m)* partiel

instance : instance *(f)*

    court of first ~ : tribunal *(m)* de première instance

instantaneous offence : infraction *(f)* instantanée

instigation : excitation *(f)*

instigator : instigateur *(m)*

institute : (1) engager, entamer, déclencher (2) institut *(m)*

    ~ **proceedings** : engager/entamer/déclencher des poursuites, intenter une action, intenter un procès

institution : établissement *(m)*

    ~ **of proceedings** : dénonciation *(f)* d'instance

instruct : instruire, donner mandat (à)

    ~ **counsel** : constituer avocat

instruction : instruction *(f)*

instructions : consigne *(f)*, directives *(fpl)*, instructions *(fpl)*

    comply with ~ : se conformer aux directives

    carry out ~ : exécuter les instructions

instructor : moniteur *(m)*

instrument : instrument *(m)*, acte *(m)* juridique, document *(m)* officiel

    statutory ~ : règlement *(m)* (décret, arrêté, ordonnance)

insubordinate : mutin

insubordination : refus *(m)* d'obéissance

insufficiency : insuffisance *(f)*

insult : outrage *(m)*

insurance : assurance *(f)*

    ~ **against theft** : assurance vol

    ~ **broker** : courtier *(m)* d'assurances

    ~ **certificate** : vignette *(f)* d'assurance

    ~ **policy** : police *(f)*/contrat *(m)* d'assurance

    ~ **premium** : prime *(f)* d'assurance

    life ~ : assurance sur la vie

    national ~ : assurance sociale

    (third party/comprehensive) motor ~ : assurance automobile (aux tiers/ tous riques)

insured : (1) assuré (2) assuré *(m)*

intelligence : renseignements *(mpl)*

intend : entendre

intended offence : infraction *(f)* intentionnelle

intent, intention : but *(m)*, intention *(f)*, motif *(m)*, dessein *(m)*

  criminal ~ : intention criminelle, intention délicteuse

  evil ~ : intention malveillante, intention maligne

  fraudulent ~ : intention frauduleuse

  to all ~s and purposes : sous tous rapports

  with ~ to : dans le but de, en vue de

intentional : intentionnel, prémédité

intercede : intercéder

interchange : échangeur *(m)*

intercourse : relations *(fpl)*, rapports *(mpl)*, commerce *(m)*

  sexual ~ : rapports sexuels

interest : intérêt *(m)*

  public ~ : intérêt public

interested : intéressé

interfere with : entraver, s'immiscer (dans), intervenir, contrarier

  ~ sexually : tripoter *

interference : parasitage *(m)*

interim : intérimaire, provisoire, transitoire

interlocutory : interlocutoire

intermarriage : mariage *(m)* consanguin

intermediary : contact *(m)*, entremetteur *(m)*, intermédiaire *(m&f)*

internal : intérieur *(m)*

  minister for ~ affairs : ministre *(m)* de l'intérieur

international & organised crime branch : brigade *(f)* du crime international et du grand banditisme

internment : internement *(m)*

inter partes : contradictoire

Interpol : Interpol *(f)* (Organisation Internationale de Police Criminelle)
Contrairement à ce que disent les romans policiers, Interpol ne possède pas d'agents opérationnels mais réprésente un centre d'information et de communication pour les pays adhérents. Elle a son siège à Lyon, France.

interpret : interpréter, traduire

interpreter : interprète *(m)*

interrogate : interroger

    ~ **closely** : dépiauter

interrogation : interrogatoire *(m)*

interruption : suspension *(f)*

intervention : intervention *(f)*

interview (of suspect) : interrogatoire *(m)*

intimidation : intimidation *(f)*, menaces *(fpl)*

investigation : recherche *(f)* des preuves, enquête *(f)*, investigation *(f)*

intimidation : menace *(f)*

    ~ **of witness** : subornation *(f)* de témoin

intoxicated : en état d'ébriété, chargé, givré

intoxicating liquor : boisson *(f)* alcoolique

intoxication : ébriété *(f)*, état *(m)* d'ivresse

intoximeter : alcootest *(m)*, éthylomètre *(m)*

in–tray : plateau *(m)* dans lequel on dépose des documents à l'intention de celui qui doit les traiter

invalid : (1) nul, sans effet légal; (2) invalide *(m&f)*, malade *(m&f)*, infirme *(m&f)*

    ~ **carriage** : voiture *(f)* d'infirme

invalidity : invalidité *(f)*

inventory : état *(m)* des lieux

investigate : examiner, faire une enquête, vérifier

---

investigation : enquête *(f)*, instruction *(f)*, investigation *(f)*, recherches *(fpl)*

    ~ of a case : examen d'un dossier, instruction d'une affaire criminelle

    police ~ : enquête de police

invoice : facture *(f)*

involuntary : involontaire

    ~ conduct : comportement *(m)* involontaire

involve : impliquer, mêler, tremper, entrainer, toucher à, engager

involved : en cause, intéressé, trempé

IOU (I owe you) : "je vous dois" (reconnaissance de dette)

ipso facto : de ce fait

ipso jure : de plein droit

irrebuttable : certain, irréfragable

    ~ evidence : preuve certaine

    ~ presumption : présomption *(f)* absolue

irrefutable : inattaquable, irréfutable

irregular : irrégulier

irrelevant : hors de cours, impertinent, irrecevable

irremovability : non-révocabilité *(f)*

irresponsible : irresponsable

irreversible : irrévocable

irrevocable : irréformable, irrévocable

issue : émettre

itinerant : ambulant, forain, itinérant

J

jab * : picouse *(f)* *, piqûre *(f)*

jack : cric *(m)*

    ˜-knife : (1) eustache *(m)*, couteau *(m)* de poche; (2) se mettre en travers
      (remorque)

Jack-of-all-trades : bricoleur *(m)*

jackpot : gros lot *(m)*, bon numéro *(m)*

jail : geôle *(f)*, prison *(f)*

    ˜ break : évasion *(f)*

    ˜ breaker : évadé *(m)*

    ˜ fever : espèce de typhus, autrefois endémique dans les prisons

jailer : geôlier *(m)*, gardien *(m)* de prison

jalopy * : bagnole *(f)*, guimbarde *(f)*

jam : enrayer (une machine, une arme), brouiller (une émission
    radiophonique), bloquer, coincer

    ˜ on the brakes : freiner à bloc, freiner brutalement

    traffic ˜ : embouteillage *(m)*, encombrement *(m)*

jemmy : dingue *(m)* *, jacot *(m)* *, jacques *(m)* *, pince-monseigneur *(f)*

jeopardise : mettre en danger, compromettre

jeopardy : danger *(m)*, risque *(m)*

jeweller : bijoutier *(m)*, joaillier *(m)*

job : (1) poste *(m)*, emploi *(m)*, travail *(m)*, besogne *(f)*, tâche *(f)*, boulot *(m)* *

    ˜ description : définition *(f)* de poste

    "The ˜ " : la police *(f)* (en tant que carrière)

job * : commande *(f)*, crime *(m)*

jog : jogger

jogger : joggeur *(m)*

jogging : footing *(m)*

    ~ shoes : joggers *(mpl)*

    ~ suit : jogging *(m)*

    to go ~ : jogger

join : adhérer (à), s'affilier (à)

joinder : jonction *(f)* d'instance

joint * : drag *(m)* *, stick *(m)* *

joint and several liability : solidarité *(f)*

jointly and severally : solidairement

jostling : bousculade *(f)*

journey : voyage *(m)*

joy-riding : l'emprunt d'un véhicule sans l'accord du propriétaire
    Ce délit n'est pas considéré comme vol car il n'y a aucune d'intention de
    garder le véhicule de manière permanente.

judas : guichet *(m)*

judge : (1) juge *(m)*, magistrat *(m)* de siège; (2) juger

    circuit ~ : juge en tournée

    ~'s clerk : aide *(f)* du juge

    ~s' rules : code de procédure pour l'interrogation de suspects, etc.,
        annulé et remplacé par le **Police and Criminal Evidence Act** en 1984

judgement : condamnation *(f)*, jugement *(m)*, sentence *(f)*, arrêt *(m)*

    considered ~ : jugement sur le fond

    enforceable ~ : jugement exécutoire

    grounds of a ~ : attendus *(mpl)*, considérants *(mpl)*

    ~ handed down : jugement rendu

    pass/pronounce ~ : rendre un jugement

judicial juridique, judiciaire

    ~ decision : décision *(f)*

    ~ enquiry : enquête *(f)* judiciaire

~ **notice** : faits que le tribunal peut reconnaître sans avoir besoin d'une preuve formelle

~ **review** : contrôle *(m)* juridictionnel

judiciary : (1) judicature *(f)*; (2) la magistrature *(f)*

jumble sale : vente *(f)* de charité d'articles d'occasion

jump : (1) saut *(m)*; (2) sauter

~ **a red light** : brûler un feu rouge

~ **bail** : se soustraire à la justice (après caution)

~ **leads** : câbles *(fpl)* de démarrage

~ **suit** : combinaison *(f)* de saut

~ **to conclusions** : tirer des conclusions hâtives

junior : cadet, subalterne

~ **minister** : secrétaire *(m&f)* d'état

~ **officer** : officier *(m)* subalterne

junk : (1) bric-à-brac *(m)*, ferraille *(f)*, camelote *(f)*, pacotille *(f)*; (2) (drogue) came *(f)*

junk-dealer : brocanteur *(m)*, ferrailleur *(m)*

junkie * : camé *(m)* *, enchnouffé *

jurisdiction : compétence *(f)*, juridiction *(f)*, ressort *(m)*

court of summary ~ : tribunal *(m)* de simple police

want of ~ : incompétence *(f)*

jurisprudence : la science *(f)* du droit

comparative ~ : droit *(m)* comparé

medical ~ : médecine *(f)* légale

juriste : légiste *(m)*

juror : juré *(m)*, membre *(m)* du jury

jury : jury *(m)*

    grand ~ : jury d'accusation
        Supprimé en Angleterre en 1948, il existe toujours aux Etats-Unis.

    hung ~ : jury en désaccord

    ~ array : appel *(m)* du jury

    trial by ~ : jugement *(m)* par jury

    verdict of the ~ : verdict *(m)* du jury

just : juste, équitable, légitime

    ~ and lawful decision : un bien-jugé *(m)*

justice : (1) justice *(f)*; (2) titre donné aux magistrats

    clerk to the ~s : voir **magistrates' clerk**

    court of ~ : tribunal *(m)*

    ~ of the Peace : Juge *(m)* de Paix

    Lord Chief ~ : Président *(m)* de la Cour Supérieure

    miscarriage of ~ : erreur *(m)* judiciaire

    to pervert ~ : fausser la justice

justifiable : justifiable

    ~ force : défense *(f)* légitime

    ~ homicide : homicide *(m)* légitime

justification : justification *(f)*, faits *(mpl)* justificatifs, état *(m)* de nécessité

justify : justifier

juvenile : jeune

    ~ court : tribunal *(m)* des mineurs

    ~ delinquant : jeune délinquant *(m)*

    ~ protection unit : unité *(f)* de protection des mineurs

K

kangaroo court : tribunal *(m)* irrégulier

keep silent : se taire, s'écraser

kennels : chenil *(m)*

kerb : bord *(m)* du trottoir

    ~-crawler : automobiliste *(m)* roulant lentement à la recherche de prostituée

key : clé *(f)*, clef *(f)*, tournante *(f)*

    ~board : clavier *(m)* (de machine à écrire ou ordinateur)

    ~ money : pas-de-porte *(m)*

    ~ position : position-clef *(f)*

khaki : kaki, caca d'oie

kick : coup *(m)* de pied

    ~-start : kick *(m)*

kidnap : kidnapper

kidnapper : ravisseur *(m)*

kidnapping : enlèvement *(m)*, rapt *(m)*

kill : tuer, laminer *

kinfolk : parents *(mpl)*

kinship : consanguinité *(f)*

kiss-curl : accroche-coeur *(m)*, guiche *(f)*

kit : prêt à monter *(m)*, set *(m)*

kleptomania : kleptomanie *(f)*

kleptomaniac : kleptomane *(m&f)*

knackered * : abattu, lavé

knee-jerk reaction : réaction *(f)* instinctive, réaction *(f)* des tripes

knick-knack : babiole *(f)*

knife : (1) couteau *(m)*, arme *(f)* blanche, lame *(f)*, outil *(m)*; (2) lamer

knight : chevalier *(m)*

knock : coup *(m)*

> **~-for-knock agreement** : accord entre deux compagnies d'assurance pour dédommager séparément leurs clients respectifs

knotty problem : problème *(m)* épineux

know : connaître

know-how : savoir-faire *(m)* (technique)

knowingly : sciemment

knowledge : connaissance *(f)*

> **expert ~** : connaissance de spécialiste

> **matter of common ~** : fait *(m)* de notoriété publique

known (fact) : (fait) connu, constaté

knuckleduster : coup *(m)* de poing américain

L

label : étiquette *(f)*

laboratory : laboratoire *(f)*

labour : travail *(m)*

     hard ~ : réclusion *(f)* criminelle, travaux *(mpl)* forcés

     ~ **dispute** : conflit *(m)* de travail

lack : insuffisance *(f)*, manquement *(m)*

     ~ **of evidence** : insuffisance de motifs, manque *(m)* de preuves

ladder : échelle *(f)*

lamp : lanterne *(f)*, lampe *(f)*

land : pays *(m)*, terrain *(m)*

     ~**lord** : propriétaire *(m)*, hôtelier *(m)*, aubergiste *(m)*

     waste ~ : terrain *(m)* inculte

lane : voie *(f)*

     ~ **arrow** : présélection *(f)*

lantern : lanterne *(f)*

lapse : (1) périmer; (2) défaillance *(f)*, erreur *(f)*, méprise *(f)*, extinction *(f)*

     ~ **from one's duty** : manquement *(m)* à son devoir

lapsed : dévolu par péremption, déchu, périmé, caduc

larceny : vol *(m)*

     ~ **servant** : vol par domestique

     petty ~ : vol simple, larcin

     simple ~ : vol simple (non accompagné de circonstances aggravantes)

large : grand(e)

laser sight : visée *(f)* laser

launch : vedette *(f)*

launder (money) : blanchir (de l'argent)

law : loi *(f)*, droit *(m)*

> **adjectival** ~ : règles *(fpl)* de procédure

> **break the** ~ : enfreindre/transgresser la loi

> **case** ~ : jurisprudence *(f)*

> **civil** ~ : droit civil

> **commercial** ~ : droit du commerce, droit des affaires

> **common** ~ : droit coutumier

> **criminal** ~ : droit pénal

> **enforce the** ~ : faire respecter la loi

> **get round the** ~ : tourner la loi

> **keep within the** ~ : rester dans les limites de la loi

> ~ **abiding citizen** : citoyen *(m)* respectueux de la loi

> ~ **and order** : ordre *(m)* public

> ~ **courts** : palais *(m)* de justice

> ~ **enforcement officer** : agent *(m)* de police

> ~ **practice** : cabinet *(m)* juridique

> ~ **reports** : chroniques *(fpl)* des tribunaux, nouvelles *(fpl)* judiciaires

> **martial** ~ : loi martiale, état *(m)* de siège

> **military** ~ : droit militaire

> **practise** ~ : exercer une profession juridique

> **private** ~ : droit privé

> **public** ~ : droit public

> **repeal a** ~ : abroger une loi

> **Roman** ~ : droit romain

> ~ **Society** : Conseil *(m)* de l'ordre des juristes (habilite les **solicitors**)

> **statute** ~ : droit écrit

lawful : licite, légal, permis, légitime

> ~ **representative** : représentant légal

lawfully : à bon droit, légalement

lawless : anomique, sans loi, sans frein, désordonné

lawyer : homme *(m)* de loi, babillard *(m)*

lay information : informer

lay magistrate : juge *(m)* non rétribué

layman : profane *(m)*

lay–off (staff) : débaucher, licencier (des employés)

leader : dirigeant *(m)*, chef *(m)*, avocat principal

leadership : conduite *(f)*, domination *(f)*, direction *(f)*

leading question : question *(f)* tendancieuse
    Question posée, par un avocat ou un juge, qui tend à suggérer la réponse au témoin.

lead shot : grenaille *(f)*

leaf : feuille *(f)*

leak : coupure *(f)*, courant *(m)* d'air, fuite *(f)*

learn : apprendre

    ~ by practice : perfectionnement *(m)* par la pratique

leasing : crédit–bail *(m)*

leave (1) : congé *(m)*, permission *(f)*, vacances *(fpl)*

    maternity ~ : congé de maternité

    sick ~ : congé de maladie

    training ~ : congé–formation

    unpaid ~ : congé sans rémunération

leave (2) : quitter

    ~ without paying : planter un drapeau

ledger : grand livre *(m)*

left–hand drive : conduite *(f)* à gauche

left–luggage office : consigne *(f)*

legacy : héritage *(m)*

legal : légal, judiciaire, juridique

    ~ **adviser** : conseiller *(m)* juridique

    ~ **aid** : assistance *(f)* judiciaire

    ~ **definition** : qualification *(f)*

    ~ **document** : acte *(m)* authentique

    ~ **excuse** : excuse *(f)* légale

    ~ **instrument** : instrument *(m)*

    ~ **owner** : parade *(f)* juridique

    ~ **proceedings** : poursuites *(fpl)* judiciaires

    ~ **process** : voies *(fpl)* de droit

    ~ **redress** : recours *(m)* à la justice

    ~ **representative** : représentant *(m)* légal

    ~ **tender** : monnaie *(f)* ayant cours légal

legalise : authentifier, légaliser

legality : légalité *(f)*

legally : légalement, juridiquement

    ~ **responsible** : responsable en droit

legislation : législation *(f)*

legitimate : légitime

leisure : loisirs *(mpl)*

lend : prêter

leniency : indulgence *(f)*

lesbian : lesbienne *(f)*, gousse *(f)* *

lethal : mortel

letter : lettre *(f)*

    ~ **of request** : commission *(f)* rogatoire

    rogatory ~ : commission *(f)* rogatoire

lever : levier *(m)*

brake ~ : levier de frein

clutch ~ : levier d'embrayage

levy : lever (un impôt), imposer (une amende)

lewd : obscène

liabilities : passif, ensemble de dettes

liability : obligation *(f)*, responsabilité *(f)*, engagement *(m)*

employer's ~ : responsibilité des employeurs

joint ~ : obligation conjointe

joint and several ~ : obligation conjointe et solidaire

~ **to a fine** : risque *(f)* d'encourir une amende

limited ~ : responsabilité limitée (d'une société)

public ~ **insurance** : assurance *(f)* au tiers

liable : passible de, susceptible de, sujet à, assujetti à

~ **to prosecution** : passible de poursuites

libel : calomnie *(f)* écrite, injure *(f)*, écrit *(m)* diffamatoire

liberal : libéral

liberate : libérer

liberty : liberté *(f)*

civil ~ : liberté civile

licence : permis *(m)*, autorisation *(f)*, licence *(f)*

driving ~ : permis de conduire

firearms ~ : permis d'obtenir ou de posséder une arme à feu

game ~ : permis de chasse

~ **number** : numéro *(m)* minéralogique

~ **plate** : plaque *(f)* d'immatriculation

license : autoriser, accorder une licence/un permis/une autorisation

licensed : autorisé, patenté

~ **premises** : débit *(m)* de boisson

licensee : concessionnaire *(m&f)* d'une licence, patron(ne) d'un **public house**

licit : licite

lie : (1) mensonge *(m)*; (2) être placé, se trouver dans une situation déterminée, résider, séjourner

    ~-detector : détecteur *(m)* de mensonge

    ~ low : faire la planche

lien : privilège *(m)*, droit *(m)* de rétention, droit *(m)* de gage, hypothèque *(f)*

lieutenant : lieutenant *(m)*

    ~ general : général *(m)* de corps d'armée

life : vie *(f)*

    for ~ : à vie

    ~ insurance : assurance *(f)* sur la vie

    ~ jacket : gilet *(m)* de sauvetage

    ~ saver : maître-nageur-sauveteur (MNS) *(m)*

    ~ sentence : condamnation *(f)* à vie

    quality of life : qualité *(f)* de vie

    station in ~ : position *(f)* sociale

lifelong : à vie, de toute la vie, de toujours

lift : (1) lever; (2) * voler

lifting : levée *(f)*

light : (1) feu *(m)*; (2) léger

    ~ bar : rampe *(f)* (de signalisation)

    ~ truck : camionnette *(f)*

lighting : éclairage *(m)*

lightweight motorcycle : vélomoteur *(m)* (50 à 125 cc)

likelihood : probabilité *(f)*

limit : limite *(f)*

    age ~ : limite d'âge

exceed the speed ~ : commettre un excès de vitesse

time ~ : delai *(m)*, durée *(f)*, limite de temps

limitation : limitation *(f)*

    ~ of proceedings : forclusion *(f)*, prescription *(f)* de l'action publique

limited liability company (Ltd.) : société *(f)* à responsabilité limitée (SARL)

line : ligne *(f)*, trait *(m)*, ligne *(f)*

    ~ a route : jalonner

    ~ organisation : structure *(f)* linéaire de l'entreprise

Lion intoximeter : marque d'éthylmètre, alcootest

liquidator : liquidateur *(m)*

lisp : cheveu *(m)* lingual

list : (1) énumérer;   (2) état *(m)*, nomenclature *(f)*, liste *(f)*, tableau *(m)*

    black ~ : liste noire

    ~ of names : liste nominative

listen : entendre

listening device : écoute *(f)*

litigant : plaideur *(m)*

litigation : litige *(m)*, procès *(m)*

litter : détritus *(mpl)*, papiers *(mpl)* gras

live : vivre

livestock : bétail *(m)*, cheptel *(m)*

living on immoral earnings : proxénétisme *(m)*, tolérance *(f)* de la prostitution, vagabondage *(m)* spécial

load : (1) charge *(f)*, cargaison *(f)*;   (2) charger

loaded (1) : chargé;   (2) * : (riche) braisé *, huppé *

loan : prêt *(m)*

    ~ shark : usurier *(m)*

local : local, régional

    ~ authority : collectivité *(f)* locale
        Il existe deux niveaux de collectivité locale en Angleterre; le county
        et le district (ou London borough).

    ~ custom : usage local

    ~ government : administration locale

    ~ intelligence officer : policier, dans un commissariat, chargé du maintien
        du fichier de renseignements criminels

locality : lieu *(m)*, localité *(f)*

location : situation *(f)* (géographique)

lock : (1) boucler, enrayer, fermer à clé;   (2) serrure *(f)*

    ~-out : grève *(f)* patronale

    ~smith : serrurier *(m)*

    ~-up : cachot *(m)*

    ~-up shop : bouclard *(m)*

locum tenens : substitut *(m)*, remplaçant *(m)*

lodge : interjeter, déposer, placer, remettre

    ~ a formal complaint : porter le deuil, déposer une plainte

    ~ an appeal : interjeter un appel

lodger : locataire *(m&f)* en garni

lodgings : logement *(m)*, carrée *(f)*, hébergement *(m)*

    board and ~ : pension *(f)* complète

    furnished ~ : appartement *(m)* meublé

    let ~ : louer des chambres *(fpl)*

    ~ allowance : indemnité *(f)* de résidence/logement

log : bûche *(f)*

log(book) : (1) main *(f)* courante, journal *(m)* de bord, carnet *(m)* de vol,
    carnet *(m)*   de route, registre *(m)*; (2) carte *(f)* grise

logistics : logistique *(f)*

loiter : bagoter, balocher, tournailler

    ~ **for the purposes of prostitution** : faire du racolage

    ~ **with intent to commit crime** : rôdailler

long : long, étendu, prolongé

    ~-**distance lorry driver** : routier *(m)*

    ~ **range** : (de, à) longue portée

    ~ **range plans** : projets *(mpl)* à long terme

    ~-**term prospects** : perspectives *(fpl)* à long terme

lookout : guet *(m)*, guetteur *(m)*

loophole : lacune *(f)*, échappatoire *(f)*

loose : détendu, relâché, mobile, en vrac

    ~ **change** : petite/menue monnaie *(f)*

    ~ **chippings** : gravillons *(mpl)*

    ~ **leaf binder** : classeur *(m)*

    ~ **sheet of paper** : feuille *(f)* volante

    ~ **woman** : femme *(f)* de moeurs légères, facile *(f)*

loot : (1) butin *(m)*, grisbi *(m)* *, vendange *(f)* *;   (2) piller

looter : pillard *(m)*

looting : pillage *(m)*

lorry : camion *(m)*

lose : perdre, se débarrasser, distancer, semer, paumer

loss : perte *(f)*, déficit *(m)*, dommage *(m)*, préjudice *(m)*, (assurance) sinistre *(m)*

    ~ **of a right** : déchéance *(f)* d'un droit

lost : adiré, perdu, égaré

    ~ **property (office)** : (bureau des) objets *(mpl)* trouvés

lottery : loterie *(f)*

loudspeaker : haut-parleur *(m)*, hurleur *(m)*

lounge : salon *(m)*, salle *(f)* d'attente

lout : agrinche *(m)*, voyou *(m)*

lower : inférieur

  ~ **limit** : seuil *(m)*

LSD : LSD (diéthylamide de l'acide lysergique), acide *(m)*

luck : hasard *(m)*

lucky charm : grigri *(m)*

lucrative : lucratif

luggage : bagages *(mpl)*

  ~ **carrier** : porte-bagages *(m)*

lump sum : prix *(m)* forfaitaire, versement *(m)* global

lunatic : dément *(m)*, aliéné *(m)*

luncheon voucher : ticket-restaurant *(m)*, chèque-repas *(m)*

lying : (1) faisant des mensonges *(mpl)*; (2) être placé, se trouver, s'allonger

  he is ~ : il est menteur, il dit des mensonges

  he was ~ **in the road** : il était étendu au milieu de la route

lynch law : loi *(f)* de Lynch, justice *(f)* sommaire

M

machine : machine *(f)*, appareil *(m)*, organisation *(f)*

~ **down time** : équipement *(m)* non utilisé (par suite d'une défaillance)

~-**gun** : mitrailleuse *(f)*

~ **piston** : pistolet-mitrailleur *(m)*

~ **shop** : atelier *(m)*

madness : folie *(f)*

magazine : (1) magazine *(m)*; (2) chargeur *(m)*

magisterial : judiciaire

magistracy : (la) magistrature *(f)*

magistrate : juge *(m)* d'instance
*La plupart des **magistrates** sont bénévoles, siègant à temps partiel. Ils ne siègent seuls que dans certains cas rares. D'autres (**stipendiaries**) sont des juges professionnels qualifiés qui siègent seuls.*

~ **clerk** : greffier *(m)*

~**s court** : tribunal *(m)* de police, tribunal *(m)* d'instance

Magna Carta : Grande Charte *(f)*
Grande Charte des libertés, signée en 1215, et qui donne des droits de liberté et de justice aux citoyens britanniques.

magnetic tape : bande *(f)* magnétique

maid : (1) jeune fille; (2) servante *(f)*, domestique *(f)*

maiden : demoiselle *(f)*, vierge *(f)*

~ **name** : nom *(m)* de jeune fille

Maiden : espèce de guillotine
Utilisée en Ecosse et dans une partie de l'Angleterre jusqu'au XVIIème siècle.

mail : (1) courrier *(m)*, poste *(f)*; (2) envoyer par la poste

~ **order sales** : vente *(f)* par correspondance

registered ~ : lettre *(f)* recommandée

maim : mutiler, estropier

maimed : mutilé

main : principal

    ~ **beam** : feu *(m)* de route

    ~ **residence** : domicile principal

    ~ **road** : grande route

mainline (drugs) : shooter

maintain : maintenir, entretenir

maintenance : entretien *(m)*

    ~ **crew** : équipe *(f)* d'entretien

    ~ **of public order** : maintien *(m)* d'ordre (public)

    ~ **order** : décision *(f)* en matière d'obligation alimentaire

    ~ **work** : travail *(m)* d'entretien

major : (1) personne *(f)* majeure, aîné; (2) majeur, important, essentiel; (3) commandant (grade militaire)

    ~ **disaster** : sinistre *(m)* majeur, catastrophe *(f)*

majority : (1) majorité *(f)*; (2) majoritaire

    ~ **verdict** : verdict *(m)* non-unanime

make : (1) marque *(f)*; (2) fabrication *(f)*; (3) faire, construire

    ~ **a complaint** : porter plainte

maker : constructeur *(m)*, fabricant *(m)*

making : construction *(f)*, fabrication *(f)*, confection *(f)*

    ~ **off (without paying)** : filouterie *(f)*, grivèlerie *(f)*

maladministration : forfaiture *(f)*, mauvaise administration *(f)*

mala fides : mauvaise foi *(f)*

malefactor : malfaiteur *(m)*

malevolence : malveillance *(f)*

malfeasance : acte *(m)* illégal

malice : malice *(f)*, préméditation *(f)*

    ~ **aforethought/prepense** : intention *(f)* malicieuse, avec préméditation *(f)*

malicious : malveillant, criminel

    ~ **damage** : sabotage *(m)*

    ~ **prosecution** : poursuites *(fpl)* abusives

    ~ **wounding** : coups *(mpl)* et blessures *(fpl)*

malign : (1) porter atteinte à l'honneur, calomnier; (2) pernicieux, nuisible

malpractice : malversation *(f)*, faute *(f)*, négligence *(f)* professionnelle

malversation : (1) malversation *(f)*; (2) mauvaise gestion *(f)*

man : homme *(m)*

    ~ **of straw** : homme de paille

manage : diriger, conduire, gérer

management : (1) direction *(f)*, gestion *(f)*, gérance *(f)*; (2) voir **managerial staff**

    ~ **by objectives** : gestion par objectifs

    ~ **services** : services *(mpl)* auxiliaires de direction

manager : directeur *(m)*, dirigeant *(m)*, gérant *(m)*

    departmental ~ : chef *(m)* de service

    sales ~ : directeur commercial

    works ~ : chef *(m)* d'usine

managerial staff : cadre *(m)*, personnel *(m)* dirigeant

managing director : administrateur *(m)* délégué

mandamus (order of ~ **)** : "nous ordonnons"
    *Ordre décerné par le **High Court** pour l'exécution d'un devoir public.*

mandate : autorisation *(f)*

mandatory : obligatoire

mania : folie *(f)*

manning : effectifs *(mpl)*

manor * : fief *(m)*, circonscription *(f)*

manpower : effectifs *(mpl)*, main-d'oeuvre *(f)*

mansion : (1) hôtel *(m)* particulier; (2) immeuble *(m)* de rapport, divisé en appartments

manslaughter : homicide *(m)* par imprudence

manufacture : (1) fabrication *(f)*, construction *(f)*, manufacture *(f)*;
(2) manufacturer, fabriquer, confectionner

manufacturer : industriel *(m)*, fabricant *(m)*

manufacturing firm : établissement *(m)* industriel

map out (a policy) : déterminer une politique, tracer une ligne de conduite

march : défilé *(m)*

marginal note : mention *(f)* en marge

marijuana : marijuana *(f)*, banga *(m)*, bhang *(m)*, merde *(f)* *

marine : marin, maritime, marine

marital : marital, matrimonial

~ **status** : état matrimonial

mark : (1) notation *(f)*; (2) marque *(f)*, signe *(m)*, croix *(f)* (signature d'un
illettré)

hall ~ : poinçon *(m)* de contrôle sur les objets d'orfèvrerie

~ **out** : délimiter, borner, aborner

post ~ : cachet *(m)* de la poste

trade ~ : marque de fabrique

marker : repère *(m)*, témoin *(m)*

market : marché *(m)*

black ~ : marché noir

common ~ : marché commun

find a ~ **for** : trouver un débouché pour

~ **overt** : marché public

~ **research** : étude *(f)* de marché

~ **square** : place *(f)* du marché

~ **survey** : étude *(f)* de marché

~ **trader** : marchand *(m)* forain

stock ~ : marché des valeurs, la Bourse *(f)*

~ **value** : valeur *(f)* vénale, valeur *(f)* marchande

marksman : tireur *(m)* d'élite

marriage : mariage *(m)*

~ **certificate** : acte *(m)* de mariage

marshal : (1) maréchal *(m)*; (2) marshal *(m)* (magistrat et officier de police fédérale aux Etats Unis); (3) membre *(m)* du service d'ordre (à une manifestation, etc.); (4) ranger, mettre en ordre, rassembler, canaliser, trier

~ **the facts** : rassembler des faits et les présenter ordonnés

marshalling : (1) maintien *(m)* de l'ordre (parmi une foule de manifestants); (2) triage *(m)*

~ **yard** : gare *(f)*/centre *(m)* de triage

martial law : loi *(f)* martiale

mask : (1) masque *(m)*; (2) dissimuler

masked : cagoulé

massacre : massacre *(m)*, égorgerie *(f)*

master : (1) maître *(m)*; (2) maîtriser

~ **mind** : instigateur *(m)*

mate : camarade *(m)*, compagnon *(m)*, copain *(m)*; (2) officier *(m)* en second (dans la marine)

material : (1) matériel, pertinent; (2) matière *(f)*, substance *(f)*, matériel *(m)*

building ~**s** : matériaux de construction

~ **damage** : dégâts matériels

~ **evidence** : preuve matérielle

~ **fact** : fait essentiel

~ **witness** : témoin *(m)* de fait

raw ~**s** : matière *(f)* première

maternity leave : congé *(m)* de maternité

matrimonial home : domicile *(m)* des conjoints

matter : matière *(f)*, substance *(f)*

legal ~ : question *(f)* juridique

~ **of fact** : point *(m)* de fait

~ **of form** : formalité *(f)*

maturity : échéance *(f)*

maximum number : nombre *(f)* maximum

mayhem : (1) mutilation *(f)* du corps humain; (2) grabuge * *(m)*, destruction *(f)*

mayor : maire *(m)*

mean : (1) entendre, avoir l'intention; (2) moyen *(m)*; (3) avare, mesquin

meaning : sens *(m)*, signification *(f)*

means : moyens *(mpl)*, ressources *(fpl)*

    lawful ~ : moyens légaux

    live beyond one's ~ : vivre au-dessus de ses moyens

    ~ **of conveyance** : moyens de transport

    private ~ : fortune *(f)* personnelle

measure : mesure *(f)*, démarche *(f)*

    emergency ~ : mesure d'urgence

mechanic : mécanicien *(m)*, mécano *(m)* *

medal : décoration *(f)*, médaille *(f)*

media : moyens *(m)* de communication de masse

mediation : médiation *(f)*, intervention *(f)* amicale, procédure *(f)* de conciliation

medical : médical

    ~ **evidence** : expertise médicale

    ~ **examination** : visite médicale

    ~ **jurisprudence** : médecine *(f)* légale

    ~ **officer** : médecin *(m)* du travail

    ~ **officer of health** : médecin *(m)* sanitaire, directeur *(m)* de la santé publique

    ~ **profession** : corps médical

    ~ **record** : fiche médicale

medicine : médecine *(f)*

>   **forensic** ~ : médecine légale

medium : médium *(m)*

>   **fraudulent ~s** : médiums frauduleux
>   *Proscrits par la loi de 1961 qui a révoqué la loi ancienne contre la sorcellerie.*

meet : (1) se réunir, se rencontrer, se joindre à; (2) répondre (à un besoin), faire face (à des exigences)

meeting : assemblée *(f)*, rendez-vous *(m)*, réunion *(f)*

Member of Parliament : député *(m)*

memorandum : bordereau *(m)*, note *(f)*

menace : menace *(f)*

>   **demand with ~s** : chantage *(m)*, extorsion *(f)*

mens rea : dol *(m)*, intention *(f)* délictueuse

mental : mental, moral

>   ~ **anguish** : souffrance morale

>   ~ **capacity** : discernement *(m)*

>   ~ **defectiveness** : débilité mentale (comportant l'irresponsabilité pénale)

>   ~ **distress** : préjudice moral

>   ~ **disturbance/derangement** : aliénation mentale

>   ~ **hospital** : asile *(f)* psychiatrique, maison *(f)* d'aliénés

>   ~ **patient** : malade mentale

mentally defective : irresponsable

merchant : marchand *(m)*, commercant *(m)*, négociant *(m)*

mercy : merci *(f)*, miséricorde *(f)*, grâce *(f)*, clémence *(f)*

>   ~ **killing** : euthanasie *(f)*

>   **petition for** ~ : pourvoi/recours *(m)* en grâce

merger : confusion *(f)*, fusion *(f)*, unification *(f)*

merit : mérite *(m)*, fond *(m)*, substance *(f)*

> **go into the ˜s of** : discuter le pour et le contre de

> **˜ system** : avancement *(m)* fondé sur le mérite

meritorious : méritant, valable

message : message *(m)*

> **˜ received** : message reçu

mete out (punishment/rewards) : assigner (des punitions), décerner (des récompenses)

meter : compteur *(m)*

> **speedo˜** : compteur de vitesse

method : système *(m)*, méthode *(f)*, procédé *(m)*

> **˜ of payment** : modalités *(f)* de paiement

microcomputer : micro-ordinateur *(m)*

middle : moyen

> **˜ age** : âge *(m)* mûr

> **˜ class** : classe moyenne

> **˜man** : intermédiaire *(m)*

> **˜ management** : cadres *(mpl)* intermédiaires de direction

mileage : parcours *(m)*, kilométrage *(m)*

> **˜ allowance** : indemnité *(f)* pour frais de transport

milestone : borne *(f)*

military : (1) militaire; (2) force *(f)* armée

> **˜ law** : code *(m)* de justice militaire, droit *(m)* militaire

> **˜ pay** : solde *(f)*

> **˜ policeman** : gendarme *(m)*

militia : milice *(f)*

mill : moulin *(m)*, fabrique *(f)*, usine *(f)*

mine : (1) mine *(f)* (de charbon, d'or); (2) mine *(f)* (explosive); (3) creuser, extraire (le charbon), exploiter

~field : (1) champ *(m)* de mines; (2) (fig.) sac *(m)* d'embrouilles

~ of information : source *(f)* inépuisable de renseignements

miner : mineur *(m)*

~s' strike : grève *(f)* des mineurs

minicab : taxi *(m)* qu'on doit commander par téléphone

minister : ministre *(m)*

Defence ~ : Ministre de la Défense

ministry : ministère *(m)*

~ of Defence : ministère de la Défense

minor : (1) enfant *(m&f)*, mineur *(m)*; (2) mineur

~ changes : changements *(mpl)* de peu d'importance

~ offence : contravention *(f)*

~ repairs : petites réparations *(fpl)*

mint (money) : battre (monnaie)

in ~ condition : à l'état neuf

minutes (of meeting) : procès-verbal *(m)* (d'une réunion)

mirror : miroir *(m)*, glace *(f)*

rear-view ~ : rétroviseur *(m)*

misadventure : accident *(m)*

misappropriate : malverser

misappropriation : abus *(m)* de confiance, concussion *(f)*, détournement *(m)*

~ of funds : détournement de fonds

miscarriage : avortement *(m)*

~ of justice : erreur *(m)* judiciaire, déni *(m)* de justice

miscellaneous : divers, mêlé, mélangé

mischief : mal *(m)*, tort *(m)*, dommage *(m)*

misconduct : inconduite *(f)*

professional ~ : faute *(f)* commise dans l'exercice de ses fonctions

miscreant : délinquant *(m)*

misdemeanour : délit *(m)*, acte *(m)* délictueux
La distinction entre **misdemeanour** et **felony** (crime) fut supprimée en 1967
et tous les deux sont classés comme **arrestable offences.**

misfit : (personne) inadapté(e)

misgiving : doute *(m)*

misinformation : faux renseignements *(mpl)*

mislaid : adiré

mismanage : mal gérer

mismanagement : mauvaise gestion *(f)*

misprision (of a felony) : non-dénonciation *(f)* (d'un crime)

misrepresentation : déclaration *(f)* ou conduite *(f)* tendant à induire en erreur

    fraudulent ~ : fraude *(f)* pénale

    wilful ~ : fraude *(f)* civile

missile : projectile *(m)*

missing person : disparu *(m)*

mission : opération *(f)*, mission *(f)*

mistake : erreur *(f)*, faute *(f)*, méprise *(f)*, inadvertance *(f)*

mistaken identity : erreur *(f)* sur la personne

mistrial : erreur *(f)* judiciaire

mistrust : méfiance *(f)*

misunderstanding : malentendu, erreur *(f)*, méprise *(f)*

misuse : (1) abus *(m)*; (2) abuser

    ~ of authority : abus d'autorité, abus de pouvoir

    ~ of funds : détournement *(m)* de fonds

mitigate : adoucir, atténuer

mitigation : atténuation *(f)*, modération *(f)*, adoucissement *(m)*, réduction *(f)*

    ~ of sentence : atténuation de peine

mob : grande foule *(f)*, cohue *(f)*

mobile : mobile

> **~ support unit** : groupe *(m)* d'intervention

mock : imitation, contrefait, faux

> **~ auction** : fausse vente aux enchères
>
> **~ trial** : simulacre *(m)* de procès
>
> **~-up** : maquette *(f)*

modesty : pudeur *(f)*

modify : modifier

modus operandi : méthode *(f)*

molest : importuner, tracasser, molester, brutaliser

molestation : tracasserie *(f)*, brutalités *(fpl)*, attentat *(m)* à la pudeur

money : argent *(m)*, fonds *(m)*, monnaie *(f)*

> **come into ~** : faire un héritage *(m)*
>
> **~ lender** : prêteur *(m)* d'argent
>
> **~ order** : mandat-poste *(m)*
>
> **public ~** : fonds public
>
> **ready ~** : argent comptant
>
> **withdraw ~ (from the bank)** : retirer de l'argent (de la banque)

moneyed : riche, qui a de l'argent

> **~ classes** : classes *(fpl)* possédantes

monitor : (1) exercer une surveillance; (2) moniteur *(m)*

monkey business * : quelque chose *(f)* de louche, affaire *(f)* malhonnête, singeries *(fpl)*

month : mois *(m)*

monthly : mensuel

moonlight flit : déménager à la cloche de bois

moonlighting : travail *(m)* au noir

moonshine * : pétrole *(m)* *, distillation *(f)* illégale

moot : discutable

moped : cyclomoteur *(m)*

morality : bonnes moeurs *(fpl)*

moral : morale

morality : moralité *(f)*

morals : moeurs *(fpl)*, moralité *(f)*

mores : moeurs *(fpl)*

mortgage : hypothèque *(f)*

mortuary : morgue *(f)*, frigo *(m)* *

MOT : (Ministry of Transport): = Ministère *(m)* des Transports

~ **certificate** : certificat *(m)* de contrôle technique

~ **test** : contrôle *(m)* périodique obligatoire des véhicules

mother : mère *(f)*

~-**in-law** : belle-mère

motion : (1) mouvement *(m)*, marche *(f)*; (2) geste *(m)*; (3) motion *(f)*, proposition *(f)*

motive : mobile *(m)*, motif *(m)*, raison *(f)*

motor : moteur *(m)*

~ **car** : voiture *(f)*, auto(mobile) *(f)*

~ **home** : camping-car *(m)*, autocaravane *(f)*

~ **insurers' fund** : fonds *(m)* de garantie automobile

~ **scooter** : scooter *(m)*

motorboat : vedette *(f)*

motorcade : cortège *(m)* d'automobiles

motorcycle : motocyclette *(f)*, moto *(f)*

~ **combination** : (motocyclette à) sidecar *(m)*

~ **patrol** : motard *(m)*

~ **section** : unité *(f)* motocycliste

motorcyclist : motocycliste *(m&f)*, motard *(m)*

motorway : autoroute *(f)*

~ **patrol unit** : unité *(f)* d'autoroute

mountain bike : (vélo) tout-terrain *(m)*

mountaineer : montagnard *(m)*

mounted branch : unité *(f)* montée, cavalerie *(f)*

mourning : deuil *(m)*

moustache : moustache *(f)*

handlebar ~ : moustache en croc

toothbrush ~ : moustache en brosse

walrus ~ : moustache gauloise

mouthpiece * : babillard *(m)* *

movable : mobile, mobilier, meuble

move : (1) mouvement *(m)*, démarche *(f)*, décision *(f)*; (2) se déplacer, proposer

~ **house** : déménager

movement : déplacement *(m)*

muck-raker : fouille-merde *(m&f)* *

mudguard : garde-boue *(m)*

mug * : pante *(m)* *

mugging : dépouille *(f)*, vol *(m)* à l'arraché, agression *(f)*

mug-shots * : album *(m)* de famille *, trombinoscopes *(mpl)*, photos *(fpl)* de criminels

multiple pile-up : carambolage *(m)*

mum (to keep ~ **)** : ne pas piper mot, se taire

municipal : municipal

municipality : municipalité *(f)*

munitions : munitions *(fpl)*

murder : (1) assassinat *(m)*, meurtre *(m)*; (2) assassiner
Crime d'homicide illicite avec préméditation.

~ **squad** : = brigade *(f)* criminelle

murderer : assassin *(m)*, meurtrier *(m)*

muscular : musclé, costaud

mush : (1) sentimentalité *(f)*; (2) visage *(m)*, gueule *(f)*; (3) gars *(m)*, mon vieux *(m)*

mute : muet

mutilate : mutiler

mutineer : mutiné *(m)*, mutin *(m)*

mutiny : (1) mutinement *(m)*, mutinerie *(f)*, sédition *(f)*; (2) se mutiner

mutual consent : gré-à-gré

muzzle : (1) (arme) bouche *(f)*; (2) gueule *(f)*; (3) (anti-mordre) muselière; (4) empêcher quelqu'un de parler

mystery : mystère *(m)*

N

nab * : pincer *, choper *, poisser *

name : (1) nom *(m)*; (2) nommer, présenter, désigner, élire

    assumed/false/fictitious ~ : nom supposé

    fore~ : nom de baptême, prénom *(m)*

    full ~ : nom et prénoms *(mpl)* (en toutes lettres)

    go by the ~ **of** : être connu sous le nom de

    have a bad ~ : avoir mauvaise réputation *(f)*

    maiden ~ : nom de jeune fille

    ~**less** : innommé

    sur~ : nom de famille

namely : à savoir, c'est-à-dire

narcotics : stupéfiants *(mpl)*

nasty : désagréable, méchant, mauvais

    ~ **piece of work** : vilain bonhomme *(m)*, sale type *(m)*

national : (1) national; (2) ressortissant *(m)*

    ~ **assistance** : assistance *(f)* publique

    ~ **central bureau (Interpol)** : bureau *(m)* central national (Interpol)

    ~ **co-ordinator of ports policing** : coordinateur *(m)* de police des ports

    ~ **defence** : défense nationale

    ~ **drugs intelligence unit** : office *(m)* central pour la repressin du trafic illicite des stupéfiants

    ~ **football intelligence unit** : unité *(f)* centrale de renseignements concernant le maintien de l'ordre sur les stades de football

    ~ **health service** : service national de santé

    ~ **identification bureau** : service central *(m)* d'identité judiciaire

    ~ **insurance** : sécurité *(f)* sociale

    ~ **interest** : raison *(f)* d'état

~ **service** : service national

nationalisation : étatisation *(f)*

NATO helmet : casque *(m)* de protection

natural : naturel

    ~ **child** : enfant naturel

    ~ **person** : personne *(f)* physique

    ~ **wastage** : diminution naturelle des effectifs (par retraite, vieillesse, etc.)

nature : caractère *(m)*

naval : naval

    ~ **base** : port *(m)* de guerre, base navale

navigation : navigation *(f)*

    inland ~ : navigation fluviale

navy : marine *(f)* de guerre

    ~ **blue** : bleu marine

near miss : quasi-collision *(f)*

need : besoin *(m)*

needle : (1) aiguille *(f)*; (2) asticoter, agacer

    to be on the ~ : se shooter *

    to get the ~ : se ficher en boule

needy : indigent

ne'er-do-well : vaurien *(m)*, rien-du-tout *(m)*

negative : négatif

    answer in the ~ : répondre par la négative

    ~ **evidence** : preuve négative

neglect : négligence *(f)*

negligence : négligence *(f)*

    criminal ~ : négligence criminelle, faute grave de caractère pénal

    gross ~ : négligence de nature délictuelle

negligent : négligent, fautif

negotiations : pourparlers *(mpl)*, négotiations *(fpl)*

negotiator : négotiateur *(m)*

neighbour : voisin(e) *(m&f)*

neighbourhood : voisinage *(m)*, quartier *(m)*, alentours *(mpl)*

~ **watch** : surveillance du quartier par les habitants

nervous breakdown/depression : dépression *(f)* nerveuse, déprime *(f)*

nest-egg : planque *(f)*

net : ramasser dans les filets

network : réseau *(m)*, système *(m)*

new-born child : part *(m)*

news : nouvelle(s) *(f)*, information(s) *(f)*, renseignement *(m)*

~ **agency** : agence *(f)* d'information

~ **conference** : conférence *(f)* de presse

newspaper : journal

~ **advertisement** : annonce *(f)* de journal

~ **cutting** : découpure *(f)* de journal

~ **heading** : rubrique *(f)* de journal

next : prochain, suivant.   ~-**of-kin** : parents *(m&fpl)* les plus proches

nick (1) * : (voler) barboter *, chiper *, faucher *, lever *, récupérer *, subtiliser *, tirer *

nick (2) * : (appréhender) accrocher *, baiser *, coiffer *, coincer *, empoigner *, épingler *, pincer *

nick (3) * (commissariat de police/prison) bing *(m)* *, cabane *(f)* *, cage *(f)* *, cambron *(m)* *, château *(m)* *, taule *(f)* *, tôle *(f)* *

nickname : surnom *(m)*, sobriquet *(m)*, diminutif *(m)*

niece : nièce *(f)*

night : nuit *(f)*, borgne *(f)*, sorgne *(f)*

~ **club** : boîte *(f)* de nuit, night *(m)* *

~ **duty** : surveillance *(f)* nocturne

~ **safe** : coffre *(m)* de nuit

~ **shift** : poste/service *(m)* de nuit, équipe *(f)* de nuit

~ **stick** : matraque *(f)*

~**watchman** : veilleur *(m)* de nuit

nil : (1) nul; (2) néant *(m)*, zéro *(m)*

nobble * : (1) acheter, soudoyer; (2) droguer; (3) pince *, choper *, happer *

nobody : personne *(f)*, aucun *(m)*

no change : statu *(m)* quo

no-claims bonus : bonus *(m)*, prime *(f)* de non-casse

no criminal record : casier *(m)* judiciaire vierge

nod : signe *(m)* affirmatif de la tête

noddy * : policier *(m)* en tenue

no entry : sens *(m)* interdit

no fixed abode : sans domicile fixe

no funds : défaut *(m)* de provision

no further action : sans suite

no indication : aucun signe *(m)*

no injuries : aucune blessure *(f)*

noise : bruit *(m)*

nolle prosequi : désistement *(m)*

nominal : nominal, nominatif

~ **damages** : dommages-intérêts *(mpl)* symboliques

~ **fine** : amende *(f)* pour la forme

~ **rent** : loyer *(m)* pour la forme, loyer *(m)* insignifiant/symbolique

~ **roll** : contrôle/état *(m)* nominatif

nominate : désigner, nommer

nomination : désignation *(f)*, élection *(f)*

non-appearance : non-comparution *(f)*

non-commissioned officer (NCO) : gradé *(m)*, sous-officier *(m)*

non-cooperation : refus *(m)* de coopération

non-existence (of evidence) : inexistence *(f)* (de preuve)

non-payment : défaut *(m)* de paiement

non-profit making organisaton : société *(f)* sans but lucratif (loi 1901)

non-skid : sans-déraper, anti-dérapant

non-stop : sans arrêt

nonsuit : débouter, cessation *(f)* de poursuites

noose : noeud *(m)* coulant, corde *(f)* (de bourreau)

no previous convictions : casier *(m)* judiciaire vierge

normal : normal, régulier

nose : nez *(m)*

    ~ about/around : fouiller, fureter, fouiner *

    to have a good ~ : avoir du flair *(m)*

    to poke/stick one's ~ into something : mettre/fourrer son nez dans quelque chose

    you'd better keep your ~ clean! * : il vaut mieux que tu te tiennes à carreau! *

not allowed : interdit, défendu

notary public : notaire *(m)*

note : billet *(m)*, note *(f)*, observation *(f)*, bordereau *(m)*

    bank-~ : billet de banque

    credit ~ : facture *(f)* de crédit

    ~ book : calepin *(m)*, carnet *(m)*, main *(f)* courante

    ~ down : noter, inscrire, écrire

not guilty : non coupable

nothing : rien

    ~ to report : rien à signaler

notice : (1) affiche *(f)*, avis *(m)*, sommation *(f)*;
(2) délai-congé *(m)*, préavis *(m)* (de licenciement, de congé)

    formal ~ : mise *(f)* en demeure

    give ~ (to employer) : demander son congé, donner sa démission

    give ~ (to employee) : signifier son congé (à un employé)

    judicial ~ : fait de notoriété *(f)* publique

    ~ of appeal : avis d'appel

    ~ board : panneau *(m)* d'affichage

    public ~ : avis au public

    written ~ : avis par écrit

notifiable (disease) : (maladie) dont la déclaration est obligatoire

notify : notifier, annoncer, signaler

notoriety : notoriété *(f)*

notorious : mal famé

no trace : aucune trace *(f)*

notwithstanding : nonobstant

novice : blanc bec *(m)*

nowhere : nulle part

nuisance : nuisance *(f)*, acte *(m)* dommageable, désagrément *(m)*

    public ~ : atteinte *(f)* aux droits du public (par ex. à la libre circulation)

null (and void) : nul (et non avenu)

nullify : rendre nul, annuler

number : nombre *(m)*, quantité *(f)*, chiffre *(m)*, numéro *(m)*

    ~ plate : plaque *(f)* d'immatricualtion

    reference ~ : numéro de référence

    registration ~ : numéro d'immatriculation

    telephone ~ : numéro de téléphone

    wrong ~ : faux numéro

numerous : nombreux

nurse : (1) infirmier(ière) *(m/f)*;   (2) soigner

   children's ~ : bonne *(f)* d'enfants

nursing home : maison *(f)* de santé

nut-case : dingue *(m)*, fou *(m)*

nuts and bolts * : tous les détails pratiques

nymphomaniac : hystérique *(f)*

O

oath : serment *(m)*

    on ~ : sous serment

obedience : obéissance *(f)*

object : (1) sujet *(m)*; (2) but *(m)*, objet *(m)*, objectif *(m)*, fin *(f)*;
    (3) objet *(m)*, chose *(f)*

objection : exception *(f)*, récusation *(f)*, opposition *(f)*

objectionable : répréhensible

obligation : obligation *(f)*, devoir *(m)*

obligatory : obligatoire

obliterate : oblitérer, effacer

obscene : obscène

    ~ **language** : chants, cris ou discours *(mpl)* contraires aux bonnes moeurs

    ~ **publication** : publication obscène/pornographique

observation : observation *(f)*, surveillance *(f)*

observe : observer

observer : observateur *(m)*, spectateur *(m)*

obsolescence : désuétude *(f)*

obsolete : désuet, tombé en désuétude

obstruct : encombrer, obstruer, entraver, gêner

    ~ **a constable in the exercise of his duty** : faire obstacle à un agent de
    police, entraver une enquête policière

    ~ **the traffic** : entraver la circulation

obstruction : encombrement *(m)*, obstruction *(f)*, obstacle *(m)*

    to cause an ~ : entraver (la circulation)

obtaining : obtention *(f)*

    ~ **property/services by deception** : carambouillage *(m)*, escroquerie *(f)*

occupant : (1) titulaire *(m)*, occupant *(m)*, locataire *(m)*

occupation : emploi *(m)*, métier *(m)*, occupation *(f)*, profession *(f)*

occupational : professionnel

    ~ **disease** : maladie *(f)* professionnelle

    ~ **hazards** : risques *(fpl)* du métier

occur : se produite, avoir lieu, arriver

occurrence : événement *(m)*, occurrence *(f)*,

    ~ **book** : main *(f)* courante des événements (tenue au commissariat de police)

odd : (1) impair; (2) bizarre.   ~ **jobs** : bricolage *(m)*

off : (au) loin, séparé, écarté

    day ~ : jour *(m)* de liberté, jour *(m)* de congé

    ~**-the-job training** : formation *(f)* professionnelle externe

    ~ **licence** : autorisation *(f)* permettant seulement la vente des boissons alcooliques à emporter

    ~ **peak** : creux

    ~ **the record** : officieusement

    ~ **season** : hors saison *(f)*

    ~ **shore** : au large, extraterritorial

    ~ **shore banking** : unité *(f)* bancaire opérant outre-mer

    ~ **shore company** : société *(f)* n'ayant pas d'activité dans l'état du siège social

    ~ **shore oil field** : gisement *(m)* pétrolier sous-marin

    well-~ : à l'aise (financièrement)

offence : infraction *(f)*, agression *(f)*, faute *(f)*

    continuing ~ : contravention *(f)*/délit *(m)* à l'état permanent

    indictable ~ : crime *(m)* ou délit *(m)*, acte *(m)* délictueux

    minor ~ : contravention *(f)*

    ~**s known to the police** : criminalité *(f)* apparente

    serious ~ : faute grave

technical ~ : quasi-délit *(m)*

unnatural ~ : crime *(m)* contre nature

offender : contrevenant *(m)*, délinquant *(m&f)*, malfaiteur *(m)*, offenseur *(m)*, repris *(m)* de justice, auteur *(m)*

first ~ : délinquant primaire

habitual ~ : délinquant d'habitude, récidiviste

joint ~ : complice *(m&f)*

juvenile ~ : mineur délinquant

offensive : offensant, repoussant, grossier,

~ language : chants, cris ou discours *(mpl)* contraires aux bonnes moeurs

~ weapon : arme *(f)* offensive

office :   bureau *(m)*, étude *(f)*; office *(m)*, fonctions *(fpl)*

branch ~ : succursale *(f)*

Foreign ~ : Ministère *(m)* des Affaires Etrangères

Home ~ : Ministère *(m)* de l'Intérieur

~ staff : personnel *(m)* de bureau

~ premises : bureaux, immeuble *(m)* commercial

police ~ : bureau de police, poste *(m)* de police

public ~ : fonctions publiques

registered ~ : siège *(m)* social

registry ~ : bureau de l'état-civil

tourist ~ : bureau de tourisme, syndicat *(m)* d'initiative

officer : officier *(m)*, agent *(m)*

local government ~ : fonctionnaire *(m&f)* de l'administration locale

police ~ : agent de police

official : (1) officiel, d'office; (2) fonctionnaire *(m&f)*, responsable *(m&f)*

in his ~ capacity : ès-qualités

~ agency : office *(m)*

~ **channels** : voie *(f)* hiérarchique

~ **document** : acte/document *(m)* officiel

~ **receiver** : administrateur *(m)* (liquidateur *(m))* judiciaire

~ **seal** : cachet *(m)* réglementaire

~ **secrets** : secrets *(mpl)* d'Etat

~ **stamp** : estampille *(f)*

officially : d'office, officiellement

officious : officieux, -euse

oil : pétrole *(m)*, huile *(f)*

old : vieux, ancien

~ **age** : vieillesse *(f)*

~ **age pension** : pension *(f)* vieillesse

~ **Bailey** : nom familier du **Central Criminal Court**

~ **Bill** * : les flics *(mpl)* *, bigorne *(f)* *

~ **hand** : briscard *(m)*

~ **lag** : cheval *(m)* de retour

~ **soldier** : ancien soldat *(m)*, (fig.) briscard *(m)*

ombudsman : médiateur *(m)*

omission to discharge a legal duty : négligence *(f)* à s'acquitter d'un devoir imposé par la loi

one-armed bandit : bandit-manchot *(m)*

one way (street) : (rue à) sens unique

on-the-job training : formation *(f)* professionnelle interne

one-off : exceptionnel, unique

onus of proof : charge *(f)* de la preuve

open : (1) ouvrir, débrider, délourder, entamer; (2) ouvert, public, libre

~ **cheque** : chèque *(m)* non barré

~ **court** : audience publique

~ **day** : portes ouvertes

~ **trial** : jugement public

~ **verdict** : décision *(f)* par le jury d'un **inquest** laissant ouverte la question de comment le défunt est décédé.

opening : ouverture *(f)*

~ **of the courts** : rentrée *(f)* des tribunaux

~ **of the case** : exposé *(m)* des faits

~ **of the investigation/enquiry** : ouverture de l'instruction/de l'enquête

~ **speech** : plaidoirie *(f)* initiale du procureur

operation : opération *(f)*, fonctionnement *(m)*

~ **of the law** : application *(f)* d'une loi

~**s room** : salle *(f)* opérationnelle, centre *(m)* d'opérations

operational section : unité *(f)* territoriale

opiate : opiat *(m)*

opinion : opinion *(f)*, avis *(m)*, consultation *(f)* juridique, arrêté de la **House of Lords**

expert ~ : avis d'expert

counsel's ~ : avis motivé

dissenting ~ : avis de la minorité

public ~ : opinion publique

opium : opium *(m)*

~ **poppy** : pavot *(m)* somnifère

oppression : oppression *(f)*, tyrannie *(f)*, abus *(m)* d'autorité

optional : facultatif, loisible

oral evidence : voir **évidence, oral**

ordain : statuer

ordeal, trial by : ancienne procédure par laquelle on faisait appel à Dieu pour savoir si l'accusé était coupable. L'accusé devait, par exemple, prendre à la main une barre de fer chauffée sans provoquer de brûlure grave, ou bien il était trempé dans l'eau pour voir s'il flottait ou non.

order : arrêté *(m)*, commande *(f)*, consigne *(f)*, directive *(f)*, ordonnance *(f)*

> **by ~ of** : sur ordre *(m)* de

> **by ~ of the court** : par autorité *(f)* de justice

> **~ for costs** : condamnation *(f)* aux dépens

> **~ form** : bon *(m)* de commande

> **~ in council** : arrêté ministériel

> **traffic ~** : règlement *(m)* de circulation

ordinance : ordonnance *(f)*

ordinary : ordinaire

> **~ courts** : tribunaux *(mpl)* ordinaires

> **~ law** : droit *(m)* commun

> **out of the ~** : exceptionnel

order : (1) ordonner; (2) ordre *(m)*, commande *(f)*

organisation : organisation *(f)*, organisme *(m)*, institution *(f)*, système *(m)*

> **~ chart** : organigramme *(m)*

organised : organisé

> **~ crime** : banditisme *(f)*

> **~ labour** : syndicats *(mpl)* ouvriers

organiser : animateur *(m)*

origin : provenance *(f)*, origine *(f)*

originate : donner naissance à, tirer son origine de

orphan : orphelin *(m)*

others/other people : autrui *(m)*

otherwise : autrement, par ailleurs

> **unless ~ provided** : sauf dispositions *(fpl)* contraires

oust : évincer

"out" (radio) : "terminé"

outcome : résultat *(m)*, issue *(f)*

outcry : clameur *(f)*

outer harbour : avant-port *(m)*

outfit : équipement *(m)*, habillement *(m)*

outlaw : (1) hors la loi *(m)*; (2) proscrire, prohiber

outlook : perspective *(f)*

outlying : éloigné, isolé

out of court : extrajudiciaire

out of date : prescrit, périmé, désuet, démodé

    ~ **cheque** : chèque prescrit

out of order : en dérangement

out of the question : inadmissible

out of work : en inactivité, sans occupation, en chômage

output : rendement *(m)*, production *(f)*

outrage : attentat *(m)*

outraging public deceny : attentat *(m)* public à la pudeur

outright : pur et simple, à forfait

outside : hors

outstanding : (1) saillant, marquant, éminent; (2) impayé, échu, en retard

    ~ **offences** : infractions *(fpl)* non jugées
        Infractions qui peuvent être prises en compte dans la condamnation
        pour une autre infraction semblable.

overalls : bleus *(mpl)* de travail

overcharge : estamper, majorer, surfaire

overdose : surdose *(f)*

overdraft : découvert *(m)*, facilités *(fpl)* de caisse

overdrawn account : compte *(m)* à découvert

overdrive : surmultiplié *(m)*

overleaf : verso *(m)*

overmanning : sureffectif *(m)*

overriding : primordial

overrule : décider contre, annuler (une décision), passer outre (une objection)

overseas : outre-mer

oversteer : survirage *(m)*

overt : manifeste, évident, patent

overtime : heures *(fpl)* supplémentaires, travail *(m)* supplémentaire

over the wall * : prendre la clé des champs

overturn (a vehicle) : faire la crêpe *(f)*

overweight : excédent *(m)* de poids

owe : devoir

owing : dû, exigible, arriéré

own : posséder

    ~ up : reconnaître, avouer

owned by : appartenant à

owner : propriétaire *(m&f)*

    at ~s risk : aux risques et périls du propriétaire

    lawful ~ : propriétaire légitime

    rightful ~ : ayant *(m)* droit

ownership : propriété *(f)*, droit *(m)* de propriété

    proof of ~ : preuve *(f)* de propriété, titre *(m)* de propriété

oyer : audition *(f)*

oyez : ouïr

P

padlock : cadenas *(m)*

pain : peine *(f)*, douleur *(f)*

    on ˜ of death : sous peine de mort

    ˜ and suffering : indemnités *(fpl)* pour blessures et souffrances

palm print : empreinte *(f)* de paume

Panda car : voiture *(f)* pie

panel : tableau *(m)*, groupe *(m)*, comité *(m)*, commission *(f)*

    instrument ˜ : tableau de bord

    ˜ of experts : commission d'experts

parade : parade *(f)*, défilé *(m)*

paragraph : alinéa *(m)*

parachutist, paratrooper : parachutiste *(m)*, para *(m)*, chuteur *(m)*

pardon : (1) amnistie *(f)*, grâce *(f)*, pardon *(m)*; (2) gracier

parentage : filiation *(f)*

parents : parents *(mpl)*, ascendants *(mpl)*

parish : paroisse *(f)*, commune *(f)*

    ˜ council : conseil *(m)* communal

park : (1) parc *(m)*; (2) stationner, garer

    car ˜ : parking *(m)*

parked : en stationnement

parking : stationnement *(m)*

    no ˜ : défense de stationner

    ˜ lights : feux *(mpl)* de position

    ˜ meter : parcmètre *(m)*

    ˜ place : lieu *(m)* de stationnement

parliament : parlement *(m)*

    act of ~ : loi *(f)*

    member of ~ : parlementaire *(m&f)*, député *(m)*

parliamentary privilege : immunité *(f)* parlementaire

parole : libération *(f)* conditionnelle

    ~ board : comité *(m)* consultatif de la libération conditionnelle

parricide : parricide *(m)*

parry : (1) parade *(f)*; (2) parer, détourner, éluder

particulars : libellé *(m)*, signalement *(m)*

partnership : société *(f)* en commandite

part–time work : travail *(m)* à mi-temps

party : partie *(f)*

    injured ~ : partie lésée

    ~ to a crime : impliqué dans un crime

    third ~ : tiers *(m)*

pass : (1) passer, voter, transmettre; (2) laissez-passer *(m)*, coupe-file *(m)*
(3) être reçu (examen)

    ~ book : livret *(m)* de banque

    ~ key : passe-partout *(m)*

    ~ sentence : prononcer condamnation

    ~ word : mot *(m)* du guet

passage : passage *(m)*, trajet *(m)*

passenger : passager *(m)*, voyageur *(m)*

passing–off : écoulement *(m)*, supposition *(f)*
Délit commis en vendant des marchandises, en traitant des affaires, etc.
sous un nom, une description, etc., propres à faire croire qu'il s'agit d'un
autre article ou d'une autre personne.

passport : passeport *(m)*

    ~ control : contrôle *(m)* des passeports

paste jewellery : burmas *(mpl)*, strass *(m)*

pasting * : rossée *(f)* *

path : chemin *(m)*, sentier *(m)*

patrol : (1) patrouille *(f)*, ronde *(f)*, surveillance *(f)*; (2) patrouiller, faire une patrouille

paunch : bide *(m)*, ventre *(m)*, panse *(f)*, bedaine *(f)* *

pauper : indigent *(m)*, économiquement faible

pavement : trottoir *(m)*, bitume *(m)*, macadam *(m)*, pavé *(m)*

paving stone : pavé *(m)*

pawn : (1) gage *(m)*, mise *(f)* en gage; (2) mettre en gage

   ~ **broker** : prêteur *(m)* sur gages

pay : (1) appointements *(mpl)*, salaire *(m)*, paie *(f)*; (2) verser, payer

   ~ **as you earn (PAYE)** : impôt *(m)* sur le revenu
      Système de retenue à la source de l'impôt sur les salaires.

   ~ **back** : rendre, rembourser

   ~ **day** : jour *(m)* de paie

   ~ **freeze** : blocage des salaires

   ~ **in** : verser

   ~ **load** : charge *(f)* utile

   ~ **roll** : bordereau *(m)* de paie, état *(m)* des salaires, montant *(m)* global des salaires

   sick ~ : indemnité *(f)* de maladie

   unemployment ~ : secours *(m)* de chômage

paying-in slip : feuille *(f)* de versement

payee : destinataire *(m)*

payment : paiement *(m)*, rémunération *(f)*, règlement *(m)*, versement *(m)*

   order for ~ : ordre *(m)* de paiement

   ~ into court : consignation *(f)* en justice

peace : paix *(f)*, tranquillité *(f)*, calme *(m)*, ordre *(m)* public

   breach the ~ : troubler l'ordre public

~ **officer** : agent *(m)* de police

(the) Queen's ~ : l'ordre public

peak hours : heures *(fpl)* de pointe

peccadillo : faute *(f)* légère

peculation : péculat *(m)*, malversation *(f)*

peculiarities : signes *(mpl)* particuliers, traits *(mpl)* distinctifs

pecuniary : pécuniaire, financier

~ **advantage** : avantages *(mpl)* matériels

pedal : pédale *(f)*

pederast : pédéraste *(m)*, pédé *(m)* *

pedestrian : piéton *(m)*

~ **crossing** : passage *(m)* clouté, passage *(m)* piétons

~ **precinct** : zone *(f)* piétonnière

pedestrianize : transformer en zone *(f)* piétonnière

pedlar : marchand *(m)* ambulant, colporteur *(m)*

peeler : sergent *(m)* de ville
*Policier du XIXème siècle, surnommé en souvenir de Sir Robert Peel,
premier ministre de l'époque.*

peephole : housard *(m)*, oeilleton *(m)*

Peeping Tom : voyeur *(m)*, guette-au-trou *(m)*

peer : (1) pair *(m)* (du royaume et égal social); (2) regarder (attentivement, d'un
air interrogateur ou inquiet, avec des yeux de myope)

pelt : bombarder, cribler

penal : pénal

~ **servitude** : travaux *(mpl)* forcés (peine abolie en 1948)

~ **settlement** : colonie *(f)* pénitentiaire

~ **system** : régime *(m)* pénitentiaire

penalty : peine *(f)*, sanction *(f)* pénale

pending : en cours

penetration : pénétration *(f)*

penitentiary : pénitentiaire

penknife : canif *(m)*

penniless : fauché, lavé, sur le pavé, sans ressources

penology : pénologie *(f)*

pension : pension *(f)*, rente *(f)*

    old-age ~ : pension de vieillesse

    ~ off : mettre à la retraite

    retirement ~ : pension de retraite

    retire on ~ : prendre sa retraite

pensionable : qui donne droit à une pension

pensioner : retraité *(m)*

people : gens *(mpl)*, peuple *(m)*

pep talk * : paroles *(fpl)* d'encouragement

per : par, selon, conformément à

    ~ annum : par an

    ~ capita : par personne

    ~ pro : par procuration

    ~ se : de (en) lui-même

peremptory : péremptoire, impératif, décisif, absolu

    ~ challenge : récusation *(f)* pure et simple de jurés

    ~ notice : mise *(f)* en demeure

    ~ proof : preuve *(f)* libératoire

    ~ question : interpellation *(f)*

performance : exécution *(f)*

period : délai *(m)*, durée *(f)*, période *(f)*

periodical : magazine *(m)*, publication *(f)* périodique

perjury : faux serment *(m)*

    subornation of ~ : subornation *(f)* de témoin

perks * : gratte * *(f)*, avantages *(mpl)* accessoires

permanent : permanent

    ~ address : résidence *(f)* fixe, séjour *(m)* habituel

    ~ disability : incapacité *(f)* permanente

    ~ under–secretary : secrétaire *(m&f)* général de ministère

permissible : admissible, loisible

permission : permission *(f)*

permissive : (1) permissif; (2) facultatif

permit : autorisation *(f)*, permis *(m)*, laissez-passer *(m)*;   permettre, autoriser

perpetrate : commettre, perpétrer

perpetrator : auteur *(m)*

perpetuity : perpétuité *(f)*

perquisites : émoluments *(mpl)*, casuel *(m)*

perseverance : diligence *(f)*

persistence : diligence *(f)*

persistent : persistant

    ~ complainer : râleur *(m&f)*

    ~ offender : multi récidiviste *(m&f)*, repris *(m)* de justice

person : personne *(f)*, individu *(m)*

    artificial ~ : personne morale

    natural ~ : personne physique

    ~ unknown : un tiers non-identifié

    private ~ : (simple) particulier *(m)*

    third ~ : tierce personne, tiers

personal : personnel, privé

~ **assistant** : secrétaire *(m&f)* particulier, attaché *(m)* de direction

~ **effects** : affaires *(fpl)*

~ **file** : dossier *(m)* de personnalité

~ **history** : situation personnelle

~ **identification number (PIN)** : numéro *(m)* de code secret

~ **injury accident** : accident *(m)* corporel

~ **privacy** : vie privée

~ **radio** : talkie-walkie *(m)*

~ **service** : service *(m)* à personne

~ **status** : statut personnel

~ **use** : usage personnel

personally (liable) : personnellement (responsable)

personation : supposition *(f)* de personne, usurpation *(f)* de nom

personnel : effectif *(m)*, personnel *(m)*

~ **department** : service *(m)* du personnel

persuasive authority : jurisprudence qui n'est pas obligatoire (par ex. décisions de tribunaux inférieurs, étrangers ...)

pertinent : pertinent, utile, opportune

perturbation : trouble *(m)*

perverse verdict : décision *(f)* du jury qui est contraire aux preuves

perversion : perversion *(f)*

pervert : pervertir

~ **the course of justice** : égarer la justice (en subornant un témoin)

pest : casse-pieds *(m&f)*, empoisonneur *(m)*

pester : importuner, harceler

pet : animal *(m)* familier

peter * : coffiot *(m)*, coffre-fort *(m)*

peterman * : arquin *(m)* *

Peter principle : principe *(f)* de Peter
    Théorie selon laquelle les gens sont promus jusqu'à un poste qu'ils sont incapables d'assumer.

petition : (1) pétition *(f)*, requête *(f)*, demande *(f)*; (2) adresser une pétition, faire une demande

petrol : essence *(f)*

    ~ **bomb** : cocktail *(m)* Molotov

    ~ **can** : bidon *(m)* d'essence

    ~ **station** : station-service *(f)*

    ~ **tank** : réservoir *(m)* d'essence

    ~ **tanker** : camion-citerne *(m)*

petty : sans importance, mineur, insignifiant

    ~ **cash** : petite caisse *(f)*

    ~ **larceny** : larcin *(m)*

    ~ **offence** : contravention *(f)*

    ~ **sessions** : session *(f)* des juges de première instance, tribunal *(m)* de police

    ~ **theft** : vol *(m)* simple, carottage *(m)*, larcin *(m)*,

pharmacy : pharmacie *(f)*

phone : (1) téléphone *(m)*;   (2) téléphoner, passer un coup de fil

    ~ **card** : télécarte *(f)*

    ~ **tap** : écoute *(f)*

phoney * : (1) faux, balourd, bidon;   (2) charlatan *(m)*, poseur *(m)*

photo : voir **photograph**

photocopie, photostat : photocopie *(f)*

photofit picture : portrait *(m)* robot

photograph : photographie *(f)*, photo *(f)*

photographer : photographe *(m&f)*

physical : physique, matériel, corporel

    ~ **dependence** : dépendance physique

   ~ **disability** : incapacité *(f)*, invalidité *(f)* physique

   ~ **impossibility** : impossibilité *(f)* matérielle

   ~ **training** : entraînement *(m)* physique

physician : médecin *(m)*, docteur *(m)*

pick (a lock) : chatouiller (une serrure), crocheter

pickaxe : pioche *(f)*

   ~ **handle** : manche *(f)* de pioche

picket : (mil.) factionnaire *(m)*, (indust.) piquet *(m)* de grève

picklock : rossignol *(m)*

pick out : distinguer, choisir, désigner

pick-pocket : tireur *(m)*, fourchette *(f)*, pick-pocket *(m&f)*

pick-pocketing : vol *(m)* à la tire, vol *(m)* de la bousculade

pick-up : (1) prendre (des passagers); (2) ramasser; (3) arrêter, cueillir *,
   pincer *

   ~ **truck** : camionnette *(f)* ouverte

piece : (1) morceau *(m)*, pièce *(f)*; (2) * arme à feu

pie-chart : fromage *(m)*, camembert *(m)*
   *Graphique sous forme de cercle coupé en tranches comme un pâté et
   permettant de comparer des résultats.*

pier : jetée *(f)*, quai *(m)*

pig : flicard *(m)*, la flicaille *(f)*

pile-up * : (1) carambolage *(m)*; (2) s'écraser, bousiller

pile in * : s'entasser *, s'empiler *

pilfering : larcin *(m)*

pill : pilule *(f)*

pillage : rapine *(f)*

pillaged : saccagé

pillar box : boîte *(f)* aux lettres

pillion : siège *(m)* arrière

~ **passenger** : passager *(m)* arrière

pillory : pilori *(m)*

pimp : protecteur *(m)*, souteneur *(m)*, alphonse *(m)* *, barbe *(m)* *,
barbillon *(m)* *, hareng *(m)* *, maquereau *(m)* *, poisson *(m)* *

pin : (1) épingle *(f)*; (2) épingler

~ **money** : argent *(m)* de poche

they tried to ~ **the crime on him** * : ils ont essayé de lui mettre le crime
sur le dos/de lui coller *

to ~ **one's hopes on something** : mettre tous ses espoirs dans quelque
chose

you can't ~ **it on me!** : vous ne pouvez rien prouver contre moi!

pinball machine : flipper *(m)*

pinstripe : rayure *(f)* très fine

~ **suit** : costume *(m)* rayé

pinch (1) * : (arrêter) agrafer *, coiffer *, coincer *, empoigner *, épingler *

pinch (2) * : (voler) chiper *, chauffer *, faire *, faucher *, griffer *,
ratisser *, soulever *

piracy : piraterie *(f)*

piss * : pisser *

~ **off** * : foutre le camp

pistol : pistolet *(m)*, pétard *(m)* *

automatic ~ : pistolet automatique

machine ~ : pistolet-mitrailleur

Verey ~ : pistolet lance-fusées, pistolet de signalisation

pit : fosse *(f)*, mine *(f)*

~ **bull terrier** : espèce de bull-terrier (chien) très féroce

pitch (market trader's) : placarde *(f)*, place *(f)* habituelle

~ **in** : s'attaquer au boulot, s'y coller

~ **into** : tomber sur

    sales ~ : baratin *(m)* de vendeur

pitfall : trappe *(f)*, piège *(m)*, embûche *(f)*

pity : pitié *(f)*, compassion *(f)*

place (1) lieu *(m)*, endroit *(m)*; (2) placer, poser

    parking ~ : lieu de stationnement

    ~ of abode : lieu de séjour, domicile, résidence

    public ~ : lieu public

placing : mise *(f)*

plainclothes : (en) bourgeois

    ~ officer : policier *(m)* en civil, perdreau *(m)* *

plain cover : pli *(m)* neutre

plaint : plainte *(f)*

plaintiff : accusateur *(m)* privé, demandeur *(m)*, plaignant *(m)*

plan : projet *(m)*, plan *(m)*, dessein *(m)*

plant * : (1) coup *(m)* monté, agent *(m)* infiltré;
(2) cacher (des objets pour incriminer)

plate : plaque *(f)*

    number ~ : plaque d'immatriculation, plaque minéralogique

    ~ glass : verre *(m)* à vitre très épais

platform ticket : laissez-passer *(m)*

plea : défense *(f)*, cause *(f)*, procès *(m)*, demande *(f)*

    ~ bargaining : procédure informelle dans laquelle l'accusé peut accepter de faire un aveu de culpabilité concernant un crime ou délit moins grave au lieu de nier sa culpabilité d'une infraction plus sérieuse.

    ~ of guilty : aveu de culpabilité fait à l'audience.

plead : plaider, protester

pleasure boat : bateau *(m)* de plaisance

plod : avancer d'un pas lent/lourd

    Mister ~/ PC ~ * : policier *(m)* en tenue

plonk * : pinard *(m)* *

plot *(conspiracy)* : (1) conspiration *(f)*, complot *(m)*, machination *(f)*;
  (2) comploter, conspirer

plot *(land)* : terrain *(m)*, lot *(m)*, lotissement *(m)*

  building ~ : terrain à bâtir

plum job : planque *(f)*, boulot *(m)* en or

plump : grassouillet, empâté

ply for hire : marauder, faire un service de taxi

poacher : braconnier *(m)*

poaching : braconnage *(m)*

pocket : (1) poche *(f)*;   (2) empocher, mettre dans sa poche

  hip ~ : poche-revolver

  ~ **book** : calepin *(m)*

  ~ **money** : argent *(m)* de poche

point : (1) pointe *(f)*, point *(m)*, lieu *(m)*, sujet *(m)*, question *(f)*;
  (2) braquer, pointer

  case in ~ : en cas d'espèce

  ~ **at issue** : question (en litige)

  ~ **of law** : point de droit

  ~ **of no return** : point de non retour

  ~ **of order** : objection *(f)* préalable sur la façon dont seront menés les
    débats

point-blank : (à) bout-portant *(m)*

pointer : indice *(m)*

pointless : gratuit, inutile, injustifié

poison : (1) poison *(m)*;   (2) empoisonner

  ~**-pen letter** : lettre *(f)* anonyme venimeuse, bafouille *(m)* de chiotte *

poisonous : toxique, asphyxiant

poke (about/around) : fourrager, fureter, fouiner

police : (1) police *(f)*;   (2) faire la police

British Transport ~ : police des chemins de fer

~ **and Criminal Evidence Act** : loi *(f)* de procédure pénale

~ **authority** : comité *(m)* de l'administration régionale chargé du contrôle de la police.
*Avec le **Chief Constable** et le **Home Secretary** ils constituent le système "tripartite" de contrôle.*

~ **cadet** : jeune gardien *(m)* auxiliaire (non-assermenté)

~ **cells** : violon *(m)*

~ **complaints authority** : direction *(f)* des plaintes contre la police

~ **constable** : gardien *(m)* de la paix

~ **court** : tribunal *(m)* de police, tribunal d'instance

~ **custody** : garde *(f)* à vue

~ **force** : corps *(m)* de police
Il en existe une quarantaine en Angleterre, Pays de Galles et Ecosse, en principe un pour chaque comté ou grande agglomération.

~ **Gazette** : bulletin *(m)* de police criminelle

~ **headquarters** : quartier-général *(m)* de police
*Le quartier-général de la **Metropolitan Police** de Londres se trouvent à **Scotland Yard**.*

~ **informer, informant** : indicateur *(m)* de police

~ **inspector** : officier *(m)* de la paix

~ **investigation** : enquête *(f)* de police

~ **national computer** : système *(m)* informatique national de la police

~ **office** : bureau *(m)* de police, poste *(m)* de police

~ **officer** : agent *(m)* de police, agent *(m)* de la force publique

~ **raid** : descente *(f)* de police, coup *(m)* de filet, descente *(f)*, emballage *(m)*, coup *(m)* de torchon, coup *(m)* de serviette

~ **record** : casier *(m)* judiciaire

~ **requirement support unit** : direction *(f)* des études logistiques, informatiques et de matériel

~ **scientific development branch** : direction *(f)* des études scientifiques de la police

    ~ **staff college** : école *(f)* nationale supérieure de la police

    ~ **station** : commissariat/hôtel *(m)* de police

    ~ **superintendent** : commissaire *(m)* principal

    ~ **training centre** : école *(f)* régionale de police

    ~ **trap** : souricière *(f)*

    ~ **vehicle** : véhicule *(m)* de police, voiture *(f)* de police

    river ~ : police fluviale

policeman : policier *(m)*

policewoman : policière *(f)*

policy : (1) police *(f)*; (2) politique *(f)* générale, ligne *(f)* de conduite

    insurance ~ : police d'assurance

political : politique

    ~ **offence** : infraction *(f)* de nature politique (en matière d'extradition)

    ~ **uniform** : uniforme *(m)* de nature politique (dont le port est interdit)

poll : scrutin *(m)*, par tête, sondage *(m)*, enquête *(f)*

pollute : polluer

pollution : pollution *(f)*

polygraph : détecteur *(m)* de mensonge

ponce * : protecteur *(m)*, alphonse * *(m)*, hareng * *(m)*

    ~ **about** : se pavaner

poof * : tante *(f)* *, tapette *(f)* *

pool : mettre en commun

    motor ~ : parc *(m)* de véhicules

poor : pauvre *(m)*

    ~ **box** : tronc *(m)* des pauvres

    ~ **house** : hospice *(m)* des pauvres

    ~ **person** : indigent *(m)*

pop (1) * : mettre au clou *

pop (2) : faire un saut

    ~ **back** : revenir, retourner

    ~ **in** : entrer en passant

    ~ **out** : sortir pour un instant

    ~ **up (in Paris)** : réapparaître (à Paris)

poppy : pavot *(m)*

    opium ~ : pavot somnifère

population : population *(f)*, habitants *(mpl)*

    density of ~ : densité *(f)* de population

porn : voir **pornography**

pornography : pornographie *(f)*

porridge (to do ~ **)** * : faire de la taule *

port : port *(m)*

    air~ : port aérien

    sea~ : port de mer

pose (as) : se faire passer (pour)

position : état *(m)*, situation *(f)*, poste *(m)*, emploi *(m)*; (2) placer, poster

posse : détachement *(m)* d'hommes chargés de la police

possess : posséder

possession : possession *(f)*

    actual ~ : possession effective, possession de fait

    constructive ~ : possession présumée

    in ~ **of** : disposer de

    take ~ : prendre possession

    unlawful ~ **of drugs** : possession illégale de stupéfiants

possessions : effets *(mpl)* mobiliers

post : (1) apposer une affiche, afficher; (2) poteau *(m)*, pieu *(m)*; (3) situation, *(f)*, poste *(m)*, emploi *(m)*; (4) affecter (à), poster; (5) poste *(f)*, courrier *(m)*; (6) envoyer, expédier par la poste

~ **code** : code *(m)* postal

~**man** : facteur *(m)*

~**mark** : cachet *(m)* de poste

~ **office** : bureau *(m)* de poste

postage : affranchissement *(m)*, port *(m)*

~ **paid** : port payé

poster : affiche *(f)*, poster *(m)*

posting : mutation *(f)*, affectation *(f)*

post-mortem (examination) : autopsie *(f)*

postpone : différer, remettre à une date ultérieure, surseoir

postponement : ajournement *(m)*, sursis *(m)*

pot : marie-jeanne *(f)* *, marijuana *(f)*

pound : (1) fourrière *(f)*; (2) piler, concasser, réduire en miettes; (3) livre *(f)*

~ **a beat** : bagoter

power : force *(f)*, pouvoir *(m)*, puissance *(f)*, capacité *(f)*, autorité *(f)*

~ **boat** : vedette *(f)*

~ **cut/failure** : panne *(f)* d'électricité

~ **of arrest** : droit *(m)* d'arrestation

~ **of attorney** : procuration *(f)*, mandat *(m)*

practical : pratique

~ **application** : mise *(f)* en pratique

~ **example** : cas *(m)* concret

~ **joke** : farce *(f)*

practice : pratique *(f)*, usage *(m)*, méthode *(f)*, procédure *(f)*

practise : pratiquer, exercer

practitioner (general ~) : médecin *(m)* généraliste

prank : frasque *(f)*, fredaine *(f)*, farce *(f)*

prat * : imbécile *(m)*, andouille *(f)* *

preamble : exposé *(m)* des motifs d'une loi, attendus *(mpl)* d'un arrêt

precaution : précaution *(f)*

   ~ary measures : mesures *(f)* de précaution

precedence : préséance *(f)*, priorité *(f)*

   taking ~ : prioritaire

precedent : décision *(f)* qui fait jurisprudence, précédent *(m)*, préjugé *(m)*

precinct : circonscription *(f)* de police aux USA.

precisely : pile, précisément, exactement

preclude : empêcher, exclure, prévenir

prefer : préférer, privilégier, intenter

   ~ a complaint : déposer une plainte

   ~ an indictment : porter une accusation

pregnant : enceinte

prejudice : (1) préjudice *(m)*, tort *(m)*, dommage *(m)*; (2) préjuger

   without ~ : sans préjudice, sous toutes réserves

prejudicial : nuisible, dommageable

preliminary : préliminaire, préalable, initial

   ~ investigation : instruction *(f)*

premeditation : préméditation *(f)*

premises : local *(m)*, lieux *(mpl)*

premium : prime *(f)*

   insurance ~ : prime d'assurance

prepare (a case) : instruire (une affaire)

prepense malice : acte *(m)* criminel prémédité

prerequisite : condition *(f)* préalable

prescribe : prescrire, ordonner

prescribed : prescrit

prescription : (1) prescription *(f)*; (2) ordonnance *(f)*

presence : présence *(f)*,

    police ~ : présence policière, service *(m)* d'ordre

present : (1) don *(m)*, cadeau *(m)*;   (2) présent;   (3) présenter

presentation : présentation *(f)*, remise *(f)* (de la médaille, etc.), soumission *(f)*, exposé *(m)* oral

president : président *(m)*

presiding judge : président *(m)* du tribunal

press : (1) presse *(f)*;   (2) insister (sur), réclamer, persister, enrôler de force

    ~ **button** : bouton *(m)* poussoir

    ~ **charges** : engager des poursuites

    ~ **conference** : conférence *(f)* de presse

    ~ **gang** : racoleurs *(mpl)*

    ~ **on** : continuer, persévérer

pressure : menace *(f)*, pression *(f)*, contrainte *(f)*

    ~ **groups** : groupes *(mpl)* de pression

    under ~ : sous la contrainte

presume : présumer

presumption : présomption *(f)*

    irrebuttable ~ : présomption irréfragable

    legal ~ : présomption absolue/de droit

    ~ **of death** : présomption de décès

    ~ **of fact** : présomption de fait

    ~ **of innocence** : présomption d'innocence

    ~ **of law** : présomption légale

    rebuttable ~ : présomption réfutable

pretence : affectation *(f)*, faux semblant *(m)*, prétexte *(m)*, simulation *(f)*

    false ~**s** : moyens *(mpl)* frauduleux

pretend : frimer, prétendre, feindre, faire semblant de

pretext : prétexte *(m)*

prevarication : prévarication *(f)*

prevention : prévention *(f)*

    crime ~ : prévention de la criminalité

previous : précédent, antérieur

    ~ conviction : condamnation *(f)* antérieure, casier *(m)* spécial

prey : gibier *(m)*, proie *(f)*

pricelist : bordereau *(m)* des prix

prima facie case : affaire *(f)* qui paraît fondée

prima facie evidence : commencement *(m)* de preuve

primary : primordial, primaire, primitif, de base

principal : (1) principal; (2) principal *(m)*, directeur *(m)*, auteur *(m)*

    ~ in the first degree : auteur principal d'un crime

    ~ in the second degree : complice *(m&f)*
        Celui qui donne aide et assistance à un malfaiteur

principle : principe *(m)*

print : (1) empreinte *(f)*; (2) imprimer, publier, tirer

    finger–~ : empreinte digitale

prior : prioritaire, antérieur

priority : priorité *(f)*

prison : prison *(f)*, établissement *(m)* pénitentiaire

    ~ break : bris *(m)* de prison

    ~ calendar : livre *(m)* d'écrou

    ~ governor : directeur *(m)*

    ~ officer : gardien *(m)*

    ~ van : voiture *(f)* cellulaire

    ~ visitor : visiteur *(m)*/visiteuse *(f)* de prison

prisoner : prisonnier *(m)*, détenu *(m)*, prévenu *(m)*

    ~ **at the bar** : accusé *(m)*

private : privé, particulier

    ~ **car** : voiture particulière, voiture de tourisme

    ~ **detective** : agent privé de recherches, détective *(m)*

    ~ **income** : rente *(f)*, fortune *(f)* personnelle

    ~ **investigator** : agent privé de recherches

    ~ **member's bill** : proposition *(f)* de loi

    ~ **person** : simple particulier *(m)*

    ~ **property** : biens *(mpl)* personnels

    ~ **prosecution** : action *(f)* pénale par un particulier se substituant aux pouvoirs publics

    ~ **road** : voie privée

    ~ **secretary** : secrétaire particulier

    ~ **shoot** : chasse privée

privately-owned : particulier, qui appartient à un particulier

privilege : immunité *(f)*, privilège *(m)*

    parliamentary ~ : immunité parlementaire

probability : probabilité *(f)*

probation : probation *(f)*, délai d'épreuve *(f)*, mise à l'épreuve *(f)*, mise en liberté *(f)* surveillée

    ~ **hostel** : foyer *(m)* de semi-liberté

    ~ **officer** : agent *(m)* de probation, délégué *(m)* à la liberté surveillée, contrôleur *(m)* judiciaire

probationer : stagiaire *(m&f)*

problem : problème *(m)*

procedure : procédure *(f)*

    criminal ~ : procédure pénale

    summary ~ : procédure sommaire

proceed : procéder

proceedings : poursuites *(fpl)*, débats *(mpl)* judiciaires, délibération *(f)*, diligence *(f)*, instance *(f)*

   to take ~ : poursuivre en justice

proceeds of crime : vendange *(f)*

process : acte *(m)* de procédure, acte *(m)* de signification, instance *(f)*

   ~ server : porteur *(m)* de contraintes

procession : cortège *(f)*, défile *(m)*

procurator fiscal (Scots) : procureur *(m)*

procurer : protecteur *(m)*, poisson * *(m)*

procuring : obtention *(f)*, proxénétisme *(m)*

   ~ an abortion : manoeuvres *(fpl)* abortives

   ~ for immoral purposes : proxénétisme

produce : produire, rapporter, présenter

   ~ documents : produire des pièces

   ~ evidence : fournir des preuves

profession : métier *(m)*, profession *(f)*

professional : professionnel

   ~ ethics : déontologie *(f)*

   ~ fees : honoraires *(mpl)*

proficiency : compétence *(f)*; capacité *(f)*

proficient : versé, compétent, capable

profit : (1) bénéfice *(m)*; (2) bénéficier

profitable : lucratif

program : programme *(m)* (d'ordinateur)

programme : programme *(m)*, emploi *(m)* du temps

prohibit : interdire, défendre

prohibited : interdit, prohibé, défendu

prohibition : interdiction *(f)*, inhibition *(f)*, prohibition *(f)*

project : projet *(m)*, plan *(m)*

promulgate (a law) : promulguer (une loi)

promote : (1) promouvoir, monter en grade; (2) fomenter

promotion : avancement *(m)*

    ~ by selection : avancement au choix

    ~ by seniority : avancement à l'ancienneté

pronounce : prononcer, déclarer

proof : preuve *(f)*

    burden of ~ : charge *(f)* de la preuve

    ~ of death : constatation *(f)* de décès

    ~ of delivery : accusé *(m)* de réception

    ~ of identity : constatation/justification *(f)* d'identité

    ~ of ownership : titre *(m)* de propriété

    ~ onus of proof : charge *(f)* de la preuve

    written ~ : preuve littérale

prone : (1) sur le ventre, prostré; (2) prédisposé, sujet à

pronounce (sentence) : prononcer (la sentence)

propensity : propension *(f)*, penchant *(m)*, tendance *(f)*

properly : dûment, régulièrement

property : biens *(mpl)*, propriété *(f)*, immeuble *(m)*

    ~ of another : chose *(f)* d'autrui

    public ~ : biens collectifs, domaine *(m)* public

proprietor : propriétaire *(m)*

prop-stand : béquille *(f)*

proscription : proscription *(f)*

prosecute : exercer/engager/déclencher l'action publique, poursuivre/traduire en justice

prosecution : action *(f)*, poursuites *(fpl)*, accusation *(f)*

    criminal ˜ : poursuites pénales

    Crown ˜ Service : ministère *(m)* public, parquet *(m)*

    malicious ˜ : poursuites injustifiées

    private ˜ : action pénale par un particulier se substituant aux pouvoirs publics

    public ˜ : ministère *(m)* public

    witness for the ˜ : témoin *(m)* à charge

prosecutor : procureur *(m)*

prospects : perspectives *(fpl)*

prostitute : fille *(f)* publique, péripatéticienne *(f)*, putain *(f)*, tapineuse *(f)*

prostitution : prostitution *(f)*

protect : protéger, sauvegarder

protection : protection *(f)*

    ˜ racket : racket *(m)*, gouale *(m)*

protective measure : mesure *(f)* conservatoire

protector : protecteur *(m)*

protest : protester

prove : prouver

    to ˜ one's identity : établir son identité

proven : attesté, prouvé

provenance : provenance *(f)*

provide (for) : prévoir, prendre des dispositions

    ˜ for a child : établir un enfant

    ˜d that : à condition que, pourvu que

province : ressort *(m)*, domaine *(m)*, compétence *(f)*

provision : disposition *(f)*, prestation *(f)*, provision *(f)*

    ˜s of the criminal law ; dispositions du Code Pénal

provisional : provisoire

    ~ **driving licence** : permis *(m)* de conduire provisoire
        Obligatoire pour un élève conducteur, dont le véhicule doit porter les plaques "L".

proviso : clause *(f)* conditionnelle

provocation : provocation *(f)*
    Actes qui réduisent l'exercice de la raison et éliminent ainsi la notion de l'intention criminelle.

provoke : provoquer, pousser, inciter

provost : prévôt *(m)*, prévôté *(f)*

prowl : rôder

    ~ **car** : voiture *(f)* de patrouille (aux USA)

prowler : rôdeur *(m)*

proxy : syndic *(m)*, mandataire *(m)*, fondé *(m)* de pouvoir

prudence : discrétion *(f)*

psychological : psychique

    ~ **barrier** : limite *(f)* fatidique

    ~ **dependence** : dépendance *(f)* psychique

psychopath : désaxé *(m)*

pub : see **public house**

public : public, communal

    general ~ : (le) grand public *(m)*

    ~ **assembly** : réunion *(f)* de 20 personnes ou plus dans un endroit public en plein air

    ~ **authorities** : pouvoirs publics

    ~ **body** : organisme public

    ~ **carrier** : transporteur public

    ~ **company** : société *(f)* anonyme

    ~ **expenditure** : dépenses publiques

    ~ **funds** : fonds publics

~ **health** : salubrité publique

~ **hearing** : audience publique

~ **highway** : voie publique

~ **holiday** : fête *(f)* légale

~ **house** : débit *(m)* de boisson, bistro *(m)*

~ **interest** : intérêt public

~ **limited company (PLC)** : société *(f)* anonyme (SA)

~ **meeting** : réunion publique

~ **mischief** : délit *(m)* d'entraver l'action de la justice au préjudice de la communauté

~ **notice** : signification *(f)* par avis publique

~ **official** : fonctionnaire *(m&f)*

~ **order** : ordre public

~ **order duties** : maintien *(m)* d'ordre

~ **place** : lieu public

~ **procession** : défilé *(m)* en lieu public

~ **proclamation** : ban *(m)*

~ **property** : propriété *(f)* de l'état

~ **prosecution** : action publique, ministère public

~ **prosecutor** : accusateur public, procureur (m)g énéral, procureur *(m)* de la République

~ **records** : annales *(fpl)*

~ **records office** : dépôt public, Archives *(fpl)* Nationales

~ **relations** : relations publiques

~ **relations department** : bureau *(m)* d'information

~ **safety** : sûreté publique, protection *(f)* civile

~ **sector** : secteur public

~ **servant** : fonctionnaire *(mpl)*

~ **service vehicle (PSV)** : transport *(m)* routier en commun

~ **transport** : transport *(m)* en commun

~ **utility** : service public

~ **weal/welfare** : le bien public (commun)

~ **works** : travaux publics

publication : édition *(f)*, publication *(f)*, reproduction *(f)*

publicity : publicité *(f)*

publisher : éditeur *(m)*

publishing : édition *(f)*

pull * : arrêter, appréhender

punch : coup *(m)* de poing

puncture : (1) crevaison *(f)*; (2) piqûre *(f)*

punish : punir

punishable : délictueux, punissable

punishment : châtiment *(m)*, punition *(f)*

corporal ~ : châtiment corporel (aboli en 1948)

~ **cell** : séchoir *(m)*

punitive : punitif, répressif

~ **justice** : justice *(f)* répressive

purchase : (1) acheter; (2) achat *(m)*, acquisition *(f)*

purge : purger, se justifier, expier

purloining : détournement *(m)*, vol *(m)*

purport : sens *(m)*, portée *(f)*, teneur *(f)*

purpose : fin *(f)*, objet *(m)*, but *(m)*

pursuance (in ~ of) : en application de, conformément à

pursuant (to) : en vertu (de), conformément (à)

pursue : suivre, poursuivre

pursuit : poursuite *(f)*, recherche *(f)*

push back : repousser, faire reculer

pusher (of drugs) : revendeur *(m)*, revendeuse *(f)*

put : mettre, présenter (une motion), poser (une question)

    ~ **down** : déposer, inscrire

    ~ **in for** : poser candidature pour, solliciter

    ~ **into effect** : mettre en vigueur

    ~ **off** : remettre (à plus tard)

    ~ **up with** : supporter, tolérer

putting : mise *(f)*

puzzle : énigme *(f)*, mystère *(m)*

Q

qualification : qualification *(f)*, compétence *(f)*, qualité *(f)* requise, aptitude *(f)*

qualified : qualifié, reçu, admis, posséder les qualités requises

~ **person** : personne *(f)* compétente

quality : qualité *(f)*, vertu *(f)*

~ **of life** : qualité de vie

quarantine : quarantaine *(f)*

quarter : (1) quartier *(m)*; (2) trimestre *(m)*; (3) quart *(m)*

~ **light** : déflecteur *(m)*

~ **sessions** : tribunal *(m)* de grande instance qui siègeait chaque trimestre
   —   remplacé par le Crown Court.

quartermaster : garde-magasin *(m)*

quarry : proie *(f)*

quash : annuler, casser, infirmer

quashing : annulation *(f)* d'un acte judiciaire, cassation *(f)*

Queen : reine *(f)*

~'s **Bench Division** : chambre *(f)* du **High Court**

~'s **Counsel** : avocat *(m)* de l'ordre supérieur

~'s **Regulations** : code *(m)* de justice militaire

turn ~'s **evidence** : dénoncer ses complices contre promesse d'immunité

queer : (1) bizarre, suspect; (2) * homosexuel

~ **bashing** * : chasse aux pédés *

query : question *(f)*

quest : recherche *(f)*

question : (1) interroger, berluer, interpeller; (2) question *(f)*,

leading ~ : question tendancieuse
      Question posée par un avocat tendant à suggérer la réponse voulue.

~ **of fact/law/procedure** : question de fait/de droit/de procédure

supplementary ˜ : question subsidiaire

questionable : contestable, douteux, discutable

questioning : interrogatoire *(m)*
Un policier a le droit d'interroger toute personne qu'il croit susceptible de donner des renseignements utiles.

queue : file *(m)* d'attente, queue *(f)*

quid * : livre *(f)* (sterling)

quiet : calme, tranquille

quietly : doucement

to come ˜ : se rendre paisiblement

quit : quitter, cesser, vider les lieux

R

rabbit punch : coup *(m)* du lapin

rabble : fripouille *(f)*, cohue *(f)*, foule *(f)*

race (1) : course *(f)*

> **horse˜** : course hippique

race (2) : race *(f)*

> ˜ **relations** : relations *(fpl)* inter-raciales

> ˜ **relations board** : commission *(f)* pour les relations inter-raciales

racial hatred : haine *(f)* raciale
Inciter à la haine raciale est un délit.

racing : courses *(fpl)*

> ˜ **on the highway** : faisant une course sur la voie publique

rack : porte-bagages *(m)*

racket : racket *(m)*, escroquerie *(f)*

racketeer : racketteur *(m)*

radar trap : piège *(m)* radar

> **to get caught in a** ˜ : se faire piéger par un radar

radiator : radiateur *(m)*

> ˜ **grille** : calandre *(f)*

radical : extrémiste

radio : radio *(f)*

> **personal** ˜ : talkie-walkie *(m)*

> ˜ **alarm** : alarme *(f)* digitale

> ˜ **link** : pont-radio *(m)*

> ˜ **set** : poste *(m)* de radio

> ˜ **transmission** : transmission *(f)*

radius : rayon *(m)*

raffle : tombola *(f)*

raid : descente *(f)*, emballage *(m)*, rafle de police, razzia *(f)* de bandits

    smash and grab ~ : rafle après bris de devanture

railway : chemin *(m)* de fer

    ~ track : voie *(f)* ferroviaire

raincoat : imperméable *(m)*

raise : lever

raising : levée *(f)*

rake–off : gratte *(f)*, profit *(m)* malhonnête

rally : rassemblement *(m)*, rallye *(m)* (auto.)

ram : percuter

    ~ raider : celui qui brise une devanture au moyen d'une automobile, afin d'en voler le contenu

ramble : balade *(f)*

ramp : casse–vitesse *(m)*

range : éventail *(m)*, portée *(f)*

    ~ of salaries : éventail de salaires

rank : rang *(m)*, grade *(m)*

ransacked : saccagé

ransom : rançon *(f)*

rap * : inculpation *(f)*

    ~ sheet : casier *(m)* judiciaire

rape : (1) viol *(m)*;   (2) violer

rapine : rapine *(f)*

rapist : violeur *(m)*

rascal : fripon *(m)*

rashness : imprudence *(f)*

rate : taux *(m)*, proportion *(f)*

rates : taxe *(f)* d'habitation, taxe *(f)* d'utilisation

ratification : homologation *(f)*

ratify : entériner, ratifier

ratio decidendi : fondement *(m)* d'une décision

rat race: foire *(f)* d'empoigne

rattle (someone) : déconcerter, démonter

ravaged : saccagé

ravishment : rapt *(m)*

ray : rayon *(m)*

re : concernant, relatif à, au sujet de

      in ~ : en l'affaire de

reach : (1) portée *(f)*, atteinte *(f)*; (2) parvenir, atteindre, toucher, prendre

      ~ a decision : prendre une décision

react : réagir

read : lire

      ~ and confirmed : lu et approuvé

      ~ the Riot Act : faire les trois sommations légales

readies * : pognon * *(m)*, oseille * *(f)*

ready cash : liquide *(m)*

real : effective

      ~ estate : biens *(mpl)* immeubles, propriété *(f)* immobilière

rear : arrière, derrière

      ~ door : porte *(f)* de derrière (maison), portière *(f)* arrière

      ~ lamp : feu *(m)* arrière

      ~ spoiler : déporteur *(m)*

      ~-view mirror : rétroviseur *(m)*

      ~ window : lunette *(f)* arrière

reason : motif *(m)*, droit *(m)*, raison *(f)*

reasonable : raisonnable

    ~ **doubt** : doute *(m)* bien fondé

    ~ **force** : force *(f)* raisonnable

rebellion : mutinerie *(f)*, rébellion *(f)*

rebut : réfuter, repousser, rebuter, riposter

rebuttable presumption : présomption *(f)* réfutable

rebutting evidence : preuve *(f)* contraire qui réfute la preuve prima facie

recall a witness : rappeler un témoin

recant : (se) rétracter

recapitulation : récapitulation *(f)*

receipt : réception *(f)*, reçu *(m)*, récépissé *(m)*, quittance *(f)*, accusé *(m)* de réception

receive : recevoir, toucher

receiver : receleur *(m)* (d'un vol)

receiving : recel *(m)*
    Délit remplacé par celui de **handling stolen property.**

recent possession : possession *(f)* récente (d'objets volés)

recess : vacations *(fpl)*, vacances *(mpl)* judiciaire, suspension *(f)* d'audience

recidivism : récidive *(f)*

recidivist : récidiviste *(m&f)*, délinquant *(m)* d'habitude, repris *(m)* de justice

recipient : destinataire *(m)*

reckless driving : conduite *(f)* imprudente ou téméraire

recklessness : imprudence *(f)*, dol *(m)* éventuel

recognizance : reconnaissance *(f)*, engagement *(m)*

recoil : reculer

recognize : reconnaître, retapisser, tapisser

recommendation : avis *(m)*, conseil *(m)*

reconstruction (of a crime) : reconstitution *(f)* (d'un crime)

record : document *(m)*, dossier *(m)*, état *(m)*, registre *(m)*;   (2) enregistrer,
    recenser

    criminal ~ : casier *(m)* judiciaire

    off the ~ : confidentiel, officieux

    police ~ : casier *(m)* judiciaire

    ~ of attendance : feuille *(f)* de présence

    ~ of evidence : procès-verbal *(m)* de témoignage

recorded : enregistré, noté

Recorder : juge *(m)* du **Crown Court**

recording : enrôlement *(m)*

records : archives *(fpl)*, annales *(fpl)*

    criminal ~ office : casier *(m)* judiciaire

    Public ~ Office : Archives Nationales

recourse : recours *(m)*

    have ~ to : recourir à

recovery : récupération *(f)*

recruit : (1) recruter;   (2) recrue *(f)*

recruitment : recrutement *(m)*

rectify : redresser, réparer

red : rouge

    ~cap : policier *(m)* militaire

    ~-handed : en flagrant délit

    ~-herring : canard *(m)*
        Subterfuge pour engager sur une fausse piste.

    ~ light district : quartier *(m)* réservé

    ~ tape : paperasse *(f)*, bureaucratie *(f)*

redeployment : recassage *(m)*, reconversion *(f)*

redress : (1) redresser; (2) réparation *(f)*

reduce (a sentence) : adoucir (une peine)

reduction : réduction *(f)*

    ~ **in rank** : dégradation, rétrogradation

redundancy : (1) licenciement *(m)*; (2) surplus *(m)*, excédent *(m)*, surnombre *(m)*

    ~ **payment** : indemnité/prime *(f)* de licenciement

reefer * : drag *(f)*, stick *(m)* *

re-enact : remettre en vigueur, reconstituer

re-enlist : (se) rengager

re-establish : rétablir

re-examination : réplique *(f)*, nouvel examen *(m)*, nouvel interrogatoire *(m)*
    Nouvel interrogatoire du témoin par la partie qui l'a cité, au cours de l'interrogatoire contradictoire.

refer : rapporter, référer de quelque chose (à une autorité), renvoyer (une affaire devant un tribunal)

    " ~ **to drawer**" : "voir le tireur"
    Formule inscrite sur les chèques sans provision.

reference : référence *(f)*, renvoi *(m)*, attribution *(f)*

    by ~ to : en fonction de

    cross- ~ : renvoi, appel

reflector : cataphote *(m)*

reform : réformer

reformatory : maison *(f)* de correction

refrain (from) : s'abstenir (de)

refresher course : cours *(m)* de recyclage

refreshing memory : un témoin peut demander l'accord du juge pour rafraîchir sa mémoire, au cours de la déposition, en consultant ses notes ou des documents

refrigerator : frigo *(m)*

refuel : réalimenter (en combustible)

refuge : refuge *(m)*, abri *(m)*, asile *(m)*

    women's ~ : asile pour les femmes abusées

refugee : réfugié *(m)*

refusal : déni *(m)*, refus *(m)*

    ~ **to give evidence** : refus de témoigner

    ~ **to speak** : mutisme *(m)*

refuse (1) : refuser, décliner

refuse (2) : détritus *(mpl)*, ordures *(fpl)*, déchets *(mpl)*

    ~ **dump** : décharge *(f)* publique

refute : réfuter

regard : (1) considération *(f)*; (2) considérer

    having ~ **to** : compte tenu de

    ~**ed as** : considéré comme

    without ~ **to** : indépendamment de

regarded as : réputé

regime : régime *(m)*, forme de gouvernement *(m)*

regina : reine *(f)*
The Queen v. Smith (la Reine contre Smith) – *formule des procès de l'Etat contre les particuliers.*

region : région *(f)*

regional crime intelligence office : bureau *(m)* régional de renseignements criminels

regional crime squad : service *(m)* régionale de police judiciaire

register : (1) enregistrer; (2) registre *(m)*, sommier *(m)*

    commercial ~ : registre de commerce

    ~ **a birth** : déclarer une naissance

    ~ **a company** : faire enregistrer une société

    ~ **of births, marriages and deaths** : actes *(mpl)* d'état-civil

    ~ **office** : bureau *(m)* de l'état-civil

registered : enregistré, inscrit, immatriculé

    ~ **capital** : fonds *(m)* social

    ~ **letter** : lettre *(f)* recommandée

~ **mail** : pli *(m)* recommandé

~ **office** : siège social

registering : enrôlement *(m)*

registrar : juge *(m)* du **County Court,** officier *(m)* de l'état civil, secrétaire-archiviste *(m)* (d'une   université)

~ **General's Office** : archives *(fpl)* de l'état-civil

to marry before a ~ : se marier civilement

registration : enregistrement *(m)*, inscription *(f)*, immatriculation *(f)*

~ **document** (auto.) : carte *(f)* grise

~ **fee** : droit *(m)* d'inscription

~ **form** : feuille *(f)* d'inscription

~ **number** : numéro *(m)* d'immatriculation

registry : casier *(m)*,   ~ **office** : bureau *(m)* de l'état civil

regrading : reclassement *(m)*

regular : régulier, habituel, ordinaire

~ **customer** : habitué *(m)*

~ **police** : la police *(f)* de métier

~ **soldier** : soldat *(m)* de métier

regulations : règlement *(m)*

rehabilitation : reclassement *(m)*, rééducation *(f)*, réadaptation *(f)*

reimbursement : remboursement *(m)*

reinforce : renforcer

reject : rejeter, repousser

relate : rapporter

relationship : rapport *(m)*, degré *(m)* de parenté

relatives : parents *(mpl)*

relax : assouplir

relay : relais *(m)*

release : (1) libération *(f)*, mise *(f)* en liberté;   (2) libérer, relâcher

~ **of prisoner** : levée *(f)* d'écrou, élargissement *(m)*

~ **on bail** : libération sous caution, mise en liberté sous caution

~ **on licence** : libération conditionnelle

relevant : utile, pertinent, applicable, approprié

all ~ **information** : tous renseignements *(mpl)* utiles

~ **authority** : l'autorité *(f)* compétente

~ **document** : les pièces *(fpl)* justificatives à l'appui

~ **evidence** : preuve *(f)* concernant les faits applicables

to be ~ **to** : se rapporter à

reliability : fiabilité *(f)*, esprit *(m)* de sérieux, sûreté *(f)*, précision *(f)*

reliable : digne de confiance, sûr, sérieux, efficace

reliance : confiance *(f)*

relict : veuve *(f)*

relief : (1) décongestion *(f)*; (2) unité *(f)* de roulement

~ **road** : itinéraire *(m)* de délestage

reluctant (witness) : (témoin) réticent

remain silent : se taire, s'écraser

remand : ajournement *(m)*, renvoi *(m)* d'un prévenu à une autre audience

~ **centre** : centre *(m)* pénitentiaire pour les jeunes de 14 à 20 ans

~ **in custody** : détention *(f)* préventive, détention *(f)* provisoire

~ **on bail** : mise *(f)* en liberté sous caution

reminder : mémento *(m)*, rappel *(m)* "pour mémoire"

remission : pardon *(m)*, remise *(f)* (de la peine)

remit : remettre, renvoyer

remittance : versement *(m)*

remorse : repentir *(m)*

remote control : télécommande *(f)*

removal : déménagement *(m)*, levée *(f)*, mainlevée *(f)*, déplacement *(m)*, enlèvement *(m)*

    ~ **from office** : destitution *(f)*, révocation *(f)*

remuneration : émoluments *(mpl)*, rémunération *(f)*

render : rendre

    ~ **judgment** : prononcer le jugement

rendez-vous : (1) rendez-vous *(m)*;   (2) rejoindre, se réunir

renounce : renoncer

renown : renommée *(f)*

rent : loyer *(m)*, prix *(m)* de location

    ~ **allowance** : indemnité/prime *(f)* de logement

    ~**-a-mob** : agitateurs *(mpl)* professionnels

    ~ **boy** : garçon *(m)* de passe

    ~ **collector** : receveur *(m)* des loyers

    ~ **restriction** : blocage *(m)* des loyers

rental : loyer *(m)*, prix *(m)* de location

renting : location *(f)*

re-open (a case) : rouvrir (une affaire)

reorganisation : réorganisation *(f)*, réforme *(f)*

repair : (1) réfection *(f)*, réparation *(f)*;   (2) réparer

reparation : réparation *(f)*

repayment : remboursement *(m)*

repeal : (1) annuler, casser;   (2) abrogation *(f)*, cassation *(f)*, révocation *(f)*

repent : se repentir

repentance : repentir *(m)*

reply : (1) répondre;   (2) réponse *(f)*

report (1) : procès-verbal *(m)*, rapport *(m)*, bulletin *(m)*, constat *(m)*, compte-rendu *(m)*, constatation *(f)*, déclaration *(f)*, état *(m)*, exposé *(m)*

    Law ~**s** : recueil *(m)* de jurisprudence

make a ~ : faire/rédiger un rapport

police ~ : procès-verbal

~ of investigation : constatation d'une enquête

to ~ someone to the police : dénoncer quelqu'un à la police

report (2) : rendre compte, rapporter, verbaliser, relater

nothing to ~ : rien à signaler

~ an accident : signaler un accident

~ someone to the police : dénoncer quelqu'un à la police

~ to someone : se présenter à

reprehensible : répréhensible

representative : délégué (m), représentant (m), syndic (m)

legal ~ : représentant légal

repressive : répressif

reprieve : (1) disculpation (f), grâce (f), sursis (m); (2) gracier

reprimand : admonestation (f), blâme (m), réprimande (f), déshabillage (m) *, emballage (m) *, engueulade (f) *, tatouille (f); (2) engueuler *

reprisal : représaille (f), rebiffe (f)

repudiation : refus (m), reniement (m), rejet (m)

reputation : réputation (f)

repute : notoriété (f), renommée (f), réputation (f)

request : (1) réclamation (f), requête (f), demande (f), sommation (f); (2) demander

at the ~ of : sur les instances (fpl) de

on ~ : sur demande

require : enjoindre, exiger

requirement : besoin (m), exigence (f), obligation (f)

requisition : demande (f), requête (f), réquisition (f) (de vivres, etc.)

reroute : dérouter, changer d'itinéraire

res : une chose (f)

rescind : annuler, rapporter

rescinding : révocation *(f)*

rescission : annulation *(f)* d'un jugement

rescue : (1) secours *(mpl)*, sauvetage *(m)*, délivrance *(f)*; (2) sauver, délivrer

rescuer : sauveteur *(m)*

research : recherche *(f)*

    ~ **and development** : recherche et développement

resemblance : ressemblance *(f)*

reservation : réserve *(f)*, réservation *(f)*

    central ~ : bande *(f)* médiane

reserve : (1) provision *(f)*, réserve *(f)*; (2) réserver, retenir

res gestae : les faits *(mpl)* matériels d'une affaire

reshuffle : remanier (personnel)

reside : résider

residence : demeure *(f)*, résidence *(f)*, domicile *(m)*

    actual ~ : résidence effective

    customary ~ : résidence habituelle

    main ~ : résidence principale

    secondary ~ : résidence secondaire

resident : résident *(m)*, habitant *(m)*

resignation : démission *(f)*

resin : résine *(f)*

resist : résister

    ~ **arrest** : offrir de la résistance à l'appréhension (de quelqu'un)

res judicata : affaire *(f)* jugée

res nullius : chose qui n'appartient à personne

resolution : résolution *(f)*, délibération *(f)*, proposition *(f)*, ordre *(m)* du jour

resort : (1) recourir; (2) recours *(m)*

    ~ **to violence** : avoir recours/recourir à la violence

resource : moyen *(m)*, recours *(m)*, ressource *(f)*

respect : rapport *(m)*, égard *(m)*

    in other ~**s** : à d'autres égards

    in ~ **of** : relatif à, au titre de

    with ~ **to** : quant à, en ce qui concerne

respirator : respirateur *(m)*, masque *(m)* à gaz

respite : délai *(m)*, répit *(m)*, sursis *(m)*

response : réplique *(f)*, réponse *(f)*

responsibility : responsabilité *(f)*

    criminal ~ : responsabilité pénale

    ~ **for one's actions** : imputabilité *(f)*

responsible : responsable, compétent

    the ~ **quarters** : les milieux autorisés

    to be ~ **for** : avoir à charge

rest day : jour *(m)* de congé

restitution : restitution *(f)*, réparation *(f)*

restore : rapporter, rétablir

    ~ **order** : rétablir l'ordre public

restrain : contraindre

restraint : contrainte *(f)*, restriction *(f)*, entrave *(m)*, empêchement *(m)*

restricted : restreint, limité, borné

    ~ **area** : zone *(f)* où la vitesse des automobiles est limitée

restriction : limitation *(f)*

result : effet *(m)*

    to get a ~ * : réussir à appréhender l'auteur d'un crime

resume : reprendre

resumption : reprise *(f)* (de négotiations, de travail etc.)

retail : détail *(m)*, vente *(f)* au détail

    ~ **price** : prix *(m)* de détail

    ~ **trade** : petit commerce *(m)*

retailer : détaillant *(m)*

retain : retenir, arrêter

retainer : honoraires *(mpl)*

retired : retiré, à la retraite

    ~ **pay** : pension *(f)* militaire

    ~ **person** : retraité *(m)*

retirement : (départ à la) retraite *(f)*, non-activité *(f)*

    compulsory ~ : retraite d'office

    early ~ : retraite anticipée

    ~ **fund** : fonds *(m)* de retraite

    ~ **home** : maison *(f)* de retraite

    ~ **of the jury/of the court** : période *(f)* durant laquelle les jurés/les juges considèrent leur décision

    ~ **on account of age** : retraite par limite d'âge

    ~ **pension** : pension *(f)* de retraite

retract : désavouer, rétracter

retraining : recyclage *(m)*

retread : pneu *(m)* rechapé

retrial : nouveau procès *(m)*

retribution : châtiment *(m)*, récompense *(f)*

retroactive : rétroactif

retrospective : rétroactif

return : (1) état *(m)*, relevé *(m)*; (2) retour *(m)*; (3) revenir

    monthly ~ : état mensuel

official ~ : relevé officiel

~ **a verdict** : rendre un verdict

revenge : vengeance *(f)*, rebiffe *(f)* *

~ **killing** : règlement *(m)* de comptes

reversal (of traffic flow) : basculement *(m)*

reverse : (1) marche *(f)* arrière; (2) verso *(m)*

review : (1) examiner;   (2) révision *(f)*, revue *(f)*, examen *(m)* à nouveau, révision *(f)*

court of ~ : cour *(m)* d'appel, de cassation

police ~ : revue *(f)* de la police (magazine hebdomadaire)

revise : réactualiser, réviser, modifier

revision : révision *(f)*

revival : renaissance *(f)*, remise *(f)* en vigueur

revocation : révocation *(f)*, abrogation *(f)*

revoke : rapporter, rétracter, révoquer

~ **a licence** : retirer un permis

revolt : rébellion *(f)*

revolting : dégueulasse

revolver : revolver *(m)*

reward : rémunération *(f)*, récompense *(f)*

for hire or ~ : à titre commercial

rid : débarrasser, délivrer

riddle : énigme *(m)*, mystère *(m)*

ride : aller à cheval/à bicyclette/à moto

rider : (1) annexe *(f)*, ajout *(m)*; (2) cavalier *(m)*, (moto)cycliste *(m&f)*

pillion ~ : passager arrière

riff-raff : fripouille *(f)*

rifle : (1) fusil *(m)*; (2) fouiller, fourailler, vaguer

~ **fire** : fusillade *(f)*

~**man** : tireur *(m)*

rig : monter un coup

right : (1) droit *(m)*, titre *(m)*, privilège *(m)*, liberté *(f)*; (2) redresser

act as of ~ : agir de plein droit

civic ~**s** : droits politiques

civil ~**s** : droits civils

civil ~**s movement** : campagne pour les droits civils

human ~**s** : droits de l'homme

~**-hand drive** : conduite *(f)* à droite

~ **of access** : droit d'accès

~ **of assembly** : liberté *(f)* de réunion

~ **of entry** : droit d'accès

~ **of sanctuary** : droit d'asile

~ **of way** : droit de passage

rightful : légitime, équitable

~ **claimant** : ayant droit *(m)*

~ **owner** : propriétaire légitime

ring : bague *(f)*, alliance *(f)*;   changer, troquer

~ **a car** : changer l'aspect d'une voiture volée

~ **road** : ring *(m)*, route *(f)* de ceinture, boulevard *(m)* périphérique

~ **the changes** : faire un cambut *(m)*, faire un chanstique *(m)*, vol *(m)* au rendez-moi

~ **up** : donner un coup *(m)* de fil

riot : émeute *(f)*, sédition *(f)*, attentat *(m)* à l'ordre public

~ **gear** : tenue *(f)* de combat

~ **helmet** : casque *(m)* de protection

~ **shield** : bouclier *(m)*

~ **squad** : groupe *(m)* mobile, brigade *(f)* anti-émeute

rip-off : (1) plumer, filouter;   (2) vol *(m)* manifeste, arnaque *(f)* *

riposte : parade *(f)*

risk : aléa *(m)*, risque *(m)*, hasard *(m)*, péril *(m)*

risqué story : histoire *(f)* osée, une verte *(f)*

river : fleuve *(m)*, rivière *(f)*.   ~ **police** : brigade *(f)* fluviale

road : route *(f)*, chemin *(m)*, ruban *(m)*

    main ~ : grande route

    ~ **block** : barrage *(m)* routier

    ~ **check** : poste *(m)* de contrôle

    ~ **hog** : chauffard *(m)*

    ~ **holding** : garde *(f)* au sol

    ~ **safety** : prévention *(f)* routière

    ~ **safety training** : éducation *(f)* routière

    ~ **surface** : chaussée *(f)*

    ~ **tax** : impôt *(m)* de voirie

    ~ **traffic** : circulation *(f)* routière

    ~ **traffic accident** : accident *(m)* de la circulation

    ~ **traffic law** : code *(m)* de la route

    ~ **traffic patrols** : police *(f)* de la route

    ~ **transport** : transport *(m)* routier

    ~ **works** : travaux *(mpl)*

rob : dérober, friponner

robber : brigand *(m)*, larron *(m)*

robbery : rapine *(f)*, vol *(m)* avec violence

    armed ~ : vol à main armée

    highway ~ : vol de grand chemin, brigandage

rocket launcher : lance-roquettes *(m)*

rod * : flingue *(m)* *

rogatory letter : commission *(f)* rogatoire

"Roger" : "compris" (radio communications)

rogue : fripon *(m)* , coquin *(m)*, gredin *(m)*

> ~s **and vagabonds** : personnes qu'on trouve dans les lieux où elles sont
> pour des buts illégaux ou qui prétendent dire la bonne aventure

roll : (1) tableau *(m)*, liste *(f)*, rôle *(m)*; (2) rouleau *(m)*; (3) rouler

> **nominal** ~ : état nominatif

> ~ **a car** : faire un tonneau *(m)*

> ~ **a client** : vol *(m)* à l'entôlage

> ~ **call** : appel *(m)* (nominal)

> ~**-on**, ~**-off** : espèce de ferry sur lequel les véhicules s'embarquent et se
> désembarquent par leurs propres moyens

Roman law : droit *(m)* romain

romany : manouche *(m&f)*

roof : toît *(m)*

> ~ **rack** : galerie *(f)*

> ~ **top** : toît

rook * : estamper

rookie * : bleu *(m)* *

room : (1) salle *(f)*, pièce *(f)*; (2) place

roster (duty ~ **)** : contrôle *(m)* (de service)

rough : grossier

> ~ **notes** : brouillon *(m)*

round : (1) balle *(f)*; (2) rond, autour (de); (3) tournée *(f)*

> ~ **table discussion** : table *(f)* ronde

> ~ **trip** : aller-retour *(m)*

roundabout : rond-point *(m)*

round-up (of suspects) : emballage *(m)*, rafle *(f)*

rout : attroupement *(m)* illégal
Délit intermédiaire entre une réunion illégale et un attroupement séditieux
(abrogé en 1986)

route : itinéraire *(m)*, chemin *(m)*, parcours *(m)*, route *(f)*

~ **marker** : flécheur *(m)*

routine : traintrain *(m)*

rowdyism : chahut *(m)*, bagarre *(f)* , violence *(f)*

royal : royal

~ **Automobile Club (RAC)** : club de tourisme automobile

~ **Canadian Mounted Police (RCMP)** : Gendarmerie Royale du Canada

~ **Ulster Constabulary** : Gendarmerie d'Irlande du Nord

rozzer * : flic *(m)* *, poulet *(m)* *

rubber : caoutchouc *(m)*

~ **buller** : balle *(f)* en caoutchouc

~ **cheque** : chèque *(m)* en bois

~ **stamp** : entériner

rub out * : descendre *, liquider *

rude : impoli, insolent

rule : (1) règle *(f)*, disposition *(f)* générale;   (2) régir, gouverner, décider

~ **of law** : état *(m)* de droit

~ **out** : éliminer (une possibilité)

~**s of evidence** : droit *(m)* judiciaire, code *(m)* de procédure

ruling : décision *(f)* d'un juge

~ **classes** : classes *(fpl)* dirigeantes

rumble * : flairer, subodorer *, piger *

rummage : (1) farfouiller, fouiller, fourailler, trifouiller; (2) fouille *(f)*

rumour : bruit *(m)*

run : encourir, courir, diriger, gérer

    on the ~ : recherché par la police

    ~away : (1) fugue *(f)*, fugitif *(m)*; (2) s'évader, patiner *;
        (3) uncontrôlable, galopant

    ~ down : renverser, écraser

    ~ into : rencontrer par hasard, tomber sur

    ~ out of road : planter

    ~ over : écraser

rural : rural, champêtre

    ~ beat officer : policier *(m)* affecté à une région rurale

    ~ constable : garde *(m)* champêtre

    ~ section : brigade *(f)* territoriale responsable d'une région rurale

rush hour : heure *(f)* de pointe

rustling : vol *(m)* de bétail

rusty : rouillé

rut : ornière *(f)*

ruthless : impitoyable, cruel, sans pitié

S

sabotage : sabotage *(m)*

sabre : sabre *(m)*

sack : mettre à la porte, licencier, balancer, donner congé

sacking : mise *(f)* à pied

sacrilege : cambriolage *(m)* dans une église

saddle : selle *(f)*

sadistic : sadique

safe : (1) coffre-fort *(m)*; (2) hors de danger; (3) sans danger, sûr

    ~ **and sound** : sain et sauf

    ~**-breaker** : perceur *(m)* de coffre-fort, arquin *(m)* *

    ~ **conduct** : sauf-conduit *(m)*

    ~ **custody** : dépôt *(m)* en garde

    ~**-deposit** : dépôt *(m)* de coffres-forts

safeguard : (1) sauvegarde *(f)*;   (2) sauvegarder

safety : sûreté *(f)*, protection *(f)*, sécurité *(f)*

    public ~ : sécurité/sûreté publique

    road ~ : sécurité routière

    ~ **at work** : la sécurité aux lieux de travail

    ~ **belt** : ceinture *(f)* de sécurité

    ~ **catch** : cran *(m)* de sécurité, arrêtoir *(m)*

    ~ **-chain** : bride *(f)*

    ~ **margin** : marge *(f)* de sécurité

    ~ **measure, precaution** : mesure *(f)* de sécurité

    ~ **standards** : normes *(fpl)* de sécurité

said : susdit, susvisé, susnommé, susmentionné

    the ~ : ledit, ladite, lesdits, lesdites

sailing : navigation *(f)*

salaried : appointé, salarié

salary : appointement *(m)*, émoluments *(mpl)*, traitement *(m)*, salaire *(m)*

    basic ~ : salaire de base

    ~ grade : échelon *(m)* de salaire

    ~ range : échelle *(f)* des traitements

    ~ scale : grille/échelle *(f)* de salaire, barème *(m)* des traitements

    starting ~ : traitement initial

    to draw a ~ : toucher un traitement

sale : vente *(f)*

    ~ by auction : vente publique

    ~ room : salle *(f)* de vente

salesman : vendeur *(m)*

    travelling ~ : voyageur *(m)* de commerce

saloon : (1) salle *(f)*, salon *(m)*; (2) (débit de boissons) bar *(m)*, saloon *(m)*; (3) (auto.) berline *(f)*, voiture *(f)* de tourisme

salt away : mettre (de l'argent) à gauche

salute : (1) saluer; (2) salut *(m)* (militaire)

salvage : prime *(f)* de sauvetage
Accordée aux personnes ayant sauvé, du danger ou de la perte en mer, un navire, une cargaison ou la vie de personnes embarquées.

Samaritans : S.O.S. Amitié

sample : prélèvement *(m)*, échantillon *(m)*

    blood/urine sample : prélèvement de sang/urine

    intimate ~ : prélèvement intime
Avec son accord, on a le droit de prélever des échantillons de sang, de sperme ou autre tissu, fluide, urine, salive, poils du pubis ou prélèvement d'un orifice corporel d'un individu en état d'arrestation.

sanction : sanction *(f)*, autorisation *(f)*, approbation *(f)*

sanctuary : sanctuaire *(m)*, asile *(m)*

>   **right of** ~ : droit d'un suspect à chercher asile dans une église
>   *Ce droit a été supprimé définitivement en 1723.*

sandwich course : stage *(m)* de formation professionnelle alterné

save : (1) sauver; (2) épargner

savings : épargne *(f)*, pécule *(m)*

>   ~ **bank** : caisse *(f)* d'épargne

>   ~ **certificate** : bon *(m)* d'épargne

sawn-off : scié

>   ~ **shotgun** : fusil *(m)* (de chasse) à canon scié

saw resistant : anti-sciage *(m)*

scab * : briseur *(m)* de grève, jaune *(m)*

scaffolding : échafaud *(m)*

scale : (1) échelle *(f)*, barème *(m)*; (2) escalader

scalp * : crâne *(m)*

scam * : fraude *(f)*, escroquerie *(f)*, arnaque *(f)* *

scandal : tapage *(m)*, scandale *(f)*, honte *(f)*

>   ~**monger** : fouille-merde *(m&f)*

scanner : explorateur *(m)*

scar : cicatrice *(f)*, balafre *(f)*

scarcity : rareté *(f)*, pénurie *(f)*, insuffisance *(f)*, manque *(m)*

scare : peur *(f)*, alarme *(f)*, panique *(f)*

>   **bomb** ~ : alerte *(f)* à la bombe

scared : effrayé, affolé, avoir peur

scenario : cas *(m)* de figure

scene of the crime/accident : lieu *(m)* du crime/de l'accident

schedule : annexe *(f)* (à une loi), bordereau *(m)*, tableau *(m)*, liste *(f)*

>   **ahead of/behind** ~ : en avance/en retard sur le programme

scheme 222

~ **of cases** : rôle *(m)* des causes

work ~ : horaires *(mpl)* de travail

scheme : projet *(m)*, arrangement *(m)*, système *(m)*, plan *(m)*, intrigue *(f)*

scheming : manoeuvres *(fpl)*

school : école *(f)*

science : science *(f)*

forensic ~ : médecine *(f)* légale

scientific : scientifique

~ **research** : recherche *(f)* scientifique

~ **support unit** : service *(m)* d'identité judiciaire
Comprend les unités de visite aux lieux des crimes, d'empreintes digitales et de photographie.

scooter (motor- ~**)** : scooter *(m)*,

scope : ressort *(m)*, rayon *(m)*, portée *(f)*, champ *(m)* d'action, compétence *(f)*

matters within the ~ **of ...** : questions qui sont du ressort de ...

of limited ~ : dont le champ d'action est limité

~ **of activity** : rayon d'action

Scotland Yard (New ~ **)** : = Préfecture de Police
*Quartier-général de la **Metropolitan Police** de Londres*

Scots : écossais

~ **law** : droit *(m)* écossais

scoundrel : rien-du-tout *(m)*

scram * : se barrer, s'en aller, vingt-deux!

scrambled : brouillé

scrambler : appareil *(m)* de brouillage

scrambling : cryptage *(m)*

scrap : (1) ferraille *(f)*, rebuts *(mpl)*, déchets *(mpl)*; (2) petit bout *(m)*, bribe *(f)*, fragment *(m)*, débris *(mpl)*; (3) jeter, bazarder, envoyer à la ferraille; (4) bagarre *(f)*, baroud *(m)*, baston *(m)*

~ **dealer, merchant** : marchand *(m)* de ferraille

~ **heap** : décharge *(f)* publique, tas *(m)* de ferraille

~ **metal** : ferraille

~ **value** : valeur *(f)* de rebut, valeur *(f)* résiduelle

~ **yard** : chantier *(m)* de ferraille

scream : (1) cri *(m)* aïgu, hurlement *(m)*;   (2) crier, hurler, pousser des cris

screech : (freins) grincement *(m)*, (pneus) crissement *(m)*

screen : (1) écran *(m)*; (2) cacher, dérober; (3) passer au crible, faire subir un test de dépistage

~ **washer** : lave-glace *(m)*

wind ~ : pare-brise *(m)*

screening : procédure *(f)* de sélection sur dossier, tri *(m)*, test *(m)* de dépistage

screw * : (1) artoupan *(m)* *, maton *(m)* *;   (2) baiser *

~ **around** * : coucher à droite et à gauche *

scribble : gribouiller

scrote * : fripopuille *(f)* *, vaurien *(m)*, crapule *(f)*

scrubber * : putain *(f)* *

scrumping * : maraudage *(m)*

scuffers * : les flics *(mpl)* *

scuffle : bagarre *(f)*, rixe *(f)*

scum * : salaud *(m)* *, ordure *(f)* *

scrutiny : recherche *(f)* minutieuse, investigation *(f)*

sea : mer *(f)*

the four ~**s** : les mers qui entourent la Grande-Bretagne

the seven ~**s** : toutes les mers du monde

seal : sceau *(m)*, cachet *(m)*

sealed : scellé

~ **letter** : lettre *(f)* close

search : (1) perquisition *(f)*, fouille *(f)*; (2) recherche *(f)*; (3) fouiller, fourailler

    intimate ~ : fouille intime
> *Un **Superintendent** peut autoriser la fouille des orifices corporels d'un individu en état d'arrestation dans le cas où il a des raisons de croire qu'un objet dangereux ou des narcotiques s'y trouvent.*

    right of ~ : droit *(m)* de visite

    ~ party : expédition *(f)* de secours

    ~ warrant : mandat *(m)* de perquisition

season : saison *(f)*

    off ~ : hors saison

seat : siège *(m)*, place *(f)*

    ~-belt : ceinture *(f)* de sécurité

    ~ of a fire : foyer *(m)* d'incendie

second : (1) détacher; (2) appuyer, soutenir, approuver, seconder; (3) deuxième, second

    ~ a motion : appuyer une motion

    ~ best : numéro *(m)* deux

    ~ hand : d'occasion

    ~ hand dealer : fripier *(m)*, revendeur *(m)*, brocanteur *(m)*

    ~ hand goods : friperie *(f)*, objet *(m)* de vente

    ~ hand shop : friperie *(f)*, boutique *(f)* d'occasions/de brocanteur

    ~ offender : récidiviste *(m&f)*

secondary : secondaire, accessoire

    ~ evidence : présomption *(f)*

    ~ income : revenus *(mpl)* accessoires

    ~ motive : mobile *(m)* secondaire

    ~ matter : affaire *(f)* d'intérêt secondaire

    ~ picket : piquet *(m)* de grève constitué par des travailleurs non directement concernés par le conflit

    ~ residence : résidence *(f)* secondaire

secondly : deusio, deuxio, deuxièmement, en second lieu

secondment : détachement *(m)*, affectation *(f)* provisoire

secrecy : secret *(m)*

secret : clandestin, occulte, secret, caché

~ **agent** : agent secret, barbouse *(f)* *

~ **police** : police secrète

~ **service** : services secrets

secretary : secrétaire *(m&f)*

permanent ~ : secrétaire général de ministère

private ~ : secrétaire particulier

~ **of state** : ministre *(m)* d'état
Chef d'un service gouvernemental et souvent membre du cabinet.
*Il est secondé par des **Ministers**.*

section : (1) article *(m)* (d'une loi); (2) brigade *(f)*, peloton *(m)*, section *(f)*

~ **house** : logement *(m)* pour les policiers célibataires

sector : secteur *(m)*

secure : sûr, de tout repos

Securicor : société *(f)* de surveillance et de convoi de fonds

security : sûreté *(f)*, sécurité *(f)*

~ **firm** : société *(f)* de surveillance

~ **forces** : forces *(fpl)* de sécurité

~ **leak** : fuite *(f)* (des documents, des secrets)

~ **of tenure** : inamovibilité *(f)*

social ~ : sécurité sociale

sedative : dépresseur *(m)*

sedition : sédition *(f)*

seduce : débaucher

seduction : séduction *(f)*, corruption *(f)*

seek : chercher

seize : saisir, confisquer

    ~ **up** : se gripper

seizure : mainmise *(f)*, saisie *(f)*

select : choisir, élire

    ~ **committee** : commission *(f)* d'enquête parlementaire

selection board : comité *(m)* de sélection

self : moi-même

    ~**-addressed envelope** : enveloppe-réponse *(f)*

    ~**-defence** : défense *(f)* de soi, légitime défense *(f)*

    ~**-employed person** : travailleur *(m)* indépendant

    ~**-incrimination** : incrimination *(f)* de soi-même

    ~**-inflicted injury** : mutilation *(f)* volontaire

    ~**-propelled** : autotracté *(m)*

    ~**-service** : libre-service *(m)*

sell : vendre

    ~**-by date** : date limite d'utilisation (d'un produit)

seller : vendeur *(m)*

selling : vente *(f)*

semi-skilled worker : ouvrier *(m)* spécialisé

send : envoyer, expédier, adresser

senior : supérieur, aîné, doyen, principal

    ~ **judge** : doyen des juges

    ~ **clerk** : chef *(m)* de bureau, commis *(m)* principal, premier clerc *(m)*

    ~ **staff** : cadres *(mpl)* supérieurs

seniority : ancienneté *(f)*, priorité *(f)* d'âge

    promotion by ~ : avancement *(m)* à l'ancienneté

    right of ~ : droit *(m)* à l'ancienneté

sense : sens *(m)*, sentiment *(m)*, opinion *(f)*

~ **of justice** : sens de la justice

sensitive : sensible, délicat, épineux

sentence : condamnation *(f)*, jugement *(m)* criminel/pénal, sanction *(f)* pénale, sentence *(f)* criminelle, peine *(f)*

commutation of ~ : commutation de peine

cumulative ~ : cumul *(m)* des peines

life ~ : condamnation à vie

pass ~ : prononcer condamnation

remission of ~ : remise *(f)* de peine

~ **in absence/in absentia** : ordonnance *(f)* de contumace, condamnation par contumace, sentence par défaut

serve one's ~ : purger sa peine

sentry : factionnaire *(m)*

~ **-box** : guitoune *(f)*, guérite *(f)*

sequestration : saisie *(f)* conservatoire, mise *(f)* sous séquestre

sergeant : brigadier *(m)* (police), maréchal des logis-chef *(m)* (gendarmerie)

serial : en série

~ **killer** : assassin *(m)* en série

series : série *(f)*, gamme *(f)*

serious : grave

~ **arrestable offence** : crime *(m)*

~ **crimes squad** : brigade *(f)* de recherche et d'intervention, brigade *(f)* anti-gang, brigade *(f)* criminelle, brigade *(f)* de répression de banditisme

~ **Fraud Office** : office *(m)* central pour la répression de la grande délinquance   financière
Bureau national formé des experts comptables judiciaires qui font des enquêtes sur les fraudes les plus graves.

~ **offence** : faute *(f)* grave, crime *(m)*

servant : domestique *(m&f)*, serviteur *(m)*

    civil ˜ : fonctionnaire *(m&f)* d'Etat

serve : (1) signifier (un acte); (2) purger (une peine), tirer son temps

    ˜ **on a jury** : faire partie d'un jury

    ˜ **notice** : signifier un arrêt

    ˜ **a prison term** : purger sa peine

service : (1) service *(m)*, prestation *(f)*, (2) signification *(f)* (d'un procès)

    address for service : domicile *(m)* élu

    ˜ **at place of abode** : signification à domicile

    ˜ **by post** : signification ordinaire

    ˜ **road** : accès *(m)* de service

    ˜ **station** : station-service *(f)*

servitude : servitude *(f)*

    penal ˜ : travaux *(mpl)* forcés (transformés désormais en réclusion)

session : session *(f)*, séance *(f)*, audience *(f)* du tribunal

    closed ˜ : séance à huis clos

    petty ˜**s** : session du tribunal d'instance

set : ensemble *(m)*, groupe *(m)*

    ˜ **back** : (1) retarder;   (2) coûter *

    ˜ **in motion** : déclencher

    ˜ **upon** : attaquer

settle : décider, régler

    ˜ **a matter** : trancher une question

    ˜ **a score** : s'arranger, régler des comptes

settlement : règlement *(m)*, arrangement *(m)*, résolution *(f)*, décision *(f)*

    ˜ **of account** : règlement de compte

severance pay : prime *(f)* de licenciement

severe : sévère, dur

sewn–up * : dans la poche *

sex : sexe *(m)*

    ~ **discrimination** : discrimination *(f)* sexuelle, sexisme *(m)*

    ~ **establishment** : cinéma *(m)* ou boutique *(f)* pornographiques

    ~ **shop** : boutique *(f)* porno

sexual : sexuel

    ~ **assault** : abus *(m)*

    ~ **deviancy** : déviance sexuelle

    ~ **intercourse** : acte sexuel

    ~ **offence** : attentat *(m)* aux moeurs, attentat *(m)* à la pudeur

shackle : (1) entraver;   (2) chaîne *(f)*, entrave *(f)*

shades * : lunettes *(fpl)* de soleil

shadow : (1) ombre *(f)*;   (2) ficelle *(f)* (policier qui file quelqu'un);
(3) filer, pister, suivre

shadowing : filage *(m)*, filature *(f)*

shady : interlope, véreux, douteux, louche, suspect

    ~ **deal** : combinaison *(f)*

shake off : semer

shaky : peu solide, faible

sham : factice, simulé, faux, feint, en toc *

shame : honte *(f)*

shandy : panaché *(m)*

shanty : bicoque *(f)*

    ~ **town** : bidonville *(m)*

shape : (1) former, façonner;   (2) forme *(f)*

share : (1) part *(f)*, portion *(f)*;   (2) partager

    ~ **out** : partager, distribuer

sharpshooter : tireur *(m)* d'élite

sheet : feuille *(f)*

shelter : (1) abri *(m)*, asile *(m)*; (2) héberger, protéger

shelve : décrocher, enterrer, mettre en suspens

sheriff : shérif *(m)*
   Principal représentant de la Couronne, dans un comté. Aux Etats-Unis, il assume les fonctions de chef de police dans les districts ruraux.

shield : bouclier *(m)*

   ~ **training** : formation *(f)* de maintien d'ordre avec boucliers

shift : relais *(m)*, poste *(m)*, équipe *(f)*, service *(m)*, période *(f)* de travail d'une équipe

   ~ **system** : système *(m)* e travail par roulement

shiner * : oeil *(m)* poché *

ship : bateau *(m)*, navire *(m)*, vaisseau *(m)*

   ~**s log** : journal *(m)* e bord

   ~ **wreck** : naufrage *(m)*

shipping : navigation *(f)*

   ~ **company** : entreprise *(f)* de navigation

shipyard : chantier *(m)* naval

shire : comté *(m)*

shirt : chemise *(f)*

shit * : merde *(f)* *, marijuana *(f)*

shock-absorber : amortisseur *(m)*

shoestring (on a ~) : à peu de frais

shoot : fusiller

shooter * : artillerie *(f)*, azor *(m)*, bouledogue *(m)*, calibre *(m)*, flingue *(m)*

shooting : chasse *(f)*, tir *(m)*

   ~ **brake** : brake *(m)*

   ~ **range** : stand *(m)* e tir

shoot–out : fusillade *(f)*

shop (1) : magasin *(m)*, boutique *(f)*, atelier *(f)*

    ~ assistant : employé *(m)* de magasin

    ~ keeper : marchand *(m)*

    ~ steward : délégué *(m)* syndical

shop (2) * : se mettre à table (voir aussi **grass**)

shoplifter : voleur *(m)* à l'étalage

shoplifting : vol *(m)* à l'étalage *(m)*

shopping centre/precinct : centre *(m)* commercial

short : de petite taille *(f)*

shortage : insuffisance *(f)*, manque *(m)*, pénurie *(f)*

    housing ~ : crise *(f)* de logement

    labour ~ : pénurie de main-d'oeuvre

short–back–and–sides : coupe *(f)* à la Deibler

shortcoming : faute *(f)*, faiblesse *(f)*, point *(m)* faible

shortfall : déficit *(m)*

shorthand : sténographie *(f)*

    ~ –typist : sténo-dactylo *(m&f)*

shot : (armes) coup *(m)*, décharge *(f)*;   (narcotiques)   dose *(f)* *

shotgun : fusil *(m)* de chasse

    pump–action ~ : fusil à pompe, fusil à répétition

    sawn–off ~ : fusil à canon scié

shoulder : épaule *(f)*

    hard ~ : accotement *(m)* stabilisé

    ~ strap : patte *(f)* d'épaule

shout : gueuler, crier

shove : pousser

show : spectacle *(m)*, exposition *(f)*, salon *(m)*

shredder : destructeur *(m)* de documents, déchiqueteuse *(f)*

shrewd : perspicace

shunt * : collision *(f)*

shutter : volet *(m)*

shutting : fermeture *(f)*

sickening : dégueulasse

sick : malade

> ~ **leave** : congé *(m)* de maladie

> ~ **pay** : indemnité *(f)* de maladie

sickness : maladie *(f)*

> ~ **benefit** : prestation *(f)* maladie

side : côté *(m)*

> **have a bit on the** ~ : avoir une concubine, coucher hors du lit conjugal

> **make a bit on the** ~ : faire un peu (d'argent) en plus

> ~**boards/~burns** : pattes *(fpl)* rouflaquettes

> ~**car** : sidecar *(m)*

> ~ **door/~ entrance** : entrée *(f)* latérale

> ~ **effect** : effet *(m)* secondaire

> ~**kick** : sous-fifre *(m)* *

> ~ **street** : petite rue *(f)*, rue *(f)* transversale

> ~**walk** : trottoir *(m)*

> ~**light** : feu *(m)* de position

> ~**line** : activité *(f)* annexe/d'appoint

siege : siège *(m)*

sight (weapon) : visée *(f)*

> **laser** ~ : visée laser

> **telescopic** ~ : lunette *(f)* de visée, visée télescopique

sighting : mire *(f)*

sign : (1) signer, apposer une signature; (2) signe *(m)*, panneau *(m)*

    ~ language : langage *(m)* par signes

    ~ on : se faire embaucher, s'engager, pointer

signal : signal *(m)*

    traffic ~ : feu *(m)* de circulation

signature : signature *(f)*, visa *(m)*

significance : portée *(f)*, importance *(f)*, conséquence *(f)*, gravité *(f)*

    matter of great ~ : affaire *(f)* de la plus haute importance

significant : significatif, important

signing : émargement *(m)*

signpost : poteau *(m)* indicateur

    the road is badly ~ed : la route est mal indiquée

silence (right of accused to ~) : droit *(m)* au silence
*En principe, un suspect a le droit de ne pas répondre aux questions qui
lui sont posées par la police.*

silencer : silencieux *(m)*

silly : bête, idiot, sot(te)

silver : argent *(m)*

simmer (emotions) : être excité, bouillir (de mécontent), fermenter, couver

sin : péché *(m)*

    to live in ~ : vivre en concubinage

sine die : indéfiniment, ajournement pour un temps indéfini

sine qua non : condition *(f)* indispensable

single : (1) séparé, seul; (2) célibataire

sinister : sinistre, menaçant

siren : sirène *(f)*, avertisseur *(m)* à deux tons

sister : soeur *(f)*

    ~ -in-law : belle soeur

    step-~ : belle-soeur

sit : siéger

    ~-in : grève *(f)* sur le tas

    ~ in camera : siéger à huis clos

    ~ in judgement : se faire juge des actes d'autrui

    ~ on a committee : être du comité

site : site *(m)*, situation *(f)*, emplacement *(m)*

    building ~ : chantier *(m)* de construction

sitting : session *(f)*, séance *(f)*, audience *(f)*

situation : (1) situation *(f)*, emplacement *(m)*; (2) emploi *(m)*, poste *(m)*, place *(f)*

    ~ report : rapport *(m)* de situation

    ~s vacant : offres *(fpl)* d'emploi

    ~s wanted : demandes *(fpl)* d'emploi

size : importance *(f)*, dimension *(f)*, format *(m)*, mesure *(f)*, taille *(f)*

    ~ up : juger, jauger, mesurer

skeleton : squelette *(m)*

    ~ key : passe-partout *(m)*, crochet *(m)*, rossignol *(m)*, frou-frou *(m)*

skid : déraper

    ~lid : casque *(m)* (de moto)

    ~mark : trace *(m)* de dérapage

skilled : qualifié, habile, expérimenté, spécialisé

    semi-~ : spécialisé

    ~ worker : ouvrier *(m)* qualifié

skim off : mettre à part

skindiver : plongeur *(m)*

skin-flick : film *(m)* pornographique

skinful (to have a ~) * : être bourré *, être noir *

skint * : lavé, fauché

skip * : (1) faire défaut en justice; (2) benne

skull : crâne *(m)*

sky-high : astronomique

skyjacking : piratage *(m)*, piraterie *(f)* aérienne

skylarking * : rigolade *(f)* *, chahut *(m)*

skylight : lucarne *(f)*

slag * : putain * *(f)*, salope *(f)* *

    ~ off * : engueuler *

slam : claquer, fermer violemment

    ~ on the brakes : freiner à mort

slammer * : prison *(f)*, cellule *(f)*, taule *(f)*

slander : calomnie *(f)* orale, diffamation *(f)* orale, injure *(f)*

slang : argot *(m)*

slap : claque *(f)*, gifle *(f)*

    ~ bang * : en plein

slash : balafrer

slaughter : carnage *(m)*, massacre *(m)*, égorgerie *(f)*

slave driver : employeur *(m)* exigeant

sleeper (spy) : espion *(m)* en sommeil

sleeping policeman : bande *(f)* ralentisseuse, gendarme *(m)* couché, casse-vitesse *(m)*

sleuth : limier *(m)*

slide (photo.) : diapositive *(f)*

slim : mince, svelte

slip road : bretelle *(f)*, voie *(f)* d'accès/de sortie

slippery : glissant

    ~ customer : homme *(m)* fuyant, insaisissible

    ~ road : chaussée *(f)* glissante

slip-up : gaffe *(f)*

slog : travail *(m)* pénible

slop–out (prison) : vider les seaux hygiéniques

slow down : ralentir

slum : taudis *(m)*

slush fund : caisse *(f)* noire

small fry : menu fretin *(m)*

smart card : carte *(f)* à mémoire, carte *(f)* à puce

    ~ **reader** : lecteur *(m)* de carte à mémoire

smash and grab raid : rafle *(f)* (après bris de devanture)

smashed * : dynamité *

smell out : découvrir, dépister

smoke: fumée *(f)*

    ~ **bomb** : obus *(m)* fumigène

    ~ **out** : dénicher

    "The ~" : Londres

smuggle : trafiquer, faire de la contrebande

smuggler : contrebandier *(m)*

smuggling : contrebande *(f)*, fraude *(f)* douanière

    arms ~ : contrebande d'armes

smutty : obscène, grossier

snack : casse–croûte *(m)*

snag : accroc *(m)*

snare : (1) piège *(m)*; (2) attraper

snarl–up : embouteillage *(m)*

snatch : vol *(m)* (à l'arraché)

    ~ **thief** : arracheur *(m)* de sacs

    wages ~ : vol de fonds (à main armé)

sneak thief : chapardeur *(m)*

sniff : aspirer, respirer

    to ~ glue/solvents : respirer de la colle/des solvants

sniper : tireur *(m)* d'élite

snitch * : (1) mouchard *(m)*; (2) chiper *

snoop : rôder, fureter, fouiller

    ~ around : jeter un coup d'oeil discret

    ~ on someone : surveiller quelqu'un, espionner quelqu'un

snort (drugs) : sniff *(m)*

snout * : informateur *(m)* (voir aussi **grass**)

snow * : blanc *(m)*, chnouf *(f)*, cocaine *(f)*, neige *(f)*

sobering-up : dégrisement *(m)*

soccer : foot *(m)*

social : social

    ~ benefits : prestation *(f)* de caractère social

    ~ class : mileu *(m)*

    ~ deviant : marginal *(m)*

    ~ insurance : assurance sociale

    ~ unrest : agitation sociale

    ~ security : assistance sociale

    ~ services : services sociaux

    ~ standing : situation sociale

    ~ work : assistance sociale (en tant que profession)

    ~ worker : assistant social

society : association *(f)*

    building ~ : société *(f)* pour le financement de l'habitation

    law ~ : association d'avocats

sod * : con *(m)* *, couillon *(m)* *, salaud *(m)*

   ~ **off!** * : foutre le camp! *

   ~**'s law** * : loi de l'emmerdement maximum *

sodomy : sodomie *(f)*

soft drugs : drogues *(f)* douces

soften-up * : attendrir, bonimenter *, intimider, malmener

software : logiciel *(m)*

sojourn : demeure *(f)*

soldier : soldat *(m)*, militaire *(m)*

solicit : fouler le bitume

soliciting (for prostitution) : racolage *(m)*, tapinage *(m)*

solicitor : avocat *(m)*, notaire *(m)*
   Un homme de loi, autorisé à déclencher des poursuites, dresser des actes et donner des conseils juridiques. En cela il combine, en partie, les qualités d'un avocat et celles d'un notaire.

solitary confinement : isoloir *(m)*

solvent : (1) solvable; (2) solvant, dissolvant

   ~ **abuse** : usage de solvants hallucinogènes (colle, etc.)

son : fils *(m)*

   ~ **-in-law** : beau-fils

   step-~ : beau-fils

sordid : sordide, misérable, crapuleux

sound : (1) sain, sûr, solide, bien fondé; (2) bruit *(m)*

   ~ **argument** : argument *(m)* solide

   ~ **management** : gestion *(f)* rationnelle

souped-up : gonflé

source : provenance *(f)*

span : portée *(f)*

spanner : clé *(f)* à écrous

spare : (1) de secours, de trop, disponible; (2) épargner, faire grâce

~ **parts** : pièces *(fpl)* de rechange

~ **wheel** : roue *(f)* de secours

special : spécial

~ **Air Service Regiment (SAS)** : groupement d'intervention militaire

~ **Branch** : Service des Renseignements Généraux et de Contre-espionnage

~ **constabulary** : service auxiliaire de police

~ **patrol group** : unité/groupe d'intervention

~ **weapons and tactics (SWAT) team** : service de recherche, assistance, intervention et de dissuasion

specialist group : formation *(f)* spécialisée

specimen : spécimen *(m)*, modèle *(m)*, exemplaire *(m)*, échantillon *(m)*

~ **charges** : accusations *(fpl)* types

specious argument : argument *(m)* faux/captieux

speech : discours *(m)*, allocution *(f)*

speed : vitesse *(f)*

high ~ : grande vitesse

maximum ~ : vitesse limite

~ **limit** : limitation *(f)* de vitesse

~ **trap** : piège *(m)* de police pour contrôle de vitesse

speeder : automobiliste *(m&f)* coupable d'excès de vitesse

speedometer : compteur *(m)* de vitesse

speeding offence : infraction *(f)* d'excès de vitesse

spent conviction : condamnation *(f)* qui, après un certain laps de temps, ne peut pas être évoquée pour des motifs professionnel ou judiciaire

spin off effects : effets *(mpl)* induits, retombées *(fpl)*

spinster : femme *(f)* célibataire

spite : malveillance *(f)*

split * : se barrer, s'en va, vingt-deux!

spoiler (auto.) : spoiler *(m)*

spokesman/spokesperson/spokeswoman : porte-parole *(m&f)*

sponsor : parrain *(m)*

sports car : voiture *(f)* de sport

spot : (1) lieu *(m)*;   (2) tache *(f)*;   (3) repérer *, remarquer

spouse : époux *(m)*, mari *(m)*, épouse *(f)*

sprain : entorse *(f)*

spread : (1) étaler; (2) éventail *(m)*

spring : ressort *(m)*

    coil ~ : ressort hélécoïdal

spurious : faux, falsifié

spy : (1) espion *(m)*;   (2) espionner

    ~ **-hole** : guichet *(m)*, oeilleton *(m)*

spying : espionnage *(m)*

squad : brigade *(f)*, peloton *(m)*

squadron : escadron *(m)*

squander : gaspiller

squat : squattage *(m)*

squatter : celui qui s'établit sans droit dans les lieux d'autrui

squeal * : informer

squealer * : indicateur *(m)*

stab : poignarder, lamer

stabbing : coup *(m)* de couteau

staff : effectif *(m)*, personnel *(m)*

    clerical : personnel administratif, personnel de bureau

    senior ~ : cadres *(mpl)* supérieurs

    ~ **officer** : officier *(m)* d'état-major,

    ~ **shortage** : insuffisance *(f)* de personnel

stagger : (1) étaler;   (2) chanceler

staging : échafaud *(m)*

stag party : réunion *(f)* entre hommes

stake : enjeu *(m)*, pari *(m)*

    ~ out : mettre sous surveillance

stall : (1) caler; (2) éventaire *(m)*, stand *(m)*

    ~ holder : marchand *(m)* forain

stamp : cachet *(m)*, estampille *(f)*, timbre *(m)*

stand : stand *(m)*

    ~-in : doublure *(f)*

standard of living : niveau *(m)* de vie

stand-by : remplaçant *(m)*, de réserve

    to be on ~ : être sur pied d'intervention, être de garde

standing : (1) permanent, établi, fixe, stable; (2) situation *(f)*

    social ~ : situation sociale

    ~ committee : commission permanente

    ~ crops : récoltes *(fpl)* sur pied

    ~ orders : règlements *(mpl)* intérieurs, règlement *(m)* de service

stand surety : garantir

stand trial : comparaître

Stanley knife : cutter *(m)*

start : commencer, ouvrir, lancer

starting : mise *(f)* en marche

stash * : cacher, planquer *

state : (1) état *(m)*, situation *(f)*; (2) déclarer, régler

    head of ~ : chef d'état

    ~ of emergency : état d'urgence

stated cases : jurisprudence *(f)*

stateless person : apatride *(m)*

statement : (1) déclaration *(f)*, déposition *(f)*, dire *(m)*, (2) relevé *(m)*,
rapport *(m)* (de situation)

~ **of witness** : déposition

sworn ~ : déclaration sous serment

station : station *(f)*, gare *(f)*

police ~ : commissariat *(m)* de police, gendarmerie *(f)*

~ **duty officer** : policier *(m)* de permanence au commissariat

statistics : statistique *(f)*

statute law : droit *(m)* écrit

status : standing *(m)*, état *(m)*, rang *(m)*, situation *(f)*, statut *(m)*

civil ~ : état-civil

marital ~ : état matrimonial

statute : statut *(m)*, acte *(m)* législatif, loi *(f)* écrite (opp. droit coutumier)

~ **book** : titre collectif de toutes les lois en vigueur

statutory : imposé par la loi, légal

~ **holiday** : fête légale

~ **instrument** : règlement *(m)*

~ **provision** : disposition légale

stay : (1) demeure *(f)*, séjour *(m)*; (2) sursis *(m)*, arrêt *(m)*, entrave *(f)*;
(3) surseoir

period of ~ : durée de séjour

~ **of execution** : opposition *(f)* à un jugement, sursis, ordonnance *(f)*
à surseoir

~ **of proceedings** : suspension *(f)* d'instance

steal : dérober, voler

stealing : vol *(m)*

going equipped for ~ : possession *(f)* des outils de cambriolage, de vol ou
de fraude

~ **by finding** : appropriation *(f)* frauduleuse d'objets trouvés

stealthily : furtivement

steaming * : vol *(m)* de l'encerclement
Vol par une bande de malfaiteurs qui courent dans une foule (au marché, par exemple) en volant des objets et, par leur nombre et rapidité, empêchent qu'on les arrête.

steep : raide

steer : diriger, conduire

steering : direction *(f)*

   ~ **committee** : comité *(m)* directeur

   ~ **wheel** : volant *(m)*

step : démarche *(f)*, pas *(m)*, mesure *(f)*

   ~-**brother** : beau-frère *(m)*

   ~-**daughter** : belle-fille *(f)*

   ~-**father** : beau-père *(m)*

   ~-**mother** : belle-mère *(f)*

   ~-**sister** : belle-soeur *(f)*

   ~-**son** : beau-fils *(m)*

   to take ~s : faire des démarches

steward(s) : service *(m)* d'ordre (à une réunion), suivette *(f)* (à une défilé)

   shop ~ : délégué *(m)* syndical

stick : coller, afficher

   ~ **no bills** : défense d'afficher

   ~ **together** : se serrer les coudes

   ~-**up** : dévaliser à main armée

sticker : (1) vignette *(f)*, autocollant *(m)*; (2) affaire difficile à résoudre

sticking point : impasse *(f)*

sticks (in the ~) * : (dans le) bled *(m)*

sticky : (1) gluant, poisseux; (2) épineux, délicat

   ~ -**fingered** * : porté sur la fauche

stiff : macchabée *(m)*

still-born : mort-né

stimulant : dopant *(m)*, stimulant *(m)*

sting * : coup *(m)* monté, arnaque *(f)* *

stint : ration *(f)* de travail

stipendiary magistrate : juge *(m)* de police qualifié et permanent

stir * : bal *(m)*, taule *(f)*

stirrup : étrier *(m)*

stir-up : fomenter

stitch-up * : monter un coup (contre quelqu'un)

stock : parc *(m)*

stocking mask : bas *(m)* (d'un bandit masqué)

stocks : pilori *(m)*

stolen : volé

    ~ **property** : lamedus *(mpl)*

    ~ **vehicle index** : fiche *(f)* des véhicules volés

stop : arrêter, stopper

    bus ~ : arrêt *(m)* d'autobus

    ~ **a cheque** : faire opposition à un chèque

    ~ **and rear light cluster** : feu *(m)* arrière complet

    ~ **and search** : contrôle *(m)* et fouille *(f)* par un policier

    ~ **check** : contrôle *(m)* d'identité

    ~-**gap measures** : bouche-trou *(m)*

    ~ **line** : bande *(f)* stop

    " ~ **thief!**" : "au voleur!"

store : entrepôt *(m)*, magasin *(m)*

    ~**man** : garde-magasin *(m)*

story : histoire *(f)*, version *(f)* des faits

straight : régulier

> **~ talking** : parler-vrai

strain : entorse *(f)*, tension *(f)*, embarras *(m)*, difficulté *(f)*

stranger : étranger *(m)*, inconnu *(m)*

strangle : étrangler

strangling : étranglement *(m)*

strangulation : étranglement *(m)*

stray (animal) : animal *(m)* égaré, bête *(f)* épave

street : rue *(f)*

> **~-lamp** : réverbère *(m)*

> **~ lighting** : éclairage *(m)*

> **~ market** : marché *(m)* à ciel ouvert

> **~ offences** : contravention *(f)* aux règlements concernant l'encombrement
> de la rue ou à d'autres règlements de police.

> **~ trader** : marchand *(m)* ambulant

> **~ value** : valeur *(f)* au niveau du revendeur

> **~ walker** : rôdeuse *(f)*

> **~ wise** : futé, réaliste

strength : (1) effectif *(m)*; (2) force *(f)*, vigueur *(f)*; (3) résistance

> **actual ~** : effectif réel

> **full ~** : effectif au complet

stress : tension *(f)*

stretch (prison ~) * : score *(m)* *

strict : rigoureux, rigide, strict

> **~ construction** : interprétation *(f)* littérale

> **~ liability** : responsabilité *(f)* sans faute

strike : (1) grève *(f)*; (2) frapper

> **call a ~** : appeler à la grève

go on ~ : se mettre en grève

hunger ~ : grève de la faim

official ~ : grève officielle, sanctionnée par le syndicat

sit-down ~ : grève avec occupation

~ breaker : briseur *(m)* de grève, jaune *(m)* *

~ force : force *(f)* de frappe, commando *(m)*

token ~ : grève symbolique

wildcat ~ : grève sauvage

work to rule ~ : grève du zèle

stringent : strict, rigoureux

strip : (1) bande *(f)*;   (2) dévêtir

~ down : démonter complètement

~ search : fouille *(f)* d'une personne dévêtue

~-off : se déshabiller

tear off a ~ : réprimander

stripe : galon *(m)* (en form de chevron)

sergeant's ~s : les galons d'un brigadier chef

stripper : effeuilleuse *(f)*

stroll : balade *(f)*

strong : résistant, fort

~ arm : brutal

stroppy * : contrariant, difficile

struggle : lutte *(f)*, combat *(m)*

stubble : (1) chaume *(m)*, éteule *(f)*;   (2) barbe *(f)* de plusieurs jours

stubborn : mordicus, entêté, têtu

study : cabinet *(m)* de travail, étude *(f)*;   (2) étudier, examiner

~ trip : voyage *(m)* d'étude

stuff * : came *(f)* *, drogue *(f)*

stumble upon : tomber sur

stunt–man : casse-cou *(m)*

subaltern : officier *(m)* subalterne

sub–committee : sous-commission *(f)*

sub–contractor : sous-traitant *(m)*

sub–division : sous-circonscription *(f)*

subject : (1) sujet *(m)*, objet *(m)*; (2) ressortissant *(m)*

    ~ **to** : sous réserve de

subjection : sujétion *(f)*

sub judice : affaire pendante ou en cours

    ~ **rule** : règle qui défend la publication d'articles touchant à une affaire et qui sont susceptibles d'entraver la justice

sub–machine gun : mitraillette *(f)*

submission : (1) conclusion *(f)*, soumission *(f)*, plaidoirie *(f)*; (2) obéissance *(f)*

subordinate : (1) sous-ordre *(m)*, (2) inférieur, subalterne

    ~ **legislation** : règlements *(mpl)* (décisions prises par le pouvoir exécutif)

subornation : corruption *(f)*, séduction *(f)*, subornation *(f)*

sub–paragraph : sous-alinéa *(m)* (d'une loi)

sub–section : paragraphe *(f)* (d'une loi)

subsequent (to) : consécutif (à)

subsequently : par la suite *(f)*

subsistence : subsistance *(f)*

substance : substance *(f)*

    harmful ~ : substance nuisible

substantial : important, sérieux

substantiate : fournir des preuves à l'appui de, justifier

substitute : succédané *(m)*

suburb : faubourg *(m)*, banlieue *(f)*

subversive : subversif

successful : heureux, fructueux

sucker * : pante *(m)* *, pigeon *(m)* *

sudden death : mort *(f)* subite

sue : intenter un procès

suffer : subir, éprouver, supporter

suicide : suicide *(m)*

suit : requête *(f)*, procès *(m)*, action *(f)* civile

summary : résumé *(m)*, récapitulation *(f)*, sommaire *(m)*

    ~ jurisdiction : pouvoir *(m)* des juges du tribunal d'instance

    ~ offence : contravention *(f)*

    ~ proceedings/trial : procédure *(f)* sommaire

summing-up : résumé *(f)* par le juge, à l'intention du jury, des points importants des témoignages produits

summons (1) : acte *(m)* de procédure introductif d'instance, demande *(f)* en justice, mandat *(m)* d'amener, mandat *(m)* de comparution, exploit *(m)*, sommation *(f)* à comparaître

summons (2) : assigner, citer, appeler en justice

superannuation : mise *(f)* à la retraite, pension *(f)* pour cause de limite d'âge

    ~ contribution : retenue *(f)* pour retraite

    ~ plan : régime *(m)* de retraite

super-bike : gros-cube *(m)*

super-grass : super-mouchard *(m)*

superintendence : surveillance *(f)*

superintendent : commissaire *(m)* principal

    chief ~ : commissaire divisionnaire

    detective ~ : commissaire principal de la police judiciaire

superior : supérieur

supermarket : supermarché *(m)*, grande surface *(f)*

supernumary : surnuméraire *(m)*

supersede : remplacer, supplanter

supervision : surveillance *(f)*, contrôle *(m)*, direction *(f)*

~ **order** : liberté *(f)* surveillée

supervisor : responsable *(m)*, surveillant *(m)*

supplement : annexe *(f)*

supplementary : annexe

~ **question** : question *(f)* subsidiaire

supplies : matériel *(m)*

supply : (1) fourniture *(f)*, approvisionnement *(m)*; (2) subvenir, approvisionner, fournir

support : (1) entretien *(m)*, appui *(m)*; (2) appuyer, entretenir, subvenir

~ **group** : groupe *(m)* d'intervention

suppress : abolir

suppression : suppression *(f)*

supreme : suprême

~ **court** : tribunal *(m)* suprême
Comprend la *Court of Appeal*, la *High Court of Justice* et la *Crown Court.*

sure : (1) sûr; (2) sans aucun doute, certain

surety : (1) caution *(f)*, cautionnement *(m)*, garantie *(f)*, sûreté *(f)*; (2) répondant *(m)*

surname : nom *(m)* de famille, patronyme *(m)*

surprise : surprendre

surrender : se livrer à la police, se constituer prisonnier

surround : ceinturer

surveillance : surveillance *(f)*

survey : rapport *(m)* de situation

survivor : survivant *(m)*

---

suspect : (1) suspect *(m)*, suspecte *(f)*; (2) interlope; (3) soupçonner, suspecter

    ~ activities : magouille *(f)*

suspected : être en suspicion

suspend : surseoir, suspendre

suspended : suspendu, interrompu provisoirement

    ~ from duty : exclu temporairement de ses fonctions

    ~ sentence : condamnation *(f)* avec sursis (à l'exécution de la peine)

suspension : suspension *(f)*

    ~ from duty : exclusion *(f)* temporaire de fonctions

suspicion : méfiance *(f)*, soupçon *(m)*, suspicion *(f)*

    arrest on ~ : arrêter quelqu'un pour cause de suspicion légitime

    detention on ~ : détention *(f)* préventive

suspicious : suspect

    ~ death : mort suspecte

swag : butin *(m)*

swear : jurer

    ~ on oath : lever la main

sweatshop system : sentier *(m)*
    Atelier ou usine où les ouvriers sont exploités.

sweep : ratissage *(m)*

swindle : (1) biber, blouser, engailler, entourer, escroquer, flouer, feinter, rouler;   (2) repassage *(m)*

swindler : escroc *(m)*

swipe * : calotter , piquer *

switchboard : standard *(m)* (téléphonique)

    ~ operator : standardiste *(m&f)*

switch on/off : mettre/couper le contact, allumer/éteindre

swoop : descente *(f)*

sword : épée *(f)*, sabre *(m)*

    ~play : escrime *(f)*

    ~-stick : canne *(f)* à épée

sworn : assermenté, juré

    ~ statement : déclaration *(f)* sous serment

syringe : seringue *(f)*

system : réseau *(m)*, système *(m)*, régime *(m)*

table   252

T

table : (1) table *(f)*, tableau *(m)*; (2) déposer (un projet de loi, une résolution)

tabs (keep ~ on) * : tenir à l'oeil *

tacit : tacite

tactical : tactique

    ~ support unit : groupe *(m)*/unité *(f)* d'intervention

tail : (1) queue *(f)*; (2) ficelle *(f)*; (3) faire le train à quelqu'un

tailgate : hayon *(m)*

tailing : filage *(m)*, filature *(f)*

tainted : corrompu, infecté, souillé

    ~ with fraud : entaché de dol

take : prendre

    ~ advantage : tirer parti

    ~ an oath : prêter serment

    ~away : café qui fait des plats à emporter

    ~ away : soustraire

    ~ down : inscrire (au procès-verbal)

    ~ effect : prendre effet

    ~ evidence : recueillir des témoignages

    ~ home pay : salaire *(m)* net

    ~ in * : rouler *, avoir *

    ~ into account/consideration : prendre en considération

    ~ legal advice : consulter un avocat

    ~ out : retirer, obtenir

    ~ over : prendre en charge, se charger de, assumer

    ~ proceedings : poursuivre en justice

    ~ sides : prendre parti

~ **up duties** : entrer en fonction

taking : prise *(f)*

    ~ **and driving away** : vol *(m)* d'usage

    ~ **charge** : prise en charge

    ~ **into account** : en égard à, compte tenu

    ~ **of evidence** : audition *(f)*

    ~ **on staff** : embauchage *(m)*

tall : grand

tamper (with) : corrompre (un témoin), tripoter, altérer, falsifier, toucher sans permission

tangible : tangible, palpable, sensible, réel

tank : char *(m)* blindé/de combat

tanker : camion-citerne *(m)*

tantamount (to) : équivalent à

tap : taper

    telephone ~ : téléphone *(m)* sur écoute

tape : (1) bande *(f)* magnétique, bande *(f)* d'enregistrement; (2) enregistrer

    ~ **recorder** : magnétophone *(m)*

    ~ **recording** : enregistrement *(m)* magnétique

target : cible *(f)*, point *(m)* de mire

tart : demi-mondaine *(f)*, prostituée *(f)*

task : tâche *(f)*, mission *(f)*

    ~ **force** : commando *(m)*, détachement *(m)* spécial

tattoo : (1) tatouer; (2) tatouage *(m)*

tax : (1) taxe *(f)*, impôt *(m)*, contribution *(f)*; (2) taxer, imposer; (3) accuser

    road ~ : impôt de voirie

    ~ **avoidance** : dérobade *(f)* fiscale

    ~ **disc** : vignette *(f)*

~ **evasion** : fraude *(f)* fiscale

~ **exemption** : immunité *(f)* fiscale

~ **haven** : paradis *(m)* fiscal

taxation : imposition *(f)*

taxi : taxi *(m)*

team : équipe *(f)*, brigade *(f)*

~ **work** : travail *(m)* en équipe

tearful : larmoyant, éploré, pleunichard

tear gas : gaz *(m)* lacrymogène

technical : professionnel, technique, de pure forme

quashed on a ~ **point** : cassé pour vice de procédure ou de forme

~ **assault** : quasi-aggression *(f)*

~ **offence** : quasi-délit *(m)*

~ **training** : formation *(f)* technique

technicality : technicité *(f)*, caractère *(m)* technique, terme *(m)* technique

technological response : parade *(f)* technologique

teenager : jeune adolescent *(m)* (de 13 à 19 ans)

teetotal : personne qui ne boit jamais d'alcool

telephone : (1) téléphone *(m)*, appareil (téléphonique); (2) téléphoner, appeler, passer un coup de fil

~ **box** : cabine *(f)* téléphonique

~ **exchange** : central *(m)* (téléphonique)

~ **extension** : poste *(m)* (téléphonique)

~ **number** : numéro *(m)* de téléphone

~ **tap** : bretelle *(f)*, table *(f)* d'écoute

telephoto lens : téléobjectif *(m)*

teleprinter : télétype *(m)*, téléscripteur *(m)*

telescopic : télescopique

~ **forks** : fourche *(f)* téléhydraulique

~ **sight** : lunette *(f)* de visée, visée *(f)* télescopique

telex : télex *(m)*

temp. * : voir **temporary replacement**

temporary : temporaire, intérimaire, suppléant, provisoire, passager

~ **appointment** : engagement/avancement *(m)* à titre temporaire

~ **effect** : effet *(m)* transitoire

~ **insanity** : demi-folie *(f)*

~ **replacement** : suppléant, intérimaire, secrétaire qui fait de l'intérim

~ **suspension** : mise *(f)* à pied

tenant : locataire *(m&f)*, tenancier *(m)*

tendency : tendance *(f)*, orientation *(f)*

tenement block : immeuble *(m)* de rapport

tentative : expérimental

tenure : tenure *(f)*, période *(f)* de jouissance ou d'occupation

~ **of office** : stabilité d'emploi dans le cadre de la fonction publique, période d'occupation d'un office ou d'un emploi

term : (1) trimestre *(m)*, session *(f)*; (2) échéance *(f)*; (3) terme *(m)*, expression *(f)*

legal ~ : terme de droit

~s **of reference** : mandat *(m)*, attributions *(fpl)*

to come to ~s : arriver à un accommodement *(m)*

terminal : terminal, situé à l'extrémité

terminate : résilier, terminer, mettre fin, dénoncer, résoudre

termination : fin *(f)*, terminaison *(f)*, cessation *(f)*, extinction *(f)*, résolution *(f)*, résiliation *(f)*

terminology : nomenclature *(f)*

terrier * : fouineur *(m)*, furat *(m)* (policier tenace)

territorial : territorial

   ~ **division** : unité *(f)* territoriale, circonscription *(f)* policière

   ~ **waters** : eaux *(fpl)* territoriales

territory : territoire *(m)*

terror : terreur *(f)*, épouvante *(f)*

terrorism : terrorisme *(m)*

terrorist : terroriste *(m&f)*

terrorize : terroriser

test : épreuve *(f)*, essai *(m)*, examen *(m)*, test *(m)*; (2) mettre à l'essai, essayer, mettre à l'épreuve

   blood ~ : analyse *(f)* de sang

   driving ~ : examen de permis de conduire

   ~ **case** : cas dont la solution fait jurisprudence

testify : rendre témoignage *(m)*, témoigner

testimonial : attestation *(f)*

testimony : déposition *(f)*, témoignage *(m)*

text : libellé *(m)*, texte *(m)*

   ~ **book** : manuel *(m)*

theft : vol *(m)*

   petty ~ : vol minime

   ~ **by mobbing** : vol à l'encerclement

   ~ **from motor vehicle** : vol à la roulotte, vol dans une voiture

   ~ **from the person** : vol à la tâche, vol à la fourchette

   ~ **of a motor vehicle** : vol d'une voiture

theory : théorie *(f)*, thèse *(f)*, hypothèse *(f)*

there : là, y

   ~**after** : après cela, par la suite

   ~**from** : de là, de cela, de ceci

~**inafter** : plus loin, plus bas, ci-dessous

~**of** : dudit, de la dite

thermal imaging : thermographie *(f)*

thick : épais, gros

~ **as two short planks** * : bête comme ses pieds *

~ **skinned** : peu sensible

thief : voleur *(m)*, arcan *(m)*, larron *(m)*

thin : fin, mince, maigre

~ **out** : se disperser

thing : chose *(f)*, objet *(m)*, affaire *(f)*, article *(m)*

think tank : laboratoire *(m)* d'idées, groupe *(m)* de réflexion

third : troisième

~ **degree** : tabassage *(m)* *, passage *(m)* à tabac *

~**-party** : tiers, tierce personne, autrui

~ **party insurance** : assurance *(f)* en responsabilité civile

third world : tiers-monde *(m)*

thorough : complet, absolu, achevé, approfondi

~ **enquiry** : enquête *(f)* approfondie

~ **measures** : mesures *(fpl)* radicales

thrashing : raclée *(f)*, tatouille *(f)*, trempe *(f)*

threat : menace *(f)*, outrage *(m)*, intimidation *(f)*

threaten : menacer

threatening : menaçant

~ **behaviour** : conduite *(f)* menaçante

~ **letter** : lettre *(f)* comminatoire

~ **words** : menaces *(fpl)* verbales

three : trois

~**-card trick** : jeu *(m)* de bonneteau

~ **shift system** : trois-huit (système de trois équipes de huit heures)

threshold : seuil *(m)*

throat : gorge *(f)*,

throttle : (1) serrer la gorge; (2) papillon *(m)* de gaz, accélérateur *(m)*

at full ~ : à pleins gaz

throughout : durant

throw : jeter, lancer

~ **one's weight about** : faire l'important

~ **out** : rejeter, repousser

~ **up** * : vomir

thug : voyou *(m)*, gangster *(m)*, casseur *(m)*

thumb : pouce *(m)*

rule of ~ : d'une façon empirique

~ **a lift** : faire du stop

~ **print** : empreinte *(f)* digitale

~ **screws** : poucettes *(fpl)*

thwart : contrecarrer

ticket : billet *(m)*, ticket *(m)*, contravention *(f)*, papillon * *(m)*

~ **of leave** : tutelle *(f)* pénale

tick over : tourner au ralenti

tide : marée *(f)*

high/low ~ : marée haute/basse

tie :   lien *(m)*; nouer, ficeler, lier;   cravate *(f)*

~**-up** : ligoter

tight * : soûl *, gris *, rond *

till : tiroir-caisse *(m)*, caisse *(f)* enregistreuse

tilt : bâche *(f)*

time : temps *(m)*

    period of ~ : délai *(m)*

    ~ immemorial : de temps immémorial
        Dans le sens du droit coutumier, fixé à l'an 1189.

    ~ limit : délai *(m)*, péremption *(f)*

    ~table : horaire *(m)*, ordre *(m)* du jour

    to do ~ : faire de la prison

timer (for explosives) : minuteur *(m)*

tip : (1) pourboire *(m)*, gratification *(f)*, cadeau *(m)*; (2) tuyau *(m)*

    ~-off : avertir, prévenir (par une dénonciation)

tipper lorry : camion *(m)* à benne basculante

tip–off : coupure *(f)*

tipsy * : allumé *, attendri *

T–junction : embranchement *(m)*

tobacco : tabac *(m)*
    La vente de tabac aux mineurs de moins de 16 ans est interdite.

toe the line : marcher droit

together : ensemble

    get ~ : se réunir

token : (1) jeton *(m)*; (2) symbolique, nominal, fictif

    ~ salary : salaire *(m)* nominal

    ~ strike : grève *(f)* symbolique

tolerance (to drugs, etc.) : accoutumance *(f)*, tolérance *(f)*

toll : péage *(m)*

    ~ booth : péage *(m)*

    ~ bridge : pont *(m)* à péage

    ~ motorway : autoroute *(f)* à péage

    ~ of the roads : mortalité *(f)* sur les routes

tom * : catin *(f)*, demi-mondaine *(f)*, prostituée *(f)*

tonneau : couvre-capote *(m)*

tool : outil *(m)*, instrument *(m)*

tooled-up * : enfouraillé *

top : haut *(m)*, partie *(f)* supérieure, sommet *(m)*

    ~-brass * : hiérarque *(m)*, les huiles * *(fpl)*

    ~less : aux seins *(mpl)* nus

    ~ secret : ultra-secret

    ~-security prison : prison *(f)* centrale

torch : lampe *(f)* de poche, torche *(f)* électrique

tort : injure *(f)*, préjudice *(m)*

torture : torture *(f)*

torturer : bourreau *(m)*

totalisator : pari-mutuel *(m)*

totting-up : faisant le total, l'addition
*Les contraventions aux **Road Traffic Acts** provoquent une peine supplémentaire qui consiste en l'allocation de points de pénalisation. Une fois
un total donné atteint, le permis peut être suspendu pour une période
déterminée.*

touch : toucher

    ~ off : déclencher

tough : (1) robuste, résistant; (2) dur *(m)*

tourist : touriste *(m)*

    ~ agency : agence *(f)* de voyages

    ~ office : office *(m)* de tourisme, syndicat *(m)* d'initiatif

tout : batteur *(m)*, rabatteur *(m)*, racoleur * *(m)*

tow : remorquage

    ~away zone : zone *(f)* de stationnement interdit avec mise en fourrière

    ~-rag * : fripouille *(f)*, vaurien *(m)*, crapule *(m)*

    ~ rope : cable *(m)* de remorquage

towing unit : camion-tracteur *(m)*, tracteur *(m)* routier

town : ville *(f)*, commune *(f)*, cité *(f)*

    new ~ : ville nouvelle

    ~ clerk : secrétaire *(m&f)* de mairie

    ~ council : conseil *(m)* municipal

    ~ hall : hôtel *(m)* de ville, mairie *(f)*

    ~ planning : urbanisme *(m)*

trace : filière *(f)*

track : filière *(f)*, piste *(f)*, trace *(f)*, voie *(f)*

    ~ down : traquer

    ~ suit : jogging *(m)*

tractor : tracteur *(m)*, camion-tracteur *(m)*, tracteur *(m)* routier

trade : métier *(m)*, commerce *(m)*, trafic *(m)*, négoce *(m)*

    ~ description : appellation *(f)* de commerce
        Une loi de 1968 protège les consommateurs contre la publicité et les
        appellations mensongères.

    ~ directory : bottin *(m)*

    ~ dispute : conflit *(m)* entre le patronat et les ouvriers

    ~ mark : marque *(f)* déposée

    ~ union : syndicat *(m)*

trader : marchand *(m)*, commerçant *(m)*, négociant *(m)*

tradesman : artisan *(m)*

tradition : tradition *(f)*

traffic : (1) circulation *(f)* routière, trafic *(m)*; (2) trafiquer, négocier

    drug ~ : trafic de stupéfiants

    road ~ : circulation routière

    ~ accident : accident *(m)* de circulation

    ~ cone : balise *(f)*, biroute *(f)*

    ~ division : groupement *(m)* de police de la route

    ~ flow : flot *(m)* de circulation, flux *(m)* routier

~ **hold-up** : bouchon *(m)*, embouteillage *(m)*

~ **island** : refuge *(m)*

~ **jam** : bouchon *(m)*, embouteillage *(m)*

~ **lights** : feu *(m)* de circulation, feu *(m)* rouge, feu *(m)* tricolore

~ **patrol section** : peloton *(m)* motorisé

~ **ramp** : bande *(f)* ralentisseuse

~ **regulations** : police *(f)* de la voirie, code *(m)* de la route

~ **sign** : panneau *(m)* de signalisation

~ **warden** : contractuel (-le) *(m&f)*

white slave ~ : traite *(f)* des blanches

trail : piste *(f)*

trailer : remorque *(f)*

train : (1) train; (2) former

trainee : apprenti *(m)*, stagiaire *(f)*

trainers : joggers *(mpl)*

training : formation *(f)*, éducation *(f)*, entraînement *(m)*, instruction *(f)*

further ~ : formation continue

on-the-job ~ : formation pratique

physical ~ : entraînement physique

road safety ~ : éducation routière

~ **centre** : école *(f)*, centre *(m)* de formation

~ **department** : service *(m)* de formation de personnel

~ **leave** : congé-formation *(m)*

vocational ~ : formation professionnelle

traitor : traître *(m)*

tramp : clochard *(m)*, vagabond *(m)*

transaction : transaction *(f)*

transcript : transcription *(f)* en clair d'un sténogramme d'une audience

transfer : (1) mutation *(f)*; (2) virer, transférer

    ~ funds : virer des fonds

transgress : enfreindre, transgresser, violer

transgression : offense *(f)*, faute *(f)*

transient : transitoire, passager, éphémère

    ~ effect : effet *(m)* transitoire

transit : transit *(m)*, passage *(m)*

transitory : passager, transitoire, fugitif

translate : traduire

translation : traduction *(f)*

translator : traducteur *(m)*, traductrice *(f)*

    sworn ~ : traducteur assermenté

transmission (radio) : transmission *(f)*

transmit : émettre, diffuser

transmitter : émetteur *(m)*

transparency : diapositive *(f)*

transport : (1) transport *(m)*, (2) transporter

    road ~ : transport routier

transportation (penalty) : relégation *(f)*

transporter : entrepreneur *(m)* de transports

trap : piège *(m)*, guet–apens *(m)*

travel : (1) déplacement *(m)*, voyage *(m)*; (2) voyager, faire un voyage

    ~ agency : agence *(f)* de voyage

    ~ expenses : frais *(mpl)* de déplacement

traveller's cheque : chèque *(m)* de voyage

travelling fair : foire *(f)* foraine

tread pattern : profil *(m)*, sculpture *(f)* (de pneu)

treason : atteinte *(f)* à la sûreté de l'Etat, trahison *(f)*

treasure trove : trésor *(m)* (dont le propriétaire est inconnu)

treasury : trésor *(m)*, ministère *(m)* des Finances

trend : tendance *(f)*, orientation *(f)*

trespass : (1) atteinte *(f)* au droit de propriété, violation *(f)* de propriété, entrée non autorisée; (2) s'introduire sans permission

    criminal ~ : violation de domicile

trespasser : intrus *(m)*

trial : (1) audition *(f)*, débats *(mpl)* judiciaires, procès *(m)*; (2) essai *(m)*, épreuve *(f)*

    awaiting ~ : en instance de jugement

    committal for ~ : mise *(f)* en accusation

    criminal ~ : procès criminel

    held for ~ : prévenu

    ~ by jury : jugement *(m)* par jury

tribunal : tribunal *(m)*, conseil *(m)*

trick : artifice *(m)*, ruse *(f)*, strategème *(m)*

trigger : détente *(f)*, gâchette *(f)*

    ~-happy : à la gâchette facile, prêt à tirer pour un rien

    ~ off : déclencher, provoquer

trilby : feutre *(m)*

trip : (1) voyage *(m)*, excursion *(f)*; (2) (drogues) trip *(m)* *

triplicate : triplicata *(m)*

trivial : insignifiant, dérisoire

trouble : peine *(f)*, souci *(m)*, dérangement *(m)*, ennuis *(mpl)*

    ~ spot : point *(m)* de conflit

truck : camion *(m)*

true : effectif, vrai, exact

    certified ~ copy : pour copie *(f)* conforme

    ~ copy : copie *(f)* conforme

~ **owner** : propriétaire *(m)* légitime

trump up (a charge) : forger une accusation, déposer une fausse plainte

truncheon : bâton *(m)*, matraque *(f)*

trust : confiance *(f)*

trusteeship : curatelle *(f)*

trustworthy : digne de confiance

truth : vérité *(f)*

the ~, **the whole** ~ **and nothing but the** ~ : la vérité, toute la vérité et rien que la vérité

try : (1) juger; (2) essayer, éprouver, expérimenter

turning : route *(f)* latérale

turn off : embranchement *(m)*

turn Queen's Evidence : bonir
Porter témoignage contre ses complices.

turnstile : guichet *(m)*

turnover : chiffre *(m)* d'affaires

staff ~ : renouvellement *(m)* du personnel

turpitude : turpitude *(f)*

twist–grip : poignée *(f)* tournante/d'accélération

two–stroke : deux-temps *(m)*

two–tone horn : avertisseur *(m)* à deux tons

type : taper (à la machine)

typing : dactylographie *(f)*

typist : dactylo *(m&f)*, dactylographe *(m&f)*

shorthand– ~ : sténo-dactylo *(m&f)*

typewriter : machine *(f)* à écrire

tyre : pneu *(m)*

~ **pressure** : pression de gonflage

U

ugly : laid, vilain

    ~ **customer** : os *

Ulster : Ulster (Irlande du Nord)

ultra high frequency (UHF) : hyperfréquence *(f)*

ultralight (aircraft) : ultra-léger *(m)* (motorisé)

ultrasonic : ultrasonique, ultrasons

ultra vires : au-delà de (leurs) pouvoirs, hors de (leur) compétence

unaccompanied : non accompagné

    ~ **learner driver** : conducteur *(m)* non-qualifié sans moniteur

unaccounted for : non expliqué, non retrouvé

unallotted : non réparti

unaltered : inchangé

unanimous : unanime

unarmed : non armé

unassailable : inattaquable

unauthorised : abusif, sans autorisation, non autorisé

unavoidable : incontournable

unavoidability : état *(m)* de nécessité

unbalanced : déséquilibré

unbiased : désintéressé

unblemished : sans tache

unbridled : non contrôlé, débridé, déchaîné

uncertainty : doute *(m)*, incertitude *(f)*

unchallenged (witness) : (témoin) non récusé

unchanged : inchangé

unchecked : non contrôlé, non vérifié

unclaimed : non réclamé

unclothed : sans vêtements, nu

unconditionally : à discrétion, sans réserve

unconscious : sans connaissance

uncontested : incontesté

uncontrollable : non contrôlable

uncooperative : peu coopératif

uncorroborated : non corroboré

uncouple : détacher

uncouth : grossier, fruste

uncover : découvrir

undefended : sans défense

  ˜ **prisoner** : accusé *(m)* comparaissant sans avocat

undeniable : incontestable

under : sous, en vertu de, aux termes de, d'après

  ˜ **age** : enfant *(m&f)* mineur(e)

  ˜ **estimation** : sous-estimation *(f)*

  ˜ **oath** : assermenté, sous serment

  ˜ **penalty/pain of** : à peine de

  ˜ **sub-section 4** : aux termes du paragraphe 4

underclothes : sous-vêtements *(mpl)*

undercover : secret, clandestin

under-developed : sous-développé

under-employment : sous-emploi *(m)*

undergo : subir

Underground : Métropolitain *(m)*

underhand : sournois

underlying : fondamental

undermanned : à court de personnel

under-mentioned : sous-dit *(m)*

undersecretary : sous-secrétaire *(m&f)* d'état, adjoint *(m)* de ministre

undersigned : soussigné *(m)*

understaffed : à court de personnel

understand : entendre, comprendre

understanding : accord *(m)*, entente *(f)*

understeer : sous-virage *(m)*

understudy : doublure *(f)*

undertake : s'engager

undertaker : entrepreneur *(m)* de pompes funèbres

undertaking : entreprise *(f)*, engagement *(m)*, promesse *(f)*

underwater : sous-marin, sous l'eau

    ~ **search and recovery unit** : unité *(f)* des hommes-grenouilles

underworld : le milieu *(m)*, pègre *(f)*

underwriter : assureur *(m)*

undesirable : peu souhaitable, indésirable

    ~ **alien** : étranger *(m)* indésirable

undetected : non décelé, non détecté

    ~ **crime** : crime *(m)* dont l'auteur reste inconnu

undisclosed : caché, occulte

undisturbed : non dérangé, non déplacé

undone : défait

undue : illégitime, indu

    ~ **influence** : intimidation *(f)*

unduly : à tort, sans raison, illégalement

unemployed : en inactivité

    ~ **person** : chômeur *(m)*

unemployment : chômage *(m)*

    ~ benefit : allocation *(f)* de chômage, solde *(f)* de non-activité

unexpected : imprévu

    ~ problem : os * *(m)*

unexploded bomb : bombe *(f)* non explosée

unfair : déloyal, inéquitable

    ~ dismissal : licenciement *(m)* abusif/injustifié

unfashionable : démodé

unfit : inapte, impropre, qui n'est pas en forme

    ~ for work : pas en état de reprendre le travail, incapable de travailler

    ~ to drive : pas en état de conduire

    ~ to plead : pas en état de plaider

unforeseen : imprévu

    ~ circumstances : cas imprévu, force *(f)* majeure

unfounded : sans fondement, injustifié

    ~ appeal : fol appel *(m)*

unfriendly : inamical

unharmed : indemne, sain et sauf

unhurt : indemne

unidentified : non-identifié

uniform : tenue *(f)*, uniforme *(m)*
    Le port des uniformes politiques est interdit.

uniformed : en tenue, habillé

unimpeachable : indéboulonnable

unimportant : sans importance

unintentional offence : infraction *(f)* praeterintentionnelle

union (trade ~) : syndicat *(m)*

unique reference number : numéro *(m)* de référence unique

unit : groupe *(m)*, unité *(f)*

United Kingdom : Royaume-Uni *(m)*
  Comprennant l'Angleterre, le Pays de Galles, l'Ecosse et l'Ireland du Nord

United Nations : (Organisation des) Nations *(fpl)* Unies

United States of America (USA) : Etats-Unis *(mpl)* d'Amérique

universal declaration of human rights : déclaration *(f)* universelle des droits de l'homme

university : université *(f).*   ~ **degree** : licence *(f)*

unjust : injuste

unkempt : négligé, débraillé

unknown : inconnu

unlawful : anomique, illégal, illicite, contraire à la loi

 ~ **arrest** : arrestation illégale, détention *(f)* arbitraire

 ~ **assembly** : attroupement *(m)*, rassemblement *(m)* illicite

 ~ **entry** : entrée *(f)* dans le domicile d'autrui sans autorité légale

 ~ **means** : moyens *(mpl)* illicites

 ~ **sexual intercourse** : relations *(fpl)* sexuelles avec une mineure ou un aliéné

 ~ **wounding** : coups *(mpl)* et blessures *(fpl)* avec l'intention de mutiler

unlawfully : sans droit *(m)*, san motif *(m)* légal

 ~ **at large** : évadé, fugitif (de prison)

unless : à moins que

 ~ **otherwise provided** : sauf disposition *(f)* contraire

 ~ **I hear to the contrary** : sauf stipulation *(f)* contraire

unlicensed : illicite, non autorisé

unlikely : peu probable, peu plausible

unlimited : illimité

 ~ **liability** : responsabilité *(f)* illimitée

unlit : (lampe) non allumée, (route) non éclairée, (véh.) sans feux

unload : décharger

unloading : délestage *(m)*

unlock : ouvrir

unlocked : pas fermé à clef

unmanned : sans surveillance, non occupé

unmarked : sans tache, sans marque,

      ~ police car : voiture *(f)* banalisée

unmarried : célibataire

      ~ mother : fille-mère *(f)*

unnamed : innomé

unnatural offence : synonyme de **buggery**

unofficial : inofficiel, officieux, noir

      ~ strike : grève *(f)* sauvage (non déclenchée par les syndicats)

unpaid : bénévole, impayé

      ~ bill : drapeau *(m)* *

      ~ leave : congé *(m)* sans rémunération

unpickable (lock) : incrochetable

unprovoked : sans provocation

unquestionable : certain, incontestable

unreadable : indéchiffrable

unreasonable : excessif, démesuré

unrelated : n'ayant aucun rapport (avec)

unreservedly : sans réserve

unrestricted : illimité

unroadworthy : qui n'est pas en état de marche

unruly : mutin, indiscipliné

unscrupulous : sans scrupules, indélicat, malhonnête

unshakeable : indéboulonnable

unsolved case : affaire *(f)* classée

unsound : défectueux

~ **mind (person of ~)** : aliéné *(m)*, débile *(m)* mental

unsubstantial : immatériel

unsuccessful crime : délit *(m)* manqué

unsuitable : inapte

unsuspecting : qui ne se méfie pas

unsworn evidence : témoignage *(m)* sans serment
Peut être admis dans le cas d'un enfant d'âge tendre.

untrustworthy : véreux

unwarranted interference : ingérence *(f)*

unworkable : inexécutable

unwritten law : loi *(f)* non écrite, droit *(m)* coutumier et jurisprudentiel, ce qui
est   tacitement admis

update : réactualiser, mettre à jour

upheaval : bouleversement *(m)*

upkeep : entretien *(m)*

upon : sur

~ **application** : sur demande *(f)*

upper : (1) supérieur;   (2) (narcotiques) dopant *(m)* *, stimulant *(m)* *

uprising : soulèvement *(m)*, insurrection *(f)*, révolte*(f)*

uproar : clameur *(f)*, tapage *(m)*

upstairs : en haut (d'un escalier)

up-to-date : à jour

urban : urbain

~ **clearway** : axe *(m)* rouge

urgency : cas *(m)* de nécessité

urgent : urgent

~ **measure** : mesure *(f)* conservatoire

urine test : analyse *(f)* d'urine

use : usage *(m)*, emploi *(m)*, utilisation *(f)*

      personal ~ : à usage personnel

useful : utile

usefulness : utilité *(f)*

usher : huissier–audiencier *(m)*

usual : habituel

usually : d'habitude

usurpation : usurpation *(f)*

usury : usure *(f)*

utility : utilité *(f)*

      public ~ : service *(m)* public

uttering : écoulement *(m)*, émission *(f)* (de fausse monnaie)

V

vacancy : vacance *(f)*, poste *(m)* à pourvoir

vacation : vacances *(fpl)* judiciaires

vagabond : clochard *(m)*, vagabond *(m)*

vagrancy : vagabondage *(m)*

vagrant : itinérant *(m)*, vagabond *(m)*

valid : valide, régulier

valour : vertu *(f)*

value : valeur *(m)*

     ~ **added tax (VAT)** : taxe *(f)* à la valeur ajoutée (TVA)

van : fourgon *(m)*, camionnette *(f)*

vandal : vandal *(m)*, loulou *(m)*

vandalism : vandalisme *(m)*

vanish : disparaître, se volatiser

vault : chambre *(f)* forte

vehicle : véhicule *(m)*

     ~ **excise licence** : vignette *(f)*

     ~ **fleet** : parc *(m)* de véhicules

     ~ **registration document** : carte *(f)* grise

vending machine : distributeur *(m)* automatique

vengeance : rebiffe *(f)* *

venture : entreprise *(f)*

venue : lieu *(m)*, juridiction *(f)*

verbal : aveux *(mpl)* faits oralement

verdict : verdict *(m)*

    guilty ~ : verdict de culpabilité

    not guilty ~ : verdict d'acquittement

majority ~ : décision *(f)* prise par au moins 10 des 12 jurés (en l'absence de l'unanimité)

open ~ : jugement *(m)*, dans une enquête de **Coroner,** qui ne formule aucune conclusion sur les circonstances dans lesquelles la mort est survenue

verge : accotement *(m)*

very pistol : pistolet *(m)* lance-fusées

verification : contrôle *(m)*, récolement *(m)*, vérification *(f)*

verify : vérifier

veritable : vrai

versus : contre

vest : (1) gilet *(m)*; (2) investir d'un droit

bulletproof ~ : gilet pare-balles

~ **someone with authority** : revêtir quelqu'un d'une autorité

vet : (1) vétérinaire *(m&f)*; (2) examiner soigneusement

positive ~**ting** : enquête *(f)* de sécurité
Examen sérieux précédant l'autorisation d'accès aux données secrètes ou concernant la sûreté de l'état.

vice : vice *(m)*

~ **(and clubs) squad** : brigade *(f)* des moeurs, brigade *(f)* mondaine

vicinity : voisinage *(m)*, environs *(mpl)*

vicious : brutal, violent

victim : victime *(f)*, sinistré *(m)*

~ **support scheme** : système *(m)* benévole d'aide aux victimes des crimes

video : vidéo *(f)*, magnétoscope *(m)*, vidéocassette *(f)*

vigour : vigueur *(f)*

village square : placarde *(f)*

villain : malfaiteur *(m)*, truand *(m)*, scélérat *(m)*

vindication : justification *(f)*

violate : violer

violation : abus *(m)*, violation *(f)*

violence : violence *(f)*, rififi *(m)* *

      resort to ˜ : se livrer à des voies de fait

violent : violent

      ˜ disorder : rixe *(f)*, ou menace *(f)* de troubles, dans laquelle au moins trois personnes sont impliquées

VIP : gros bonnet *(m)*

virtue : vertu *(f)*, qualité *(f)*

      by ˜ of : en vertu de

visit : (1) visite *(f)*; (2) se rendre, aller voir

      ˜ to the scene of the crime : descente *(f)* sur les lieux

visor : garde-vue *(m)*, visière *(f)*

vitriol : vitriol *(m)*

vocational : professionnel

      ˜ guidance : orientation professionnelle

      ˜ training : formation professionnelle

void : nul

volition : volonté *(f)*

      act of ˜ : acte *(m)* délibéré

Volkswagen (VW) : vévé *(f)* *

voluntarily : volontairement

voluntary : bénévole, volontaire, spontané

      ˜ statement : déclaration *(f)* faite volontairement

volunteer : volontaire *(m&f)*, bénévole *(m&f)*

vote : (1) voix *(f)*; (2) voter

voucher : bon *(m)*, fiche *(f)*

voyeur : voyeur *(m)*

vulnerable : vulnérable

W

wad : liasse *(f)*

wage differentials : grille *(f)* des salaires

wager : enjeu *(m)*, pari *(m)*

wages : salaire *(m)*, paye *(f)*, paie *(f)*

waif : enfant *(m&f)* abandonné(e)

waistcoat : gilet *(m)*

      bullet-proof ~ : gilet pare-balles

wait : (1) attente *(f)*; (2) attendre

      lying in ~ : guet-apens

waiter : garçon *(m)* de café

waitress : serveuse *(f)*

waive : déroger, renoncer

waiver : dispense *(f)*

walkie-talkie : talkie-walkie *(m)*

walk-out : faire grève *(f)*

      to stage a ~ : débrayer, organiser une grève, un débrayage

walrus moustache : moustache *(f)* à la gauloise

wandering : itinérant

wander-light : baladeuse *(f)*

wanted : recherché par la police

      situations ~ : demandes *(fpl)* d'emploi (dans la presse)

      ~ **person index** : fiche *(f)* des personnes recherchées

war : guerre *(f)*

ward : (1) canton *(m)*; (2) pupille *(m&f)*

warden : directeur *(m)*, directrice *(f)*

warder : gardien *(m)* de prison

warehouse : entrepôt *(m)*, magasin *(m)*

wares : marchandises *(fpl)*

warn : prévenir, avertir, alerter

warning : avertissement *(m)*, mise *(f)* en garde

warrant : mandat *(m)*, ordre *(m)*

     arrest ~ : mandat d'amener

     search ~ : mandat de perquisition

warranted : justifiable

watch : (1) guet *(m)*, surveillance *(f)*; (2) repérer

     to keep a close ~ on : surveiller de près

     to be on the ~ for : guetter

     ~ committee : commission municipale de surveillance de la police

     ~ dog : chien *(m)* de garde

     ~man : garde *(m)*

water–bailiff : garde-pêche *(m)*

water–cannon : autopompe *(f)*, arroseuse *(f)*

water–tight case : cas *(m)* d'espèce

way : voie *(f)*, route *(f)*, chemin *(m)*

     by ~ of : sous forme de

     ~–in : entrée *(f)*

     ~s and means : voies *(fpl)* et moyens *(mpl)*

weak : faible

weakness : faiblesse *(f)*

weal (the public ~) : le bien *(m)* public

wealth : richesse *(f)*

weaning : sevrage *(m)*

weapon : arme *(f)*

wear and tear : dégradation *(f)*, usure *(f)* normale, déterioration *(f)*

wearing : port *(m)*

weekly : hebdomadaire

    ~ **return** : bilan *(m)* hebdomadaire

weighbridge : pont-bascule *(m)*

welfare : bien-être *(m)*

Welsh : gallois

welsh : lever le pied * (en emportant l'enjeu de quelqu'un)

wharf : quai *(m)*, embarcadère *(m)*

wheel : roue *(m)*

    ~ **clamp** : sabot *(m)* d'Anvers

    spare ~ : roue *(f)* de secours

wheels * : guinde *(f)*

where : où, lorsque, quand, au cas où

whereas : attendu (que), considérant, vu que

whereby : en vertu de, par le fait que

wherefore : par conséquent, pourquoi

whiplash : coup *(m)* du lapin*, syndrome *(m)* cervical traumatique

whip–out : sortir brusquement

whip-round * : collecte *(f)*

whisky : scotch *(m)*

white : blanc

    ~-**collar crime** : délinquance *(f)* en col-blanc, criminalité *(f)* d'affaires

    ~-**collar worker** : col-blanc *(m)*, employé *(m)* de bureau

    ~ **line** : bande *(f)* matérialisée

    ~ **slave trader** : marchand *(m)* de viande

    ~ **slave traffic** : trafic *(m)* d'êtres humains

whole : plein

wholesale : vente *(f)* en gros

whore : putain * *(f)*

Who's Who? : bottin *(m)* mondain

wicked : mauvais, méchant, vilain

widow : veuve *(f)*

widower : veuf *(m)*

wife : épouse *(f)*, femme *(f)*

wilco : message reçu et sera observé

wild : sauvage

    ~-cat strike : grève *(f)* sauvage

wilful : intentionnel, volontaire, destiné, prémédité

    ~ damage : dommage intentionnel

wilfully : volontairement

will : (1) volonté *(f)*; (2) testament *(m)*

willie * : zizi * *(m)*

winch : treuil *(m)*

    ~ up (by helicopter) : hélitreuiller

wind down : baisser (la vitre), ouvrir (la fenêtre)

windfall : fruit *(m)* abattu par le vent, aubaine *(f)*, manne *(f)* (tombée du ciel)

winding-up : liquidation *(f)* d'une société

windscreen/windshield : pare-brise *(m)*

    ~ wiper : essuie-glace *(m)*

wind up : (1) monter, fermer (la fenêtre)

    it's a ~ * : on vous taquine, c'est une blague

wine bar : bistro *(m)*

wing : aile *(f)*

witchcraft : sorcellerie *(f)*

witch hunt : chasse *(f)* aux sorcières

withdraw : se désister, retracter, soustraire

withdrawal : déchéance *(f)*, mainlevée *(f)*, retraite *(m)*

    ~ of a complaint : retrait d'une plainte

    ~ symptoms : manque *(m)*, symptômes *(mpl)* de sevrage

withholding : refus *(m)*, détention *(f)*, rétention *(f)*

    ~ the truth : dissimulation *(f)* de la vérité

within : sous, dans, au cours de

    ~ the meaning of section 2 : au sens de l'article 2

without : sans

    ~ prejudice : sous réserve, sans préjudice

witness : témoin *(m)*

    eye ~ : témoin oculaire

    false ~ : faux témoin

    hostile ~ : témoin se révélant hostile à la partie qui l'a convoqué

    material ~ : témoin de fait

    reluctant ~ : témoin réticent

    to bribe, suborn, tamper with a ~ : suborner un témoin

    ~ box : barre des témoins

    ~ for the defence : témoin à décharge

    ~ for the prosecution : témoin à charge, fargueur

    ~ statement : déposition *(f)*

    ~ summons : collante *(f)*

wog * : sale étranger *(m)*, métèque * *(m)*

woman : femme *(f)*

Womens' Lib. : mouvement *(m)* de libération de la femme (MLF)

Woolsack : le Sac de Laine
    Siège du Lord Chancellor à la Chambre des Lords.

wording : libellé *(m)*

work : travail *(m)*

    ~–out : (1) entrainement *(m)* physique; (2) sporter; (3) élaborer, étudier

    ~ permit : permis *(m)* de travail

    ~s : travaux

    ~ to rule : grève *(f)* du zèle

worker : ouvrier *(m)*

    semi–skilled ~ : ouvrier spécialisé

    skilled ~ : ouvrier qualifié

    ~s' representative : délégué *(m)* du personnel

working : de travail, actif, qui marche

    ~ class : classe *(f)* ouvrière

    ~ day : jour *(m)* ouvrable

    ~ party : groupe *(m)* de travail

    ~ week : semaine *(f)* de travail

workman : ouvrier *(m)*

    ~s hut : guitoune *(f)*

workshop : atelier *(m)*

worry : (1) souci *(m)*; (2) s'inquiéter; (3) harceler

wound : (1) blesser, léser; (2) blessure *(f)*

wounding : coups *(mpl)* et blessures *(fpl)*, mutilation *(f)*

    ~ with intent : blessure *(f)* voluntaire

wreck : épave *(f)*, voiture *(f)* accidentée

wrecked : sinistré

wrestle : lutter corps à corps

    to ~ with a problem : se débattre avec un problème

writ : acte *(m)* de procédure, acte *(m)* de signification, demande *(f)* en justice

    ~ of attachment : exploit *(m)* de saisie

    ~ of summons : assignation *(f)*

write : écrire

    ~ **down** : consigner par écrit

    ~ **off** : amortir, défalquer

writing : écrit *(m)*

wrong : (1) mal *(m)*, tort *(m)*, injure *(f)*, lésion *(f)*, préjudice *(m)*, injustice *(f)*; (2) léser;   (3) erroné, faux

wrongful : injustifié

    ~ **arrest** : arrestation *(f)* arbitraire

    ~ **dismissal** : renvoi *(m)* injustifié

wrongfully : à tort

X

x-ray : rayon *(m)* X, radiographie *(f)*

Y

yard : chantier *(m)*, cour *(f)*

year : an *(m)*, année *(f)*

    calendar ~ : année civile

yearly : annuel

yeomanry : régiment *(m)* de cavalerie (volontaire)

yob * : voyou *(m)*, agrinche *(m)*, petit caïd *(m)*

yobbo * : loulou *(m)*, blouson *(m)* noir

yokel : rustre *(m)*, péquenaud *(m)*

young offender : jeune adulte délinquant *(m)*

young offenders institution : centre *(m)* de détention pour mineurs

youth : jeunesse *(f)*

    ~ custody centre : centre *(m)* pénitentier pour les jeunes de 15 à 20 ans.

    ~ hostel : auberge *(f)* de jeunesse

Z

zebra crossing : passage *(m)* (pour) piétons, passage *(m)* clouté

zero : zéro

    ~ hour : heure H

zip fastener : fermeture *(f)* éclair

ACRONYMS

A.A.	Automobile Association, Alcoholics Anonymous
A.B.H.	Actual Bodily Harm
A.F.I.S.	Automatic Fingerprint Identification System
A.R.V.	Armed Response Vehicle
A.S.F.	Automatic Search Facility
C.C.T.V.	Closed Circuit Television
C.I.D.	Criminal Investigation Department
C.O.T.	Computerised Organic Tracer
C.P.S.	Crown Prosecution Service
C.P.U.	Central Planning Unit
C.R.O.	Criminal Record Office
D.E.A.	Drugs Enforcement Agency
D.N.A.	Deoxyribonucleic Acid (Genetic Molecule in Body Fluids)
E.C.	European Community
E.C.S.T.	European Convention for the Suppression of Terrorism
F.A.C.E.S.	Facial Analysis Comparison & Elimination System
F.A.R.	False Alarm Rate
F.B.I.	Federal Bureau of Investigation
F.L.I.R.	Forward-looking Infra-red
G.B.H.	Grievous bodily harm
H.E.D.	Hydrogenous Explosive Detection
H.G.V.	Heavy goods vehicle
H.M.C.I.	Her Majesty's Chief Inspector of Constabulary
H.M.I.	Her Majesty's Inspector of Constabulary
H.O.L.M.E.S.	Home Office Large & Major Enquiry System
H.Q.	Headquarters
I.D.	Identity
I.R.A.	Irish Republican Army
L.F.C.	Local Force Computer
L.G.M.B.	Local Government Management Board
L.I.O.	Local Intelligence Officer
M.I.5	Military Intelligence, Section 5 (British Domestic Intelligence Service)
M.I.6	Military Intelligence, Section 6 (British Foreign Intelligence Service)
M.P.	Member of Parliament, Military Police(man)
M.S.X.	Message Switch Exchange
N.A.T.O.	North Atlantic Treaty Organisation
N.C.I.S.	National Criminal Intelligence Service
N.D.I.U.	National Drugs Intelligence Unit
N.F.I.U.	National Football Intelligence Unit
N.I.X.	Criminal Intelligence Computer System
O.S.P.R.E.	System of Promotion Examinations
P.A.C.E.	Police & Criminal Evidence Act
P.I.N.	Personal Identification Number
P.L.C.	Public Limited Company
P.M.	Post-mortem examination
P.N.C.	Police National Computer
P.P.	Per Pro
P.R.	Public Relations
P.S.V.	Public Service Vehicle
P.T.17	Police Firearms Team
Q.C.	Queen's Counsel
R.& P.	Research and Planning

R.A.C.	Royal Automobile Club
R.C.I.O.	Regional Criminal Intelligence Office
R.C.S.	Regional Crime Squad
R.I.O.	Regional Intelligence Officer
R.T.A.	Road traffic accident, Road Traffic Act
R.U.C.	Royal Ulster Constabulary
S.A.P.S.	Skill-assessment Processing System
S.A.S.	Special Air Services Regiment
S.E.A.	Single European Act
S.P.G.	Special Patrol Group
S.W.A.T.	Special Weapons and Tactics Team
T.D.A.	Taking and Driving away
T.I.C.	Taken Into Consideration
T.S.G.	Tactical Support Group
U.D.R.	Ulster Defence Regiment
U.H.F.	Ultra-High Frequency
U.N.	United Nations
U.S.A.	United States of America
V.A.T.	Value Added Tax
V.C.R.	Video Cassette Recorder
V.E.L.	Vehicle Excise Licence
V.H.F.	Very High Frequency
V.I.P.	Very Important Person
W.P.C.	Woman Police Constable
W.R.V.S.	Womens Royal Voluntary Service
Y.H.A.	Youth Hostels Association

FRANÇAIS - ANGLAIS

FRENCH - ENGLISH

A

abaissement (m) : demotion

abandon (m) **de famille** : desertion of family
Misdemeanour committed by (i) a parent who leaves the family home, thus avoiding his or her parental responsibilities, (ii) the desertion of an expectant mother by her husband, (iii) the moral abandonment of children by the mother and father, thus endangering their health, safety or moral welfare, or (iv) failure to pay maintenance determined by a court.

abattage (m) * : (1) reprimand, bollocking*; (2) winning throw at **passe-anglaise,** an underworld dice game; (3) stall goods displayed in the open air

~ **d'arbres** : felling or damaging trees
It is an offence to fell, mutilate, cut or debark so as to cause to die, any tree belonging to another. Tree includes shrubs such as roses and vines.

maison d'~ * : brothel, cat-house

abbaye (f) **de Monte-à-regret** * : guillotine

abbesse (f) * : "madam" of a brothel

aberration (f) : aberration.   ~ **mentale** : insanity

abjurer : to forswear

abloquer * : to hand over money (as in a mugging)

abolir : to suppress, to abolish

abolition (f) : abolishment, abolition, repeal (of a decree)

à bon droit : lawfully, rightfully

abortifs (fourniture de moyens ~) : supplying the means to procure an abortion

abouler * : to hand over, to give

aboyeur (m) * : (1) shooter*, hand gun; (2) fairground barker, nightclub tout

abraquer * : to obtain by force or deception

abréger (des debats) : to summarize (proceedings)

abreuvoir (m) * : pub, "local" (from the nickname given by lawyers to the bar in the Palais de Justice in Paris)

abri (m) : shelter.   **sans** ~ : homeless

abrogation (f) : abrogation, cancellation, rescission

    ~ **d'une loi** : repeal of a law

absent (m) : an individual unheard of for 7 years and thus presumed dead

absolution (f) : see **excuse absolutoire**

absolutoire : absolving.   **decision** (f) ~ : acquittal

s'abstenir (de) : to refrain (from)

abstention (f) **délicteuse** : see **non-assistance à une personne en danger**

abus (m) : abuse, misuse, infringement, violation

    ~ **d'autorité** : misuse of authority
        Moral pressure brought to bear to cause a person to complete a legal document. It constitutes a defect of consent and renders the document nul and void.

    ~ **de biens sociaux** : misuse of corporate assets
        Misdemeanour committed by a director of a company who wilfully applies the property or stock in trade of that company to a purpose which he knows is not in the company's best interest, for his own use or for the benefit of another firm in which he has an interest.

    ~ **de blanc-seing** : misuse of a blank, signed document
        Offence committed by a person who inserts fraudulent details above a signature to the prejudice of the signatory. Punishable as fraud or false pretences where committed by the person to whom the document has been entrusted, and as forgery in all other cases.

    ~ **de confiance** : misappropriation, embezzlement
        Misdemeanour committed by a person who misappropriates or disposes of property previously entrusted to him by way of lease, deposit, mandate, rental or loaned to him for his use as an employee or otherwise.

    ~ **de droit** : abuse of a right, misuse of the law, abuse of process

    ~ **de droits** : infringement of rights

    ~ **de la puissance paternelle** : misuse of parental authority

    ~ **de pouvoir** : abuse of discretion, *ultra vires*

    commettre un ~ **de pouvoir** : to over-ride one's commission

    reformer un ~ : to redress an abuse

abuser : to misuse, to deceive, to act improperly

    ~ **d'une fille** : to sexually assault a girl

abusif : improper, unauthorised

abusivement : improperly, fraudulently

acagnarder/accagnarder * : to lie low, to hide

accès (m) : access, approach

      ~ de service : service road

      droit d'~ : right of access

      voies d'~ : approaches

accident (m) : accident

      ~ corporel : personal injury accident

      ~ de la circulation : road traffic accident

      ~ de personne : personal injury accident

      ~ du travail : industrial accident

      ~ mortel : fatal accident

      constat d'~ : accident report

      par ~ : fortuitously

accidentel : accidental

accidenté (m) : casualty, victim of an accident, the damaged vehicle

accipiens (m) : the beneficiary

accise (f) : excise.   **droits d'~** : excise duties

accommoder * : to beat up (someone), to verbally abuse (someone), to (mis)use

accomplissement (m) : accomplishment, achievement, carrying out

      dans l'~ de ses devoirs : in the exercise of one's duties, whilst on duty

accordéon (m) * : string of convictions, a long record (of convictions)

accorder : to allow, to grant.   **~ une autorisation** : to license

accordeur (m) **des flûtes** * : magistrate

accoucher * : to confess, to "come clean", to own up

accoutumance (f) : tolerance (to a drug), habit formation

accoutumé : customary

accroc (m) : hitch, snag

accrochage (m) * : (1) prang*, scrape (of cars); (2) clinch (in boxing); (3) skirmish, set-to, argument

accroché * : hooked, addicted (to drugs)

accroche-coeur (m) : kiss-curl

accrocher * : (1) to nick*, to arrest someone; (2) to prang* (motor vehicle); (3) to hock, to pawn

~ un paletot : to lie, to tell a fib

accusateur (m) : accuser.

~ privé : plaintiff

~ public : public prosecutor

accusation (f) : accusation, charge, prosecution

acte d'~ : bill of indictment, charge

chef d'~ : count of indictment, particulars of a charge

l' ~ : the case for the prosecution

mise en ~ : arraignment, committal for trial

accusatoire : see procedure accusatoire

accusé (m) : the accused, the prisoner, the defendant
Person charged with having committed a felony and brought before the court of assize for trial.

~ défaillant/contumax : absconder

~ de réception : proof of delivery

accuser : to accuse, to charge with a crime

à faux : to accuse falsely

~ le coup * : to flinch, to show a reaction, to be upset

acide (m) : acid, LSD (drugs)

acolyte (m) : accomplice

acompte (m) : deposit

acoquiner : to debauch, to degrade

à-côtés (mpl) * : perks

acquit (m) : (1) acquittal; (2) receipt

acquittement (m) : acquittal, verdict of not guilty, dismissal, discharge (at Court
of Assize)

acquitter : to acquit, to discharge, to dismiss (a prisoner)

acré! * : look out!, watch out!

" ~ , **v'là les cognes!**" : "Look out, it's the cops!"

acrobate (m) * : (1) cat-burglar; (2) someone who always falls on his feet

acte (m) (1) : outward act

~ **anticonstitutionnel** : unconstitutional action

~ **conservatoire** : protective action
Measure taken in order to protect a situation or right (inventory,
seals, etc.).

~ **constitutionnel** : constitutional act or action

~ **criminel** : crime

~ **d'administration** : administrative action

~ **de barbarie** : barbaric act

~ **de cruauté envers les animaux** : cruelty to animals

~ **délictueux** : misdemeanour

~ **d'instruction** : investigative measure
Measures taken or ordered by an examining magistrate in order to
determine the truth.

~ **d'usage** : normal, customary act

~ **frauduleux** : fraudulent act

~ **illicit** : illicit/forbidden act

~ **préparatoire** : act of preparation to the commission of a crime
As such, these actions do not constitute an attempt per se.

~ **punissable** : punishable act

~ **sexuel** : sexual intercourse

faire ~ **d'autorité** : to act with full powers

acte (m) (2) : instrument
Written proof of a legal action or transaction.

~ **authentique** : certified document
> *Document drawn up by a public official (bailiff, court clerk, registrar of births, deaths and marriages, notary, etc.). Subject to proof of forgery, it is accepted as good evidence of the matter contained therein.*

~ **d'accusation** : bill of indictment

~ **de baptême** : baptism/christening certificate

~ **de bonne vie et moeurs** : certificate of good character

~ **de décès** : death certificate

~ **de l'état civil** : birth, marriage and death certificates

~ **de mariage** : marriage certificate

~ **de naissance** : birth certificate

~ **de notoriété** : declaration of established facts
> *Document drawn up by a notary or examining magistrate, recording the declarations made to him by several persons as to the existence of generally known facts. It is used, for example, to identify the heirs of a deceased person for inheritance purposes.*

~ **de poursuite** : document opening a criminal investigation
> *Any instrument such as an **avertissement, réquisitoire introductif, citation directe, comparution immédiate, convocation par procès verbal, plainte avec constitution de partie civile**, which triggers a criminal investigation or facilitates the conduct of such an investigation.*

~ **de procédure** : writ, process, summons

~ **en double** : instrument drawn up in two originals

~ **officiel** : official document

~ **public** : public document

prendre ~ : to take legal note, to take formal notice

action (f) : action, case, suit

~ **civile** : civil action
> *Action taken by an individual for damages arising out of a criminal act (in its widest sense). The injured party has the right to choose whether to institute his action in conjunction with the criminal proceedings or separately in the civil courts. To be distinguished from **constitution de partie civile** which enables the victim to institute proceedings in the criminal courts, notwithstanding his right to claim damages.*

~ **collective** : corporate action
> *Proceedings instituted by a disinterested legal entity such as a professional body, association or union, to protect the interests of its members.*

~ **publique** : public prosecution
> *Although the prosecution may be initiated by the injured party, only the public prosecutor's department (or certain other official bodies such as the Inland Revenue). may actually conduct the prosecution.* cf **action civile**

déclencher/exercer/engager l'~ publique : to prosecute, to bring a prosecution, to institute criminal proceedings

actionner (en justice) : to institute proceedings against someone

adiré : lost, mislaid.   **titre ~, pièce ~e** : document which has gone astray

adjoint (m) : assistant, deputy

adjudant (m) : warrant officer (senior gendarmerie NCO)
> *The rank is indicated by two wide stripes and one narrow one on the cuff.*

adjudant-major (m) : adjudant (usually a captain)

adjupète (m) * : familiar name for an **adjudant**

administration (f) administration, application

~ **de substances nuisibles** : administration of noxious substances
> *Distinguished from poisoning in that the substances are not such as to cause death but are injurious to health.*

~ **publique** : the Administration, the civil service and local government officers

admissible : allowable, permissible, eligible

admonestation (f) : admonishment, reprimand
> *Action which a juvenile court judge may take against a minor prosecuted for a criminal offence.*

adoption (f) : adoption, passing

~ **des motifs** : taking up the grounds considered in the lower court

~ **d'une loi** : passing, carrying of a law

adoucir : to mitigate, to reduce (a sentence)

adultère (m) : adultery
> *Adultery was a criminal offence until the reform of the divorce laws in 1975.*

aérodrome (m) : airfield, airport, aerodrome

> **dommages aux ~s** : criminal damage to airfield buildings or installations

aéronef (m) : aircraft, airplane, aeroplane

> **détournement d' ~** : see **détournement d'avion**

> **dommage aux ~s** : criminal damage to aircraft on an airfield

affaire (f) : case

> **~ classée** : case filed "no further action"

> **~ en état** : case ready for hearing

> **instruire une ~** : to authorise the investigation of a case

affaires (fpl) : (1) business, personal matters; (2) personal belongings

> **~ criminelles** : criminal matters

> **sous-direction des ~ criminelles** : department of criminal affairs

> **sous-direction des ~ économiques et financières** : fraud office

affaler * : to sing*, to confess, to spill the beans

affichage (m) : bill-sticking.   **droit d'~** : duty paid for the right to post bills

affiche (f) : (1) poster, bill; (2) * fairy*, pansy*, queer* (obvious homosexual)

affirmation (f) : declaration of truth and fidelity
This is only required where the law so demands, e.g. by a lawyer for taxation purposes, creditors in liquidation proceedings, the writers of certain official reports (water bailiffs, gamekeepers, etc.), guardians of infants.

afflictive (peine ~) : punishment involving death, personal restraint or penal servitude

affligé (m) * : cripple, disabled person

afflure (f) * : gain, profit

affranchi (m) * : one of the lads, one who is accepted by the criminal fraternity as one of them, an acknowledged member of the 'underworld'

affranchir : (1) to stamp, to frank; (2) to put someone in the picture; (3) to initiate in sexual matters

affreux (m) * : (1) ugly character;   (2) mercenary, soldier of fortune

affûter * : to lure, to entice, to trick, to swindle

~ **la forme** : to get into shape, to get fit, to train hard

agent (m) : agent, officer

~ **de contributions indirectes** : excise officer

~ **de la force publique** : police officer, member of the armed forces

~ **de police** : police officer, law enforcement officer

~ **de police judiciaire** : agent of the Criminal Court (see also **officier de police judiciaire**)
   *Assistant crime investigators who work under the instructions of an **examining magistrate** and are divided into two categories :*
   *(a) <u>senior category</u> (ordinary **gendarmes**, **inspecteurs** of the Police Nationale) and, (b) <u>junior category</u> (all personnel of the Police Nationale other than those in the senior category above or who are classified as **officiers de police judiciaire**). The junior category covers all uniformed members and **enquêteurs** of the Police Nationale and municipal police officers. On a practical level, the difference between these two categories is that senior agents may carry out preliminary investigations into crimes, report flagrant breaches of the law by way of **procès verbal** and, under the supervision of an OPJ, carry out interviews and identity checks. Junior agents do not have this authority.*

~ **de police municipale** : borough police officer
   Policeman employed by the municipality and having limited police powers, mainly orientated towards the enforcement of road traffic and parking regulations and local bye-laws.

~ **de probation** : probation officer

~ **de renseignements** : informer

~ **privé de recherches** : private investigator, private detective

~ **provocateur** : agent provocateur, instigator, provoker

agglomération (f) : built-up area

aggravation (f) : increase, augmentation

~ **d'une peine** : increase in penalty

circonstances aggravantes : aggravating circumstances

agir : to act

~ **d'autorité** : to act with full authority

~ **d'office** : to act ex officio, by virtue of one's office

~ **és qualités** : to act in one's capacity

avoir qualité pour ~ : to have the necessary powers to act

agissements (mpl) **(frauduleux)** : (fraudulent) dealings, activities

agitation (f) **(sociale)** : (social) unrest, disturbance

agobilles (fpl) * : housebreaking instruments, tools of the trade

agrafer * : (1) to pinch (arrest or steal); (2) to reprimand, to tear off a strip

agréer : to accept, to approve

agresseur (m) : aggressor. **agresser** : to assault. **agression** (m) : assault

agricher * : to collar*, to nab*, to arrest

agrinche (m) * : lout, yob*

agrincheur (m) * : thief, crook

s'agripper : to come to blows

aide (f) : aid, assistance, relief.

~ **et assistance** : aiding and abetting, principal in the second degree

~ **judiciaire** : legal aid

~ **sociale** : social security, public assistance

aieul (m) : grandfather. **aieux** (mpl) : ancestors

aigrefin (m) : fraudsman, con-man

aigrette (f) **(avoir son** ~ **)** * : to be tipsy, to be slightly drunk

aiguille (f) : (1) needle; (2) key (always in context of dishonest use)

aile (f) : (1) wing (automobile); (2) * arm

avoir un coup dans l' ~ : to be tipsy

croquer de l' ~ : to slipstream (racing cyclists' slang)

air (m) : air, appearance

jouer la fille de l' ~ * : to escape from custody, from a captive situation

mettre en l' ~ * : to kill, to bump off*

s'envoyer en l' ~ * : to get high on drugs

ajisme (m) * : the Youth Hostel movement (**Auberges de la Jeunesse**)

   faire de l'~ : to go youth hostelling

ajournement (m) : adjournment, postponement

   ~ du prononce de la peine : deferment of sentence, conditional discharge
   *Option open to judges in criminal and summary courts where a
   defendant has been found guilty of the offence but there are
   grounds for believing he has reformed, that the injury has been
   rectified and that the social perturbation caused by the offence has
   ceased.*

à juste titre : as it should be, as was only fair

à la condition que : provided that

alarmiste (m) * : guard dog

album (m) **de famille** * : set of "mug shots", photos of known criminals

alcool (m) : alcohol, alcoholic liquor, spirits

   débit d'~ : premises licensed for the sale of alcohol

alcoolémie (f) : alcohol level (in blood, urine or breath)

alcootest (m) : (1) alcotest, breathalyser, intoximeter;   (2) breath test

aléa (m) : hazard, risk

à l'encontre de : to the contrary, in opposition

   aller ~ : to go against

alevin (m) * : young pimp

algarade (f) * : quarrel, row

alibi (m) : alibi

aliénation (f) **mentale** : mental disturbance, derangement

aliéné (m) : insane person, non compos mentis

   ~ interdit : certified mental defective

s'aligner * : to quarrel, to row

alinéa (m) : paragraph

alléguer : to plead, to assert, to claim

alliance (f) : (1) relationship through marriage; (2) wedding ring

allié (m) : in-law, person related by marriage

allocation (f) : allowance, benefit

allonger * : to kill, to bump off*

    s'~ * : to confess, to spill the beans*

allumé * : (1) tipsy, slightly drunk; (2) sexually excited

allumeur (m) * : accomplice (of con man, swindler)

almanach (m) * : copious criminal record

alpague (m) : coat, jacket

    avoir sur l' ~ * : to be blamed for a crime, to be on the "wanted" list

alpaguer * : to nick*, to collar*, to arrest

alpagueur (m) * : heavy*, muscle-man, mobster

alphonse (m) * : pimp, ponce, procurer

amadouer : (1) to coax, to entice; (2) to calm someone dowm

amazone (f) * : high class prostitute who solicits from an expensive car

ambier : to run away (from something or someone)

ambulant : itinerant

âme (f) : small red tag stapled to postal bags describing the contents

amende (f) : fine, financial penalty

    ~ fiscale : tax penalty
        Includes a measure of reparation for having deprived the Inland
        Revenue of the sum involved, as well as a penalty.

    ~ forfaitaire : fixed penalty
        Applicable only to minor matters, the offender may pay the
        reporting police officer or make use of a **timbre amende**. *If the*
        facts are contested the normal courts procedure is invoked.

amender (un projet de loi) : to amend, alter (a bill)

amiral (m) * : chiv*, blade, knife

amnistie (f) : pardon
    Without prejudice to the material facts and their consequences as regards
    civil redress, a pardon annuls the prosecution and quashes the penalty
    imposed. Pardoned offences no longer appear on criminal records or in
    the previous convictions index.

amochage (m) * : beating-up, bashing, thrashing

amocher * : to "push someone's face in", to beat up, to bash someone

amortisseur (m) : shock absorber

ampliation (f) : duplicate, copy.   **"pour ~ "** : "certified a true copy"

amusette (f) * : small-time fiddle, amateur confidence trick (perjorative)

analogie (f) : see **interprétation stricte**

analyse (f) : analysis

ancien : former

    ~ soldat : old soldier

    faire l' ~ : to be in the antiques trade

ancienneté (f) : seniority, length of service

    avancement à l'~ : promotion in order of seniority

ange (m) : angel.   **faiseuse d' ~s** * : back-street abortionist

anglais : English

    capote ~e : French letter, condom

    filer à l'~e : to take French leave

angle (m) **mort** : blind spot

angliche (m) * : "Brit.", British subject

animateur (m) : organiser, group leader

    ~ de centre de loisirs des jeunes : youth centre leader

animaux (mpl) : animals

    dommages aux ~ : causing injury to animals
        Until 1959 this was only an offence if committed publicly - ie. the
        law was designed to protect the sensibilities of the onlooker rather
        than the animal.

    expériences sur les ~ : conducting experiments on animals
        Only legal if they comply with certain requirements.

    mauvais traitements aux ~ : ill-treating animals
        This offence does not extend to wild animals not in captivity.

annals (fpl) : annals, public records, archives

annexe (1) : supplementary

> **activité ~** : sideline, second job

> **document ~** : enclosure

> **lettre ~** : covering letter

annexe (f) (2) : supplement

> **~ à une loi** : schedule to an Act of Parliament

> **~ d'un document** : rider

annoté : annotated,   **code ~** : annotated text of a code

annulability (f) : voidability
Describes a document which contains a defect in form or in substance such as to render it liable to be cancelled or rescinded

annulation (f) : annulment

> **~ d'un acte judiciaire** : abatement

> **~ d'un jugement** : quashing, rescission of a judgement

annuler : to cancel

> **~ un arrêté** : to overrule an order

> **~ une ordre** : to withdraw, cancel an order

> **~ une loi** : to repeal, rescind, revoke a law

anomique : anomic, unlawful, lawless, arbitrary

anquilleuse (f) * : female shoplifter
So called because she hides the goods between her legs, or "quilles".

antécédents (mpl) : antecedents, record.   **~ d'un accusé** : defendant's record

antenne (f) : subordinate operational unit

anthropométrie (f) : anthropometry
Method of identifying criminals based on body measurements and certain particular individual signs, such as the shape of certain parts (nose, feet, ears, etc.).

anthume : preceding/occurring before death

antiblocage (m) : anti-lock (brakes)

anti-bouchons : designed to prevent traffic jams

antidate (f) : antedate
> *The error or fraud which occurs when a legal document is given a date prior to that on which it was signed. Antedating is only punishable where the dating of the document is a material factor, either to determine the priority of two concurrent rights or to indicate the date of commencement of a legal or judicial situation.*

antidater : to antedate

anti-effraction : burglar-proof

antigang (brigade ~) : Serious Crimes Squad
> *Popular name for the **brigade de recherche et d'intervention**).*

antipatinage (m) : anti-spin (wheels)

antiprohibitionniste (m) : person in favour of decriminalising the use of drugs

antisciage (m) : saw-resistant
> *Describes the metal rollers incorporated in the bolt of a lock to thwart the use of a saw to cut through the bolt.*

antistups (m) * : drugs squad, narcotics bureau, anti-drugs office

aoûtien (m) : August holidaymaker
> *Person who takes his holiday in August (despite official exortations to stagger holidays)*

apache (m) * : heavy*, gangster

apaiser * : to top*, to bump off*

apatride (m) : stateless person

à peine de : under pain of, under penalty of

apparent : evident, apparent, obvious

> **mort ~e** : apparent (not real) death

appartenir : to belong, to be owned

> **ainsi qu'il appartiendra** : as befitting

> **~ de droit** : to belong rightfully

> **~ en propre** : to possess something in one's own right

> **à tous ceux qu'il appartiendra** : to all whom it may concern

appel (m) : (1) appeal; (2) roll-call
> *There is only one possible form of appeal – on questions of both law and fact – and the French word is correspondingly narrower in meaning than its English formal equivalent.*

~ **a minima** : appeal by prosecutor against too mild a sentence

~ **des témoins** : roll call of witnesses

~ **du jury** : jury array

~ **d'une décision** : appeal against a decision

~ **incident** : appeal on a point of law

~ **joint** : appeal on a point of law

~ **principal** : principal appeal
Lodged by the party which lost a case in the court of first instance, whether as plaintiff or defendant.

~ **tardif** : appeal out of time

avis d' ~ : notice of appeal

casser un jugement en ~ : to quash a sentence on appeal

délai d' ~ : time limit for lodging an appeal

demandeur en ~ : appellant

fol ~ : unfounded appeal

interjeter ~ : to lodge an appeal

jugement frappé d' ~ : judgement under appeal

juger en ~ : to hear an appeal

un ~ n'est pas suspensif : "an appeal is not a stay"

appelant(e) : appellant.   **se porter ~** : to appeal

appeler : to call

~ **en justice** : to summons, to sue someone

~ **en témoignage** : to call someone as a witness

être appelé à un emploi/à exercer des fonctions : to be appointed to an office, given a task or duties

application (f) : application

~ **de la loi** : enforcement of the law

~ **des règlements** : administration of regulations

~ **d'une peine** : determination of a penalty

arrêté d' ~ : statutory instrument quoting measures for the implementation of a law

en ~ de : in pursuance of

appliquer : to apply

~ le maximum de la peine : to impose the severest penalty provided for

~ les dispositions de la loi : to enforce the law

~ une politique : to implement a policy

s'~ à : to apply to

appoint (activité d'~) : sideline, secondary occupation

appointé : salaried

appointements (mpl) : salary, pay.   toucher des ~ : to draw a salary

apposer : to affix, to place, to put

~ une affiche : to post a bill

~ une signature, un sceau : to sign, to seal

~ les scellés : to affix seals (by a magistrate or police official)

appréhender : (1) to dread, to fear; (2) to arrest, to apprehend someone

apprenti (m) : apprentice, novice, trainee

approbation (f) : (1) approval, approbation; (2) authentication of a document, certification

approcher : to approach

~ avec caution : approach with care/caution

appropriation (f) : appropriation (of property)

~ frauduleuse d'objets trouvés : stealing by finding

approvisionnement (m) : supply, supplying

appui (m) : support

accusation avec preuves à l' ~ : accusation supported by real evidence

~ -tête : head-rest

documents, pièces à l'~ d'un procédure : documents in support of a case

appuyer : (1) to support; (2) to lean; (3) to bear upon

    ~ sur la meule : to pedal hard (cycling)

    ~ sur le champignon : to accelerate, to get a move on

après-ski (m) : Moon boots
Warm boots worn after skiing sessions and, as a fashion item, in towns and cities

apte : fit, suited, qualified.   **~ aux fonctions** : fit for the office

aptitude (f) : aptitude, ability, qualification

    brevet/certificat d'~ : certificate of competence

à qui de droit : to whom it may concern, the party concerned, the appropriate authority

aquilienne (responsabilité ~) : liability for wilful damage to property

arabe (m) : arab, arabic

    fourbi ~ : tricky business

    téléphone ~ : grapevine, bush telegraph

aramon (m) * : cheap red wine, plonk*

arbi (m) * : wog*
Perjorative term used to describe North Africans.

arcan (m) * : thief, crook

arcat (m) : elaborate con trick (usually involving a letter)

arceau (m) **de protection** : crash bar, roll bar (automobiles)

archer (m) * : cop, copper, policeman
*Law-enforcement officers in France in the 15th/16th c., known as **archers de guet**, were armed with bows and arrows and controlled by the provost through elected grand masters, constables and masters.*

archevêché (m) * : Marseilles central police station
So called because of its nearness to the cathedral.

archiviste (m) : keeper of the public records, filing clerk

arcpincer * : to nick*, to collar*, to arrest

ardoise (f) : slate

    mettre sur l' ~ : to put it on the slate, to give credit

poser une ~ : to eat in a restaurant without intending to pay
(see also **grivèlerie**)

prendre une ~ : to use a street urinal or **pissotière**

arêtes (fpl) * : shoulder blades, ribs

argoter : to speak argot, to talk slang

argousin (m) * : (1) copper, cop;   (2) screw, prison officer;   (3) gaffer, boss

arguincher * : to nick*, to collar*, to arrest

argument (m) : argument
The discussion of legal or other points by counsel.

~ concluant : conclusive argument

~ faux, ~ captieux : fallacious, specious argument

refuter/retorquer un ~ : to refute an argument

Argus (m) : Glass's Guide
*Motor magazine catering mainly for the trade and giving the current
prices of used cars.*

ARIANE : One of the Gendarmerie's computer networks

arme (f) : weapon
*Instrument which by its nature may cause physical injury to someone,
the possession and sale of which is controlled and the carrying of which
constitutes an aggravation of certain offences such as theft.*

~ blanche : knife or other cutting or stabbing weapon

~ contondante : blunt instrument

~ d'épaule : shoulder weapon (eg rifle, shotgun)

~ de poing : hand gun

~ neutralisée : weapon rendered incapable of being fired

permis de port d'~ : licence to carry a firearm

armoire * (f) : heavy*, strong-man

arnac (m) * : copper*, cop*, policeman

arnaque (m) * : (1) secret police;   (2) arrest; (3) fraud, con trick, swindle

arnaquer : (1) to trick, to diddle; (2) to grass*, to betray;   (3) to bash*, to
beat up;   (4) to nick*, to arrest

arnaqueur (m) * : con man, swindler

arpèges (fpl) * : dabs*, fingerprints

arpenteuse (f) * : prostitute, street walker

arquepincer : to steal, to pinch

   La maison-je-t'arquepince : the fuzz*, the police

arquin (m) * : peterman, safe-breaker

arquincher * : to nab*, to collar*

arracher : to tear, to pull out.

   ~ des aveux : to extort a confession

   s'~ : to "go over the wall", to break out of prison

arracheur (m) de sacs : bag snatcher, snatch thief

arrangemaner * : (1) to con*, to diddle*, to swindle; (2) to beat someone up

s'arranger * : to settle an old score

arrestation (f) : arrest
   The act of apprehending a person, by force if necessary, in order that he might be brought before a judicial or administrative authority or be incarcerated. Except in cases of flagrante delicto, a warrant is necessary in all cases.

   ~ arbitraire : false arrest

   ~ illégale : unlawful arrest

   ~ préventative : detention on suspicion

   en état d'~ : under arrest, in custody

   ordre/mandat d'~ : arrest warrant

arrêt (m) : (1) judgement delivered by a superior court (i.e. Cour de Cassation, Cour d'Assises, Conseil d'Etat), decree

      ~ d'accusation : commital for trial on indictment (at the assizes)

      ~ de mort : death sentence

      ~ de non lieu : discharge

      ~ pénal : judgement in a criminal case

      ~ de renvoi : committal for trial (at the tribunal d'instance)

(2) stop, stoppage

   ~ **des poursuites** : *nolle prosequi* (to be unwilling to prosecute)

   ~ **de la procédure** : abatement

(3) arrest, seizure

   mandat d'~ : arrest warrant

arrêté (m) : decree, order, bye-law

  ~ **d'exécution** : order providing for the implementation of a law

  ~ **ministériel** : order in council (order made by a minister)

  ~ **municipal** : bye law (issued by the mayor)

  ~ **préfectoral** : order made by the *Préfet* of a *département*

arrêter : (1) to arrest;   (2) to draw up, to settle

arrêtoir (m) : safety catch

arriviste (m) : careerist, highly ambitious person

arrondissement (m) : administrative district

arrosage (m) * : booze-up*, drinking party, celebration

arroseuse (f) : water cannon

arsenal (m) : arsenal, collection, gear*

   l'~ législatif : the body of the law

arsonner * : to frisk*, to search someone

s'arsouiller * : to frequent the underworld

Arthur : Arthur (proper name)

   se faire appeler ~ : to get told off, to be reprimanded

   Madame ~ : Parisian night club famous for its "drag" clientele

artichaut (m) * : wallet, purse
  The word has a built-in pun in that it keeps l'artiche au chaud.

artiche (f) * : (1) brass*, loot*, money; (2) alibi; (3) bum*, backside

article (m) : section (of a law)

articulat (m), **articulation** (f) : written statement of facts

artifice (m) : artifice, trick

artificier (m) : bomb disposal expert

artillerie (f) * : artillery, shooter*, hand-gun

artiste (m) : geezer*, bloke*, burk*, person

artoupan (m) * : screw*, prison officer

as (m) : (1) ace, expert; (2) alibi

> **avoir un carré d' ~** : to have a good alibi

> **passer à l' ~** : to vanish into thin air

> **veiller à l' ~** : to keep ones eyes peeled, to keep a sharp lookout

ascendant (m) : relatives in the ascending line (parents, grandparents, uncles, aunts, etc.)

> **~ par alliance** : relatives in the ascending line by marriage

> **pension d'~ direct** : allowance paid to parent

asile (m) : shelter, home, place of safety.   **~ d'aliénés** : mental hospital

aspine (f) * : loot*, brass*, money

assabouir * : to knock down, to bowl over

assaisonner * : (1) to beat someone up;   (2) to "tear a strip" off someone

> **se faire ~** : to get sent down for a long stretch, a long sentence

assassin (m) : murderer

assassinat (m) : murder
Homicide committed with malice aforethought or by ambush.

assassiner : (1) to murder; (2) to overcharge; (3) to bore someone to death

assemblée (f) : meeting, assembly

> **~ du contentieux** : judicial assembly

> **~ générale dans certaines juridictions de l'ordre judiciaire** : general meetings held in the appeal courts and higher courts
> *The task of these is to organise the work of the court and prepare court lists, etc. The meetings are of five types, (i) meetings of the judges, (ii) meeting of the prosecutors, (iii) meeting of both judges and prosecutors, (iv) meeting of court officials (clerks and prosecutors) and (v) a meeting of all of these in plenary session.*

~ **plénière** : plenary meeting
> *A formation of the* **Cour de Cassation** *consisting of the five civil chambers and the criminal divisions (25 judges). It is obliged to intervene whenever a second appeal is lodged, based on the same grounds as the first. Its involvement may be invoked where there are divergent opinions between the judges hearing the initial case or between these and the judges of the* **Cour de Cassation.** *In all cases its decision is binding on the court to which the case is referred. Exceptionally, it may pronounce judgement without referring the case back.*

assermentation (f) : administration of oaths

assermenté : sworn.   **traducteur** ~ : sworn translator

assesseur (m) : assessor

juge ~ : associate judge, assistant judge
> *In the higher courts, the presiding judge is assisted in his deliberations by two* **assesseurs.**

(Les) Assiettes (fpl) * : The Assize Court

assignation (f) : writ of summons

assigner : (1) to assign, to allocate;   (2) to summons, to cite (a witness, etc)

~ **à résidence** : to assign a compulsory residence

assis : seated

la magistrature ~**e** : the Bench (cf **la magistrature debout** – the Public Prosecutors)

assises (fpl) : assizes

cour d'~ : assize court

renvoi devant la cour d'~ : committal for trial at the assizes

assistance (f) : aid, assistance, relief

~ **judiciaire** : legal aid

~ **publique** : National Assistance

assistant (m) **social** : social worker

association (f) **de malfaiteurs** : conspiracy

assommoir (m) * : seedy pub

(Les) Assottes (fpl) * : The Assize Court

assouplir : to relax, to ease

> ~ **les règlements sur ...** : to relax the regulations on ...

assuétude (f) : addiction, dependence

assurance (f) : insurance

> ~ **automobile aux tiers** : third party motor insurance
>
> ~ **automobile tous risques** : comprehensive motor insurance
>
> ~ **sociale** : national insurance
>
> ~ **vol** : insurance against theft
>
> **attestation d'**~ : certificate of insurance
>
> **contrat d'**~ : insurance policy
>
> **police d'**~ : insurance policy
>
> **prime d'**~ : insurance premium

assuré (m) : insured person

assureur (m) : insurer

astiquer * : (1) to beat up, to bash*; (2) to nag, to pester; (3) to tease

> **s'**~ : (1) to dress up; (2) to argue, to quarrel

atelier (m) : workshop, machine shop

atiger : see **attiger**

atouser : to lead on, to encourage

atout (m) * : (1) blow, wound; (2) courage, bottle*; (3) strength; (4) trump card

attaché (m) : attaché, assistant

> ~ **d'administration** : junior civil servant
>
> ~ **d'ambassade** : attaché in the Diplomatic Service
>
> ~ **de cabinet** : departmental assistant

attacher : to attach, to fix, to fasten

> ~ **un bidon, une gamelle** : to squeal*, to grass*

atteinte (f) : strike, blow, attack

    ~ au droit de propriété : trespass

    ~ à la sûreté de l'Etat : treason, offence against national security
        Any crime which compromises national defence, foreign relations, or
        state security and public tranquility.

    ~ à l'autorité de la justice : contempt of court

    ~ à la vie privée : invasion of privacy, eavesdropping
        Torts or crimes prejudicial to the rights of every citizen as regards
        his personality within the framework of his private life.

    porter ~ à l'honneur de qn. to malign someone, defamation

    porter ~ aux intérêts de qn. to act against the interest of someone

atteler * : to live off women,

    s'~ : to set up home together

attendri * : tipsy, slightly drunk

attendu (m) : whereas
    Those parts of a judgement containing the grounds on which it is made.
    *Each paragraph commences with the words **"Attendu que ..."***

attentat (m) : outrage, criminal attempt

    ~ à la bombe : bomb attack, terrorist bombing

    ~ à la pudeur : indecent assault

    ~ aux moeurs : sexual offence, offence against public decency
        Any crime where an essential element is an immoral or sexual act
        which involves the victim (either sex). A clear distinction is made
        between those involving violence and those which do not.

    ~ contre la sûreté de l'Etat : conspiracy against the security of the State

    ~ public à la pudeur : indecent exposure, outraging public decency

attenter à ses jours : to inflict injury on oneself, to endeavour to commit suicide

attention! : caution!, look out!

atténuation (f) : mitigation

    ~ de peine : mitigation of punishment or sentence

atténuant : extenuating

    circonstances ~es : extenuating circumstances (taken into account at the
        court's discretion)

excuses ~es : statutorily recognised extenuating circumstances

atténuer : to mitigate

attestation (f) : testimonial, certificate

~ d'assurance : certificate of (motor) insurance
In France, the certificate takes the form of a "sticker" which must
be displayed on the windscreen.

~ de bonne vie et moeurs : certificate of good character

~ sous serment : affidavit

attesté : proven

attiger * : (1) to wound; (2) to overcharge; (3) to exaggerate

attrapade (f) * : reprimand, severe scolding

attrape (f) : trick, practical joke.   ~ -couillons * : confidence trick, swindle

attrimer * : to pinch*, to nick*, to steal

attriquer * : to handle stolen property, to fence

attroupement (m) : unlawful assembly
A spontaneous or organised assembly of people in a public place and likely
to result in disorder and damage. An armed assembly is always an offence
but an unarmed one is only an offence where it is likely to result in a
breach of the peace.

auber (m) * : dough*, lolly*, money

aubergine (f) * : traffic warden, meter-maid
Until 1980 these officials wore an aubergine-coloured uniform.

audience (f) : court session, court sitting, hearing (in court)

lever l'~ : to close the sitting

suspendre l'~ : to adjourn the sitting

auditeur (m) : hearer, listener

~ à la Cour de Cassation : junior judge (performing administrative tasks
for the court (documentation, work in support of the decision, etc.)

audition (f) : examination, taking of evidence

~ contradictoire : cross examination

~ des témoins : examination of witnesses

~ **sur commission rogatoire** : taking evidence under authority of a commission rogatoire

"au secours!" : "Help!"

auteur (m) : author, creator, originator

~ **d'un accident** : party at fault in an accident

~ **d'un crime** : perpetrator of a crime

authentifier : to certify, to legalise

authentique : authentic, genuine

acte ~ : certified document (drawn up by a notary, etc.)

copie ~ : true copy

document ~ : authentic deed

en forme ~ : duly certified

texte ~ : official wording

titre ~ : valid document

autobus (m) : (1) bus;   (2) * part-time prostitute

~ **à impériale** : double-decker bus

autocar (m) : coach.   **autocariste** (m&f) : coach (tour) operator

automobile (f) : automobile, motor car

automobilité (f) : ownership and use of a car

autopompe (f) : water cannon

autopsie (f) : autopsy, post mortem examination

autorisation (f) : licence, authorisation, permit

~ **d'établissement** : permit to take up domicile

~ **d'exploiter un debit de tabac/une salle de spectacle** : tobacco/theatre licence

~ **provisoire de séjour** : temporary stay/residence permit

autorité (f) : authority

~ **judiciaire** : judicial power

~ **parentale** : parental authority

autotracté : self-propelled

autrui : others, other people, third party

"au voleur!" : "stop thief!"

avortement (m) : abortion

auxiliaire : auxiliary, assistant

> ~ de (la) justice : officer of the court

> gendarme ~ : auxiliary gendarme
> *Person performing his/her compulsory military service in the
> National Gendarmerie*

> policier ~ : auxiliary policeman, cadet
> *Men and women called for national service may elect to perform this
> in the police. They wear a normal uniform but with a green cap
> band and epaulettes.*

avancement (m) : promotion

> ~ à l'ancienneté : promotion by seniority

> ~ au choix : promotion by selection

avaro (m) * : accident, snag, hitch, run of bad luck

avertissement (m) : (1) invitation to appear before a court; (2) caution, warning
*(1) Informal means used by the public prosecutor to initiate a prosecution.
This document, which specifies the offence, brings the matter before the
courts without need for a formal summons where the accused agrees to
appear voluntarily. (2) Disciplinary sanction which may be applied to
police officers, lawyers and public officials, amongst others.*

> lettre d'~ : letter of caution

avertisseur (m) : horn, hooter

> ~ à deux tons : two-tone horn, siren

aveu (m) : confession, admission
*Acceptance by a wrongdoer of the illegal acts which he is alleged to have
committed.*

> passer à la chambre des ~x spontanés * : to undergo the "third degree"

à vie : lifelong, for life

avion (m) : aircraft, airplane, aeroplane

> détournement d'~ : hijacking

avis (m) : advice, recommendation, opinion
Legal term which applies to the mandatory or voluntary seeking of advice from a wide range of bodies (persons, councils, qualified civil servants, Council of State, etc). Such consultations are rarely binding on other courts. The resulting decision therefore states "judgement will be made according to the opinion given by ..."

~ **au public** : public notice

~ **d'expert** : expert opinion

~ **officiel** : official notice

un ~ : a piece of advice

avocat (m) : advocate, counsel, barrister
*In criminal cases, an **avocat** represents the defendant or the **partie civile**. He presents a **plaidoirie** in which he seeks to establish his client's innocence or put forward extenuating circumstances. Where he is representing the **partie civile** he seeks to obtain damages for his client who has suffered injury as a result of the criminal action.*

~ **aux conseils** : barristers at the Court of Cassation

~ **conseil** : consulting lawyer, legal expert

~ **d'office** : duty solicitor
Lawyer appointed to assist an impecunious person

~ **Général** : state advocate, advocate-general
*Member of the public prosecutor's department appointed to the court of appeal or the **Cour de Cassation,** assistant to the **Procureur Général.** He is responsible for conducting the prosecution's case at the assize court.*

avoiner * : to travel at high speed in a car

avortement (m) : (1) miscarriage;   (2) procuring an abortion
Misdemeanour committed by a person who procures or attempts to procure the termination of a pregnancy, whether real or believed to exist, whether the woman consents or not. Justifiable where carried out before the end of the tenth week or under certain conditions prescribed by the Public Health Code.

avoué (m) : attorney
Formerly a separate legal profession, now largely merged with that of **avocat.**

avouer : to confess, to admit

axe (m) **rouge** : red route, urban clearway
Specially marked through routes in Paris on which stopping is strictly prohibited.

ayant droit (m) : beneficiary, rightful claimant

B

babillard (m) * : mouthpiece*, lawyer

babiole (f) * : knick-knack, item of little value

bac * : see **baccalauréat**

baccalauréat (m) : examination, roughly equating to A-levels

bâche (f) : canvas cover, tilt

bâcheur/bâcheuse (m/f) : keeper of low class hotel or lodging house

bachot (m) * : see **baccalauréat**

badaboum (m) * : free-for-all, rough-house

badgé : wearing a badge

baffe (f) : (1) slap in the face;   (2) moustache

bafouer : to flout (justice)

bafouille (f) : letter, item of correspondence

    ~ **de chiotte** : poison-pen letter

bagaf (m) * : shooter*, handgun

bagarre (f) : scuffle, fight, affray, brawl

bagnard (m) : convict

bagne (m) : convict prison, penal servitude, penal settlement

bagnole (f) : old banger, dilapidated motor car

bagof (m) * : shooter*, handgun

bagoter : (1) to loiter aimlessly; (2) to pound a beat

bahut (m) : (1) one's place of work; (2) motor car; (3) taxi, cab

bailli (m) : bailiff, magistrate

bailloner : to gag

bain (m) : bath

    Le Grand ~ : the Central Criminal Records Office

baïonnette (f) : bayonet

baiser : (1) to con, to deceive; (2) to pinch, to steal; (3) to nick*, to arrest

bakshich (m) : backhander, bribe, tip

bal (m) * : nick*, stir*, prison

balade (f) : ramble, stroll, run in a car

       être en ~ : to be on the run from prison, to be high on drink or drugs

baladeuse (f) : inspection lamp, wander-light

balaise (m) : heavy*, muscleman

balançage (m) : grassing*, informing

balance (f) : sacking, dismissal

balancement (m) : conviction, sentence

balancer : (1) to throw away; (2) to fire, to sack; (3) to grass*, to shop*

balanceur (m) : grass*, informer

balandrin (m) : bundle, small item of baggage

balèze (m) : see **balaise**

balise (f) : traffic cone

balisage (m) : coning, beaconing, buoying (sea), ground-lighting (airports)

ballade (f) : pocket.   **faire les ~s** : to go through someone's pockets

balle (f) : (1) bullet, round; (2) * monetary unit, franc; (3) bargain

ballon (m) : (1) balloon, inflated ball; (2) balloon-shaped wine glass

      faire du ~ * : to "do porridge", to serve time in prison

balocher : to wander about in an aimless and idle manner

balourd : phoney, false
    In the plural, refers to false identity papers or counterfeit money.

baluchon (m) : bundle, small item of baggage

baluchonner : to pinch, to nick*, to steal small items of little value

baluchonneur (m) : (1) small-time crook, petty thief; (2) person visiting a prisoner and taking him provisions

ban (m) : public proclamation

      publier les ~s : to publish the banns of marriage

rompre son ban : to breach a prohibition from entering certain areas

banaliser : to make to appear normal
*Detectives often use a **voiture banalisée**, ie without police markings.*

banane (f) * : (1) overrider on car bumper; (2) medal, "gong"

peau de ~ : booby-trap

banc (m) : bench, seat

~ de jury : jury box

~ des magistrats : the bench

~ des prévenus : dock

en ~ : see **assemblée plénière**

étre sur le banc : to be down-and-out, to be a vagrant

bande (f) : (1) gang, party; (2) tape, band, strip

~ d'arrêt d'urgence : hard shoulder (on motorway)

~ d'enregistrement : tape (for tape recorder)

~ de roulement : tread (tyre)

~ matérialisée : white line marking in centre of road

~ ralentisseuse : sleeping policeman, traffic calming ramp

~ stop : stop line

banditisme (m) : organised crime, gang crime

bandit-manchot (m) : one-armed bandit, fruit machine

banga (m) : cannabis, marijuana

bannissement (m) : banishment, exile
Expulsion from the country, imposed for political crimes.

banque (f) : bank

~ de données : data bank

~ de données juridiques : judicial data bank
Judicial data held on computer. The data vary from bank to bank and cover legislation and regulations, precedents, bibliographical references, etc. The principal judicial data banks in France are the CEDIJ, SYDONI, CRIDON, JURIS-DATA, LEXIS, JURINPI and CELEX.

banquer : to pay up, to pay one's debt to society (through a prison sentence)

banqueroute (f) : criminal bankruptcy
> *Misdemeanour committed by an indebted tradesman who is unable to meet his obligations following certain dealings prescribed by law. May be either* **simple** *or* **frauduleuse** *depending on the seriousness of these dealings.*

baptiser * : to water down spirits

baraque (f) : dump*, hovel

baratiner : to chat someone up, to sweet-talk someone, to employ smooth talk

barbarie (f) : barbarism

    actes de ~ : barbaric acts

barbe (f) : (1) beard, bearded person;   (2) bore, nuisance

barbe, barbeau, barbillon, barbiquet (m) * : pimp, person living on immoral earnings

barbelouses (fpl) : barbed wire

barbichette (f) : goatee beard

barbote (f) * : (1) body search (of prisoner); (2) prostitutes' medical examination

barboter * : to nick*, to pinch* to steal

barboteur (m) * : petty thief, kleptomaniac

barbotin (m) * : loot, booty, proceeds from a robbery

barbouse, barbouze (f) * : secret agent, secret policeman

bargeot (m) : nut-case*, crazy individual

barillet (m) : cylinder (of a revolver)

barjo (m) * : mug*, sucker*, dupe

barlu (m) * : gang-bang*, collective rape

baron (m) * : plant*
> *The accomplice of a con-man or swindler who mingles with the crowd to encourage potential victims.*

baroud (m) : fight, scrap

barrabille (f) : brawl, disturbance

barrage (m) : road block

barraqué : well-built, muscular

barre (f) : bar
   *The place in the court where the **avocats** stand to make their pleas.*

   ~ **des témoins** : witness box

   entendre à la ~ : to give a hearing (in a trial)

   mander/traduire à la ~ : to summons, to prosecute someone

   paraître à la ~ : to appear before the court

barreau (m) : bar
   *The professional body of **avocats**. There is one for each court of **grande instance**.*

se barrer * : to make off, to scram, to skedaddle

barreur (m) : bouncer

bascule (f) * : grass*, informer

   ~ **à Charlot** * : the guillotine

basculement (m) : reversal (of traffic flow, etc.)

base (f) **de données** : data base

basique : crude, basic

basoche (f) : the legal fraternity

baston (m)/**bastonnade** (f) * : punch-up, brawl, fight

batellerie (f) : inland water transport

bâtiment (m) **et travaux publics (BTP)** : the building and civil engineering
   industry

bat-la-dèche (m) * : tramp, vagabond

bâton (m) : baton, truncheon

bâtonné : to be subject of an **interdiction de séjour**

bâtonnier (m) : elected President of the Bar

batterie (f) : corps of drums

   ~ **-fanfare** : combined brass band and corps of drums

batteur (m) : tout (usually outside shady night clubs)

battoir (m) **d'oeufs** : helicopter, chopper*

bauche (m) * : safe, strong box

bavard, bavocheux (m) * : (1) "brief", barrister; (2) shooter*, handgun

baveux (m) : newspaper, rag*

bayard (m) : bullet-proof shield

beauf (m) : see **beau-frère**

beau-fils (m) : son-in-law, stepson

beau-frère (m) : brother-in-law,

beau-père (m) : father-in-law, stepfather

bécane (f) : (1) bicycle; (2) typewriter

Beccaria (Cesare ~) : Italian jurist (1738-94)
Author of the influential work on criminal law reform, "Crimes and Punishment". He condemned torture, criticized the death penalty and urged that punishment should fit the crime.

bedeau (m) : beadle

becquet (m) : front spoiler (automobile)

bédi (m) * : gendarme, rural policeman
Romany slang term.

béguineuse (f) * : prostitute
Specifically, one who might give of her services free of charge, out of love for her client.

beigne (f) : blow, punch

belle (f) * : release from prison

   se faire la ~ * : to break out of prison

belle-fille (f) : daughter-in-law, stepdaughter

belle-mère (f) : mother-in-law, stepmother

belle-soeur (f) : sister-in-law,

bénéfice (m) : profit, gain, advantage, benefit, privilege

bénéficier : to profit, to benefit

   ~ d'un non-lieu : to be discharged

bénévole : benevolent, voluntary, unpaid

benne (f) **basculante** : tipping body (on a truck)

béquillarde (f) * : the guillotine
So-named because its shape is reminiscent of someone on crutches.

béquille (f) : (1) crutch; (2) prop-stand; (3) lever-type door handle

~ **à roues** : undercarriage (of a semi-trailer)

berges (fpl) : years

berline (f) : saloon car, old pram used by tramps

berlue (f) : cover (for bed or for illegal activities)

berluer : to quiz, to question

bertelot (m) * : vice-squad officer, member of the **brigade des moeurs**

betting (m) : place where illegal bookmakers assemble on a racecourse

beuglant (m) * : seedy cabaret, second-rate nightclub

beur (m) : second generation Arab immigrant

beurette (f) : feminine of **beur**

beurgeois (m) : Arab immigrant councillor

beurré * : sozzled, drunk

bhang (m) * : cannabis, marijuana

bibelots (mpl) * : housebreaking implements

biber : to swindle, to cheat

bibis (mpl) * : skeleton keys

bic, bicot (m) * : wog*, North African arab (perjorative)

bichotter * : to nick*, to pinch*, to steal

bicoque (f) : shack, shanty, hovel

bicorps (m) : hatchback
So-called because it is of "two-box" construction, rather than "three-box" (tricorps).

bicyclette (f) : bicycle

bidasse (m) * : private soldier, "Tommy Atkins"

bide (m) * : paunch, belly

bidon (m) : (1) can; (2) phoney, fake, false; (3) paunch, belly

bidonneur (m) : con man, swindler

bidonville (m) : shanty town

bien (m) : good, welfare, weal

    le ~ **public** : the public good, the public weal

biens (mpl) : estate, property, assets, goods and chattels

    ~ **collectifs** : public property

    ~ **corporels** : tangible assets

    ~ **de la succession** : estate, hereditaments

    ~ **domaniaux** : state property

    ~ **immeubles, immobiliers** : immovable property, real estate

    ~ **incorporels** : intangible assets

    ~ **meubles, mobiliers** : personal estate, personalty, chattels, movables

    ~ **vacants, sans maître, à l'abandon** : ownerless property, derelict

    reprise de ~ : recovery of property

bien-fondé (m) : the merits of a case or claim, the grounds for such

bienfaisance (f) : charity

biffer (un mot, un nom) : to erase a word, to strike off a name

biffin (m) : (1) foot soldier; (2) tramp paid to put out rubbish for collection; (3) rag-and-bone man, junk dealer

biffure (f) : cancellation

bigamie (f) : bigamy
Misdemeanour committed by a person who, being legally married, contracts a marriage with another before the first has been dissolved.

bigleur (m) : witness to a crime

biglotron (m) : (1) magnifying peephole in door; (2) room where suspects may be observed without their knowledge.

bigne (m) * : nick*, prison

bignolon (m) * : screw*, prison officer

bignou, bigophone (m) * : telephone, blower*

bigorne (f) * : the fuzz*, the "Old Bill"*, the police

bigorneau (m) * : tapped telephone

bigorneur (m) * : brawler, street-fighter

bijoutier (m) : jeweller

~ du clair de lune * : cat-burglar

bilan (m) : balance sheet

déposer son ~ * : to croak*, to snuff it*, to die

faux ~ : fraudulent balance sheet

billet (m) : note, ticket.   ~ de banque : banknote

bing (m) * : nick*, prison

binôme (m) : couple, associated pair

biroute (f) : plastic traffic cone

bisaïeuls (mpl) : great-grandparents

biscuit (m) * : ticket*, fine for traffic offence

choper un ~ * : to get booked for an offence

bisenesseuse (f) * : prostitute, tart

Bison Futé (m) : holiday traffic route

bistro/bistrot (m) : pub, bar

bite, bitte (f) * : truncheon, staff

bitume (m) : pavement, footpath.   fouler le ~ * : to go soliciting

bitumeuse (f) * : prostitute, street-walker

bizeness (m) * : "racket", shady activity
The word is a corruption of the English "business".

faire le ~ * : to be "on the game", to solicit for prostitution

black-out (m) : (press) blackout

blâme (m) : reprimand

blanc (m) : (1) snow*, cocaine; (2) white wine

blanc : (1) blank;   (2) innocent

> **~ bec** : novice, tyro

> **~-seing** : document signed in blank (eg. a signed blank cheque)

> **les ~s** : the blank spaces in a document

> **mariage ~** : unconsummated marriage

> **signer un document en ~** : to sign an incompleted document

blanche (f) : glass of clear fruit liqueur

Blanche (f) : nickname for the **gendarmerie départementale**

blanchir (de l'argent) : to launder (money)

blanco * : clean*, innocent of any wrongdoing, without form*

blase, blaze (m) * : name, handle*

blé (m) * : bread*, cash, money

bled (m) : small village, in the country, in the sticks*

blesser : to injure, to wound

> **~ les intérêts** : to be prejudicial to

blessure (f) : wound, injury, battery

> **~ aux animaux** : causing injury to animals

> **~ involuntaire** : unintentional wounding

> **~ voluntaire** : wounding with intent

> **coups et ~** : assault and battery

bleu : blue

> **~ gendarme** : navy blue

> **zone ~e** : restricted parking zone

bleus (mpl) **de travail** : overalls, dungarees, boiler suit

blindé : armoured

bloc (m) : solitary confinement

blocus (m) : blockage

bloquer : to put away, to imprison

blouser : to deceive, to swindle

> **se ~** : to make a mistake, to slip up

blouson (m) : bomber jacket

> **~ noir** : yob*, lout, greaser*

> **~ doré** : wealthy lout, hooligan from good background

bob/bobinard (m) : brothel, whorehouse

bock (m) : small glass of beer

bocson (m) * : brothel, whorehouse

boisson (f) : drink, liquor

> **~ alcoolisée** : intoxicating liquor, alcoholic beverage

boite (f) **de nuit** : night club

bombardier (m) * : reefer*, joint*, cannabis cigarette

bombe (f) : bomb, grenade

> **~ à gaz lacrymogène** : tear gas grenade

bomber : to go very fast, to bomb along

bon (m) : voucher, bill, bond

> **~ de caisse** : cash voucher

> **~ de commande** : order form

> **~ de Trésor** : Treasury bill

bon : good, proper, sound

> **aux ~s soins de ...** : care of (c/o)

> **" ~ pour ..."** : "good for ...", I.O.U.
> *Formula used by a debtor over his signature showing the amount or thing due, or the purpose of the document*

> **~ne foi** : good faith

> **~nes moeurs** : morality
> *Those rules imposed by social conventions at any given time. Where the disregard of these involves a breach of the criminal law, it may be grounds for terminating a contract.*

> **~s offices** : good offices

certificat de ˜nes moeurs : certificate of good character

de ˜ne foi : bona fide

en ˜ état : in good condition

en ˜ne et due forme : in due and proper form

témoin de ˜ne foi : reliable witness

bondir : to arrest someone

boniment (m) : tall story, sales patter

bonir : to spill the beans, to turn Queens evidence

bonisseur (m) : hawker, street vendor

bonnet (m) : (1) cap, headgear, bonnet; (2) three-card trick

gros ˜ : VIP, big shot

bonneteau (m) (**jeu de** ˜) : three-card trick

bonnir : see **bonir**

bonus (m) : no claims bonus

book (m) : bookmaker (illegal in France)

bordel (m) : brothel, bordello

bordereau (m) : memorandum, docket, detailed statement, consignment note, abstract, schedule, voucher

˜ **de crédit** : credit note

˜ **de paye** : payroll

˜ **des pièces d'un dossier** : docket

˜ **des prix** : price list

˜ **d'expédition** : dispatch note

bordille (f) * : copper, policeman, copper's nark, informer

bordurer : to ban, to withdraw permission to be somewhere

borgne (f) : night, night-time

borgne : suspicious, shady.   **café** ˜ : low dive.   **compte** ˜ : fishy account

borne (f) : boundary stone, milestone

bottin (m) : trades directory.   ~ **mondaine** : Who's Who

bottine (f) * : lesbian

bouc (m) : goatee beard

bouche-trou (m) : stop-gap measure

bouchon (m) : (1) traffic jam, traffic hold-up; (2) corner café

bouclage (m) : imprisonment

bouclard (m) : lock-up shop

boucle (f) : imprisonment

boucler : to lock, to close down, to close (a deal), to imprison

bouclier (m) : shield

boudin (m) : (1) sausage, black pudding; (2) * cosh, truncheon; (3) tyre;
      (4) * low-class prostitute

boueux (m) : dustman, bin-man

bouge (m) : low-class pub, dive

bougre (m) : chap, fellow, bloke

bouiboui (m) : low-class pub, dive

bouic (m) * : low-class brothel

bouilleur (m) **de cru** : home distiller

bouledogue (m) * : shooter*, handgun

boulevard (m) **périphérique** : ring road, orbital motorway

boumiane (m&f) * : Romany, gipsy

bourdille (m) * : copper, policeman, informer, copper's nark

bourgeois (m) : (1) burgess, burgher, citizen; (2) plain clothes policeman

     en ~ : in plain clothes

bourre, bourreman (m) * : cop, policeman, "Old Bill"*

bourreau (m) : executioner, hangman, torturer, tormenter

bourrer * : (1) to beat someone up; (2) to speed along

se bourrer : to get drunk, to get high on drugs

bourrés (mpl) : loaded dice

bourrique (f) * : cop, policeman

bousculade (f) : jostling, bumping, elbowing

      vol de la ~ : pick-pocketing by jostling

bousillage (m) : (1) underworld killing; (2) excessive drinking or drug taking

bousin (m) * : sleazy pub, brothel

bousine/bouzine (f) * : banger*, decrepit motor car

bout-portant : point-blank

bouzillage (m) * : tattoo

bouzin (m) * : boozer, pub, low-class brothel

bracelets (mpl) : handcuffs, handbolts

braconnage (m) : poaching
The taking of game or fish without a licence, or at a prohibited time or place or by prohibited means.

braco (m) : see **braconneur**

braconnier (m) : poacher

braguette (f) * : low-class, short-time prostitute

braises (fpl) : vital evidence

braisé : loaded*, very rich

branche (f) : branch

     ~ de l'administration : branch of the civil service

braquage (m) : hold-up, armed robbery

braquer : (1) to aim a gun at someone; (2) to carry out a hold-up; (3) to turn the steering wheel

braqueur (m) : gangster, armed hoodlum

brasseur (m) **d'affaires** : tycoon, big businessman

break (m) : shooting brake, estate car

brème (f) : identity papers

     être en brème : to be registered with the police health service (prostitute)

bretelle (f) : (1) shoulder strap, sling, braces;   (2) telephone tap

~ **d'accès** (f) : motorway slip road

brelica (m) * : shooter*, handgun

brevet (m) : diploma, certificate

breviaire (m) : A - Z street plan of Paris

bricard (m) : senior prison officer

bricoleur (m) : Jack-of-all-trades, small-time crook

bride (f) : safety chain.   ~**s** : handcuffs

brigade (f) : section, team, squad
> *A small unit of police or gendarmerie, usually commanded by a **brigadier** (Police) or **Maréchal de Logis Chef** (Gendarmerie). Also a small team or squad of specialist detectives.*

~ **anti-commando** : hostage release team (Paris)
> *See also the **Groupe d'Intervention de la Police Nationale.***

~ **anti-criminalité/anti-gang** : serious crimes squad

~ **canine** : dog section

~ **criminelle** : serious crimes squad (Paris police)

~ **de recherche et d'intervention** : special investigation and operations team (Paris police)

~ **de repression du banditisme** : organised crime squad (Paris police)

~ **des mineurs** : juvenile crime squad (Paris police)

~ **des moeurs** : vice squad

~ **des recherches** : investigation squad (Gendarmerie)

~ **des stupéfiants et du proxénétisme** : drugs and vice squad (Paris)

~ **des stups** : see **brigade des stupéfiants**

~ **de surveillance et de recherches** : crime investigation section (Belgian Gendarmerie)

~ **de surveillance nocturne** : night patrol unit

~ **frontière mobile** : border crime investigation unit
> *Section of the PAF (frontier police) which conducts enquiries into criminal or immigration matters away from the passport control posts.*

~ **mobile** : Flying squad

~ **mondaine** : vice squad
*Former name for the **brigade des stupéfiants et du proxénétisme**.*

~ **territoriale** : rural section (Gendarmerie)
A unit of Gendarmerie which covers a given area of the countryside for general police purposes.

brigadier (m) : police sergeant, corporal in the **Gendarmerie Auxiliaire**

~ **-chef** (m) : station sergeant (police), senior corporal (**Gendarmerie Auxiliaire**)

brigadiste (m) : member of the anti-terrorist brigade

brigand (m) : brigand, (armed) robber

briocher : to fill in a very detailed crime report

brique (f) * : 10,000 francs (one million old francs)

bris (m) : breaking, rupture

~ **de clôture** : breaking down fences

~ **de prison** : prison break

~ **de scellés** : breach of seals

briscard, brisquard (m) : veteran, old soldier, old hand

brocanteur, broc (m) : junk-dealer

brocard (m) : (1) jibe, lampoon; (2) any legal term in current use by laymen

broderie (f) (**argentée**) : (silver) braid

brouette (f) : jalopy, old banger, decrepid old car

brouillard (m) : fog

brouillage (m) (**appareil de ~**) : communications scrambler

brouiller les pistes : to confuse the scent, to baffle the hunters

brouillon (m) : rough notes, draft

bru (f) : daughter-in-law

bruit (m) : (1) noise; (2) rumour

~ **et tapage nocturne** : breach of the peace by night

le ~ **court** : it is rumoured

brûler : (1) to burn (down);   (2) to kill (usually by shooting)

~ **le dur** : to travel by train without a ticket

~ **un feu rouge** : to jump a red light

brume (f) : mist

bucolique (f) * : prostitute who works the public parks and gardens

bulletin (m) : bulletin, report, paper, form

~ **de police criminelle** : Police Gazette
Official publication in which details of wanted persons, etc. are circulated.

~ **de service** : General Orders

~ **de casier judiciaire** : extract from criminal records
Three types of extract are available, depending on the status of the applicant.   The full extract is only available to the judicial authorities, an edited version can be obtained by a prefect whilst the third may only be supplied to the person concerned. As this latter version is issued so that it might be produced to a third party (e.g. a prospective employer) and every effort is made to facilitate the offender's reintegration into society, this type of extract only shows convictions for serious offences for which a custodial sentence has been passed.   Where appropriate, a blank form may be issued with a line drawn through the space for entries.

bureau (m) : office, bureau, the officers of a commercial company etc.

~ **central de recherches (BCR)** : central crime office (Belgian Gendarmerie)

~ **central national** : national Interpol office

~ **de douane** : customs office

~ **de police** : police office, sub-station

~ **des plaintes** : complaints office
Desk at a police station where complaints of crimes and offences are received and recorded

~ **d'information** : information service, public relations department

burmas (mpl) : fake jewels, paste

but (m) : aim, intent, object

dans le ~ **de (frauder)** : with intent (to defraud)

dans un ~ **lucratif** : for pecuniary advantage

butin (m) : loot, booty, proceeds of crime

C

cabane (f) : (1) nick*, clink* jail;   (2) secondary residence

cabanon (m) : modest weekend dwelling

caberlot (m) : remote country public house

cabine (f) : cab (of a truck)

cabinet (m) : small room

    ~ juridique : law firm

    ~ de travail : study, office, consulting room

cabistouille (f) : petty con-trick

cabossé : dented, battered

cabriolets (mpl) : handcuffs, bracelets*

caca d'oie * : khaki, pea green

cachet (m) : stamp, seal.   **~ de la poste** : post mark

cacheter : to seal

cachot (m) : lock-up, bridewell

cadavre (m) : corpse, cadaver

    recel de ~ : concealment of body

cadeau (m) : payment received by prostitute

cadenas (m) : padlock

cadennes (fpl) * : handcuffs, bracelets*

cador (m) * : gang leader, god-father*

cadre (m) : (1) frame; (2) executive, managerial staff
(2) An employee who belongs to the senior levels of staff by reason of his training or the exercise of a particular level of command.

    ~ noir : high-ranking police officer

cafard, cafardeur (m) * : grass*, snitch*, crawler*

cafouiller : to miss, to splutter, to misfire

cage (f) * : nick*, slammer*, jail

Cagna (f) **(La Grande ~)** : Paris Police Headquarters

cagoulé : masked

cahier (m) : (1) notebook;   (2) crime sheet

caïd (m) : gang leader, god-father*"

caillou (m) * : gem stones.   **casser des ~x** : to "do time" in prison

caisse (f) : (1) office (where cash is obtained);   (2) old banger*, decrepid
    motor car;   (3) glasshouse (military prison)

> **~ de sécurité sociale** : Social Security Office
>   *Includes* :
>
>> **caisse nationale d'allocations familiales** : family allowance office
>>
>> **caisse nationale d'assurance maladie** : sickness benefit office
>>
>> **caisse nationale d'assurance vieillesse** : retirement pensions office

calamité (f) : disaster

calandre (f) : radiator grille

caler : to stall, to come to an abrupt stop

calepin (m) : notebook

calibre (m) * : shooter*, handgun

calomnie (f): calumny, malicious representation

> **~ écrite** : libel
>
> **~ orale** : slander
>
> **dénonciation calomnieuse** : false accusation

calot (m) : forage cap (as worn by the CRS)

cambriolage (m) : burglary

cambriole (f) : the brotherhood of burglars

cambrioler : to burgle

cambrioleur (m) : burglar

cambron (m) * : nick*, jail, prison

cambut (m) **(faire un ~)** : to switch goods, to ring the changes
    A popular con trick where inferior articles are substituted for those
    originally purchased.

came (f) : see **camelote**

camelote (f) : (1) trash, shoddy goods;   (2) drugs, narcotics;   (3) cash, money

camé (m) * : drug addict, junkie*

camembert (m) * : round and flat traffic bollard

camionnage (m) : cartage, haulage, transport by truck

camion (m) : lorry, truck

   ~ **-grue** : breakdown truck

   ~**-tracteur** : tractor, towing unit

   ~**-citerne** : tanker

camionnette (f) : light truck.   ~ **-plateau** : platform truck

camphre (m) **(sentir de la** ~ **)** : (1) to be gathering dust;   (2) trouble brewing

campo (m) : a short break, a day off

canadienne (f) **en sapin** : "wooden overcoat", coffin

canal (m) : (1) canal;   (2) channel (radio, TV)

canaque (m) * : coon*, nigger* (pejorative)

canard (m) : (1) rag*, newspaper;   (2) red herring, misleading clue

canarder * : to gun down, to shoot

cancan (m) : gossip, the "grapevine"

candidat (m) : candidate, applicant

cané (m) * : stiff*, corpse

canelles (fpl) * : handcuffs, bracelets*

canif (m) : penknife

cannabis (m) : cannabis, Indian hemp, marijuana

canne (f) : cane, walking stick

   ~ **à épée** : swordstick

   ~ **plombée, ferrée** : weighted cane

   être en ~ : to be subject to an **interdiction de séjour**

canon (m) : barrel (of gun).   ~ **scié** : sawn-off barrel

cantine (f) : canteen

canton (m) : ward
> *Electoral division of a **département** for the purpose of electing members*
> *of the **Conseil Général**. Also, in Switzerland, a province or state. In*
> *Canada, a land registry division of about 100 square miles.*

cantonnement (m) **(des CRS)** : temporary accommodation (for the CRS)

capacité (f) : capacity, (legal) ability, competence, qualification

> **avoir ~ de faire quelque chose** : to be entitled (qualified) to do something

> **~ d'ester en jugement** : capacity to go to law

> **~ d'exercer** : entitlement to practise

> **~ de payer** : ability to pay

> **~ de traitement** : data handling capacity (computers)

capiston (m) * : captain (military), **officier de la paix principal** (police)

capital : capital

> **crime ~** : capital crime

> **peine ~e** : capital punishment, death sentence

> **question ~e** : essential (main) issue

capsule (f) **représentative des droits (CRD)** : "tax-paid" seal (on wines, etc.)

car (m) : coach

carabine (f) : carbine.   **~ à air comprimé** : air-gun

capot (m) : bonnet (automobile)

capote (f) : hood (automobile)

caractère (m) : character, nature, disposition

> **~ spécifique d'un délit** : the facts of the case
> *(Also called the **éléments constitutifs de délit**).*

carambolage (m) : pile-up*, multiple shunt*, serious traffic accident

carambouillage (m) : obtaining property by deception, "moonlighting"
> *Dishonest business practice whereby the offender purchases goods on*
> *credit, sells them off cheaply for a quick profit and then absconds without*
> *paying the original suppliers.*

carenage (m) : fairing (motorcycle)

cargaison (f) : cargo, load, freight

carluche (f) * : nick*, jail, prison

carmouille (f) : payment (often for illicit transactions)

carnet (m) : note book

carottage (m) : petty theft

carouble (f) : pick-lock, skeleton key

caroubler : to break in, to burgle

carrée (f) : digs*, lodgings

carrer : to hide, to stash*

carreuse (f) * : professional female shoplifter

carrière : (f) : career

carrosse (m) : black maria, paddy wagon, police van

carrousel (m) : ante-chamber and waiting hall at the Paris Law Courts

carte (f) : card, sheet of paper

    ~ à mémoire : smart card, intelligent card

    ~ à puce : smart card

    ~ de commerçant : work permit
       For a craftsman or a self-employed worker in industry or commerce.

    ~ de crédit : credit card

    ~ de séjour : residence permit, aliens certificate
       *Document issued to aliens over sixteen years of age residing in France and not the subject of a special arrangement. Since 1984 these have been of two types : **carte de résident** - valid for 10 years and automatically renewable, giving the holder the right to exercise in France the profession of his choice, within the existing legal provisions: **carte de séjour temporaire** - valid for the duration of the document or visa required to enter France, not exceeding one year, permanently renewable.   Only acts as a combined residence/ work permit if the words "salarié" are included.*

    ~ de travail : work permit (for an employee)

    ~ d'exploitant agricole : work permit (for farm workers)

    ~ grise : grey card, vehicle registration document, log book

~ **nationale d'identité** : national identity card
> *Document issued by the authorities on demand to any person. The details contained therein enable the holder to establish his or her identity in the event of this being required by the police or any other body. Its possession is optional and identity may be proved by any other means.*

~ **professionnelle** : work permit
> *Any alien who wishes to take up a vocational activity, paid or unpaid, in Metropolitan France, must hold a work permit (see **carte de travail, carte de commerçant, carte d'exploitant agricole**.)*

~ **verte** : "green card"
> *International certificate of motor insurance.*

être en ~ : prostitute registered with the police

cartouche (f) : cartridge

cartouse (f) : identity card

cas (m) : case, instance

au ~ **où** : in the event of

~ **de figure** : hypothesis, scenario

~ **de nécessité** : urgency, emergency

~ **d'espèce** : watertight case, copybook case

~ **fortuit** : accident, accidental case

~ **imprévu** : emergency, unforeseen circumstances

~ **juridique** : legal case

~ **urgent** : emergency

en aucun ~ : on no account, under no circumstances

en ~ **d'urgence** : in an emergency

hormis le ~ **de** : barring the case of

le ~ **échéant** : should the occasion arise, in case of need

case (m) : form*, criminal record
> *Abbreviation of **casier judiciaire**.*

case (f) : (1) house, home;   (2) nick*, prison

caserne (f) : barracks

casier (m) registry

> ~ **judiciaire** : criminal record, criminal records office
> *The same term is used to indicate both the actual record and the*
> *office where the criminal records are held.*

> ~ **spécial** : record of previous convictions
> *This record is maintained for minor offences relating to alcoholism*
> *and road traffic matters only.*

> **extrait de** ~ **judiciaire** : CRO form
> *Extract from the national computerized criminal records, used to*
> *establish an offender's antecedents. Three types of extract (known*
> *as **bulletins**) are available, the content being more or less complete,*
> *according to the status of the enquirer.*

casque (m) : helmet

> ~ **de protection** : riot helmet, NATO helmet

casquette (f) uniform cap

cassation (f) : annulment, repeal, quashing (by the Supreme Appeal Court)

> **cour de** ~ : Supreme Court of Appeal

> **pourvoir/recours en** ~ : appeal on a point of law

casse-cou (m) : daredevil, madcap, stuntman

casse, cassement (m) : break-in, burglary

casser : (1) to quash;   (2) to dismiss

> ~ **un fonctionnaire** : to dismiss a civil servant

> ~ **un jugement en appel** : to quash a sentence on appeal

casserole (f) * : (1) jalopy, banger, old car;   (2) trollop,
low-class prostitute;   (3) snout*, grass*, police informer

casse-tête (m) : (1) bludgeon, cosh;   (2) puzzle, enigman, tiring brainwork

casseur (m) : (1) burglar; (2) muscle-man, heavy*; (3) car-breaker (for spares)

castagne (f) : brawl

castagner : to brawl, to come to blows with

castration (f) : castration
The amputation of any organ necessary for procreation (male or female).
A felony, it may be classified as excusable if it is immediately provoked
by a violent assault of a sexual nature.

casuel : fortuitous, accidental, casual

casuel (m) : perquisites, fees (in addition to salary)

    faire le ~ : to let a hotel room for use by prostitutes

cataphote (m) : reflector

catastrophe (f) : disaster

catin (f) : prostitute, whore

cause (f) : suit, action, trial, brief, case

    affaire en ~ : case before the court

    être chargé d'une ~ : to hold a brief

    être en ~ : to be party to a case, to be involved

    hors ~ : unquestioned, undoubted

    mettre en ~ : to call into question

    mettre hors de ~ : to rule out of court

    mettre quelqu'un en ~ : to summons or sue someone, to implicate someone

    véhicule en ~ : vehicle involved (in an accident)

caution (f) : bail, surety, indemnity

    mettre en liberté sous ~ : to release on bail

    donner/fournir/se porter ~ pour quelqu'un : to stand bail for someone

cautionnement (m) : surety.   **~ judiciaire** : bail

cautionner (quelqu'un) : to stand bail for, to stand as surety for (someone)

cavalendour (m) * : outsider, not part of the **milieu**

cavalerie (f) : cavalry, mounted troops (including gendarmerie)

C.C.C. (m) : raincoat
C.C.C., a famous rainwear firm, gave its name to all types of raincoats.

ceinture (f) **de sécurité** : seat-belt

ceinturer : to surround, to encircle, to arrest

célibataire (m&f) : bachelor, spinster

cellule (f) : cell.   **voiture cellulaire** : prison van, Black Maria

Centaure (f) : real-time computer system used by the Gendarmerie

central (m) : main office

   ~ **téléphonique** : telephone exchange

   commissariat ~ : central (main) police station

   prison ~**e** : top-security prison

centre (m) : centre

   ~ **commercial** : shopping centre, shopping precinct

   ~ **d'accueil** : remand centre for young offenders

   ~ **de détention** : rehabilitation prison
      Open or closed prison for long-term prisoners, the aim of which is
      rehabilitation and re-entry into society.

   ~ **de documentation et d'information de la Police Nationale** : Police
      information and documentation centre
      This service forms part of the facilities provided by the ENSP
      (National Police Staff College).

   ~ **de formation de la police** : police training centre
      Created in 1982, these local training centres are controlled by one
      of the **Ecoles Nationales de Police** *and provide initial training for*
      uniformed constables.

   ~ **de rétention administrative** : detention centre for illegal immigramts

   ~ **des affaires** : business centre

   ~ **de semi-liberté** : parole hostel, semi-custodial centre

   ~ **de soins palliatifs** : hospice (for the terminally ill)

   ~ **d'études et de la formation de la Police Nationale** : Police research and
      training centre
      Carries out research into legal, administrative and general policing
      matters.

   ~ **d'études et de recherche de la Police Nationale** : National Police research
      and planning unit
      This central unit performs much the same function as the Home
      Office Police Requirements Support Unit and the Scientific Research
      and Development Branch. It is concerned with the development of
      equipment for police use and the application of science and
      technology to policing matters.

   ~ **d'observation** : observation centre
      Centre to which young offenders are sent for medical, psychological
      or educational observation and report.

   ~ **national de préparation aux concours et examens** : police national
      examinations preparation centre

~ **pénitentiaire** : young offenders prison

~ **régional** : short-sentence prison
For convicted prisoners who do not have more than three years left to serve.

~ **technique de la Gendarmerie Nationale** : Gendarmerie technical research centre.

certain : certain, sure, unquestionable, irrebuttable

date ~e : fixed date

à jour ~ : on the stated day

preuve ~e : irrefutable evidence

un ~ M. Untel : a certain Mr So-and-so

certificat (m) : certificate

~ **d'aptitude professionnelle (C.A.P.)** : certificate of professional competence

~ **de bonne vie et moeurs** : certificate of good character

~ **médical** : medical certificate

chacail (m) * : snout*, grass*, informer

chahutage (m) * : rowdy behaviour

chambre (f) : chamber, division
Sitting of several judges of the same court for judicial purposes, either examination or judgement. As a general rule, the chambers within the courts of the same jurisdiction have no competence of their own and the decision made is regarded as a decision of all the courts.
*The term can also be used to describe the representative and controlling body for each of the various types of court auxiliaries, such as **avoués, agréés, notaires, commissaires-priseurs.***

~ **civile** : civil division
*That division of the **tribunal de grande instance** which deals with civil cases (where one party is seeking redress against another party). As such it may award damages and issue injunctions but has no punitive powers.*

~ **correctionnelle** : criminal division, criminal court
*That division of the **tribunaux d'instance** and the **tribunal de grande instance** which deals with offences against the **Code Pénal**, the **Code de la Route**, etc. The **chambre correctionnelle** of the **tribunal d'instance** (sometimes referred to as the **tribunal de police** deals with **contraventions** (minor matters or summary offences). The **chambre correctionnelle** of the **tribunal de grande instance** hears prosecutions for **delits** (arrestable offences).*

~ **criminelle** : criminal division of the supreme court of appeal
*Chamber of the **Cour de cassation** which hears appeals against decisions where it is held there has been a violation of the law, where the court's powers have been exceeded, or there has been incompetence, a failure to observe the proper procedure, a lack of legal grounds, a contrary judgement or a lack of judicial cause.*

~ **d'accusation** : indictment division, indictment review court
Division of the court of appeal deliberating mainly on (1) matters arising from the examining magistrate's decision and (2) as a second examining chamber in the case of felonies. Also acts as the disciplinary body for police officers and deals with certain other matters such as extraditions, legal rehabilitation, supervision of judges, etc.

~ **des appels correctionnels** : criminal appeals division
*Division of the court of appeal hearing appeals against matters heard in the first instance by the **tribunaux correctionnels** and **tribunaux de police***

~ **des mineurs** : juvenile division

~ **des mises en accusation** : Grand Jury
*Where cases are to be heard by the assize court, the committal proceedings are reviewed by this chamber. If there is deemed to be insufficient evidence, a **non-lieu** may be issued. Where it is considered that there is a prima facie case, the chamber issues an **arrêt de mise en accusation**. The **inculpé** then becomes the **accusé**.*

~ **mixte** : joint bench, composite bench
*A sitting of the **Cour de Cassation** consisting of judges belonging to at least three of the court's six chambers (at least 13 judges, the senior president, and the president, dean and two counsellors from each chamber). Matters <u>must</u> be referred to it where the judges of a particular chamber are equally divided on a matter and <u>may</u> be referred to it where the case raises questions falling within the competence of more than one chamber, or where a case has given rise to differing decisions, or is likely so to do.*

~**s réunies** : joint division
*Division of the **cour de cassation**, replaced by the **assemblée plénière** in 1967.*

chambre-forte (f) : strong room

champignon (m) : accelerator

chancellerie (f) : the departments of the Ministry of Justice

chansonnette (f) * : con-man's spiel, patter

avoir quelqu'un à la ~ : to extract a confession by sheer verbal persuasion

chanstique (faire un ~ **)** (m) : to ring the changes, to switch goods

chantage (m) : blackmail

> *Obtaining or attempting to obtain a signature, an undertaking or a renunciation, or the handing over of money or money's worth, by violence or by verbal or written threats to make revelations or defamatory allegations.*

chants (mpl), **cris ou discours contraires aux bonnes moeurs** : using obscene, indecent or offensive language in public

chanvre (m) hemp.   ˜ **indien** : Indian hemp, cannabis

chanvré : to be "high" on marijuana

chaparder : to pilfer

chapelets (mpl) * : bracelets*, handcuffs

char (m) : (1) waggon;   (2) jalopy*, old banger*

   ˜ **blindé/de combat** : tank

charge (f) : (1) burden, charge, responsibility;   (2) practice (of an *officier ministériel*)

   ˜ **de la preuve** : burden of proof

   témoin à ˜ : witness for the prosecution

chargé : intoxicated (alcohol or drugs)

chargement (m) : loading

charger : (1) to load, to fill; (2) to entrust, to instruct; (3) to charge (advance impetuously, attack); (4) to charge (with an offence)

chargeur (m) : magazine (firearms)

charlotte (f) : bolt croppers

charrette (f) : (1) old banger*, jalopy*;   (2) black maria*, police van

chasse (f) : hunting, shooting (game)

   ˜ **gardée** : private shoot (land)

   ˜ **-neige** : snow plough

   fusil de ˜ : shotgun

   louer une ˜ : to rent a shoot

   permis de ˜ : hunting/shooting permit

châtaigner : to hit, to punch

châtain : brown (hair), brunette

château (m) * : nick*, prison

châtiment (m) : punishment, chastisement

chatouiller (une serrure) : to pick (a lock)

chauffard (m) : road-hog, reckless driver

chauffer : to nick*, to pinch*, to steal

chaussettes (fpl) : tyres

> ~ **à clous** : plain clothes policeman
> *This expression dates from the time when plain clothes policemen could be recognised by their regulation, hob-nailed boots.*

chef (m) : (1) head, chief, leader;   (2) heading, item, count

brigadier ~ : station sergeant

~ **d'accusation** : count of an indictment

~ **de dépense** : expense item

commissaire en ~ : chief superintendent (Belgium)

chemin (m) : path, road

~ **de grande randonnée** : long-distance footpath

~ **public** : public highway

chemise (f) : (1) shirt;   (2) file cover

en bras de ~ : in shirt-sleeves, shirt-sleeve order

chèque (m) : cheque

bénéficiaire d'un ~ : payee of a cheque

~ **bancaire** : banker's draft

~ **en blanc** : blank cheque

~ **en bois** : rubber cheque*, cheque endorsed "return to drawer"

~ **postal** : giro cheque

~ **sans provision** : bad cheque, dud cheque, NSF (not sufficient funds)
> *It is a misdemeanour to issue a cheque without adequate funds, or where all or part of the provision is witheld after issue, or where payment is stopped, with intent to prejudice the rights of another.*

faux ~ : forged cheque

 toucher un ~ : to cash a cheque

chetard/chtard (m) * : nick*, prison

cheval (m) horse

 ~ de retour : old lag

cheveu (m) : hair.   **~ lingual** : lisp

chevilleur (m) : go-between, intermediary

chevreuil (m) : grass*, police informer

chien (m) : dog

 ~ de fusil : hammer

 ~ renifleur : sniffer-dog

chiffre (m) **noir** : dark figure, black figure, unreported crimes
 The difference between the actual number of crimes committed and those known to the police.

chignole (f) * : (1) car, old banger*;   (2) electric or hand drill

chignoleur (m) * : safe-breaker

chignoleuse (f) * : tart, prostitute

chine (f) **(aller à la ~)** : to go on the knock (call at houses to buy antiques)

chinoiseries (fpl) : red tape, bureaucracy

chioteur (m) * : bent copper, corrupt policeman

chiotte (f) * : old banger*, dilapidated motor car

chiourme (f) : prison staff

chiper : to steal

chipeur (m) : petty thief

chnouf (f) * : snow*, cocaine

choc (m) : shock, impact

choléra (m) : nasty piece of work*, evil person

chômage (m) : unemployment

 allocation de ~ : unemployment benefit, dole

 ~ conjoncturel : short-term unemployment

chomeur (m) : unemployed person

chopeur (m) : pilferer, petty thief

chose (f) : a chose, a thing, property
> *English law distinguishes between a "chose in possession" or movable chattel, and a "chose in action" or rights to intangible property such as debts, trade marks, etc.*

> ~ **consomptible** : consumable
>> *Items which are destroyed the first time they are used, such as foodstuffs.*

> ~ **d'autrui** : property of another

> ~ **jugée** : *res judicata*, closed case, autrefois convict/autrefois acquit
>> *The status of an accused once judgement has been delivered and the period for appeal has expired. He may not be brought before the courts on the same facts again, even under a different charge.*

> ~ **sans maître** : derelict (bona vacantia)

choupette (f) : mop of hair

chourin (m) * : chiv*, knife

chronique (f) **des tribunaux** : Law Reports

chroumer * : to strip parked vehicles of parts and accessories

chuteur (m) : parachutist, paratrooper

ci-après : hereafter

cible (f) : target

ciblot (m) **(en ~)** : in plain clothes

cicatrice (f) : scar

ci-dessous : hereinafter

ci-inclus : enclosed

ci-joint : herewith

cimetière (m) : cemetery, graveyard

> ~ **à bagnoles** : car-breaker's yard

cinq-sur-cinq : loud and clear, five by five
> *Formula used to report radio reception*

circonscription (f) : (police) division

    ~ **électorale** : parliamentary constituency

circonstances (fpl) : circumstances

    ~ **aggravantes** : aggravating circumstances
        Certain specified circumstances which result in a heavier than normal sentence (e.g. possession of a firearm when committing burglary).

    ~ **atténuantes** : extenuating circumstances, mitigating circumstances
        Certain circumstances surrounding the commission of an offence, or personal factors relating to the offender which merit a lower than normal penalty.

circonstancié (rapport ~) : detailed report

circulaire (f) : circular, memorandum
    Service instructions, issued by a superior authority to its agents.

circulation (f) **routière** : road traffic

    ~ **par blocs** : movement of traffic in blocks
        A system used by the Belgian Gendarmerie on heavily-used motorways. Blocks of vehicles are escorted by a motorcyclist who maintains a steady, predetermined speed at the head of the convoy in order to keep an even flow of traffic.

circuler : to circulate, to move about.   **"Circulez!"** : "Move along there!"

citation (f) **directe** : simple summons, direct summons
    Procedural document by which the prosecutor or the victim of a criminal offence may take a matter to the court <u>direct</u> simply by notifying the defendant of the date and time of the hearing. Applicable to straightforward matters which do not warrant going through the "instruction" phase.

citer : (1) to quote, to cite; (2) to summons; (3) to mention in dispatches

citoyen (m) : citizen

civelot (m) : see **ciblot**

civière (f) : stretcher

civil : civil

    action ~e : civil action

    capacité ~e : (legal) capacity

    droit ~ : civil law

    droits ~s : civil rights

en ~ : in plain clothes

état ~ : civil status (also the office of the Registrar of births, deaths and marriages)

jour ~ : 24 hours

mariage ~ : civil marriage (without religious ceremony)

civiliser : to try a case under civil law (where the criminal proceedings are closed)

clac/claque (m) * : low-class brothel

clameur (m) : outcry

~ publique : hue and cry
Where an offender, immediately after committing the offence, is pursued by members of the public, it is regarded as being a case of flagrant délit.

clandestin : clandestine, secret, covert

immigré ~ : illegal immigrant

clarinette (f) * : (1) rifle;   (2) jemmy, crowbar or other tool

classe (f) : class

~ moyenne : middle class

~ ouvrière : working class

~ sociale : social class

être de la ~ : to be ready for demobilisation from National Service

classement (m) : arrangement, classification, order

~ sans suite : file "no further action" (N.F.A.)
An administrative decision taken by the public prosecutor not to prosecute where he considers it inappropriate. The matter may be reopened at a later date if desired.

classer : to file, to classify

affaire classée : unsolved case

classeur (m) : file

classification (f) : classification

~ des infractions : classification of offences
The classification of offences into crimes, délits and contraventions.

~ **des juridictions** : jurisdictional classification
The distinction made between the various courts hearing criminal matters.

~ **des peines** : classification of sentences
The classification of sentences into imprisonment, fine, or other sanction.

clause (f): clause, section, provision (of an Act)

~ **belge** : waiver of the non-extradition rule for political matters in the event of the assasination of a head of state

clavier (m) : keyboard (on musical instrument, typewriter, computer, etc.)

clé/clef (f) : key

vol avec fausse ~ : theft by duplicate key

clerc (m) : clerk
Employee in the office of a public official such as a bailiff, notary, public auctioneer, etc.

clochard (m) : tramp, vagabond
*The word derives from the expression **déménager à la cloche de bois** implying a "moonlight flit", the lodging house doorbell having been silenced to aid a silent departure.*

cloporte (m) : doorkeeper, janitor, caretaker

clôture (f) : enclosure, fence, enclosed land

bris de ~ : breach of close, breaking down fences

~ **des débats** : the point after which no further representation may be made to the court

coaccusé (m) : co-defendant

coaction (f) : coercion, compulsion

co-activité (f) : complicity
Participation in an offence as a principal in the first degree.

coauteur (m) : accomplice

coccinelle (f) : "Beetle", Volkswagen car

coco (f) * : coke*, cocaine

code (m) : a collection of laws of a similar nature and which form part of the same branch of the law

~ **de justice militaire** : = Queen's Regulations

~ **de la route** : road traffic law

~ **de procédure pénale** (m) : rules of criminal evidence and procedure

~ **pénal** : the criminal law

en ~ : dipped headlights
As in "obligation de mettre en code dans les villes" (requirement to use dipped headlights in built-up areas).

codéfendeur (m) : co-defendant

codétenu (m) : fellow-prisoner

codification (f) : codification, classification of laws

coercition (f) : coercion, duress

coffiot (m) * : peter*, safe, strongbox

coffre (m) : boot (automobile)

coffre-fort (m) : safe

coffrer : to collar*, to arrest

cogne (m) * : copper, cop, the filth*
A pejorative term, implying brutal treatment.

coiffer : (1) to head, to be the boss of;   (2) to arrest

coincer : to collar*, to arrest

col-blanc (m) : white collar worker

délinquance en ~ : white collar crime

colère (f) : anger, rage

collaborateur (m) : fellow-worker, colleague

collante (f) : witness summons issued by the police

collation (f) : collation (of documents)

collecte (f) : collection (for charity)

collectivité (f) **locale** : local authority
Départements, communes (or groups of these) which administer a public service.

collège (m) : (1) college;   (2) prison, the nick*

~ **des magistrats** (m) : college of judges
Judges elected by all the judges of a Court of Appeal. Their role is to nominate those amongst them who will be proposed as members of the Promotions Board or the Disciplinary Board.

collégialité (f) : bench system,
Principle under which justice is dispensed by more than one judge or magistrate.

collègue (m) : colleague, (learned) friend
*Mode of address between peers, e.g. **avocats.***

collimater : to keep a watchful eye on someone or something

collusion (f) : collusion

colombienne (f) : high-grade marijuana

colonne Morris (f) : advertising pillar
The well-known, circular structures to be seen in Paris, on which advertisements are posted and are used to contain street-cleaning equipment, etc.).

colporteur (m) : hawker, door-to-door salesman (see also **démarchage**)
One who visits other men's houses to seek customers or solicit orders on behalf of a firm.

combat (m) **de coqs** : cock-fighting

combinaise/combinaison (f) : scheme, ploy, shady deal, questionable transaction

comité (f) : committee

~ **consultative de la libération conditionnelle** : Parole Board

~ **de probation** : probation committee

~ **de probation et d'assistance aux libérés** : Council for the Resettlement of Offenders

commandant (m) : uniform chief inspector of police, squadron leader (air force), commander (in the sense of Supreme Commander, i.e. not a rank)

commande (f) * : job*, crime

avoir une ~ : to benefit from police immunity in return for information

commandement de l'autorité légitime (f) : acting under lawful orders
Justification for an illegal act, committed under the lawful orders of a competent, legitimate public authority (eg, a soldier who kills an enemy in time of war.

commando : strike force, task force

commencement (m) : beginning, commencement

~ **de preuve** : prima facie evidence

~ **d'exécution** (m) : actus reas
*Action leading directly to the intentional commission of an offence
or where the immediate and direct consequences would be the
commission of the offence. It forms an attempt, punishable by law.*

commerce (m) **parallèle** : unofficial/undercover/black trading

commettre : to commit, to perpetrate, to appoint

~ **un crime** : to commit a crime

~ **une faute** : to make a mistake, to err, to act wrongfully

~ **un expert** : to appoint an expert

commis (m) : clerk

~ **greffier** : assistant clerk of the court

commissaire (m) : commissioner, senior poice officer, chief inspector (Belgium)
*There are three grades of commissaire in the French National Police (see
below). Appointment to the "corps of commissaires" is via annual,
competitive examination, open (a) to certain experienced police officers and
(b) to university graduates as direct entrants.*

~ **adjoint** : inspector (Belgium)

~ **adjoint–inspecteur** : detective inspector (Belgium)

~ **central** (m) : divisional commander
*The officer in charge of more than one commissariat in an urban
area*

~ **de la République** : see préfet
*Title given in 1982 to the Préfets. This was later abandoned and
the practice of referring to these senior civil servants as Préfets
was resumed.*

~ **de police** : assistant police superintendent (no equivalent British rank)
*The most junior grade of commissaire, he/she will frequently be a
direct graduate entrant to the Police Nationale at this rank.*

~ **divisionnaire** : chief superintendent of police
*The most senior of the commissaire grades, appointed from the more
experienced commissaires principaux.*

~ **en chef** : police superintendent (Belgium)

~ **principal** : police superintendent (French National Police)

~**-priseur** : public auctioneer

commissariat de police : police station
Staffed by members of the Police Nationale. (cf. hôtel de police, gendarmerie)

commission (f) : (1) commission;   (2) mission, task

~ **de l'application des peines** : sentence supervision board

~ **d'indemnisation des victimes d'infractions pénales** : Criminal Injuries Compensation Board

~ **permanente** : standing committee

~ **rogatoire** : letter of request, warrant, instructions to the police
*Document by which a magistrate delegates his powers to another magistrate or to an **officier de police judiciaire** to carry out an investigation on his behalf. Except in cases of **flagrant délit**, French police officers have no power to investigate crimes without such an authorisation, usually from an **examining magistrate**. A **commission rogatoire** can also be executed internationally.*

commuer : to commute (a penalty)

commun : common

droit ~ : public general law, ordinary law, general rule(s)

en ~ : joint

le bien ~ : the public weal

mettre en ~ : to pool (resources, etc)

communal : public, relating to the *commune*

communauté urbaine (f) : metropolitan district council
A public body, formed by an association of local authorities within a conurbation with over 50,000 inhabitants to provide common facilities such as fire and rescue services, public transport, water, sewage, cemeteries, markets, abattoirs, roads and road signs, car parks, planning the creation of housing and industrial estates, etc.

commune (f) : town, borough, municipality
*The smallest administrative sub-division in France, administered by a mayor and a **conseil municipal.***

communication (f) : communication

~ **de pièces** : discovery (of documents)

~ **interurbaine** : trunk call

~ **téléphonique** : telephone call

commutation (f) de peine : commutation of sentence

compagnie (f) : company
   *A unit of the CRS or of the Gendarmerie Départemental, usually commanded by a **commandant/chef d'escadron**.*

Compagnies (fpl) **Républicaines de Sécurité (CRS)** : riot police: tactical intervention units, tactical police reserve
   *The CRS is a Central Service of the National Police. Its principal function is to act as an operational reserve for other branches of the police. It is employed at most major functions (festivals, race meetings, displays, etc.) and at holiday resorts in the season but it is probably best known for its public order rôle. Trained on para-military lines and working as self-contained unit, it is very effective in quelling disorders and breaches of the peace. The Gendarmerie have an equivalent in the **Gendarmerie Mobile**.*

comparaître : to appear before a court, to stand trial

comparse (m&f) : minor accomplice in a criminal activity

comparution (f) : appearance, hearing

   ~ **immédiate** : expedited hearing
      *System introduced by the law of 10 June 1983 (amended in 1986) under which straightforward misdemeanours (other than those involving children, politics or the press, and certain other offences declared to be outside the scope of the system) may be brought before the courts with the minimum of delay. Applies in particular to many cases of **flagrant délit**.*

   ~ **personnelle** : appearance before the **chambre d'accusation** in person

   ~ **volontaire** : voluntary appearance (following notice to appear)

compétence (f) : competence, jurisdiction

   ~ **absolue/matérielle/quant au fond** : ratione materiae, competence of a court (as to subject matter)

   ~ **du lieu/locale/territoriale** : ratione loci, competence of a court (geographically)

   ~ **personnelle** : competence as regards the offender, ratione personae
      Applies to juvenile courts, etc.

compétent : (1) relevant, concerned; (2) competent, qualified

   le tribunal est ~ : the court has jurisdiction

   transmettre au service ~ : forward to the department concerned

complément (m) : complement, addition

   ordonner un ~ **d'instruction** : to order further enquiries to be made

complet (~ète) : full, complete, exhaustive

    adresse ~ : full address

compléter : to complete, to fill in (a form)

complice (m) : accomplice, accessory, abettor

    ~ par assistance : accessory after the fact

    ~ par instigation : accessory before the fact

    être ~ d'un crime : to be a party to a crime

complicité (f) : complicity, aiding and abetting
The actions of those who incite a crime, give instructions, provide the means for its commission, or who aid and assist offenders in their preparative or facilitative acts. They are dealt with in the same manner as principals in the first degree.

complot (m) : conspiracy, plot

composter : (1) to date, to perforate (ticket, etc.); (2) * to gun down, to shoot

compte (m) : account, calculation

    ~ courant : current account

    ~ courant postal (CCP) : Giro account

    ~ tenu (des circonstances) : having regard (to the circumstances)

    pour le ~ de ... : on behalf of ...

    règlement de ~ : gangland killing

compteur (m) de vitesse : speedometer

comptoir (m) : counter, bar

conception (f) : conception

    période légale de ~ : period of time during which the parents should have lived together to beget a legitimiate child

    enfant conçu : unborn child

conclusion (f) : submission

concours (m) : (1) assistance, cooperation; (2) competitive examination
In common with most French institutions, the gendarmerie and police place great emphasis on competitive examinations. Entry is always by this means, the **concours** *being open to all suitably qualified candidates.*

~ **(ou cumul) idéal d'infractions** : theoretical conflict of offences (see **conflit de qualifications**)

~ **réel d'infractions** : multiplicity of offences
Situation where an offender has, by his actions, committed several discrete offences, without these being separated by a definitive sentence.

concubine (f) : concubine

concussion (f) : misappropriation, extortion
Misdemeanour committed by any civil servant or public official who, falsely and maliciously receives, demands or orders the payment of sums claimed to be legally due.

condamnation (f) : conviction, judgement, sentence

~ **à mort** : death sentence

~ **aux dépens** : order to pay costs

~ **à vie** : life sentence

~ **par contumace** : sentence in absence

prononcer ~ : to pass sentence

purger une ~ : to serve one's sentence

condamné (m) : condemned person, convict

condé (m) * : (1) police protection from prosecution in return for information; (2) simple con trick;   (3) plain clothes policeman

condition (f) **préalable** : prior condition
Essential element for the commission of an offence but not illegal in itself, unlike the actual constituents. For example, the existence of certain contracts (hire-purchase agreement, lease, etc.) is a prior condition for the misdemeanour of **abus de confiance** *whereas the actual appropriation or diversion of the property concerned is a constituent element of the offence.*

conducteur (m), **conductrice** (f) : driver

conduite (f) **à gauche/à droite** : left-hand, right-hand drive (car)

confiance (f) : confidence, trust, reliance

abus de ~ : theft by breach of confidence or trust, embezzlement, theft as a bailee
Misdemeanour committed by any person who diverts or disposes of goods, money, effects, etc, to the prejudice of the legal owners, possessors or holders, and which were entrusted to him by way of lease, deposit, etc. on condition that he later surrenders them or replaces them, or uses them for a specified purpose.

digne de ~ : reliable, trustworthy

homme de ~ : confidential clerk

confirmation (f) : affirmative judgement by appellate court

confirmer : to corroborate (evidence), to bear out (an assertion)

confiscation (f) : confiscation, seizure of property, forfeiture
Penalty by which all or part of a person's property is transferred to the State. General confiscation is an optional additional criminal penalty which is rarely used. Confiscation of an object linked to the case is an further penalty directly associated with the principal sentence and imposed ipso jure, or it may be an additional penalty which the judge may (or must) impose. Depending on the case, it may be treated as a penalty, a safety measure or a civil reparation. Confiscation may be ordered as the main punishment where it is imposed in lieu of imprisonment.

conflit (m) : (1) conflict, dispute;   (2) concurrence

~ d'autorité : overlap of authority

~ de compétence : concurrence of jurisdiction

~ de juridiction : concurrence of jurisdiction between two courts

~ de lois : conflict of law

~ de qualification : conflict of offences
Where the same set of circumstances constitutes a number of criminal offences, eg, the production of a false document may be attempted fraud or the uttering of a forged document.

~ négatif : two courts disclaiming jurisdiction

~ positif : two courts claiming jurisdiction

être en ~ : to be in conflict

conforme : conformable, true

"pour copie ~ " : certified true copy

se conformer à : to comply with

conformément (à) : in accordance (with), pursuant (to)

confrère (m) : colleague
Term used by members of certain liberal and learned professions in their contacts with each other.

confrontation (f) : (1) confrontation (of the defendant and witnesses); (2) collation (of documents)
(1)   A stage in an examination or investigation where the judge brings together several persons with a view to comparing what they

have to say. These persons may be the witnesses alone or the prosecution or defence, or all of these. It may be tape recorded.

confusion (f) : confusion, merger

~ **de parts** : uncertain parentage
Uncertainty as to father of child born in first months of a second marriage concluded before the expiry of the legal waiting time.

~ **des peines** : two or more sentences to run concurrently

congé (m) : holiday, leave, dismissal

~ **annuel** : annual leave

~ **de maladie** : sick leave

~ **de maternité** : maternity leave

~ **-formation** : training leave

~ **payé** : holiday with pay

~ **sans rémunération** : unpaid leave

demander son ~ : to give notice

donner son ~ **à un employé**: to sack an employee

congédier : to dismiss

conjugal : conjugal, marital

domicile ~ : legal abode of a married couple

droit ~ : conjugal rights, marital intercourse

connaissance (f) : knowledge

être de la ~ **d'un tribunal** : to be within the cognizance of a court

connaître : to know

~ **de** : to hear, to have competence, to deal with

connexe : connected with, related to

connivence (f) : connivance, complicity

agir de ~ **avec quelqu'un** : to act in collusion with someone, to be in league with someone

consanguinité (f) : consanguinity, kinship

mariage consanguin : intermarriage

frère consanguin/soeur consanguine : half brother/half sister (on the father's side)

consécutif (à) : subsequent (to)

conseil (m) : council, counsel, advice

~ de discipline : discipline board

~ général : county council
The elected administrative body responsible for a *département*. Mainly concerned with social services, primary education, planning and roads, its powers have been considerably extended since the 1982 decentralisation law. Until this date the Council was presided over by the *Préfet* but now a chairman is elected by the members.

~ juridique : legal consultant, solicitor

~ municipal : town/borough council
The elected administrative body responsible for a *commune*.

~ supérieur de la magistrature : Supreme Council of Judges
Body formed to guarantee the independence of the judiciary. Presided over by the President of the Republic or the Minister of Justice (vice-chairman), it consists of nine further members nominated by the President from a list. It recommends persons for appointment to the bench and acts as their disciplinary body. It is consulted regarding reprieves and pardons.

conseiller (m) : councillor, counsel

~ à la cour d'appel, à la cour de cassation : judge of appeal

consentement (m) de la victime : consent by the victim
Acceptance by a person of circumstances which would normally constitute an offence against him. The victim's consent does not usually exclude the offender from criminal responsibility (e.g. euthanasia is still a crime).

conséquence (en ~ de) : in pursuance of, in consequence of

conservatoire : conservationary

mesure ~ : urgent measure, protective measure

saisie ~ : sequestration, arrestation

considérant : whereas
A synonym for *attendu* (which see) used when drawing up decisions made by the appeal courts.

consigne (f) : (1) orders, instructions; (2) guard room, left-luggage office

consignation (f) cash deposit

consommation (f) : completion, accomplishment, consumption, consumation

~ **d'un crime/délit** : commission of a felony/misdemeanour
*The completion of a crime by the fulfilment of all prior conditions,
by the completion of all the constituent steps and by the occurrence
of its result. Cf. an attempt.*

~ **du mariage** : consumation of marriage

conspiration (f) : conspiracy, plot

conspiratif : used for spying purposes

constat (m) : report

~ **à l'amiable** : "no–blame" accident report
*Introduced by the French Ministry of Transport to cut down on
paperwork, this form is signed by both parties in the event of a
minor accident in which no particular blame can be laid at the door
of either party.*

~ **d'accident** : accident report

~ **d'audience** : deposition

~ **de décès** : death certificate

dresser un ~ : to draw up a report

constatation (f) : (1) verification, establishment of fact; (2) report

~ **amiable** : agreed statement (as to circumstances of an accident)

~ **d'accident** : accident report

~ **d'identité** : proof of identity

~ **d'un décès** : evidence of death

~ **d'une enquête, d'une instruction** : report of an investigation

procéder aux ~s : to carry out an official enquiry

constater : (1) to determine, to establish (the facts); (2) to record

constitution (f) **de partie civile** : lodging of claim for damages in criminal cases
*The victim of a crime, when lodging his complaint, may give notice that he
wishes his claim to damages to be incorporated in the criminal case against
the defendant.*

contact (m) : go–between, intermediary,

clef de ~ : ignition key

mettre/couper le ~ : to switch an engine on/off

contractuel (m), **contractuelle** (f) : traffic warden

contradanse (f) * : ticket*, booking for a traffic offence
Popular term for a **contravention**

contradictoire : contradictory, adversarial, open argument, *inter partes*
Essential, implied rule of Roman law which governs all French court procedures. It concerns the right of every party to have access to all information necessary for its defence or the prosecution of its case. It provides that every action, every document, item or exhibit introduced in evidence by one party shall be brought to the notice of the opposing party and freely debated during the hearing. Respect for the principle of contradiction is an essential part of the rights of the defence. The judge must ensure that the principle of contradiction is observed in all cases and may only refer in his judgement to such explanations as have been brought to his notice in accordance with this principle.

> **jugement ~** : judgement after trial, judgement *inter partes*

contraindre : (1) to compel, to force; (2) to restrain; (3) to sue, bring an action

contrainte (f) : constraint, restraint, duress, compulsion

> **agir sous ~** : to act under duress
> *Where a person is acting under duress he is legally regarded as being physically or morally unable to avoid the commission of an offence and is therefore free from criminal liability.*

> **~ morale** : see **abus d'autorité**

> **~ par corps** : imprisonment in lieu of fine (or for debt)
> *Imprisonment of an adult convicted of a felony, misdemeanour or summary offence who has not met his financial obligations (fine, fiscal penalty, court costs and expenses, etc.). The period of imprisonment, which is used as a means of coercion, may vary according to the amount due and possibly the age and financial status of the offender and is determined by the judge.*

> **~ par saisie des biens** : distraint

> **mesures de ~** : compulsory measures

> **porteur de ~s** : process server, bailiff

contrat (m) : contract, agreement

> **~ d'assurance** : insurance policy, insurance contract

> **~ d'emploi** : contract of employment

contravention (f) : summary offence, minor offence
Minor infringement of the law punishable by a fine or a short period of imprisonment. Dealt with by the **tribunal d'instance** *(otherwise known as the* **tribunal de police**). *Cf.* **crime, délit.**

contrebande (f) : contraband, smuggling

   ~ **d'armes** : arms smuggling

contrebandier (m) : smuggler, ship carrying contraband

contrecarrer (un enquêteur) : to interfere with, to obstruct (an investigator)

contrecoup (m) : backlash, repercussion, spin-off

contrefaçon (f) : breach of copyright, unauthorised use of a trade mark, model
or design
*This is always a breach of the civil law and may, in some circumstances,
also be a breach of the criminal law.*

contrefacteur (m) : forger

contrefaire : to counterfeit, to forge

contre-ingérence (f) : counter-infiltration, counter-subversion

contre-preuve (f) : counter-evidence

contreseing (m) : counter-signature

   avoir le ~ **de quelqu'un** : to sign for someone

contresigner : to countersign

contrevenant (m) : offender, delinquant, trespasser

contrevenir : to contravene, to infringe

contrôle (m) : (1) roll, list;   (2) checking, verification

   ~ **de service** : duty roster

   ~ **d'identité** : name check, stop check, identity check
*Under the law of 2 February 1981 (amended by that of 10 June
1983) an **officier** or **agent de police judiciaire** is authorised to
demand proof of identity from any person in a public place.*

   ~ **judiciaire** : judicial supervision
*A measure by means of which a person charged with a crime may
be subjected to one or more legally defined restrictions on his
freedom as determined by the examining magistrate (or the court in
the case of an expedited hearing) to meet the exigencies of the
hearing or for security reasons. The numerous possible conditions
include bail (**cautionnement**).*

   ~ **juridictionnel** : judicial review

   ~ **nominatif** : nominal roll

contrôler : to check, to examine, to verify

controleur (m) général : chief police officer
*This is one of the highest ranks in the **Police Nationale**, ranking senior to a **commissaire divisionnaire**. It is approximately equivalent to an Assistant/Deputy Chief Constable (Commander/Deputy Assistant Commissioner in the Metropolitan Police).*

contumace (f) : failure to appear before the Court of Assize, contempt of court
The procedure comprises three stages :

    état de ~ : failure to appear
        Where a person due to appear before the Court of Assize fails to do so or absconds before the verdict is given.

    ordonnance de ~ : sentence in absentia
        *The pronouncing of judgement against a person in **l'état de contumace**.*

    purge de la ~ : surrender after failure to appear before the court
        The purging of the contempt of court by appearing before the court, either voluntarily or on arrest within the prescribed period of time.

convaincre : to convince, to convict, to find someone guilty

    atteint et convaincu d'un crime : guilty of crime in fact and in law

conversion (f) : conversion, change

    ~ d'un procès civil en procès criminel : conversion of a civil action into criminal proceedings

conviction (f) (pièces à ~) : exhibits (in a criminal case)

convocation (f) par procès verbal : formal notice, summons
Notice by the prosecutor inviting the accused (not being in custody) to attend the court on a given date and time.

convoi (m) exceptionnel : abnormal load

coordinées (fpl) : address and telephone number

copie (f) : copy, duplicate

    "pour ~ conforme" : certified true copy

coqueur (m) * : grass*, informer

corporel : bodily

corps (m) : body, corps

    ~ constitués : official bodies

    ~ de commissaires : police superintendent grades (see *commissaire*)

~ **de gardiens et gradés** : the corps of uniformed constables and sergeants

~ **de l'acte** : body of an instrument

~ **de métier** : trade guild, corporation

~ **de preuves** : body of evidence

~ **des lois** : body of the law

~ **d'inspecteurs** : corps of detective officers

~ **d'officiers de la paix** : the corps of uniformed officers (inspector ranks)

~ **du délit** : corpus delicti, actus reus

~ **urbain** : uniformed town police
A section of the National Police formed of those unifomed officers who have been posted to a particular town to perform normal patrol duties there. With the sûreté urbaine, it forms the police urbaine.

prise de ~ : apprehension, arrest

corréalité (f) : complicity
Participation in an offence as a principal in the first degree.

correctance (f) * : reform school (obsolete term)

correctionnalisation (f) **judiciaire** : reduced charge, plea bargaining
A judicially unlawful procedure which is nevertheless widely practised, consisting of referring what is in fact a felony to a lower court to avoid overloading the assize courts with marginal cases. This takes the form, for example, of ignoring the existence of aggravating circumstances.

correctionnel : apertaining to a misdemeanour (as opposed to felonies or summary offences)

passer en ~**le** : to appear before the **tribunal correctionnel** (= Crown Court)

corroborer : to corroborate

corrompre : to corrupt, bribe, tamper with

corruption (f) : bribery, corruption, subornation, procuring
Illegal activity whereby certain persons solicit, agree to or receive an offer, promise, gift or present. Passive corruption is committed by public officials etc. Active corruption is committed by those who try to obtain the advantage which another might give or agree to.

cortège (f) : procession

corvée (f) : forced labour, fatigues

costaud : strongly built, muscular

côte (f) : coast.   **garde-~** : coastguard vessel

cotisation (f) **sociale généralisée (CSG)** : social security contribution

cou (m) : neck

coup (m) : (1) knock, blow; (2) measure, quantity; (3) trick, dodge, ruse

~ **d'arnac** : fraud, swindle

~ **de boule** : head-butt

~ **de couteau** : stabbing, knife wound

~ **de filet** : drag-net, police raid

~ **de Jarnac** : treachery, disloyalty

~ **de lapin** : rabbit punch

~ **du père François** : strangulation

~ **de poing** : punch

~ **de poing américain** : knuckleduster

~ **s et blessures** : assault and battery, wounding, causing grievous bodily
harm
*This offence covers the whole range of assaults from one involving
very minor bodily harm to the most serious. It assumes the infliction
of a wound, burn or fracture, with or without a weapon.*

tomber sous le ~ de la loi : to fall within the provisions of the law, to fall
foul of the law

coupable : guilty, guilty person

coupe-file (m) : pass
*Document issued to VIPs, police officers, etc., enabling them to gain
immediate access to places where others have to wait.*

se couper : to give oneself away by making contradictory statements

coupure (f) : confidential information, tip-off, leak

cour (f) : court

~ **d'appel** : court of appeal
Second degree court of public general law, usually covering several
départements *(counties). It handles both civil and criminal appeals
on points of fact and of law.*

~ **d'assises** : assize court
>   *Criminal court trying felonies and consisting of two distinct elements, sitting together, viz. three judges and a jury of nine. Guilt is decided by a two-thirds majority of the combined judges and jurors and the sentence by a simple majority. The judges alone decide any damages. There is one assize court in each **département** (county). Decisions of the assize court are not subject to appeal although points of law may be referred to the **cour de cassation.***

~ **d'assises spéciale** : special asize court (to try cases of treason, espionage, etc.)

~ **de cassation** : supreme court of appeal
>   *The highest court for both civil (5 chambers) and criminal (1 chamber) matters. It only deals with matters of law, matters of fact being left to the lower courts.*

~ **de sûreté de l'état** : national security court
>   *Replaced in 1982 by the **Cour d'Assises Spéciale.***

courant (m) **d'air** : leak, disclosure of privileged information

courrier (m) : mail, post

course (f) : race, racing

~ **à l'échalotte** : eviction of someone by the scruff of the neck

~ **des lévriers** : dog racing, greyhound racing

~ **hippique** : horse race

~ **par course** : establishment providing telexed racing results

sous-direction des ~s et des jeux : police racecourse and gaming section

cousin (m), **cousine** (f) : cousin.   ~ **germain** : first cousin

couteau (m) : knife.   ~ **à cran d'arrêt** : flick-knife

coutume (f) : custom, habit

droit coutumier : common law

pays de coutume, de droit coutumier : common law countries
>   *The Anglo-Saxon countries, together with the provinces to the north of the river Loire (as opposed to **pays de droit écrit** or Roman Law provinces).*

couverte, couverture (f) : alibi (often a false one), front for shady activities

couvre-capote (m) : tonneau cover (of convertible motor car)

cracher * : to cough*, to spill the beans*, to confess

crâne (m) : skull, cranium

crânes (mpl) * : scalps*, collars*, arrests

crapaud/crapautard (m) * : wallet

crapuleux : sordid, heinous

crayonner : to accelerate rapidly, to "take off" at full speed
The term implies leaving burnt rubber tracks on the road like two large pencil marks.

crèche (f) * : digs*, bed-sitter, flatlet

crédible : convincing, credible, believable, accomplished

crédit-bail (m) : leasing

crêpe (f) * : flat cap

    faire la ~ : to overturn (a motor car)

crime (m) : serious crime, arrestable offence, felony
The more serious category of offences against the criminal law. Although the classification of felonies and misdemeanours was abolished in England by the Criminal Law Act, 1967, a similar distinction still exists in other countries, including the US and France and it is convenient to use these obsolete English terms to translate the French word (cf délit, contravention)

    ~ des foules : mob crime
    Crime committed without prior intent by one of a crowd on a sudden impulse.

    ~ passionnel : crime of passion
    Although not recognised by law, a crime committed for "noble" motives is often treated less severely by judges and juries.

criminaliser (un délit) : to classify (a misdemeanour) as a felony
To qualify a misdemeanour as a felony and transfer the case from lower court to the Court of Assize.

criminalistique (f) : criminalistics, forensic science
All those scientific disciplines which help the police and the courts determine the precise circumstances surrounding the commission of a crime and to identify the offenders. Includes forensic medicine, scenes of crime and fingerprint examinations, etc.

criminalité (f) : (1) crime statistics; (2) crime, delinquancy
All the offences committed within a given period (usually one year) in a given country. Distinction is made between :

    ~ apparente : offences known to the police, offences reported

    ~ légale : convictions

~ **réelle** : the probable total number of offences committed (including those not reported to the police)

criminel (m), **criminelle** (f) : criminal

grand ~ : felon

criminel : felonious, criminal

poursuivre au ~ : to take criminal proceedings

attentat ~ : criminal attempt

droit ~ : criminal law (the law relating to serious crimes)

criminogène : productive of crime

criminologie (f) : criminology
The scientific study of crime. Usually taken to cover the penal standard, the actual offence and the social reaction to it.

"(Le) criminel tient le civil en état" : "Civil actions are subordinate to criminal hearings"
Principle under which a civil judge, when dealing with an action for compensation arising out of a criminal act, must refrain from pronouncing judgement until such time as the criminal court judge has concluded the case brought by the public prosecutor.

crinière (f) : horsehair plume (on a ceremonial helmet)

crise (f) : (1) crisis;   (2) fit, attack

~ **cardiaque** : heart attack

~ **de conscience** : crisis of conscience

~ **de nerfs** : attack of nerves, fit of hysterics

~ **d'épilepsie** : epileptic fit

CRISTAL (m) : radio network used by the Gendarmerie

crochet (m) : hook, skeleton key

crocheter : to pick a lock

croix (f) : cross.   ~ **Rouge** : Red Cross

crosse (f) **d'appui** : butt (of firearm)

cryptage (m) : scrambling, encoding

cueille (f) * : drag-net, police raid

cuisinage (m) : "cooking the books", falsifying accounts cuisiner * : (1) to "work a fiddle", to falsify accounts; (2) to "grill" a suspect, to interrogate closely

culasse (f) : breech

    boite de ~ : breech block

    fermeture de ~ : bolt (of rifle)

culpabilité (f) : guilt

cumul (m) (des peines) : cumulative sentence, concurrence of penalties, sentences to run consecutively

curatelle (f) : trusteeship, guardianship

curieux (m) * : examining magistrate

cutter (m) : craft knife, "Stanley" knife

cyclard (m) : cyclist

cyclo, cyclomoteur (m) : moped (under 50 cc)

cylindrée (f) (grosse ~) : "super-bike", high-powered motor-cycle

cynophile : relating to dogs.

    brigade ~ : dog section

D

dactylo (m&f) : typist

    sténo~ : shorthand-typist

dactylographe (m&f) : typist

dactylographie (f) : typing

dactyloscopie (f) : identification by fingerprints

dada (m) * : (1) racehorse; (2) hobby horse, pet subject

daltonien : colour blind

dangerosité (f) : dangerousness, degree of danger

danger (m) **public** * : roadhog, dangerous driver

danse (f) : (1) dance; (2) * thrashing, beating

    entrer dans la ~ : to join in (an activity)

    mener la ~ : to take the lead

date (f) : date, time of the year

    à dater du : from

    ~ authentique : certified date

    ~ d'échéance : maturity, due date

    ~ limite : deadline

    en ~ du : dated

daubé * : infected, unfit for human consumption

daufier (m) * : pimp, ponce, procurer

daufière (f) * : prostitute, tart

dauphin (m) * : (1) jemmy, crowbar; (2) ponce, pimp; (3) heavy*, muscleman

dealer (m) : drugs dealer

débarbot (m) * : mouthpiece*, counsel for the defence

débarcade (f) * : discharge, release (from prison)

débats (mpl) : arguments
>   *That part of the court procedure which concerns the plaidoiries or verbal*
>   *representations to the court. In criminal cases the defendant has the last*
>   *word.*

~ **judiciaires** : hearing, proceedings, trial

débauche (f) : debauchery

excitation de mineur à la ~ : inducing a minor to lead a dissolute life

débaucher : (1) to entice away, to lead astray, to seduce; (2) to discharge, to
>   lay off (staff); (3) to induce workers to strike

débine (f) * : (1) utter poverty; (2) catastrophe, cock-up*

débit de tabac (m) : tobacco shop
>   *There is a fiscal monopoly on tobacco sales in France and only official*
>   *tobacco shops may sell it. The staff are subject to a complex legal system*
>   *and are, in effect, agents of the government and subject to its discipline.*
>   *Sale by an unauthorised person is an offence against the state monopoly*
>   *and may incur severe penalties.*

débonder * : to confess, to admit the truth

débouclarès * : unlocked, insecure, open

déboucleur * : safe-breaker, peterman

débouter : nonsuit, discontinuance

déboutonner * : (1) to confess; (2) to grass*, to inform

débrayer : to down tools

organiser un débrayage : to stage a walk out

débride (f) * : lifting of an **interdiction de séjour**

débrider : (1) to unlock, to open, to break open; (2) to open fire, to shoot

débringué : slovenly dressed

décale (f) : leave, holiday

décambuter * : to draw a gun

décanillage (m) : disorderly flight, hurried departure

décapiter : to behead

décapotable (f) : convertible (motor car)

décapoté : with the (car) hood down

décarpiller * : to share out the proceeds of a robbery

décarrade (f) : (1) exit, exit door; (2) prison break-out

décavé : (1) penniless, on the rocks; (2) aged, geriatric

décéder : to die, to decease

décentralisation (f) : decentralisation, devolution

décerner : to award, to decree, to issue

décès (m) : death, demise

> **acte de ~** : death certificate
> *Issued by the **officier de l'état-civil** for the area in which death occurred on the strength of a declaration made within 24 hours by a relative or other competent person.*

déchard (m) * : vagrant, penniless person

décharge (f) : (1) release, acquittal, discharge; (2) discharge (of firearm)

> **~ publique** : scrap heap, refuse dump

> **témoin à ~** : witness for the defence

déchéance (f) : downfall, forfeiture, withdrawal of rights

> **~ de la puissance paternelle** : loss of parental rights

> **~ de nationalité** : withdrawal of nationality rights

> **~ professionnelle** : disqualification, striking off, disbarring
> *Punishment, the object of which is to prevent the offender from exercising his profession. It may be imposed as the main penalty (instead of imprisonment), as a supplementary penalty (imposed by the judge in view of a link between the offence and the profession concerned) or as a secondary penalty (a consequence of the main punishment).*

décider : to decide, to settle

décision (f) : judicial decision, ruling
General term used to indicate the judgements made by a judge (or panel of judges)

> **~ avant dire droit** : interlocutory decision

> **~ (réputée) contradictoire** : judgement (deemed to be) subject to appeal

> **porter une ~** : to make a decision known, to promulgate a decision

> **prendre une ~** : to make, to reach a decision

prise de ~ : decision making

décisive (preuve ~) : conclusive (evidence)

décisoire (serment ~) : decisive (oath)
Oath sworn at the demand of the other party, upon which the decision of the court will be based.

déclarant (m) : informant
Person who notifies the appropriate authority of a fact (birth, death, etc.), an obligation, or an identity. Failure of the responsible person so to do is a punishable offence.

déclaration (f) : (1) statement of evidence; (2) report (of accident, etc.); (3) notification of birth, death, etc.; (4) formal declaration

~ **de culpabilité** : finding of guilt (recorded on the offender's criminal record)

~ **du jury** : findings of the jury

~ **en douane** : customs declaration

~ **sous serment** : sworn statement, statement under oath, affidavit

~ **universelle des droits de l'homme** : universal declaration of human rights

fausse ~ : misrepresentation

déclaré coupable : convicted

déclasser : to declassify, to downgrade a security classification

déclencher : to trigger off, to set in motion

déclinatoire (f) de compétence : plea alleging want of jurisdiction
Objection raised by a party to an action, before the case has been concluded, where he believes that the court concerned is not competent to hear the matter before it.

décliner (responsabilité) : to decline (responsibility)

décoller * : to bump off*, to kill

déconfiture (f) : insolvency (of an individual)

décongestionnant : degongesting, unclogging, relieving

décoration (f) : decoration, medal

port illégal de ~ : illegal wearing of decoration

décorer : to decorate

décret (m) : decree, edict, order
> *A statutory instrument made by the Head of State or by the Prime Minister relating to any matters which are not expressly the ambit of a loi (Act of Parliament) under the terms of the Constitution. Always subject to appeal to the Conseil d'Etat.*

> ~ **–loi** : decree-law
>> *A decree concerning a matter which should be the subject of a loi but which has been delegated to the Government by Parliament (Regarded as having the status of an Act of Parliament).*

> ~ **ministériel** : enabling decree
>> *Decree made by the prime minister to bring into effect laws passed by parliament.*

> ~ **portant règlement d'administration publique** : regulations implementing the provisions of an Act of Parliament

décriminalisation (f) : decriminalisation, legalisation

décrocher : (1) to retire from work; (2) to shelve (an enquiry); (3) to get off drugs, to kick the habit

décrochez–moi–ça (m) * : market stall selling cheap, ready-to-wear clothing

décuiter * : to sober up

de cujus : the deceased

déculpabilisant : exonerating

déculpabilisation (f) : removal of guilt, exoneration

déculpabiliser : to exonerate

dédommagement (m) : indemnification, compensation

dédommager : to compensate

dédouaner : to clear someone of a charge, to give them a clean bill of health

de droit : de jure (opposite to de facto)

défaillant (m) : absconder

défarguer : (1) to exonerate, to clear someone of a charge; (2) to dispose of incriminating evidence

défargueur (m) * : witness for the defence

défausser : to dispose of incriminating evidence

défaut (m) : absence, failure

> ~ **de comparution** : failure to appear

~ **de motifs** : lack of grounds for conviction (represents grounds for appeal)

défavorable : adverse

défectueux : faulty, unsound, defective

acte/**jugement** ~ : flawed deed/judgement

défendeur (m) : defendant

défendre : to defend

défense (f) : (1) defence; (2) stay; (3) ban, prohibition
*The term (3) is colloquially used to refer to an **interdiction de séjour**.*

~ **à exécution** : appeal court order staying the enforcement of a judgement

~ **d'autrui** : use of reasonable force in the defence of another

~ **de biens** : defence of property against attack
*This is one of the occasions where a citizen is entitled to use reasonable force to protect his property **(légitime défense).***

~ **de soi** : self-defence

~ **nationale** : national defence

~ **sociale** : concept of rehabilitation and reeducation, rather than punishment

légitime ~ : justifiable use of reasonable force in the protection of oneself or another or to protect property.

moyens de la ~ : case for the defence

défenseur (m) : counsel for the defence

~ **d'office** : defence counsel appointed by the court, duty solicitor

déférer : to hand over, to refer a case to a court, to transfer a case from a lower court to an appeal court

~ **le serment (à quelqu'un)** : to administer the oath (to someone), to swear a witness, to swear in a jury

~ **quelqu'un à la justice** : to hand over someone to justice

défilé (m) : march, procession

défiler : to slope off, to dodge an unpleasant task, to lie low, to hide

définitif (jugement ~ **)** : legally binding (judgement)

définition (f) **de poste** : job description

défoncé * : inebriated, in a state of extreme drug intoxication

défunt (m) : deceased

dégainer : to draw (a sword, pistol, etc.)

dégât (m) : damage (resulting from a violent cause)

> **~s matériels** : material damage, damage to property

> **expertise de ~s** : damage survey

déglingué : to be clapped out*, in a state of disrepair

dégommage (m) * : (1) reprimand; (2) dismissal; (3) beating up or killing

dégradation (f) : (1) (wrongful) waste, wear and tear; (2) reduction in rank

> **~ civique** : loss of civic rights
> *Punishment imposed by the courts whereby the offender loses all his rights to public office or employment, and is stripped of all civil and political rights and of certain family rights It may form the main punishment (felonies and political matters) or be complementary (all penalties for felonies under general law), in which case the loss is for life, or it may be an optional addition to a sentence of imprisonment where there are attenuating circumstances, in which case the loss is for 5 to 10 years.*

dégrafer : to wriggle loose, to escape

degré (m) : degree, level

> **~ de juridiction** : level of jurisdiction
> *The place of a court or tribunal in the judicial hierarchy Since 1958, only the court of appeal is a second level court In cases where an appeal is possible, there is said to be a **double degré de juridiction.***

> **~ de parenté** : degree of relationship

> **~ de précision** : degree of accuracy

dégrène (f) : malicious gossip, tittle-tattle

dégripper : to ease (nut or bolt), to oil the wheels*

dégrisement (m) : sobering up, cooling down

dégueulasse : revolting, sickening, disgusting

Deibler (m) (**une coupe à la ~**) : short back-and-sides, cropped haircut
Deibler was a famous executioner operating the guillotine.

de jure : de jure, by right, by lawful title

délai (m) : period (of time), time limit, respite, delay,
> Certain legal formalities must be completed within a particular period of
> time Failure to observe these time limits will result in consequences which
> vary in their severity. The day on which the period of time commences
> is not normally counted, whilst the day on which it ends may, or may not,
> be counted, depending on whether the period is referred to as **franc**
> (clear) or **non franc** (inclusive).

~ -congé : notice (period worked following notification of dismissal or
   resignation)

~ de comparution : notice of requirement to appear before the court
> The law provides that at least 10 days' notice must be given.

~ de grâce : days of grace, respite

~ d'épreuve : probation

~ de prescription : period of limitation of proceedings
> The prescribed period after which action is statute barred.

~ de procédure : procedural delay
> The time allowed a party to an action or case to carry out some
> specified formality In criminal cases it is normally accepted that
> such period of time runs from the day following the date of the
> document, event or decision granting the delay.

demande de prolongation du ~ d'opposition/d'appel) : application for
   extension of time allowed to lodge an objection/an appeal

délaissement (m) : desertion, abandonment

~ de poursuites : abandonment of prosecution

délaisser : to forgo, to relinquish, to abandon, to neglect

délateur (m) : informer, nark*, spy

délation (f) : denunciation, informing, denouncement

~ de serment (f) : dispensation from taking the oath
> Procedure under which a party to an action may be invited by the
> other party or the judge to merely attest to the accuracy of a fact
> or undertaking, rather than take the oath

délégation (f) : delegation (of authority), transfer, assignment

~ judiciaire : delegation of lawful authority
> Where an examining magistrate delegates to a police officer his
> authority to investigate an alleged crime. This takes the form of
> a **commission rogatoire**.

par ~ : on the authority of, "per pro"

délégatoire (pouvoir ~) : delegatory power

"de lege lata" : considering the law as it stands

délégué (m) : delegate, representative

    administrateur ~ : managing director

    ~ à la liberté surveillée : probation officer

    ~ à la protection de l'enfance : guardian of infants
        At every court of appeal there is a special chamber which hears
        appeals from the childrens' courts, attached to which is an adviser
        appointed for a period of three years renewable.

    ~ du personnel : workers representative

    ~ syndical : shop steward

délestage (m) : unloading

    itinéraire de ~ : alternative route, relief road

délester : to relieve someone of his money

délibération (f) : proceedings

délibéré (m) : deliberations, consideration of the verdict
    The phase in a hearing when the judges, having heard the evidence,
    retire to consider their verdict   This is always in secret but may be
    conducted "sotto voce" **sur le siège,** *ie. without actually retiring.*

    affaire mise en ~ : case adjourned for further consultation

délictueux : punishable

    acte ~ : misdemeanour

délinquant (m) : offender, miscreant, delinquant
    A person who has committed an offence against the criminal law in its
    widest sense.

    ~ d'habitude : recidivist

    ~ primaire : first offender

délit (m) : criminal offence, misdemeanour (see **crime**)
    In its widest sense, the term includes any criminal offence   Strictly
    speaking it refers to those offences which fall between **crimes** *(felonies)*
    and **contraventions** *(summary offences).*

    ~ collectif par unité de but : collective misdemeanour with a common aim
        A **délit complexe,** *committed where there are several factors, each*
        of which constitutes an offence in itself, but are considered
        together as a whole (eg. manufacture of counterfeit coin).

~ **complexe** : complex crime
Where several factors go to make up a single crime.

~ **continu** : continuing crime
Where the commission takes place over a period of time (e.g. handling stolen property, living on immoral earnings).

~ **d'audience** : contempt of court
Offence committed during a court hearing for which the judge has powers of sanction.

~ **de fuite** : failure to stop after an accident
Offence committed by the driver of a road vehicle or boat who fails to stop as soon as possible after an accident, with intent to avoid responsibility.

~ **d'entrave** : obstructing the formation of a **comité d'entreprise** or its activities

~ **disciplinaire** : disciplinary offence, breach of a code of ethics

~ **d'habitude** : habitual misdemeanour
*Where there are several factors, none of which, in isolation, constitute an offence. It is one form of **délit complexe**.*

~ **d'omission** : failure to perform a statutory duty
Includes failure to report a crime, failure to testify, failure to try to stop a crime being committed, failure to render assistance to a person in danger, etc.

~ **flagrant** : see **flagrant délit**

~ **impossible** : attempt to commit an impossible act
This includes all attempts which are doomed to failure due to lack of objective (murder of person already dead, abortion of woman who is not pregnant) or through lack of means (administering a non-toxic substance instead of the intended poison, etc.).

~ **instantané** : completed crime
Where the offence is committed at a given instant (e.g. theft).

~ **manqué** : unsuccessful crime
Where the offender carried out all the necessary steps for the commission of the crime but failed to complete the commission due to his clumsiness or other such reason, provided that his intended aim would have been possible, had he been more adroit, quicker, etc.

~ **pénal** : criminal act, misdemeanour
*In its widest sense, any offence against the criminal law. In its narrower sense, it refers to misdemeanours (as opposed to felonies). Theft is a **délit pénal** in its narrow sense.*

~ **permanent** : permanent misdemeanour
*Where a materially durable result is created, such as the
construction of an unauthorised building.*

~ **successif** : repeated offence
*This implies a guilty mind which is renewed each time the offence
is repeated (eg. the unlawful wearing of decorations).*

pris en flagrant ~ : caught in the act, caught red-handed
*The concept of **flagrant délit** is an important one as it represents
one of the rare circumstances under which a police officer of any
rank may make an arrest without the prior sanction of a **juge
d'instruction**.*

quasi ~ : technical offence

délivrer : to furnish someone with a document

délourder : to open a door
*There is no suggestion of forcible entry here and the verb is often used
in the imperative mood (**Délourdez!** – Open up!).*

déloyal : unfair

démafiosation (f) : elimination of Mafia influence

demande (f) : application, request, petition

~ **de renseignements** : inquiry

~ **en justice** : writ, summons
*Procedure by means of which one may bring a matter before a
court. The burden of proof rests with the applicant.*

demander : to ask, to request

demandeur (m), **demanderesse** (f) : plaintiff, appellant, applicant

démarchage (m) : door-to-door selling, hawking

démarcheur (m) : agent, canvasser, door-to-door salesman

démêlés (mpl) : differences, unpleasant dealings, contentions

déménager : to move house

~ **à la cloche de bois** : to do a moonlight flit, to leave without paying rent

démence (f) : diminished responsibility
*Psychic or neuro-psychological disorder of a person's mind whereby his
criminal responsibility is diminished.*

démerdeur (m) * : (1) resourceful person, "smart Alec"; (2) mouthpiece, lawyer

demeure (f) : (1) stay, sojourn; (2) dwelling, residence

    mise en ~ : formal notice to do something

demi (m) : glass of draught beer served in café
*Contrary to popular belief, the term refers to a **demi pression** and not half
a litre – the glass in fact holds 33 cl.*

demi-cercle (m) : half circle

    pincer quelqu'un au ~ : to catch someone unawares, to arrest someone

démicroter : to debug

demi-folie (f) : temporary insanity, balance of mind temporarily disturbed
Pleaded to invoke a reduced penalty as an attenuating circumstance.

demi-mondaine (f) : tart, woman of doubtful morals

demi-monde (m) : the fringes of criminality, shady*

demi-sel (m) : petty criminal, would-be tough guy

démission (f) : resignation

    ~s concertées : mass resignation
*It is an offence for public officials to agree to resign their posts
simultaneously in order to impede justice or to hinder the provision
of a particular service.*

démolir : to demolish, to destroy, to injure, to kill

démontrer (un droit) : to evidence (a right)

dénégation (f) : denial, traverse

    ~ de responsabilité : disclaimer of responsibility

déni (m) : denial, refusal

    ~ de justice : denial of justice, refusal of court to hear a case
*Where a court refuses to hear a matter which has been properly
brought before it. It constitutes a criminal misdemeanour.*

dénomination (f) **sociale** : company name, trading name

dénoncer : to inform against someone, to accuse

dénonciation (f) : denunciation, accusation, report of offence
The reporting of an offence to the authorities by a third party.

~ **calomnieuse** : false accusation, malicious prosecution
Criminal misdemeanour committed by any person who wrongfully accuses another, in writing, of having broken the law, knowing this to be untrue.

~ **d'instance** : institution of proceedings

dénoyauter (~ un suspect) : to "crack" a suspect, to get to the heart of an enquiry by skilful questioning

denrées (fpl) : foodstuffs, commodities, produce

~ **alimentaires** : foodstuffs

~ **de première nécessité** : essential goods

densité (f) **(de la population)** : population, population density

déontologie (f) : deontology, professional ethics, disciplinary regulations
These are the legal and moral rules to be observed by those exercising certain activities, including civil servants, judges and members of the liberal professions such as lawyers, doctors, etc. The rules vary from one profession to another and breaches may be result in disciplinary action.

dépanner : to render assistance, to give a helping hand

dépanneuse (f) : break-down truck

départ (m) **à la retraite** : retirement

département (m) : (1) county;   (2) Department (of State)
(1) An administrative division of the State and a local authority area There are 96 départements in France, plus a number of overseas ones (see Département d'Outre-Mer).   (2) A term synonymous with ministry used to describe a given division of the central government.

~ **d'outre-mer (DOM)** : overseas county
Local authorities created in 1946 to strengthen the links between Metro-politan France and four of its oldest colonies, Guyane, Guadaloupe, Martinique and La Réunion.   In 1976 St Pierre et Miquelon were added to the list.   They are regarded as being exactly the same as a département in Metropolitan France and are policed by detachments of the national police and gendarmerie (See also Territoire d'Outre-Mer).

dépasser : to exceed

~ **la limitation de vitesse** : to exceed the speed limit

dépénaliser : to decriminalise

dépendance (f) : dependence (e.g. on drugs, alcohol)

~ **physique** : physical dependence

~ **psychique** : psychological dependence

dépens (mpl) : costs

être condamné aux ~ : to be ordered to pay costs

dépiauter : to severely criticise a literary work or a document (e.g. a report)

~ **un suspect** : to interrogate a suspect closely, to grill* a suspect

dépistage (m) : detection, discovery

déplacement (m) : displacement, shifting, movement

~ **d'office** : compulsory transfer

frais de ~ : travelling expenses

déplanquer : (1) to retrieve an object from its hiding place; (2) to redeem a pledge from a pawnbroker

de plein droit : ipso jure, by legal right, by lawful title

dépliant (m) : folder, brochure

déport (m) : declaration of interest
Where an examining magistrate declines to deal with a case because he knows one of the parties involved.

déporteur (m) : rear spoiler (automobile)

déposant (m) : deponent, witness giving testimony

déposer : (1) to deposit, to lodge, to file, to register, to lay; (2) to make a statement, to depose

~ **un projet de loi** : to table, bring in a bill

dépositaire (m) : bailee
One who receives goods belonging to another, undertaking to look after them and return them in due course.

déposition (f) : witness statement, statement of evidence, testimony
Statement made by a third party informing the appropriate authorities (judiciary, police) what he saw, heard or learned in connection with a dispute or allegation.

~ **sous foi de serment** : sworn statement, deposition

dépossession (f) : dispossession, eviction, ouster

Dépôt (m) : court cells (in the Paris **Palais de Justice**)

dépôt (m) **public** : public record office

dépoter : (1) to exhume a corpse; (2) to drop someone, after giving a lift

dépouille (f) : mugging, robbery

dépresseur (m) : sedative, downer*

déprime (f) : nervous depression, nervous breakdown

député (m) : delegate, deputy, member of parliament

~-maire : MP and mayor (not deputy mayor)

dérangement (m) (en ~) : out of order

déranger : to disturb

déraper : to skid

sans ~ : non-stop

dératiser : to debug

dérober : to steal, to rob

déroger : to waive, to depart from (custom, the law)

désaccord (m) : disagreement

désaffection (f) : putting a public building to another purpose

église désaffectée : deconsecrated church

désamorcer (un conflit) : to defuse (a situation)

désarmer : to disarm

désaveu (m) : disavowal

désavouer : to deny, to retract

désaxé (m) : psychopath, violent mentally deranged person

descendre : (1) to knock back (a drink); (2) to gun down, to kill

descente (f) : descent, swoop, police raid

~ de justice : see ~ sur les lieux

~ sur les lieux : visit of the court or its officers to the scene

désert (m) : military deserter

déshabillage (m) : severe reprimand, dressing down

désignation (f) : designation, nomination, appointment

désigner : to nominate, to appoint, to list

désinhibant : disinhibiting (effect of certain drugs)

désintéressé : disinterested

>   **avis ~** : unbiased, unprejudiced advice

désistement (m) : nolle prosequi, desistance, nonsuit

>   **~ volontaire** : voluntary abandonment (of a criminal attempt)
>   *Where a person attempting to commit an offence desists from so
>   doing without any external coercion and before the offence is
>   complete. He is thus not guilty of any offence.*

se désister : to withdraw (an application, a complaint)

désobéir : to disobey

désordre (m) : disorder

désosser : to break down, to dismantle, to take to pieces

dessaisi : disseized, dispossessed

>   **"le tribunal s'est ~ de l'affaire"** : the court has decided not to proceed
>   with the case

dessaisissement (m) **du juge** : relieving the judge of further responsibility for
a case
*Once a judge has made a judgement he is, in principle, relieved from any
further responsibility for the case. He retains, however, the right to
interpret his decision or to correct any material error or omission.*

dessous : (1) under; (2) pimp's second woman

>   **au ~ de la normale** : below standard

>   **~ de table** : bribe, back-hander*

destinataire (m&f) : addressee, consignee, payee, recipient

destituer : to dismiss, to remove from office

destitution (f) : dismissal

destruction (f), dégradations et dommages : criminal damage
*Offence committed by any person who wilfully destroys or causes damage
to the property of another, other than a very minor defacement. The
offence may be simple or aggravated (by breaking-in, type of victim, etc.).*

désuétude (f) : disuse, desuetude, obsolescence

loi tombée en ~ : law fallen into disuse, abeyance
*The position of a law which, in fact, is not used Some legal experts
consider that this may be regarded as an implicit repeal of the law.*

détacher : to second, to attach

détaillant (m) : retailer

détaxé : duty free

détecteur (m) **de mensonge** : lie detector, polygraph

détective (m) : private detective

détenir : to detain, to hold

détente (f) : trigger

détention (f) : (1) imprisonment, detention, confinement; (2) holding, possession

~ **arbitraire** : unlawful arrest

~ **criminelle** : imprisonment for political offence (usually in a special part
of the prison)

~ **provisoire** : detention on remand, pre-trial detention
*The incarceration of a person suspected of an offence during the
judicial examination of the case, or of a person charged with a
misdemeanour under the provisions of comparution immédiate. Being
an exceptional measure, it may be invoked only in specified cases
and by a judge after he has listened to both the prosecutor and the
accused and, where appropriate, his counsel.*

détenu (m) : prisoner

~ **condamné** : convicted prisoner

déterminer : to ascertain, to determine

détonateur (m) : detonator

détournement (m) : diversion, embezzlement, misappropriation

~ **d'avion** : hi-jacking

~ **de fonds** : fraudulent conversion, embezzlement, misappropriation of
funds

~ **de fonds publics** : fraudulent conversion of public funds

~ **de mineurs** : abduction of minors

~ **de pièces** : diversion of documents

~ **de pouvoir** : abuse of authority
> *Where the local or central government pursues a purpose other than that designated by the law, thus using the power conferred upon it for other than its proper purpose. For example, a mayor who issues a bye-law to settle a personal score commits this offence.*

~ **d'objets saisis** : conversion of seized items

détriment (m) : detriment

au ~ **de** : at the expense of, to the detriment of

dette (f) : debt

deuche (f) * : Citroën 2 CV

deuil (m) : (1) mourning, sorrow; (2) risk of arrest

porter le ~ : to lodge a formal complaint

deusio, deuxio : secondly, in the second place

deux-roues (m) : bicycle, motorcycle

devers (garder quelque chose par ~ **soi)** : to keep something in one's possession

déviation (f) : diversion, deviation

devises (fpl) : foreign currency

dézinguer * : (1) to damage, to bugger up*; (2) to kill, to bump off*

diable (m) : devil

habiter au ~ : to live miles from anywhere, out in the sticks

diabolo (m) : soft drink (mixture of lemonade and fruit syrup)

DIAMANT : One of the Gendarmerie radio networks

diapo (m) : see **diapositive**

diapositive (f) : photographic slide, colour transparency

diffamer : to defame, to slander

diffamation (f) : defamation
> *Allegation or insinuation which is detrimental to the character and reputation of a person or body corporate. It becomes a misdemeanour where it is made in public or is published for public consumption.*

~ **orale** : slander

écrit diffamatoire : libel

différend (m) : difference, dispute, disagreement

différer (un jugement) : to defer judgement, to postpone sentence

dilatoire : dilatory

    moyen ~ : sham plea

diligence (f) : (1) diligence, industry, application, perseverance, persistence; (2) proceedings

diligenter (une enquête) : to interview witnesses

dindonner : to con, to swindle

dingue (m) : nut-case*, crackpot

dingue (f) : jemmy, crowbar

diplômé (m) : graduate

dire (m) : statement, assertion, allegation

    à ~ d'expert : according to expert opinion

    ~ le droit : to state the legal position

    ~ s et observations : statements and remarks

    selon les ~ s du témoin : according the the witness

directeur (m) : manager, head of department, governor (of a prison), headmaster, editor (of a newspaper), director (of a governmental service)

    ~ général : director-general, general manager

direction (f) : management, administration

    ~ de la Logistique de la Police : police procurement directorate

    ~ de la Surveillance du Territoire : State Security Directorate
    That section of the national police responsible for state security and counter-espionage matters.

    ~ des douanes : Customs service

direction (f) **centrale** : central directorate, central headquarters

    ~ de la Police Judiciaire : national headquarters of the CID.

    ~ de la Police Territoriale : national directorate of general police services
    A result of recent decentralisation measures, this directorate covers both the Service Central des Polices Urbaines and the Service Central des Renseignements Généraux.

direction générale (f) : general directorate, general headquarters

> ~ de la Police Nationale : the police department
> *A department of the Ministry of the Interior under the control of
> the Director-General of Police (a senior civil servant and not usually
> a career police officer), it is divided into ten directorates and
> operational services comprising the general inspectorate, the territ-
> orial police, the CID, the frontier police, the official transport
> service, the state security service, the CRS, the international tech-
> nical cooperation service, as well as the personnel/training and
> procurement departments.*

directives (fpl) : directions, directives, instructions, orders

dirigeant (m) : manager, executive, leader

> ~s : the establishment

> les classes ~es : the ruling classes

diriger : to direct, to manage, to operate

discontinuation (f) de poursuites : abandonment of prosecution

discrétion (f) : discretion, prudence, circumspection, secrecy

> à ~ : unconditionally

discrétionnaire : discretionary

> pouvoir ~ : full powers to act

discrimination (f) : discrimination
> *It is an offence to provoke discrimination, hatred or violence towards a
> person on the grounds of their origins, race, nationality, ethnic roots,
> religion or limited numbers.*

discriminatoire : discriminatory

disculpation (f) : acquittal, pardon, reprieve, exoneration, exculpation

> se disculper : to clear oneself

discutable : arguable, debatable

disjoncter : to dislocate, to disrupt

dispense (f) : exemption, waiver

> ~ de peine : absolute discharge
> *Measure by means of which a judge, recognising the guilt of a
> person charged with a summary offence or misdemeanour, decides
> not to impose any punishment because the offence is not likely to
> be repeated and there is no lasting detriment to the public interest.*

disponible : available

disposer : to have at one's command/disposal

   ~ **que** : to prescribe, to provide for, to enjoin

dispositif (m) : (1) disposition, order of things; (2) device

   ~ **de la loi** : enacting terms of a statute

   ~ **du jugement** : enacting terms of a judgement

disposition (f) : disposal, disposition, provision, arrangement, design

   ~ **s du Code Pénal** : provisions of the Criminal Law

   ~ **s d'une loi, etc.** : provisions of an act, etc.

   ~ **s générales** : general rules, general requirements

   mettre à la ~ **de quelqu'un** : to place at the disposal of someone

   prendre des ~ **s** : to make arrangements, to provide for

   sauf ~ **contraire** : unless otherwise provided, unless I hear to the contrary

disque (m) : disk (computer)

dissimuler : to hide, to conceal, to mask

distribution (f) **d'objets contraires à la décence** : distribution of obscene publications

district (m) : district
A voluntary association of local authorities to meet the cost of major facilities such as fire-fighting, refuse collection and disposal, public transport, etc.

dit (m) : written assertion of facts

divertissement (m) : fraudulent conversion
The diversion by a co-beneficiary of legacies under a will, or of jointly-owned property by a co-owner, to his own use.

divisionnaire (m) : see **commissaire divisionnaire**

document (m) : document,

   ~ **de sécurité** : security printed documents
Covers all documents of value which have a built-in security measure, such as cheques, banknotes, promissory notes, credit cards, passports, driving licences, etc.

   ~ **probant** : conclusive written evidence

documentique (f) : document processing (by computer)

dol (m) : mens rea, criminal intent

> ~ **éventuel** : recklessness
> *Where the person concerned did not intend the injurious results of his action but foresaw the possibility of these.*

> ~ **incident** : deception
> *Fraud relating to the ancillary provisions of a contract, in the absence of which the victim would not have entered into the contract under the same conditions.*

> ~ **indéterminé** : implicit criminal intent
> *Where the person concerned acted intentionally but without having a clearly defined result in mind. He will be guilty of the offence ultimately committed.*

> ~ **principal** : fraudulently inducing a victim to enter into a contract

> ~ **spécial** : specific intent
> *The law sometimes requires that there must be a specific intent in order to prove the offence. For example, the destruction of prints and marks at the scene of a crime must be effected with intent to "hamper the due process of law".*

dolosif : fraudulent

> **intention dolosive** : intention prejudicial to interests protected by the criminal law

doléances (fpl) : grievances

dombeur (m) : jemmy, crowbar

domicile (m) : dwelling, home, domicile
Unlike English law, domicile refers to place of principal establishment, or where one is reputed to live This is not necessarily the actual place of residence but service of documents to a person's domicile is regarded as good service

> ~ **civil** : place where a person exercises his civil rights

> ~ **conjugal** : domicile of a married couple (the husband's address)

> ~ **élu** : address nominated for the service of documents
> *Commonly the registered office of a firm, or the office of the person's lawyer*

> ~ **légale, de droit** : domicile assigned by law to certain persons not in full possession of civil rights (juvenile, convict, mentally defectives)

> ~ **réel** : actual place of residence

> ~ **social/siège social** : registered office

sans ~ **fixe** : of no fixed abode

violation de ~ : violation of the privacy of a person's home, illegal entry
Misdemeanour committed by a servant of the administrative or judicial authorities, a police officer or gendarme who enters the residence of an individual against his wishes. This misdemeanour may also be committed by an ordinary citizen if the entry is made by means of deception, threats or violence.

domicilliaire : domicillary

visite ~ : search of premises by a magistrate

dommage (m) : damage, injury

~ **aux animaux** : causing injury to animals

~ **aux biens** : criminal damage

~ **corporel** : bodily injury

~ **s–intérêts** : (award of) damages

~ **s matériels** : damage to property

don (m) : gift, present, donation

donner : (1) to give; (2) to inform on someone

se la ~ : to have suspicions about something

donneur (m) * : police informer, copper's nark"

dopant (m) : stimulant, "upper" (drugs)

dorto (m) * : "dorm", dormitory

dortoir (m) : dormitory, sleeping quarters

dose (f) : dose, shot (of drug)

dossier (m) : documents, file, record, evidence, case

avoir un ~ **lourdement chargé** : to have a very bad record

~ **de personnalité** : personal file
The examining magistrate may cause a file to be prepared covering the accused person's character, his financial, family and social position, a medical or psychological report and any other useful matters.

~ **d'une procédure** : brief

joindre une pièce au ~ : to file a document

doter : to endow (with means); to equip (with plant, etc)

douane (f) : customs

    Administration des ~ s : Board of Customs

    bureau de ~ : customs post

    droits de ~ : customs duties

    exempt des droits de ~ : duty free

    franc de ~ : duty paid

    marchandises en ~ : bonded goods

    visite de la ~ : customs examination, search

douanier (m) : (1) customs officer; (2) glass of **absinthe**

double incapacité de donner et de recevoir à titre gratuit : disqualification from right to dispose of property freely
Further penalty, added to certain general penalties, which prevents a convicted person from receiving or giving property by way of gift or legacy. It is a permanent disqualification.

doubler : to double-cross, to deceive

doublure (f) : understudy, stand-in, front man

douille (f) : (1) cartridge case; (2) * cash, money, brass*, dough*, bread*

doulos (m) * : informer, grass*, nark*

doute (m) : doubt, misgiving, uncertainty

    acquittement au bénéfice du ~ : acquittal on benefit of the doubt

douteux, douteuse : doubtful

    créance ~ : bad (dubious) debt

drag (f) * : joint*, reefer*, marijuana cigarette

drapeau (m) : (1) flag, banner, ensign; (2) unpaid bill

    planter un ~ : to leave without paying

dreauper (m) * : copper, policeman
*This is an example of **verlin** slang, in which the two syllables (of **perdreau**) are reversed.*

dresser (un procès verbal) : to draw up, write out, to prepare (a report)

driver : to drive someone somewhere, to give a lift

drogue (f) : drug

drogué (m) : drug addict

droit (m) : (1) the law

abus de ~ : misuse of the law

~ administratif : administrative law

~ civil : civil law
That branch of the law which covers transactions between individuals, not of general public concern.

~ commercial : commercial law

~ commun : ordinary law
Those rules normally applicable in law.

~ constitutionnel : constitutional law

~ coutumier : common law

~ criminel : see **droit pénal**

~ des affaires : commercial law

~ des transports : transport law
The law applicable to the transport of goods and passengers (by rail, air, inland waterways, sea and road) and governing the associated personnel, equipment, vehicles and buildings.

~ écrit : statute law

~ judiciaire : legal procedures, rules of evidence
Term used to define the body of rules and regulations governing the organisation and operation of civil and criminal jurisdictions.

~ militaire : military law

~ pénal : criminal law
That branch of the law which defines certain acts or omissions **(infractions)** *and the sanctions to be applied to these* **(peines)**.

~ pénal général : general criminal law
Those concepts which apply to all criminal offences (eg mens rea, the notion of "attempt").

~ pénal spécial : specific criminal law
The study of the various criminal offences (murder, rape, etc)

~ **positif** : current law
> *This comprises all the legal rules and regulations in force within a State at any given time, regardless of their source*

~ **privé** : private law
> *The rules which regulate relations between individuals and, in certain circumstances, between individuals and the State. It includes the civil law, the commercial law, the maritime law and the labour laws.*

~ **public** : public law
> *Those rules which govern the State and its relations with individuals. It includes constitutional law, administrative law, financial legislation, international public law, etc.*

~ **romain** : Roman law

prisonnier de ~ **commun** : common criminal (as opposed to a political offender)

droit (m) : (2) right, reason, lawful, legal

à bon ~ : with good reason

à qui de ~ : to whom it may concern

conferer un ~ **à qn** : to bestow a right on someone

de plein ~ : ipso jure, by legal right

donner ~ : to confer title

~ **à l'information** : right of access to information

~ **d'arrestation** : power of arrest

~ **de suite** : power to carry out a criminal investigation

être dans son ~ : to be within one's rights

exercer un ~ : to exercise a right

faire ~ **à une demande** : to accede to a request, to allow a claim

faire valoir son ~ : to put in a claim, to claim one's right

marcher ~ : to toe the line

par voies de ~ : by legal process

responsable en ~ : legally responsible

sans ~ : unlawfully

sauvegarder un ~ : to sustain a right

sous les peines de ~ : incurring legal penalties

droits (mpl) : (1) rights

~ **civils** : civic rights

~ **civiques** : political rights

~ **corporels** : choses in possession

~ **d'accès** : rights of access

~ **de grâce** : right of free pardon (exercised by the President of the
    Republic)

~ **de la défense** : defendant's rights

~ **de l'homme** : human rights

~ **de réunion** : right of assembly

~ **de révendication** : right to repossess

~ **d'ester en jugement** : capacity to appear in court

~ **d'établissement** : right to take up residence in a foreign country

~ **d'évocation** : right of a higher court to summon a case pending below,
    writ of certiorari

~ **de visite** : rights to enter and search

droits (mpl) : (2) duties, charges, fees, dues

~ **d'auteur** : royalties

~ **de greffe** : fees charged by the clerk of the court

~ **d'enregistrement** : registry fee

~ **de péage** : tolls

~ **de sortie** : export duty

~ **de voirie** : road tax

~ **d'exécution** : performing rights (music, etc)

~ **d'inscription** : entry fee, membership fee

~ **judiciaires, de justice** : court costs

drouille (f) * : dross, junk, unsaleable wares

duce (m) * : tip-off, secret information

duel (m) : duel

> *Duels are illegal on the basis that the consent of the victim is no justification for an illegal act (homicide, wounding).*

duplicata (m) : double

> *The second exemplar of a document which, unlike a* **copie** *is acceptable as an original.*

dur (m) * : (1) tough guy, hard man; (2) train; (3) readies*, hard cash

les ~s : hard labour

> *The distinction between an ordinary prison sentence and* **travaux forcés** *has all but disappeared but the difference to hardened criminals was, until recently, of great importance.*

dure (f) : bare ground, hard earth

coucher à la ~ : to sleep rough

"dura lex, sed lex" : "The law is severe but it is the law"

durant : during, throughout

durée (f) : duration, period (of stay), hours (of work)

dynamite (f) : (1) dynamite explosive; (2) cocaine, snow*

dynamité : high*, smashed*, drugged

E

éboulé * : deceased

ébouser * : to bump off*, to kill

ébriété (f) : intoxication

    en état d'~ : under the influence of drink

échafaud (m) : (1) scaffolding, staging; (2) gallows, gibbet

échangeur (m) : interchange, cloverleaf

échauder * : to con*, to diddle*, to cheat

échéance (f) : term, falling due, maturity, date

échelle (f) : ladder, scale

    ~ mobile : index linked

échelon (m) : grade, level

échevin (m) : (1) pre-Revolutionary municipal magistrate; (2) Belgian alderman

échevinage (m) : a tribunal where both professional judges and lay persons take an active part in the decision making

échoir (il échet, il echoit, etc) : (1) to fall (to someone's lot); (2) to fall due

éclairage (m) : (street) lighting

éclaircissement (m) : elucidation, clarification

éclater : (1) to burst, to explode; (2) to take a trip*, to be intoxicated by drugs

école (f) : school, college, training centre

    ~ classique : the classical school (of thought)
        School of thought which, in criminal matters, bases the right to punish on the idea of a social contract and thus assigns a strictly utilitarian role to the penalty imposed. This school, which offers a repressive solution to crime, incorporates twin hypotheses: the free agency of man and thus his responsibility for his actions, and the effectiveness of the penalty to combat the criminal phenomenon.

    ~ de la défense sociale : the social defence school (of thought)
        A school of thought which, in criminal matters, bases the right to punish on the concept of the necessary protection of the public against offenders. Although this school of thought was initially somewhat disinterested in the offender, current social defence movements are however marked by a clearly individualistic

attitude, taking the view that the public is best protected by the reformation of criminals and thus sentencing them to the penalty or safety measure which appears to be the most suitable, given the character and personality of the offender.

~ **des officiers de la Gendarmerie** : gendarmerie officers' training school

~ **nationale de l'administration (ENA)** : National Civil Service College

~ **nationale de la magistrature (ENM)** : National Judiciary College
The college where future judges are trained. Entry is by competitive examination or by qualification. The college also organises further training for existing judges.

~ **nationale de police** : initial training school
*There are seven such schools, one of which is dedicated to the training of **enquêteurs** (detective constables), the other concentrating on the training of uniformed **gardiens** (constables). Each school is responsible for a number of training centres (centres de formation de la police).*

~ **nationale supérieure de la police** : national police staff college
*The senior police college, located near Lyons, where future **commissaires de police** are trained.*

~ **supérieure des officiers de paix** : junior police college (uniform)
*Training centre located near Nice which provides initial and refresher courses for uniformed **officiers de paix** (inspectors) of the Police Nationale.*

~ **supérieure des inspecteurs de Police** : junior police college (CID)
*Training centre located near Nice which provides initial and refresher courses for **inspecteurs de police** (detective officers) of the Police Nationale.*

écoper * : to cop* (something), to receive (something)

écoulement (m) : uttering, passing-off, putting into circulation

écoute (f) : listening device, "bug", phone tap

écrase-merde (mpl) : "beetle-crushers", large boots

écraser : to crush, to flatten

    s'~ : to clam up, to keep silent, to adopt a low profile

    se faire ~ : to get run over

écrit (m) : document, writing

    droit ~ : statute law

    par ~ : in writing

écriture (f) : legal/commercial paper, record, document

    faux en ~s : forged document, tampering with official records, false entry

écrou (m) : entry on prison calendar of receipt of prisoner into custody or his release

    levée d'~ : discharge from prison, release of a prisoner

    livre d'~ : prison calendar

    ordre d'~ : committal to prison

écrouer : to imprison, to commit to prison

ecstasié (m) : person high on the drug Ecstasy

édicter : to enact, to decree

édifice (m) **(social)** : (social) structure

édile (m) : town councillor

éditeur (m) : publisher

    ~ responsable : person legally responsible for the content of publications

édition (f) : publication, publishing, edition, impression

    ~ des pièces : discovery of documents

édredon (m) : inducement
Promise made to criminal to induce him to inform on accomplices.

éducateur (m) : teacher, educator (especially one working with ex-offenders)

éducation (f) : education, training

    ~ routière : road safety training

    ~ surveillée : reformative education
The departments within the Ministry of Justice which are concerned with the problems posed by juvenile delinquance and young persons in moral danger.

effaroucher : to nick*, to pinch*, to steal

effectif (m) : staff, personnel, manpower, establishment

    ~ au complet : full strength

    ~ réel : actual strength

effectif, –ive : actual, true, real, effective

>   **résidence** ~ : actual residence

>   **valeur** ~ : actual value

effet (m) : effect, result

>   ~ **accordéon** : concertina effect

>   **avoir/porter/produire** ~ : to come into effect

>   **de nul** ~ : of no effect

>   **donner** ~ : to give effect

>   ~ **de droit** : legal effect

>   ~ **dévolutif** : devolutionary effect
>   *Where an appeal is lodged against a decision of an examining magistrate, the* **chambre d'accusation** *may confirm or revoke an order for remand in custody. Where other matters are concerned it may return the file to the magistrate (or another magistrate) for further enquiry, or take over the case itself.*

>   ~ **quant au fond** : fact having a bearing on the case

>   ~ **quant à la forme** : formal effect

>   ~ **rétroactif** : ex post facto, retrospective effect

>   ~**s mobiliers** : possessions, belongings, personal effects, clothes, goods and chattels

>   ~ **suspensive (d'un appel)** : the suspending of sentence pending appeal

>   ~ **transitoire** : temporary, transient effect

>   **mettre à** ~ : to carry into effect

>   **prendre** ~ : to take effect, to become operative, to come into force

>   **sans** ~ : ineffective, of no avail

effeuilleuse (f) : stripper

effraction (f) : breaking (in the sense of "housebreaking")

>   ~ **extérieure** : breach of close

>   ~ **intérieure** : breaking into premises

>   **vol avec effraction** : burglary
>   *Note that the element of "breaking" no longer applies to the crime of burglary under English law.*

égard (eu ~ à) : taking into account, consistent with

égorgerie (f) : massacre, slaughter

éjecteur (m) : ejector

élargissement (m) : release (of a prisoner)

"électa una via, non datur recursus ad alteram" : "Once a course of action has been taken, it is not possible to change to another"
Traditional legal adage, now enshrined in the Code of Criminal Procedure which, in order to prevent blackmail, forbids the victim of an offence who has started an action for compensation in the civil courts, to change his mind later and bring the matter before the criminal courts. This will not apply if the public prosecutor decides to take over the case and bring it before the criminal court before the civil court has completed its hearing.

élection (f) : election, nomination

    faire ~ de domicile : to nominate address for service
    Nominating an address for the service of documents, etc. This need not be one's place of residence but could be, for example, that of one's lawyer.

élément (m) : element, fact, factor

    ~ constitutif d'une infraction : factor constituting an offence

    ~ injuste : unjustified factor (the action of X was not justified by a right)

    ~ légal : actus reas, legal factor (the action of X is deemed an offence)

    ~ matériel : the facts of the case (X was a party to the offence)

    ~ moral : mens rea, moral factor (existence of malice)

élire : to elect

    ~ domicile : to nominate address for service
    To nominate an address for the service of documents, etc. This need not be one's place of residence but could be, for example, that of one's lawyer.

élucider : to elucidate, to clarify, to clear up

éluder : to evade

    ~ le paiement de l'impôt : to evade payment of tax

émancipation (f) : emancipation

émargement (m) : signing, initialling (a statment, paysheet, timesheet, etc)

emballage (m) : (1) police raid, round-up of suspects; (2) reprimand, dressing down

embarquer : (1) to nick*, to pinch*, to steal; (2) to arrest

embastiller * : to imprison

embaucher : to take on, to hire workers

embigner : to jail, to imprison

embourber * : to "shunt", to crash into

embouteillage (m) : traffic jam, hold-up

emboutir : to crash into, to collide with another vehicle

embrayage (m) : clutch

embringuer : to involve others in an undertaking they might later regret, to "volunteer" someone, to rope someone in

embuscade (f) : ambush

éméché * : tipsy, slightly drunk

émender : to amend, reform

émettre : to issue

émeute (f) : riot, disturbance

émietteuse (f) * : prostitute

émission (f) : emission, drawing

> ~ **de chèque sans provision** : drawing a cheque without sufficient funds
> *Misdemeanour committed by any person who knowingly and wilfully draws a cheque for a sum in excess of the funds available to meet it or withdraws the necessary funds prior to encashment or stops the cheque prior to presentation.*

> ~ **de fausse monnaie** : uttering

émoluments (mpl) : perquisities of officials, salary, remuneration, fees, conduct money, experts' fees

empalmer * : to nick*, to pinch*, to steal

empêchement (m) : hindrance, impediment

> **en cas d'**~ : if unable to do so, if prevented from doing something

empiéter : to encroach upon, to infringe

empiler * : to con*, to swindle

emplacarder * : to jail, to imprison

emploi (m) : use, employment, appointment, assignment, job, occupation, post

employé (m) : employee, worker

employeur (m) : employer

empoignarde (f) * : brawl, fight

empoigner : to arrest, to nick*, to knock off*

empoisonner : to poison

empreinte (f) : impression; print

    ~ digitale : fingerprint

emprise (f) : land acquired for public purposes

emprisonner : to imprison

emprisonnement (m) : imprisonment

énarque (f) : graduate of the Ecole Nationale de l'Administration

en-bourgeois (m) * : plain clothes policeman

encadrer : to lead, to head up

encanner : to nick*, to pinch*, to steal

encartée (f) : registered prostitute

enchetarder * : to imprison, to jail

enchnouffé (m) * : junkie*, drug addict

encouragement (m) : incentive, Dutch courage

encourir : to incur, to run

    ~ des sanctions : to be liable to penalties

    ~ un risque : to take a chance, to run a risk

endommager : to damage

endormi (m) * : beak*, judge

enfant (m&f) : child, infant, minor

    abandon d'~ : abandonment of child

    ~ conçu : child unborn

    ~ en bas âge : infant (generally under eight years of age)

~ **en danger moral** : child in moral danger

~ **mineur** : minor, under age

~ **naturel** : bastard, illegitimate child

enlèvement d'~ : kidnapping, abduction of a child

exposition d'~ : exposing a child to physical or moral danger

rapt d'~ : abduction of a minor

sans ~ : childless

suppression de part ou d'~ : concealment of birth
> *The concealment of the birth of a new-born child which, although born alive, has died, (whether from natural causes or otherwise), usually by the secret burial of the body.*

traite des ~s et des femmes : white slave traffic

enfin : finally, at last

enfouraillé * : tooled-up*, armed

enfreindre : to break, to infringe, to breach, to transgress

engager : to engage, to institute

~ **des poursuites** : to prosecute, to institute proceedings, to take legal action, to sue

s'engager (à) : to undertake (to), to agree (to)

engailler : to swindle, to con*

engerber * : to arrest, to nick*, to knock off*

engin (m) incendiaire : incendiary device

engourdir * : to nick*, to pinch*, to steal

engueulade (f) * : bollocking*, telling-off, reprimand

s'énivrer : to get drunk, to become intoxicated

enjeu (m) : stake, wager

enjoindre : to enjoin, to require (someone to do something)

enlèvement (m) : kidnapping, abduction

enquête (f) : investigation, inquiry, interview of witnesses prior to court hearing

~ **de flagrance** : investigation where offender is caught in the act
Where a person is caught red-handed committing a crime, the police officer in the case has greater powers than he would have in a preliminary investigation, carried out under the instructions of an examining magistrate.

~ **de flagrant délit** : see *enquête de flagrance*

~ **de personnalité** : character enquiries
In all felony cases, and where ordered in the case of misdemeanour, an enquiry is made into the psychological, family and social background of the accused.

~ **de police** : police investigation
The investigation carried out prior to bringing an offender before the courts. Made by specially authorised police officers, the aim is to confirm that a crime has been committed, to gather the evidence and to search for the offender.

~ **judiciaire après mort d'homme** : inquest

~ **préliminaire** : preliminary investigation
Investigation carried out by the police or gendarmerie on their own initiative or on the instructions of the public prosecutor before an official investigation has been opened, to enable the prosecution to determine whether there are prima facie grounds for a prosecution.

~ **sociale** : social enquiry (report)

enquêteur (m) : detective, detective constable
The lowest rank in the plain clothes police heirarchy

enquilleuse (f) * : female shoplifter

enrayer : to jam (machinery, a weapon), to lock (a wheel)

enregistrer : to register, to record

enrôlement (m) : enrolment, registering, recording (in official records)

entamer : to open, to breach

~ **des poursuites** : to institute proceedings

entendre : to hear, to intend, to mean, to listen, to understand, to take a statement/evidence

l'affaire sera entendue le ...: the case will be heard on ...

les parties entendues : the parties having given their evidence, the parties having been heard

s'entendre (avec) : to agree (with)

entériner : to confirm, to ratify, to rubber-stamp

enterrer : to bury, to shelve permanently

entoiler * : to jail, to imprison

entôlage (m) : theft from client (by prostitute)

entôleuse (f) * : light-fingered prostitute

entorse (f) : sprain, strain, wrench

    faire une ˜ à la loi : to stretch the law

entourer * : to con*, to swindle, to cheat

en tout état de cause : whatever the (legal) position

en tout temps : at any time

entraînement (m) : training, coaching

    ˜ physique : physical training, work-out

entraîneuse (f) : hostess (in dance hall, nightclub)

entrave (f) : hindrance
> *Misdemeanour committed by an employer who hinders a member of the work's committee, a staff representative or union official from exercising his normal functions, or prevents the free appointment of such a person.*

entraver : to shackle, to hinder, to impede

    ˜ la circulation : to hold up the traffic, to cause an obstruction

    ˜ une enquête : to hinder an investigation, to obstruct the police in the execution of their duty

entrée (f) : entry, entrance, admission, way in, input

    droit d'˜ : import duty

    ˜ en fonctions : taking up duties

    ˜ en vigueur : coming into force, effect, operation

    ˜ par ruse : burglary artifice

entremetteur (m) : go-between, intermediary

entréper : to raise an audience, to attract a crowd
> *The means used by a street vendor or hawker to attract custom.*

entrepôt (m) : warehouse, store

entrepreneur (m) : contractor, entrepreneur

    ~ de pompes funèbres : undertaker

    ~ de transports : carrier, freight forwarder

    ~ en bâtiment : builder, building contractor

entreprise (f) : undertaking, venture, firm

    ~ agricole : farm business

    ~ commerciale : business concern

    ~ de navigation : shipping company

    ~ de navigation aérienne : airline

    ~ en régie : state-managed company

    ~ industrielle : industrial concern

entretenir : to maintain, to support

entretien (m) : maintenance

    ~ de la famille : support, maintenance

    gagner son ~ : to earn one's keep

entubage * : con-trick, swindle, cheating, deception

entweedé : wearing tweeds

énumérer : to list

envelopper * : to nick*, to pinch*, to steal

épargne (f) : savings

    bon d'~ : savings certificate

    caisse d'~ : savings bank

épauler quelqu'un : to give someone a leg up, to back up someone's story

épave (f) : wreck, abandoned vehicle

épaviste (m) : car breaker

épée (f) * : expert, ace

épingler * : to arrest, to nick*, to knock off*

épouse (f) : spouse, wife (see **époux**)

époux (m&pl) : spouse, husband, couple

    communauté entre ~ : see **~ communs en biens:**

    ~ communs en biens: joint estate of husband and wife

    ~ séparés de biens : separate estates of husband and wife

équipe (f) : team

équipement (m) : equipment, plant

s'équiper : to get tooled-up*, to take up arms

équipier (m) * : accomplice

erreur (f) : error, mistake

    ~ de droit : mistake in law
      An incorrect representation of the content of a law or ignorance of the existence of such. A mistake in law only relieves a person from criminal liability if he was unable to avoid making it.

    ~ de fait : factual mistake
      An incorrect representation of a material fact or ignorance of the existence of such. A factual mistake relieves a person from criminal liability where it occurs in connection with a intentional breach of the law and where it has bearing on a circumstance essential for conviction.

    ~ judiciaire : miscarriage of justice

    ~ manifeste : obvious error

    ~ radicale : fundamental error (rendering an act invalid)

erroné : faulty

esballoner : to go over the wall, to escape from prison

escadron (m) : squadron
    *A unit in the **Gendarmerie Mobile** which equates to a company in the **Gendarmerie Départementale** and in the CRS.*

escalader : to climb, to scale (wall, etc.)

escale (f) : port of call, stop-off

escarpe (m) * : thug, underworld enforcer

escorte (f) : escort

    conduire un prisonnier sous ~ : to escort a prisoner

escorter : to escort

escrime (f) : fencing, swordplay

escroc (m) : swindler, fraud, con man

escroquer : to swindle, to cheat, to deceive

escroquerie (f) : obtaining property by deception, fraud
Misdemeanour involving the use of a false name or status or other fraudulent means to persuade someone of the existence of false activities or powers or of imaginary credit, or to give rise to the hope or fear of success, accident or other fictitious happening, with a view to causing funds, goods or choses in action to be handed or delivered to the offender, thereby depriving a third party of all or part of his estate.

espèce (f) : kind, sort, a particular court case or action, suit

    en l'~ : in this particular case

    loi applicable en l'~ : law applicable to the case in point

    un cas d'~ : a specific, concrete case

espèces (fpl) : cash, coin

    contre ~ : for cash

espionnage (m) : spying, espionage
Felony committed by a foreigner and comprising actions which represent a serious threat to the defence of the nation and which both place the nation in peril and aid the activities of hostile foreign powers. Where committed by a French national such acts will be deemed treason.

esponton (m) : spontoon, short pike
Weapon carried by the early police and gendarmerie.

essieu (m) : axle

essuie-glace (m) : windscreen wiper

estamper : to cheat, to rook*, to overcharge

estampille : official stamp

ester en justice : to go to law, to sue

estivant (m) : summer holidaymaker

estourbir : to knock unconscious, to kill

établir : (1) to ascertain (facts); (2) to draw up (a balance sheet, an account)

    ~ l'identité de quelqu'un : to establish someone's identity

~ **l'innocence de quelqu'un** : to prove someone's innocence

~ **son droit** : to establish one's rights

~ **une accusation** : to substantiate a charge

~ **un enfant** : to provide for a child

~ **un fait** : to establish a fact

établissement (m) : (1) institution; (2) taking up abode, residence

    droit d'~ : right of residence
        Right granted to a foreigner to take up residence in the country
        (usually under a treaty). EC nationals have an automatic right of
        residence in other EC countries.

    ~ **pénitentiaire** : prison

étalage (m) : display, show of goods

    vol à l~ : shoplifting

étaler : to stagger, to spread out

Etat (m) : the State
    The State consists of a nation, its territory and a political power. It may
    be a federal State (USA, Switzerland, Germany) or a unitary State (France,
    UK, China, etc). It may be a monarchy or a republic.

    affaire d~ : affair of State, matter of supreme political importance

    chef d'~ : Head of State

    Conseil d'~ : Council of State
        Administrative jurisdiction acting sometimes as court of first
        instance and sometimes as court of appeal against decisions reached
        by the administrative courts. It participates in the framing of laws
        and regulations.

    coup d'~ : coup d'état
        The sudden overthrow of a government, especially by force.

    homme d'~ : statesman

    ministre d'~ : secretary of State
        *A **ministre d'Etat** ranks directly below the prime minister and is*
        *senior to both ordinary **ministres** and **secrétaires d'Etat** (see below).*

    raison d'~ : the national interest (overriding moral considerations)

    secrétaire d'~ : junior minister
        *Note that, in France, a **secrétaire d'Etat** ranks <u>below</u> a **ministre**.*

état (m) : (1) condition, state

en bon/mauvais ~ : in good/bad repair

en tout ~ de cause : whatever the circumstances

~ dangereux : criminal propensities
> *A individual's tendency to commit offences, the circumstances of which do not always represent a danger to law and order.*

~ de choses : state of things, circumstances

~ de droit : rule of law, state where rule of law obtains

~ de fait : actual position

~ de fortune : financial standing

~ de manque : in need of a fix* (drugs)

~ de nécessité : justification,   unavoidability
> *Where a person intentionally commits an offence in order to prevent serious consequences to himself or another. It differs from **légitime défense** in that the consequences result from circumstances and not from aggression by another. An example would be where a fireman breaks into a house to extinguish a fire.*

~ de prévention : imprisonment on suspicion, on remand awaiting trial

~ des lieux : inventory

~ d'ivresse : drunkenness, intoxication

~ d'urgence : state of emergency

~ juridique : legal status

être en ~ de faire quelque chose : to be in a position to do something

hors d'~ de faire q'chose : to be unable/not in a position to do s'thing

état (m) : (2) position, profession, status

acte de l'~ civil : certificates of civil status (birth, death, marriage, etc.)

~ civil : civil status
> *Defined by birth, family name and forenames, marriage, divorce, separation, death. Also refers to the office of the registrar for births, deaths and marriages.*

~ de famille : family status (eg. relationship by marriage)

~ de fonctionnaire : status of a civil servant

~ de mariage : marital status

~ militaire : military service

officier de l'~ civil : official entitled to draw up records of civil status (eg magistrate, mayor, consul, ship's captain at sea, etc.)

état (m) : (3) statement, report, list, return, record

~ de paiements : schedule of payments

~ de répartition : allotment

~ des salaires : pay-roll, pay-sheet

~ de services : statement of posts held successively by a soldier or a civilian

~ mensuel : monthly return

rayer des ~ s : to strike off the roll

état-major (m) : headquarters, general staff

étatisation (f) : nationalisation, bringing into public ownership

étendue (f) de la couverture (sociale) : extent of (social) cover

éthylomètre (m) : intoximeter
Device which provides an instant read-out of the level of alcohol in a person.

étiquette (f) : label

étoile (f) : star (badge of rank)
*General officers in the armed forces (including the Gendarmerie) wear silver or gold stars on the cuff and on the **képi** to indicate their rank : **général de brigade** (brigadier) – two stars, **général de division** (major-general) – three stars, **général de corps d'armée** (lieut.-general) – four stars, **général d'armée** (general) – five stars.*

étouffer * : to nick*, to pinch*, to steal

étranger (m) : alien, foreigner
Under French law, in addition to subjects of foreign states, the subjects of certain countries with which France has close links are also regarded as foreigners, eg. citizens of Monaco, Andorra, etc.

étranglement (m) : strangling, strangulation, garrotting

étrangler : to strangle

être (m) : being, creature

étrier (m) : stirrup

~ de frein : brake caliper

étude (f) : (1) survey, report;   (2) office (of solicitor, notary), barrister's chambers

   ~ **de marché** : market survey

étui (m) : small case

   ~ **de pistolet** : holster

euthanasie (f) : euthanasia
Under French law euthanasia is classed as unlawful homicide.

eurêka (m) * : handgun, pistol, shooter*
Named after the trade name for a type of toy pistol.

eustache (m) : jack-knife, clasp knife

évadé (m) : escaped prisoner

s'évader : to escape, to abscond

évaluation (f) : assessment, appraisal

évasion (f) : escape, absconding

Evêché (m) : familiar name for the Marseilles central police station

événement (m) : event

éventail (m) : fan, spread, range

   ~ **des salaires** : range of salaries

éventuellement : perhaps, possibly

évocation (f) **(droit d'~)** : right of a higher court to hear a case awaiting trial before the court below

exactitude (f) : accuracy, reliability (of a statement, accounts)

examen (m) **de personnalité** : see **enquête de personnalité**

examiner : to examine, to investigate, to review

exception (f) : objection in law, incidental plea of defence

   à titre d'~ : by way of exception

   ~ **de bonne foi** : plea of having acted in good faith

   ~ **de chose jugée** : plea of **res judicata**

   ~ **de communication de pièces** : plea of non-discovery (of documents)

   ~ **de jeu** : plea of gambling debts (not recoverable at law)

~ **d'illégalité** : objection on grounds of illegality
A means of defence whereby the accused demonstrates that the administrative document on which the prosecution is based does not conform to standard. Notwithstanding the principle of separation of powers, the judge in the criminal court who recognises such a claim shall exclude from the evidence the text thus deemed to be illegal.

~ **libératoire** : see ~ **péremptoire**

~ **péremptoire** : peremptory plea (e.g. plea based on the Statute of Limitations)

~ **préjudicielle** : see **question préjudicielle**

excès (m) : excess

commettre un ~ de vitesse : to exceed the speed limit

~ **de pouvoir** : action ultra vires

exciper : to plead something

~ **de l'incompétence du tribunal** : to dispute the jurisdiction of the court

~ **de sa bonne foi** : to plead one's good faith

excitation (f) : instigation, incitement

~ **de mineur à la débauche** : procuring a minor for immoral purposes

exclure : to exclude, to leave out, to debar (from)

exclusion (f) : exclusion, expulsion

à l'~ de ... : excluding, exclusive of

~ **définitive du service** : dismissal

~ **temporaire de fonctions** : suspension from duty

excuse (f) : excuse
Circumstances or positions strictly defined in law which oblige the judge to reduce a sentence or not to impose one, depending on whether the excuse is extenuating or absolute.

~ **absolutoire** : statutory grounds for exemption

~ **atténuante** : extenuating excuse
An extenuation factor which the court is bound, by law, to accept.

~ **de minorité** : excuse of age
Where an offender between 16 and 18 years of age is convicted, the penalty may be reduced on these grounds and, where he is between 13 and 16, such penalty must be so reduced.

~ **légale** : legal excuse (eg. killing in self-defence)

~ **de provocation** : plea of provocation

exécuter : to execute, to enforce

exécution (f) : performance, enforcement, carrying out, execution (death penalty)

~ **provisoire** : the serving of a sentence pending appeal

mettre à ~ : to carry into effect

ordre d'~ : death warrant

exécutoire : enforceable

exempt (m) : cavalry warrant officer, police officer who effected arrests
These terms date from the 17th and 18th centuries and are now obsolete.
They often appear, however, in ancient laws and other documents.

exemption (f) : exemption, immunity

~ **de service militaire** : exemption from military service

~ **d'impôts, fiscale** : immunity from taxation

exempter le prévenu de toute peine : to discharge the prisoner

exercer : to exercise, to carry out

~ **l'action publique** : to prosecute

~ **un chantage** : to blackmail

~ **un métier** : to carry on a trade

exhibition (f) : indecent exposure

exhibo (m) : flasher*, indecent exposer, exhibitionist

exiger : to require

exiler : to banish, to exile

existence (f) : existence

moyens d'~ : means of support

expédition (f) **d'objets contraires à la décence** : distributing or sending
unsolicited obscene articles or publications

expérience (f) : experiment

~ **sur les animaux** : experiments on animals

expert (m) : expert, valuer, surveyor, appraiser

    ~ **comptable** : chartered accountant

    ~ **en écritures** : handwriting expert

    ~ **judiciaire** : expert appointed by the court

expertise (f) : expert valuation, appraisal, opinion
Where the judges do not have the technical knowledge necessary to judge a case properly, they may nominate an expert in the subject (doctor, engineer, architect, etc.) to carry out an enquiry on their behalf and then report back to the court.

    ~ **médico–légale** : report by forensic doctor, pathologist

expier : to expiate, to pay the penalty for

exploit (m) : (1) summons, notice, writ; (2) feat, achievement

    ~ **d'ajournement** : summons to appear

    ~ **-demande** : indictment, complaint

    ~ **de saisie** : writ of attachment

    ~ **introductif d'instance** : first process

explorateur (m) : burglar, operating mainly in small hotels

explosif (m) : explosive

exposé (m) : account (of facts, etc.)

expulser : to expel, to deport, to evict

exterritorial : off shore

extinction (f) : extinguishment

    ~ **de l'action civile** : extinguishment of civil action
A civil action may be extinguished by payment of monies claimed, renunciation of the plaintiff's claim or where there has been a settlement out of court.

    ~ **de l'action publique** : extinguishment of prosecution
Prosecution will be extinguished where the offender has died or where an amnesty has been declared.

    ~ **de la peine** : cancellation of sentence (amnesty, pardon, etc.)

extorquer : to extort

extorsion (f) : extortion

    ~ **de fonds** : obtaining money by extortion

    ~ **de signature** : obtaining a signature by extortion

    ~ **par voie de diffamation** : blackmail

    ~ **violente** : extortion by use of violence

extrader : to extradite

extradition (f) : extradition

extrait (m) : extract, excerpt, abstract

    ~ **certifié conforme** : authenticated abstract

    ~ **d'acte d'état civil** : birth, marriage or death certificate

    ~ **de compte** : statement of account

    ~ **de naissance** : birth certificate

    ~ **du casier judiciaire** : criminal record (or certificate as to lack thereof)

extrajudiciaire : extrajudicial, out of court

    serment ~ : voluntary oath

extralégal : extralegal, not legally authorised

extranéité (f) : foreign origin, alien status

F

fabrication (f) : manufacture, making (also used perjoratively to mean adulteration - eg **vin fabriqué**)

~ **de fausse monnaie** : making counterfeit coins

~ **de faux en écriture** : forgery of documents

fac-similé (m) : facsimile, exact copy (of signature, writing, etc)

factice : artificial, sham

factionnaire (m) : guard, picket, sentry

factum (m) : statement of facts of a case

facture (f) : invoice
*All commercial transactions exceeding 50 francs must, by law, be covered by a **facture**.*

facultatif : optional, permissive

fade (m) : "cut", share of booty

fader : to punish severely

fafs (mpl) * : identity papers

taper aux ~ : to check identity documents

failli (m) : undischarged bankrupt

faillite (f) : insolvency
*Since 1967 this term has been obsolete and replaced by **liquidation de biens** or **redressement judiciaire** but it is still widely used in everyday speech.*

~ **personnelle** : disqualification from commercial activity
All those forfeitures and restrictions imposed on individuals or the directors of a limited liability company subject to receivership or liquidation who are guilty of dishonest or grossly imprudent dealings.

faire : to nick*, to pinch*, to steal

faisan (m) * : crook

faiseuse (f) **d'anges** : backsteet abortionist

fesses (fpl) : buttocks

> **coller aux ~ de quelqu'un** : to stay hot on someone's trail

> **journal de ~** : girlie magazine, soft porn

> **le pain de ~** : prostitution

> **les avoir aux ~** : to have the cops on one's tail

festivalier (m) : festival goer

feu : late, deceased

> **~ mon mari** : my late husband

feu (m) : light, fire

> **brûler les ~x** : to jump the lights

> **~ anti-brouillard** : fog lamp

> **~ arrière** : rear lamp

> **~ arrière complet** : stop and tail light unit

> **~ clignotant** : (1) indicator light (on motor vehicle); (2) flashing light, warning light (at crossroads)

> **~ de circulation** : traffic light

> **~ de croisement** : dipped beam

> **~ de détresse** : hazard warning lights

> **~ de position** : sidelight

> **~ de route** : main beam

> **~ rouge** : traffic light

> **~ tricolore** : traffic light

> **~ vert** : the green light, the go-ahead

feuille (f) : leaf, sheet

> **~ d'audience** : court minutes

> **~ de présence** : record of attendance

> **~ de questions** : summing-up
> *At the end of the **débats**, the president of the court reads a written list of questions to be considered by the court and the jury.*

~ **de séance** : summary record of a meeting

~ **de versement** : paying-in slip

ficelle (f) : (1) tail*, follower, shadow*;   (2) **galon** indicating rank

fiche (f) : card, voucher, form

~ **alphabétique** : criminal record form (nominal)

~ **dactyloscopique** : fingerprint identification form

~ **de police** : hotel registration form

fichets (mpl) : handcuffs, bracelets*

fichier (m) : file, card index

~ **contre la violence, les attentats et le terrorisme** : serious crimes and terrorism file

~ **des personnes recherchées** : wanted persons index

~ **des recherches criminelles** : criminal intelligence index

~ **des véhicules volés** : stolen vehicle index

fief (m) : territory, manor*

fier-à-bras (m) : bully, tough

figure (f) : face

casser la ~ : to "push someone's face in", to beat someone up

fil (m) : wire.   **coup de** ~ : telephone call

filage (m) : tailing, shadowing,

filature (f) : shadowing, following, surveillance by a detective

file (m) : row

en double ~ : double parked

~ **d'attente** : queue

filet (m) : net, dragnet

fileuse (f) : grass*, informant

filiation (f) : parentage

~ **naturelle** : illegitimate child, natural child

filière (f) : trace, track

fille (f) : girl, daughter

    ~ **-mère** : unmarried mother

    ~ **publique** : prostitute

    nom de jeune ~ : maiden name

fillette (f) : (1) young girl;   (2) half bottle of wine

filleul (m), **filleule** (f) : god-child

filoche (f) : see **filature**

filou (m) : con man, unscrupulous person, thief, card-sharp

filoutage (m) : theft, pocket-picking

filouter : to con*, to trick, to swindle, to cheat

filouterie (f) : making off without payment

fin (f) : end, close, finish, termination, purpose

    à toutes ~**s utiles** : for all (practical) purposes

    aux ~**s de** : for the purpose of

    ~ **de mois** : part-time prostitute
       One who goes "on the game" at the end of the month when money
       is short.

    ~**s civiles en matière pénale** : civil action concurrent with criminal
       prosecution (to seek damages or compensation)

    rendre une ~ **de non-recevoir** : nolle prosequi, to dismiss a case

fine (f) : top-quality distilled alcohol

fisc (m)**, fiscal, fiscalité** (f) : Inland Revenue, the Exchequer

fixation (f) **(de la peine)** : determination (of the penalty)

fixe (m) : basic wage

fixe : fixed, determined.   **résidence** ~ : permanent address

fixer : to get a "fix", to inject with drugs

flag (m) * : colloquial term for **flagrant délit**

---

flagrant délit (m) : flagrante delicto, in the act of commiting the offence, red-handed
> *This concept is very important in French law and refers to a crime in the course of commission or which has just been committed. The investigation into such an offence is subject to a special form of procedure which permits the police to take certain courses of action without prior reference to the public prosecutor. In the case of a misdemeanour the offender may be brought before the court forthwith.*

flanc (m) : blanks (for making counterfeit coin)

flanche (m) : job*, criminal act

flanche (f) : betrayal by informant

flauper : to beat up

flèche (f) : (1) arrow;   (2) gang, association of criminals

flécher : to team up, to work in collaboration with someone

flécheur (m) : route marker, direction arrow

flibuster : to nick*, to pinch*, to steal

flic (m) : copper*, cop*, rozzer*

flicage (m) : policing

flicaille (f) : police, "boys in blue"

flicard (m) : cop*, policeman

flingoteur (m) : trigger-happy gangster

flingue (m) : shooter*, handgun

flingueur (m) : hit man, hired killer

fliquer : to police, to keep watch on

flot (m) **de circulation** : traffic flow

flottante (la population ˜) : drowned persons
> *The monthly tally of drowned persons logged by the police.*

flouer : to swindle, to cheat

fluidifier : to allow to flow freely

fluvial : appertaining to rivers

> **brigade ˜** : river police
> > *Sometimes referred to as "La Fluviale".*

flux (m) **routier/de circulation** : traffic flow

foi (f) : faith

> **de bonne ~** : bona fide, in good faith
>
> **de mauvaise ~** : mala fide, without good faith
>
> **en ~ de quoi** : in witness whereof
>
> **la bonne ~** : good faith
>
> **sous la ~ du serment** : on oath
>
> **texte qui fait ~** : authentic text

folie (f) : madness, mania

fomenter : to foment, to foster, to promote, to stir up

fonction (f) : function, office, capacity, duty

fonctionnaire (m&f) : functionary, civil servant, public official
In France, police officers are **fonctionnaires,** *as are judges and members of the public prosecutor's department but* **gendarmes** *are* **militaires** *since they come under the Ministry of Defence. There are four general grades of* **fonctionnaire,** *the entry to each grade being subject to a specified standard of education and the passing of a competitive examination.*

fonctionnariat (m) : public service

fond (m) : substance, main issue, essential features, merits (of a case)
Those elements which form the content, essence and substance of the law or the legal situation concerned. In general, it relates to the substance of the case as opposed to the procedure - questions of fact or of law which have made the case inevitable and which the judge must decide.

> **à ~ de train** : at full speed

fondé (m) **de pouvoir** : attorney (one holding a power of attorney)

fonds (m) : fund

> **détournement de ~** : misappropriation of funds, embezzlement, fraudulent conversion
>
> **~ de garantie automobile** : motor insurers' fund
>
> **~ Nationale de Solidarité** : Supplementary Pension Fund
> *Fund created in 1956 to assist elderly persons in need.*
>
> **~ social** : registered capital
>
> **placer argent à ~ perdu** : to take out a life annuity

prêt à ~ perdu : unsecured loan

virer des ~ : to transfer funds, to make a virement

foot (m) : soccer, football

footing (m) : jogging

forain : itinerant

    foire ~e : travelling fair, fun fair

    marchand ~ : stall holder, market trader

force (f) : force, strength, power

    agent de la ~ publique : constable

    ~ armée : the military

    ~ de chose jugée : res judicata
        The final decision pronounced by a competent judicial tribunal. It effectively prevents any further action in the same matter.

    ~ de loi : force of law

    ~ exécutoire : enforceable

    ~ majeure : force majeure, Act of God, an irresistable force
        *Acts committed under duress or under **force majeure** are not regarded as criminal.*

    ~ probante : power to convince

    ~ publique : armed forces, the police force
        All those forces (police, military) available to the Government to maintain order and which may be used by public officials to obtain respect for the law and the execution of legal decisions.

    maison de force : prison

forçat (m) : convict

forcé : forced

    travaux ~s : hard labour

forcer : to force, to break open

forclusion (f) : limitation of proceedings

forfait (m) : (1) heinous crime; (2) contract, agreement

forfaitaire : contractual, agreed

    prix ~ : fixed price, lump sum

forfaiture (f) : abuse of authority, maladministration
Felony committed by a public official in the performance of his duties such as embezzlement, destruction of official documents.

formalité (f) : formality, formal procedure

    ~ en douane : customs clearance

formation (f) : (1) training; (2) group, formation

    ~ continue : further education and training
Education and training for those who have left school and are at work, provided by way of approved absence from their place of employment (e.g. day release)

    ~ motocycliste urbaine : town motorcycle section

    ~ restreinte : appeal court with only three judges

    ~ professionnelle : vocational training

    ~ spécialisée : specialist group

forme (f) : form, procedural method

    avertissement dans les ~s : due warning

    en bonne et due ~ : regular, correct

    ~ authentique : duly certified

    ~ juridique : legal form

    pour la ~ : for form's sake, as a matter of form

    vice de ~ : defect, substantial flaw

formule (f) : formula, prescribed wording, printed form

    ~ digitale : fingerprint classification

formuler : to formulate, to draw up, to enunciate, to lodge

fortuit : fortuitous, by chance, accidental

fosse (f) : pit, hole, grave

    ~ aux ours * : prison exercise yard

fouille (f) : search, rummage

    ~ **à corps** : body search

    ~**-merde** : (1) muck-raker, scandalmonger; (2) private detective

fouiller : to search, to rummage

fouineur (m) : persistent and tenacious policeman

foule (f) : crowd

fouraille (f) : "shooter", handgun

fourailler : (1) to rummage, to search through; (2) to fire a gun

fourbi (m) : gear*, personal belongings

fourche (f) **de roue** : front forks

    ~ **téléhydraulique** : telescopic, teledraulic forks

fourchette (f) : pickpocket

fourgat (m) : fence, handler of stolen property

fourgon (m) : van (motor and railway)

fourgue (m) : fence, handler of stolen property

fourguer : to sell "hot" goods, to dispose of stolen wares

fourlineur (m) : pickpocket

fourniture (f) **de moyens** : provision of the means (to commit a crime)
This is one of the ways in which an accomplice may be implicated in a crime, without actually being present at the time.

fourrière (f) : compound, pound (for animals, towed-away vehicles)

foyer (m) : home, household

    abandon de ~ : desertion

    ~ **d'accueil** : foster home

    ~ **de semi-liberté** : probation hostel, hostel for released prisoners

    ~ **d'incendie** : seat of a fire

fractionnement (m) **de la peine** : split sentence
Exceptional measure which the courts may take where there are substantial medical, professional, family or social grounds, under which an offender may serve his sentence in two or more separate parts, or pay a fine by instalments, or complete some other penalty in a like manner.

frais (mpl) : costs, expenses

> **être condamné aux** ~ : to be ordered to pay costs

> ~ **de déplacement** : travelling expenses

> ~ **de déplacement de temoin** : conduct money

> ~ **de dossier** : administrative charges, fees (charged by lawyers, banks, etc)

> ~ **d'expertise** : expert's expenses, consultancy fees

> ~ **judiciaires, de justice** : court costs, legal expenses

frapper : to strike, to hit

> ~ **d'une peine** : to impose a penalty

fraude (f) : fraud, deception, deceit
*Action which reveals a wish on behalf of the perpetrator to cause injury
to another or to avoid certain legal requirements (tax evasion).*

> ~ **douanière** : smuggling

> ~ **fiscale** : tax evasion

> ~ **pénale** : fraudulent misrepresentation

> ~ **télématique** : computer fraud

frauder : to defraud

frein (m) brake

> ~ **à disque** : disk brake

> ~ **à tambour** : drum brake

> **levier de** ~ : brake lever

> **pédale de** ~ : foot brake

frelater : to adulterate (food, wine, etc)

fric (m) * : dough*, lolly*, bread*, cash

fric-frac (m) : burglary, break-in

fricfraquer : to break-in, to burgle

frigo (m) : (1) refrigerator; (2) * mortuary

frimage (m) : (1) taking photos of prisoners; (2) confrontation between suspect
and witness

frimer : to pretend, to make-believe, to show off

fripon (m) : rogue, rascal

friponner : to rob, to cheat

fripouille (f) : rabble, riff-raff, swindler, rotter

fripouillerie (f) : swindling, cheating, dirty-dealing

fromage (m) : pie chart

fromager * : to organise a robbery

frontalier : (1) pertaining to a national border; (2) persons living on a border, especially those who cross daily to work in the neighbouring country

frontière (f) : border, frontier

    carte ˜ : border pass

    trafic ˜ : local traffic and trade on either side of a border

frou-frou (m) : skeleton key

fugitif (m) : fugitive, escaper

fugue (f) : flight, escapade, runaway from home

fuite (f) : (1) flight, escape; (2) leak, indiscretion

    danger de ˜ : risk of absconding (of suspect)

    délit de ˜ : quitting the scene of a road accident, failure to stop after an accident

    préparatifs de ˜ : preparing to flee

    tentative de ˜ : attempt to escape from custody

furtivement : stealthily

fumette (f) : cannabis smoking

furat (m) : tenacious police officer, "terrier"

fusée (f) : rocket

fusible (m) : fuse

fusil (m) : rifle

    ˜ **à canon scié** : sawn-off shotgun

    ˜ **à pompe** : pump-action shotgun

~ **de chasse** : shotgun

~ **de chasse à répétition** : pump-action shotgun

fusillade (f) : fusillade, rifle fire, shoot-out

fusiller : (1) to shoot (someone); (2) to sharpen (a knife); (3) to damage something beyond repair

G

gabardine (f) * : unofficial "green light"
Verbal assurance from senior officers that the officers involved in an investigation may, for the purposes of the case, act outside the law.

gabegie (f) : (1) muddle, mess arising out of mismanagement; (2) underhand dealings, trickery

gabelou (m) * : Customs officer

gachette (f) * : hit-man, hired killer

gaffe (m) : (1) screw*, prison officer; (2) look-out during the commission of a crime

galéjade (f) * : cock-and-bull story

galette (f) * : brass*, loot*, lolly*, cash

galon (m) : stripe, bar
A metal or braid bar denoting a particular rank, depending on the colour, thickness and number.

~ **d'élite** : cap band of an elite corps
*The **Gendarmerie** wear a ½ inch braid round the tops of their **képis**, silver in the case of the **Gendarmerie Départementale** and gold in the case of the **Gendarmerie Mobile** The **Garde Républicaine** wear red, while auxiliary gendarmes wear blue The **Gendarmerie** is the only branch of the armed forces permitted to wear this distinction which marks it out as an **élite** corps.*

prendre du ~ : (1) to come up in the world; (2) to be getting on in years

galonnard (m) * : officer, top brass

galop (m) * : reprimand, roasting*

gano(t) (m) * : (1) nest-egg; (2) loot, plunder, spoils

garage (m) * : (1) hotel room used for prostitution; (2) dead-end post for unpopular or difficult employees; (3) "shelf", where documents of a sensitive nature can be left to gather dust

garce (f) * : bitch, spiteful woman

garçon (m) **de passe** : rent boy

garçonnière (f) : batchelor pad

garant (m) : guarantor, security, bail

garantir : to go bail, to stand surety

garde (m) : watchman, keeper

    chien- ~ : guard dog

    ~ **–à–vous!** : attention! (military drill command)

    ~ **–boue** : mudguard

    ~ **–champêtre** : rural constable

    ~ **–chasse** : gamekeeper

    ~ **–chiourme** : (originally) convict supervisor, slave master
        Now used to describe any brutal and unscrupulous supervisor.

    ~ **–côte** : coastguard service, coastguard cutter

    ~ **des Sceaux** : Keeper of the Seals (the Minister of Justice)
        The head of the judiciary, equivalent to the Lord Chancellor

    ~ **du corps** : bodyguard, close companion

    ~ **–forestier** : forest ranger

    ~ **–frontière** : frontier guard

    ~ **–magasin** : quartermaster, storeman

    ~ **messier** : rural policeman (in pre–Revolutionary France)

    ~ **–mites** : army slang for **garde-magasin**

    ~ **particulier assermenté** : sworn watchman, security officer

    ~ **–pêche** : (1) water bailiff;   (2) fishery protection vessel

    ~ **–vue** : visor

garde (f) : (1) guardianship, care, custody; (2) ward (of a lock); (3) guard

    avoir la ~ **de** : to have custody of

    corps de ~ : guard, guard-room
        Body of soldiers guarding a building,etc. and, by extension,
        the premises in which they are housed.

    ~ **au sol** : roadholding

    ~ **à vue** : temporary detention
        *A suspect may be held for 24 hours by an **officier de police***
        ***judiciaire** pending further enquiries, as may a witness if it is felt*
        that his remaining at liberty could result in the perversion of
        justice. This period may be extended to 48 hours under certain
        circumstances.

~ **bourgeoise** : citizen's watch

A vigilante-type body which existed in 16th century Paris and again after the Revolution.

~ **de Paris** : Paris Guard

*A body under this title was first formed in 1750 to police the capital of France and to protect the King's person. In 1849, when it had become known as the **Garde Municipale de Paris**, it was absorbed into the Gendarmerie Nationale and it took the title of **Garde de Paris** once more. This body was the forerunner of the **Garde Républicaine**).*

~ **d'honneur** : honour guard, escort

~ **d'un enfant** : custody of a child

~ **judiciaire** : legal custody of seized exhibits placed under official seal

~ **Municipale de Paris** : Paris Municipal Guard.

*Consisting of two regiments of gendarmes under the direction of the Prefect of Police, this body was formed in 1802. Disgraced in the Malet affair of 1812, it was transformed into a normal infantry regiment and replaced by the **Gendarmerie Impériale de Paris**. In 1830 the existing **Gendarmerie Royale de Paris** was renamed **Garde Municipale de Paris** once more and continued as such until 1848 when it became the **Garde Républicaine de Paris**.*

~ **nationale, mobile** : ancient titles of formations of gendarmerie

~ **Républicaine** : the Republican Guard

*The French equivalent of the Household Brigade in England, the function of this colourful section of the **Gendarmerie Nationale** is to provide honour guards and escorts and to guard certain important buildings. It consists of an infantry regiment, a cavalry regiment, a motor-cycle squadron, a band, a mounted band and a corps of drums. There is also a gymnastic section. The full dress uniform of the infantry regiment is a red-plumed shako and a long black tunic with stiff red and gold epaulettes. Cavalrymen wear a highly polished gilt helmet with a red plume and a black tuft. Blue trousers are normally worn but, in the presence of a Head of State, these are replaced by white breeches. The long black tunic has the lower part turned back to reveal the scarlet lining at the front and back. A direct descendant of the **Guet Royal** in the 13th C., it was known by various names until 1852 when it became the **Garde Républicaine de Paris**. The present title dates from 1870.*

mise en ~ : warning, caution

prenez ~ ! : look out! take care!

sous bonne ~ : in safe custody

gardian (m) : cow-boy (in the Camargue region of France)

gardien (m) : guard, caretaker, prison officer, jailer, sentinel, goalkeeper

gardien de la Paix (m) : police constable

gardiennage (m) : guarding (of car park, port area, etc.)

gare (f) : (railway) station.   ~ **routière** : bus/coach station

gargote (f) * : transport café, cheap eating place

garni (m) : furnished accommodation

    chambre ~**e** : furnished room

    police des ~**s** : hotel records police
        Those police officers whose task it was to collect the cards from
        hotels and boarding houses, showing the details of the guests.

garnots (mpl) * : see **police des garnis**

gauffrer * : to arrest, to nick*, to knock off*

gavousse (f) * : lesbian, dyke

gavroche (m) : imp, little rascal, street urchin

gay : gay, homosexual

gaz (m) : gas

    ~ **d'échappement** : exhaust gases

    ~ **lacrymogène** : tear gas

    mettre/ouvrir les ~ : to "step on the gas", accelerate violently

gélule (f) : capsule

gendarme (m) : gendarme, police officer, military policeman, constable
*A member of the **Gendarmerie Nationale**, in particular the lowest grade in*
that force.

    ~ **auxiliaire** (m) : reserve gendarme, auxiliary
        French citizens called up for compulsory national service may elect
        to perform this with the Gendarmerie and, if accepted, they serve
        in the reserve or auxiliary force.

    ~ **couché** : sleeping policeman, speed-reducing ramp

Gendarmerie (f) : a military, or military-style armed police force. The name
derives from **gens d'armes** or "men at arms" (see **Gendarmerie Nationale**)

    ~ **de l'Air** (f) : Air Force Police
        The equivalent of the RAF Police and the RAF Regiment combined,
        it is responsible for maintaining order and security at air bases.
        Members wear a uniform similar to the Air Force

~ **de l'Armement** : Armements Gendarmerie
Provides the security for armaments establishments

~ **Départementale** : Territorial Gendarmerie
*That division of the National Gendarmerie responsible for normal policing duties in rural areas, villages and small towns in France. cf. **Gendarmerie Mobile.** Sometimes referred to as "la blanche" on account of the white piping and badges worn by its members.*

~ **des Forces Françaises en Allemagne** : military police detachment in Germany

~ **des Transports Aériens** : airports police

~ **hors métropole** : overseas gendarmerie
Those gendarmes posted to the French overseas territories and départements.

~ **Impériale de Paris** : Paris Imperial Gendarmerie
*Formed in 1813 to replace the disgraced **Garde Municipale de Paris,** it became the **Gendarmerie Royale de Paris** and then the **Garde Municipale de Paris** once more in 1830.*

~ **Maritime** : Naval and Ports Police
Provides security and maintains order in naval ports, arsenals, shore establishments and bases. Members wear a naval-type uniform.

~ **Mobile** : Mobile Gendarmerie
*That division of the **Gendarmerie Nationale** which provides an emergency reserve for the **Gendarmerie Départementale** and is used, like the CRS service of the **Police Nationale,** for the maintenance and restoration of public order. As a military force, the GM can only be employed by the civil power through a requisition which leaves it free to choose the means which it will employ to attain the goals assigned to it by the civil power. Sometimes referred to as "la rouge" on account of the red piping and badges worn by its members.*

~ **Nationale** (f) : National Gendarmerie
*The **Gendarmerie** is one of the two main law-enforcing agencies in France (the other being the **Police Nationale**). A branch of the army, it is responsible for military police duties, both at home and overseas, and also has extensive civil police responsibilities. It polices all rural areas and small towns and villages in France and has detachments in most of the French Overseas Territories and Départements such as New Caledonia, French Antilles, etc. It consists of four main operational bodies; the **Gendarmerie Départementale** (approx 50,000 strong), the **Gendarmerie Mobile** (126 squadrons), the **Groupement de Sécurité et d'Intervention (GSIGN)** and the **Garde Républicaine de Paris.** There is also a **Gendarmerie Maritime,** a **Gendarmerie de l'Air,** a **Gendarmerie des Transports aériens** and the **Gendarmerie de l'Armement** It is a direct successor to the **Maréchaussée,** which it replaced in 1790.*

~ **Royale de Paris** : Paris Royal Gendarmerie
   Formed in 1815 on the restoration of the monarchy to replace the
   Gendarmerie Impériale de Paris**, it became the **Garde Municipale de
   ***Paris** fifteen years later.*

général (m) general

~ **d'armée** : general/field marshal (five star general)

~ **de brigade** : brigadier-general (two star general)

~ **de corps d'armée** : lieutenant-general (four star general)

~ **de division** : major-general (three star general)

gens (mpl) : folk, people, men and women

~ **d'affaires** : businessmen

~ **de justice** : law officers (lower grades)

– **de robe** : lawyers, "wig and gown"

~ **du monde** : society people

geôle (f) : gaol, jail, prison

geôlier (m) : jailer

gérance (f) : management

gérant (m) : manager

gerbe (f) * : year in prison

gerbier (m) * : beak*, judge

gestion (f) : administration, care and control, stewardship

gibier (m) : game

giclée (f) : burst of machine-gun fire

gifle (f) : slap in the face

gig (f) : "gig", one night stand

gilet (m) : waistcoat

~ **de sauvetage** : lifejacket

~ **pare-balles** : bullet-proof vest

giroflée (f) : slap in the face

gîter : to "hang out", to live

givré * : drunk, intoxicated

glace (f) : ice

glaiseux (m) * : "hick", peasant, someone from "the sticks"

glanage (m) : gleaning, taking ears of grain etc. left by the harvesters
A more modern usage of this old legal term relates to a shoplifting spree.

godillot (m) * : heavy boot or shoe, "beetle-crusher"

gonflé : (1) inflated;   (2) "souped-up" (engine)

gorille (m) : "heavy", enforcer, bodyguard

gouale (m) : blackmail, extortion, protection racket

gouape (m) * : lout, "yob"

gouine (f) * : lesbian, dyke*

goulot (m) **d'étranglement** : bottleneck

goumi (m) * : cosh, life-preserver

gourbi (m) * : (1) "digs", accomodation; (2) "gear", personal possessions

gourer : to con*, to swindle, to cheat

gousse (f) * : lesbian, dyke*

gouvernante (f) : housekeeper

gouvernement (m) : government
*Comprises the **ministres** and **secrétaires d'état**, presided over by the prime minister.*

goyau (m) * : low-class prostitute

grabuge (m) * : commotion, rumpus, fight

grâce (f) : grace, reprieve
Act of clemency decided by the President of the Republic by means of which a convicted person, following an application made on his behalf, is reprieved from serving all or part of his sentence or is required to undergo a lesser penalty.

~ **amnistiante** : amnesty reprieve
A hybrid measure under which the amnesty accorded to a class of convicted persons is restricted by the legislators to those individuals who have obtained a reprieve decree made by the executive (President or Prime Minister) within a specified period.

délai de ~ / jours de ~ : days of grace, time allowed

recours en ~ : petition for reprieve

gracier : to pardon, to reprieve

gradé (m) : non-commissioned officer, NCO

graffiteur (m) **(peintre ~)** : graffiti artist
The writing or painting of graffiti is a misdemeanour, punishable as criminal damage.

graffiti (mpl) : graffiti

graisse (f) * : dough*, brass*, lolly*

graisser la patte à quelqu'un : to grease someone's palm, to bribe

grand : tall, large, big, grown-up, adult

~**e foule** : crowd, mob

~**e livre** : ledger

~**e Maison** : the Paris **Préfecture de Police**

~**e surface** : department store, supermarket

~**e-route** : main road, highway

~**e-rue** : high street

~**e vitesse** : high-speed

graphique (m) : diagram, chart, graph

grappillage (m) : (1) theft of grapes in vineyard, abandoned by the pickers; (2) petty theft, scrounging, making illicit profits

gratification (f) : bonus, bounty, gratuity, tip

gratte (f) : rake-off

gratuit : gratuitous, free

accusation ~**e** : unfounded accusation

à titre ~ : free of charge, a gift

gré à gré : by mutual consent

grec (m) : (1) card-sharp, con-man, swindler; (2) delicatessen

greffe (m) : office of the clerk of the court, registry

greffier (m) : clerk of the court, assistant registrar
> *The **greffier** is a public official who assists the judges at a trial and draws up the court records. The records and files are held by the **greffier en chef** (chief clerk/registrar). Previously holding an **office ministériel**, they are now civil servants.*

grenade (f) : grenade

    ~ **lacrymogène** : tear-gas grenade

grenaille (f) : lead shot

grenouilleur (m) : gossip-monger, intriguer, schemer

grève (f) : strike

    allocation de ~ : strike pay

    briseur de ~ : strike breaker, blackleg, scab

    ~ **de la faim** : hunger strike

    ~ **de solidarité** : strike in sympathy

    ~ **du zèle** : work to rule

    ~ **générale** : general strike

    ~ **patronale** : lock-out

    ~ **perlée** : go-slow

    ~ **politique** : strike for political ends

    ~ **sauvage** : unofficial strike, wild-cat strike

    ~ **sur le tas** : strike and sit-in

    ~ **surprise** : lightning strike

    ~ **thrombose (ou bouchon)** : tactical strike, paralysing strike
> *Strike in a key sector of a firm which paralyses the whole enterprise.*

    piquet de ~ : picket

grief (m) : the injury which one suffers, grievance, grounds for complaint

    ~ **d'appel** : grounds for appeal
> *Prejudice caused to a plaintiff as a result of a formal irregularity in a judgement which entitles him to seek its annulation.*

griffe (f) : stamped signature, stamp

griffer : to nick*, to pinch*, to steal

grigri (m) : lucky charm, pendant

grille (f) : bars, railings, grille

    ~ **des salaires** : salary scale, wage differentials

griller * : to inform on, to denounce

grillot (m) : compromising document

grinche (m) * : crook, thief

grinche (f) * : thieving, larceny

grincher * : to nick*, to pinch*, to steal

grisbi (m) * : loot*, brass*, cash

grivèlerie (f) : making off without payment (for food and/or drink), bilking
    *Also known as **filouterie**, this offence consists of ordering and consuming*
    food or drink knowing that one does not have the means to pay for it.

gros bonnet (m) : big-wig, VIP

gros-cube (m) : super-bike, high-powered motorcycle

gros-cul (m) * : HGV, large lorry

groupe (m) : group, unit, body, task force

    ~ **de répression de banditisme** : Flying Squad

    ~ **de répression de la voie publique** : street patrol unit

    ~ **de sécurité de la présidence de la République** : presidential protection
       group

    ~ **d'intervention** : police tactical support unit, strike force
       *These units of the **Police Nationale** were created as a result of the*
       1972 Olympic Games in Munich. They are specially trained and
       armed and their function is to deal with acts of terrorism, serious
       assaults and gangsterism which cause serious disturbance of the
       peace or threaten the lives of one or more persons. They are the
       *national equivalent of the **brigade anti-commando** in Paris.*

    ~**s mobiles** : public order groups, riot squads (Belgian Gendarmerie)

    ~**s mobiles de réserve (GMR)** : forerunner of the CRS

groupement (m) : battalion
    A formation of several companies of gendarmes, normally commanded by
    a lieutenant-colonel.

    ~ **blindé de gendarmerie mobile** : gendarmerie armoured regiment

grouper : to nick*, to pinch*, to steal

> **se faire ~** : to get arrested, to get nicked*

gruger : to swindle, to cheat

guet (m) : watch, lookout

> **faire le ~** : to act as lookout

> **~ de la Ville de Paris** : City of Paris Watch
> *Formed in 1562 to maintain law and order in Paris, by 1688 it*
> *consisted of 4 lieutenants, some warrant officers, 50 horsemen and*
> *200 foot archers, all under the command of the **chevalier de guet**.*

> **~ Royal** : Royal Guard (police patrols formed in 1254)

> **mot du ~** : password

guet-apens (m) : ambush, trap

guette-au-trou (m) * : peeping Tom, voyeur

guetteur (m) : look-out (criminal's accomplice)

gueule (f) * : (1) mouth;   (2) face;   (3) looks, appearance

gueuler : to bawl, to bellow, to shout

guiche (f) : kiss-curl

guichet (m) : (1) spy hole, judas; (2) turnstile, barrier, counter position

guidon (m) : (1) handlebar; (2) fore sight

> **~ séparé en deux** : high-rise handlebars

guignol (m) : (1) buffoon; (2) chaotic state of affairs; (3) court of law; (4) police
> *Most of these meanings are directly related to the original meaning of*
> ***guignol** with its Punch and Judy implications.*

guillotine (f) : guillotine

guimbarde (f) * : "jalopy", "bone-shaker", ramshackle motor car

guinde (f) * : "wheels", motor car

guitoune (f) : sentry box, workman's hut, small room

gyrophare (m) : flashing (rotating) rooflamp

H

habilitation (f) **(loi d'~**) : enabling law

habiliter : to have capacity, to be empowered

    être ~ à ester en justice : to be entitled to institute proceedings

habillé (m) : uniformed policeman

habiller : to prepare a cast-iron case against someone.
This includes a comprehensive list of the charges, sworn testimonies, past criminal record and possibly a signed confession.

habitation (f) : habitation, dwelling, house, domicile, residence

    ~ à loyer modéré (HLM) : inexpensive accommodation
Usually consisting of large blocks of flats, this roughly equates to council or housing association accommodation.

habitude (f) : habit, custom, practice

    délinquant d'~ : recidivist, old lag*, habitual criminal

    d' ~ : usually

habitué (m) : regular*, regular customer

habituel (domicile ~) : usual (place of abode)

hachette (f) : hatchet, small axe

hachisch (m) : hashish, marijuana

hall (m) **d'accueil** : concourse (at station, airport)

halle (f) : covered market

hallucinogène : hallucinatory

hambourgeois (m) * : plain clothes police officer

handicapé (m) : disabled person
Persons afflicted with a physical, sensorial or mental incapacity which demands some measure of protection.

hard (m) : hard porn

hareng (m) * : pimp, ponce

harléiste (m) : owner/rider of a Harley-Davidson motor cycle, "Hells Angel"

harnaquer : (1) * : to con*, to swindle, to cheat; (2) to fix a game of chance; (3) to grass*, to inform; (4) to beat someone up; (5) to arrest, to nick*, to knock off*.

harponner * : to arrest, to nick*, to knock off*

hasard (m) : hazard, chance, luck

hausse (f) : backsight (of rifle)

hausse-col (m) : gorget, collar plate
A crescent-shaped metal plate once worn round the neck by gendarmes and still worn by the German military police.

haut : high, senior, superior

    ~e Cour de Justice : supreme court for political crimes
Consisting of 24 judges and 12 elected assistants from both houses of Parliament before which the President may be impeached for high treason as may ministers charged with crimes committed in the exercise of their office.

    ~ fonctionnaire : senior civil servant

    ~e mer : high seas
The seas outside national jurisdictions (principle of "freedom of the seas").

    ~-parleur : loudspeaker

    ~e trahison : treason by the President of the Republic
*The sole offence with which the President may be charged. Charges are heard by the **Haute Cour de Justice** which, as this crime is not defined in the laws of the land, will decide whether the facts alleged amount to treason or not.*

hayon (m) : hatch, tailgate, rear door (of hatchback car)

hebdomadaire : weekly

    bilan ~ : weekly return

héberger : to shelter and feed, to provide board and lodgings

hédonique : hedonistic

hélitreuiller : to winch up by helicopter

herbe (f) **colombienne** : cannabis, marijuana, grass*

hérisson (m) : awkward customer, suspect to be handled carefully

héritage (m) : inheritance, legacy

herse (f) : spiked device used at roadblocks to puncture tyres

heure (f) : hour, time

    ~ **de bureau** : office hours

    ~ **de pointe** : peak hour, rush hour

    ~**s creuses** : slack periods

    ~**s ouvrables, de travail** : working hours

    ~**s supplémentaires** : overtime

hiérarchie (f) : hierarchy, chain of command

hiérarque (m) : top-brass, senior officer

hirondelle (f) : policeman on a bicycle

histoire (f) : tall tale, pack of lies, cock-and-bull story

hold-up (m) : hold-up, armed robbery

holdopeur (m) * : specialist in armed robbery, blagger*

home (m) : home

    ~ **d'enfants** : children's home

    ~ **de semi-liberté** : probation hostel

homicide (m) : homicide
The killing of a human being by a human being. This may be voluntary (murder, infanticide, suicide) or involuntary (manslaughter, accident, carelessness, etc).

homme (m) : man

    ~ **d'affaires** : businessman

    ~ **de loi** : lawyer

    ~ **de paille** : (1) front man; (2) man of straw
        (1) Front man for an (often illicit) activity. A person with no capital and therefore not worth suing.

    ~ **d'état** : statesman

homologation (f) : ratification, confirmation

honoraire : honorary
Where a person has ceased to perform certain functions, but retains the title and privileges on an honorary basis, such as an honorary professor. It is customary for retired policemen to take the honorary rank next above that which they held prior to retiring.

honoraires (mpl) : fees, retainer, refresher

hôpital (m) : hospital
*Like **hospices**, public establishments provided to accommodate the sick, the injured, pregnant women, the aged and incurables. Originally it was intended that hospices should be geared towards those having need of care (the aged, incurables) and hospitals for those needing medical or surgical care. Although the distinction still exists, the growth in medical care has tended to make it less distinct.*

~ **de jour** : day hospital (for the treatment of Aids victims)

horaire (m) : (1) timetable; (2) hourly-paid worker

~ **flexible, individualisé, variable** : flexitime

horodater : to time/date stamp (as by a factory time-clock)

horodateur (m) : "Park and Display" ticket machine

hors : outside

~ **la loi** : outlaw

~ **saison** : off season

~ **taxe** : net of tax, before tax

questions ~ **de cours** : irrelevant questions

hospice (m) : hospice
*Like **hôpitaux**, public establishments provided to accommodate the sick, the injured, pregnant women, the aged and incurables. Originally it was intended that hospices should be geared towards those having need of care (the aged, incurables) and hospitals for those needing medical or surgical care. Although the distinction still exists, the growth in medical care has tended to make it less distinct.*

hôtel (m) : hotel, hostelry, large house

~ **départemental** : county hall (also known as the Préfecture)

~ **de passe** : hotel used by prostitutes

~ **de police** : police station housing more than one police service
*It is common for a **commissariat de police** in the larger towns to also accommodate other police services, such as **renseignements généraux, police judiciaire, PAF, or DST**.*

~ **de ville** : town hall

~ **particulier** : large private house

hotte (f) : car, taxi

housard (m) : voyeur's peephole in public convenience, etc.

huile (f) : (1) oil; (2) * big shot;

    de l'~ : brass*, loot*, cash

    ~ de coude : elbow grease, hard work

    mettre de l'~ sur le feu : to stir things up, to make things worse

huis (m) : door

    ~ clos : in camera, behind closed doors
        An exception to the normal principal that all court hearings must
        be in public which may be invoked where there are good grounds
        for so doing, such as possibility of public disorder or miscarriage
        of justice.

huissier (m) **de justice** : court usher, bailiff, process server

huissier (m) **de police** : police officer (in 17th C.)

huissier–priseur (m) : police officer (in 18th C.)

huit (faire les trois ~) to work (eight-hour) shifts

huppé * : loaded*, very wealthy

hurleur (m) : loudspeaker

hyperfréquence (f) : UHF

hypocrite (faire quelque chose à l'~) : to do something unexpectedly

hypothèque (f) : mortgage, charge, lien
    Security associated with the property of a debtor which gives the
    creditor, in the event of non-payment, the right to sell off the property
    and to be paid from the proceeds in preference to all other creditors.

    ~ judiciaire : judicial charge, court mortgage
        Every conviction where it notes the existence of liability on the part
        of one party, represents ipso jure a judicial charge. Not to be
        confused with a **hypothèque légale** *(statutory lien).*

hystérique (f) : nymphomaniac

I

identifier : to identify

identité (f) : identity (full name, nationality, relationships)

    carte, pièce, papiers d'~ : identity card, papers

    établir son ~ : to prove one's identity

    ~ judiciaire : forensic science and identification service
        The services which carry out the various scientific investigations into offences, such as examination of the scene of crime, fingerprint identification, pathology, laboratory analyses, photofit reconstructions, etc.

ignorer : to be unaware, not to know

illégal : illegal, unlawful

    absence ~ : absence without leave

illégitime : illegitimate, illegal, undue

    enfant ~ : illegitimate child, bastard

    mariage ~ : unlawful marriage

illicite : illicit, unlawful

illimité : unlimited, unrestricted

    congé ~ : indefinite leave

    responsabilité ~ : unlimited liability

illisible : illegible

îlotage (m) : community policing
    System of policing a given, limited area on a regular basis.

îlotier (m) : beat officer, community policeman
    The policeman who is given responsibility for a certain area in a town, typified by an îlot (block).

imitation (f) : imitation, forgery

    ~ de signature : forging of signature

immatériel : unsubstantial

immatriculation (f) : registration, enrolment

plaque d' ~ : motor vehicle number plate

immédiat : immediate, direct

cause ~e : direct cause

voisinage ~ : immediate vicinity

immeuble (m) : building, estate, property

biens ~s : real estate, realty

~ par destination : fixtures and fittings

~ de rapport : tenement building

~ à usage commercial : business premises

immobilier (-ère) : relating to real property

agence ~ : estate agency

impôt ~ : land tax

propriété ~ : real estate, property

saisie ~ : attachment of real property

immobilisation (f) (de véhicule) : impounding of vehicle
Penalty which may be imposed in lieu of a custodial sentence consisitng of depriving the owner of a vehicle of its use for a period not exceeding 6 months.

immoralité (f) : immorality

immunité (f) : immunity

~ de juridiction : diplomatic immunity

~ des plaideurs : immunity of written and verbal evidence to a court

~ diplomatique : diplomatic immunity

~ familiale : immunity from prosecution for theft from close relatives

~ fiscale : immunity from tax, tax exemption

~ judiciaire : immunity of the court from charges of defamation

~ parlementaire : parliamentary privilege

impact (m) : impact, collision

impartir : to grant, to allow

    ~ **des pouvoirs** : to grant powers

    ~ **un délai** : to allow time

impasse (f) : deadlock, sticking point

    négotiations dans l'~ : negotiations in deadlock

    se trouver dans une ~ : to find oneself in a dilemma

impayé : unpaid

impeachment (m) : impeachment
Criminal procedure under which a member of the Executive may be brought by one of the Houses of Parliament before the other house to be tried.

impense (f) : expense

impéritie (f) : incompetence

imperméable (m) : raincoat

impertinent : irrelevant

implantation (f) : setting up, establishment

impliquer : to involve, to implicate

importance (f) : importance, import, extent, size, grandeur

    ~ **d'une firme** : standing of a firm

    sans ~ : unimportant, petty

imposer : to impose, to lay on

    imposé par la loi : statutory

impôt (m) : tax, duty

    ~ **communal** : local tax, community charge

    ~ **de voirie** : road tax

    ~ **des jeux** : betting levy

    ~ **sur le revenu** : income tax

    ~ **sur les sociétés** : corporation tax

imprévision (f) : lack of foresight

imprévu : unforeseen, unexpected

imprimé (m) : form

imprudence (f) : imprudence, rashness, recklessness

    homicide par ~ : manslaughter through recklessness

    faute d' ~ : criminal recklessness

impuberté (f) : under the age for marriage, minor

impunité (f) : impunity

imputabilité (f) : responsibility for one's actions
Ability to comprehend one's actions   Assumes that one is not insane, under age or acting under duress.

imputer : to ascribe, to impute

inactivité (f) **(en ~)** : out of work, unemployed

inadmissible : inadmissible, out of the question

inamical : hostile, unfriendly

inamovibilité (f) : security of tenure
The irremovable status of judges and certain high officials.

inapte : unsuitable, unfit

inaptitude (f) **(au travail)** : incapacity (for work)
Position of a person who is unable to continue to work without serious detriment to his health and, as such, entitled to certain social security benefits.

inattaquable : irrefutable, inalienable (argument, right, etc)

incapable : incapacitated, disqualified

    ~ d'engendrer : impotent

    ~ de tester : disqualified from making a will

    ~ de travailler : unfit for work, disabled

incapacité (f) : (1) physical unfitness, disability; (2) legal disability, incapacity
*(2) Condition of a person deprived by law of the enjoyment or exercise of certain rights. It is said to be **d'exercise** where the person concerned is unfit personally to exercise or to exercise alone certain rights to which he nevertheless remains entitled. It is referred to as **de jouissance** where the person concerned is unfit to hold certain rights.*

    frappé d' ~ : disqualified by law

~ **électorale** : disenfranchisement

~ **permanente** : permanent disability

~ **s et déchéances** : incapacity of convicted person
  Security measures taken against convicted persons aimed at
  preventing them from exercising functions of a civic, civil or family
  nature.

~ **temporaire de travail (ITT)** : temporary incapacity for work

incarcération (f) : imprisonment, incarceration

incendie (m) : fire, conflagration

~ **voluntaire** : arson

inceste (m) : incest

inchangé : unaltered, unchanged

incitation (f) : incitement, encouragement

~ **de mineur à la débauche** : procuring a girl under 18 for immoral
  purposes

incompatibilité (f) **(de fonctions)** : incompatibility (of positions held)

incompétence (f) : incompetence, lack of authority or jurisdiction

~ **absolue** : complete lack of jurisdiction of a court

~ **matérielle** : incompetency ratione materiae

~ **personnelle** : incompetency ratione personae

~ **relative** : relative incompency

~ **territoriale** : incompetency ratione loci

inconduite (f) : misconduct

incontestable : unquestionable, undeniable

incontesté : uncontested

incontournable : unavoidable, impossible to get round

incorruptible : incorruptible, unbribable

incrimination (f) : accusation, law or statutory instrument under which an
  offence is defined

incrochetable : burglar-proof, unpickable

inculpation (f) : charge, accusation
Document on which the examining magistrate sets out the facts alleged against a named suspect.

~ **tardive** : delayed charge
Where an examining magistrate improperly hears a person's evidence when there are serious indications as to his guilt, in order to impede his rights to a defence. May be equated with the continued interrogation of a suspect in England without cautioning him, once it becomes clear that he may be guilty of an offence.

inculpé (m) : person charged, accused
*Person accused of having committed an offence, during the **instruction** stage of the investigation and prior to indictment.*

inculper : to charge, to accuse

indéboulonnable : unimpeachable, unshakeable

indéchiffrable : illegible, unreadable

indemnité (f) : indemnity, compensation, allowance, grant, benefit

action en ~ : claim for compensation

droit à une ~ : entitlement to compensation

~ **de cherté de vie** : cost of living allowance

~ **de déplacement** : travelling allowance

~ **de déplacement de temoin** : conduct money

~ **de fonction** : entertainment allowance

~ **de fonctionnaire** : special allowances to officials

~ **de licenciement** : dismissal allowance

~ **de logement** : rent allowance

~ **de résidence, de nourriture** : lodging allowance

~ **de route** : travelling expenses, mileage allowance

~ **d'expert** : expert's fees

~ **en cas de décès** : death benefit

~ **familiale** : family allowance

~ **forfaitaire** : statutory fixed payment in lieu of prosecution
Applied, for example, by the railway authorities to a person travelling without a valid ticket. Provided he pays the enhanced fare demanded, no prosecution will take place.

~ **pour accident de travail** : injury benefit

index (m) **(mettre à l' ~)** : to blacklist

indicateur (m) : police informer, "grass"

indice (m) : evidence, clue

indigent (m) : disadvantaged, poor person

indirecte : indirect.   **preuve** ~ : circumstantial evidence

individu (m) : individual, person.   ~ **non–admis** : prohibited alien

indivisibilité (f) : unity
> *Each member of the public prosecutor's department represents the whole prosecution service for his level and the various members of the department may replace each other for the prosecution of a single case. This compares with the rule that one judge must hear the whole of the case which he is judging.*

indu : contrary to regulations

in dubio pro reo : the accused must have the benefit of any doubt

indulgence (f) : leniency, forbearance, indulgence

industriel (m) : manufacturer, industrialist

industriel : industrial, manufacturing

centre ~ : industrial estate

établissement ~ : manufacturing firm

inexact : inaccurate, incorrect

inexécutable (projet ~**)** : unworkable (scheme)

inexistence (f) **(de preuve)** : non-existence (of item of evidence)

in extenso : in its entirety
> *The reproduction of the whole of a judicial document as opposed to an extract.*

infamant : defamatory, ignominous

peine ~**e** : penalty involving loss of civil rights

infanticide (m) : infanticide
> *The killing of a newly-born baby during the 3 day period allowed following the birth for the registration of the fact.*

inférieur : lower, subordinate, inferior, below

infirmer : to quash, to annul, to cancel

infirmité (f) disability

infliger (une amende) : to impose (a fine)

informateur (m) : informer, grass*, nark*

information (f) : see instruction

informe : not complying with the legal requirements (document, etc.)

informer (contre quelqu'un) : to inform, to lay information (against someone)

s'informer (de quelque chose) : to enquire about (something), to make enquiries

informationnel : relating to information science

informatique (f) : data processing, computer science

> ~ juridique : computerisation of legal matters (see also banque de données
> juridique)

infraction (f) : offence, infraction
*Any act or omission defined by the criminal law and punished by certain
penalties determined by the law.*

> ~ à la paix publique : breach of the peace

> ~ au devoir : breach of duty

> ~ au règlement : breach of rules, regulations

> ~ complexe : complex offence
> *Offence which involves several different material actions. An exam-
> ple could be deception cases which consist of fraudulent manoeu-
> vres and the passing of property from the victim to the accused.*

> ~ consommée : completed offence

> ~ continue : continuing offence
> *Offence typified by the fact that its commission may continue to
> take place over a period of time by the unlawful and wilful
> persistance of the offender (eg driving without licence/insurance).*

> ~ continuée : multiple offence
> *Term used to describe a number of similar illegal actions (eg theft)
> committed in succession within the framework of a single criminal
> enterprise.*

> ~ d'habitude : cumulative offence
> *Offence committed by repeating individual material actions which
> would not, in isolated cases, be an offence. E.g. the illegal practice
> of medicine.*

~ **formelle** : strict offence

> Contrary to material misdemeanours, the concept of strict offence makes it illegal to set in motion a chain of events with intent to commit an offence, even though such offence does not result therefrom. Thus the offence of poisoning consists of administering noxious substances, whether or not the death of the victim results.

~ **impossible** : impossible attempt

> An attempt which cannot be brought to fruition because of the impossibility to achieve the fulfilment of the offence. E.g. the attempt to pick an empty pocket.

~ **instantanée** : instantaneous offence

> Offence which cannot be continued over a period of time.

~ **intentionnelle** : intended offence

> Offence in which the intent alone can form the mens rea.

~ **manquée** : abortive offence

> An offence which, although commenced, fails to be completed for one reason or another, eg. clumsiness.

~ **militaire** : military offence

> Strictly speaking, neglect of duty or other disciplinary offence covered by the code of military justice and therefore inconceivable outside military life (insubordination, desertion). More widely, the term is used to refer to certain offences against general public law which are punished more severely by the code of military justice because in military life they take on a particular seriousness (e.g. striking a superior officer).

~ **naturelle ou artificielle** : natural and man-made offences

> Distinction is made between the former, which refers to those activities which most civilised societies regard as being outside the bounds of normal, acceptable behaviour, and the latter which are the offences prescribed by the legislator to create or regulate a particular social order, governed by various factors, such as the economy.

~ **obstacle** : preventive offence

> Behaviour which does not, of itself, disturb social order but which is nevertheless made an offence as a preventive measure because it is dangerous and represents the advance warning of a crime.

~ **permanente** : lasting offence

> Instantaneous offence, the effects of which continue over a period of time because of the purely passive attitude of the offender (e.g. bigamy, fly-posting).

~ **praeterintentionnelle** : unintentional offence

> A wilful, unlawful act which has consequences which the offender did not anticipate, such as an assault which results in the death of the victim. The penalty usually falls between that which would be imposed for the intended offence and that which would be applied to the offence actually committed.

~ **purement matérielle** : purely material offence
> *An unlawful act where the existence of mens rea has not been demonstrated but the facts themselves represent the guilty mind. This could be the case where the offender pleads ignorance of the law, failure to ensure that he was aware of the law being regarded as sufficient to constitute mens rea. Summary offences are usually purely material offences.*

~ **putative** : presumptive offence
> *Act or omission completed or accomplished in the erroneous belief that it constituted an offence (e.g. abduction of a person over the age of 18 in the belief that the victim was a minor).*

infrarouge : (1) infra-red; (2) I.R. gun sight

infrastructure (f) : infrastructure, facilities, basic equipment

ingérence (f) : unwarranted interference, meddling

inhibition (f) : prohibition

inimitié (f) : hostility, bias (grounds for challenging a judge, a witness)

injecter : to inject

injonction (f) : injunction, court order

injure (f) : wrong, injury, abuse, tort, libel, slander
> *In criminal law, any outrageous expression, term of contempt, or censure, not encompassing the imputation of any precise fact. In so far as it was not provoked, the offence is a misdemeanour if the matter is published and a summary offence if not.*

injurier : to insult

innocent : innocent, blameless

innomé : unnamed, nameless

inobservation des formes : failure to observe the prescribed formalities
> *This may be grounds for appeal.*

inofficiel : unofficial

inondation (f) : flooding
> *The flooding of roads and property is, under certain circumstances, a criminal offence.*

inquisitoire : see **procédure inquisitoire**

inscription (f) : enrolment, registration

    droit d' ~ : registration, entry fee

    feuille d' ~ : entry, registration form

~ **en faux** : plea of forgery

insigne (m) **de grade** : badge of rank

insoloir (m) : solitary confinement

insolvable : insolvent

insoumis (m) : absentee, deserter

inspecteur (m) : inspector, detective

~ **de police** : detective sergeant (det. constable in Belgium)

~ **divisionnaire** : detective chief inspector

~ **général de police** : inspector-general of police
   *One of the highest ranks in the National Police, equating
   approximately to a chief constable, assistant commissioner or HMI.*

~ **principal** : detective inspector (det. sergeant in Belgium)

inspection (f) : (1) inspection, close examination;   (2) inspectorate

~ **générale de la police** : General Inspectorate of the National Police
   *Sometimes referred to as the "Police des Polices", it supervises the
   police services, looks into complaints and carries out research and
   investigations aimed at improving police operations.*

instance (f) : process, action, proceedings

tribunal de grande ~ : second level court (county/crown court)

tribunal d'instance : magistrate's court

tribunal de première ~ : court of first instance

instantané (m) : snap, unposed photograph

instigateur (m) : instigator, master-mind

institut (m) : institute

~ **des Hautes Etudes de la Sécurité Intérieure (IHESI)** : Institute for
   Advanced Internal Security Studies.

~ **Médico–légal** : forensic science and pathology institute

~ **National de Formation de la Police Nationale** : National Police Training
   Institute, Central Planning Unit
   *The Institute trains instructors, advises the various police schools
   regarding training programmes and assists with teaching aids. The
   Documentation section of the Institute forms part of the central
   planning unit, covering legal, administrative, criminological, general
   policing, social sciences and training matters.*

instruction (f) : (1) instruction, training, briefing; (2) investigation, examination

    ~ **définitive** : initial stage of hearing
        Whether there has been a preliminary investigation or not, the first
        part of criminal proceedings takes the form of an **instruction**, *i.e.*
        an examination of the evidence, hearing the witnesses and the
        accused, etc. The second part consists of the **réquisitoire** *and the*
        plaidoiries *(speeches by the prosecution and defence counsels) and*
        the finding of the court.

    ~ **écrite** : written statement of the case

    ~ **préparatoire** : examination prior to committal, preliminary investigation
        An important stage in criminal proceedings which consists of an
        initial review of the evidence to establish whether there is a prima
        facie case to go before the court. This stage is optional in the case
        of misdemeanours but mandatory in the case of felony. It is
        conducted by a "juge d'instruction" to whom the matter has been
        referred by the public prosecutor.

    juge d' ~ : examining magistrate
        The **juge d'instruction** *presides over the* **instruction préparatoire**
        and directs and controls the enquiries conducted by the duly
        authorised police officers (**officiers/agents de police judiciaire**),
        usually by way of a **commission rogatoire**. *He may hear witnesses,*
        interrogate the suspect, nominate experts and issue search warrants
        and seizure orders. He also makes decisions as to **détention**
        provisoire.

    ouvrir une ~ : to open a preliminary investigation

instruire (une affaire) : to investigate (a case)

instrument (m) : legal instrument (deed, contract, writ, etc)

    ~ **authentique** : certified instrument

    ~ **de preuve** : documentary evidence

instrumenter : to draw up a document, a deed

    ~ **contre quelqu'un** : to order proceedings to be taken against someone

insuffisance (f) : insufficiency, lack, shortage

    ~ **de motifs** : lack of evidence, no case to answer

    ~ **de personnel** : staff shortage

intendant (m) : administrator

intenter : to bring, to enter

    ~ **une action/un procès** : to institute proceeding, take legal action

intention (f) : intent, intention

    ~ **criminelle/délicteuse** : criminal intent

    ~ **frauduleuse** : fraudulent intent

    ~ **malveillante, méchante, maligne** : evil intent

    dans l'~ de nuire : maliciously

intentionnel : intentional, with intent

    délit ~ : wilful misdemeanour

    dommage ~ : wilful damage

intercéder : to intercede, to stand bail

interdire : to prohibit, to forbid

interdiction (f) : prohibition, interdiction, ban
In criminal law, refers usually to the legal suspension of the civil rights of a convicted felon.

    ~ **de séjour** : banishment
An order, made by the Minister of the Interior, forbidding a convicted person to go to certain defined places after he has served his sentence. The ban may last from 2 to 20 years.

    ~ **légale** : prohibition on the disposal of property

    ~ **professionnelle** : removal of right to practice a particular profession

intéressé : interested, concerned, involved

intérêt (m) : interest, benefit

    ~ **commun** : the common good, the common weal

    ~ **public** : public interest

    ~**s civils** : damages
Awarded to private individual having instituted and won a civil action in parallel with a criminal prosecution.

    dommages– ~s : damages

intérieur (m) : internal

    ministère de l'~ : = the Home Office

    ministre de l'~ : Minister for the Interior, = Home Secretary

intérimaire : interim, acting, temporary

> **directeur ~** : acting manager

interjeter (appel) : to give notice (of appeal)

interlope : suspect, shady

intermédiaire (m) : agent, intermediary, interface

internat (m) : boarding school

internement (m) : internment (of foreigners), confinement (of mental patients)

interpellation (f) : questioning (as to identity, etc.)

interpeller : to question (as to identity, etc.)

Interpol (f) : Interpol, International Criminal Police Organisation
Contrary to popular fiction, Interpol does not have operational officers but is a centre of information and communication for member countries. Its headquarters are in Lyons, France.

interprétation (f) **stricte** : strict interpretation
Principle forbidding the judge to widen the terms of an indictment in order to sanction a matter which is not expressly covered by law.

interprète (m) **(assermenté)** : (sworn) interpreter

interrogatoire (m) : interrogation, examination, interview of suspect

> **~ contradictoire** : examination in the presence of the parties

> **~ croisé** : cross-examination

> **~ de clôture** : closing examination (by the **juge d'instruction**)

> **~ de première comparution** : first examination, initial interview (by *juge d'instruction*)

> **~ d'identité** : preliminary questions as to identity

> **procéder à un ~** : to examine

interruption (f) : interruption of the period of limitation on proceedings
*An incident which interrupts the period of limitation and retroactively cancels such time as has already passed. If the limitation recommences after the incident, the time already passed will not be included in the calculation. Appropriate incidents will include the commencement of proceedings, any **instruction** process and all judicial decisions.*

> **~ volontaire de grossesse** : intentional termination of pregnancy, abortion
> *Not an offence where performed by a doctor on serious medical grounds.*

intervention (f) : intervention

intime (conviction) : deep-seated (conviction)

intimidation (f) : undue influence

introduction (f) **d'instance** : writ of summons

invalide : invalid (not valid)

invalide (m&f) : disabled person

> ~ **de guerre** : disabled serviceman

invalidité (f) infirmity, disablement, invalidity

> ~ **permanente** : permanent disability

investigation (f) : investigation, enquiry

invétéré (délinquant ~) : incorrigible rogue

inviolabilité parlementaire (f) : immunity of Members of Parliament (from arrest and prosecution unless caught in flagrante delicto)

involontaire : involuntary

> **délit** ~ : unintentional misdemeanour

irrecevable : barred, inadmissible (means, evidence), irrelevant, immaterial (evidence)

irréformable : incorrigible, irrevocable

irréfutable : irrefutable, indisputable

irrégulier : irregular, disorderly, dissolute (life)

irresponsable : irresponsible, mentally defective, non compos mentis

irrévocable : irrevocable, final, irreversible

> **jugement** ~ : decree absolute

itinérant : itinerant, vagrant, wandering

ivresse (f) : intoxication, drunkenness

> **en état d'~ publique** : drunk in a public place

J

jacot (m) * : jemmy, crowbar

jacques (m) * : jemmy, crowbar

jalonner : to line a route

jaune (m) * : (1) scab*, blackleg*; (2) coward; (3) cuckold

jeton (m) : chip (for gaming), token (for telephone, etc.)

jeu (m) : game, gaming, gambling
Public gaming and betting in France is subject to strict control.

    concession des ~x : gaming licence

    dette de ~ : gambling debt
        Gambling debts are not recoverable at law.

    ~ de hasard : game of chance

    mettre en ~ : to call into play

jeune délinquant (m) : juvenile delinquant

jeune adult délinquant (m) : young offender
Offenders between the ages of 18 and about 25. There is a school of thought which believes that, as physiological, psychological and social maturity is not reached at 18, a level of responsibility, similar to that for minors, should be established. In practice French law and procedure makes certain concessions to offenders in this category (exclusion of certain facts from the criminal record, special penal regimes, etc.).

joaillier (m) : jeweller (selling good quality items)

jogger : to jog, to go jogging

joggers (mpl) : jogging shoes, trainers

joggeur (m) : jogger

jogging (m) : jogging suit, track suit

joncaille (f) * : (1) brass*, loot*, cash; (2) assorted items of gold jewellery

jonction (f) **d'instance** : joinder, consolidation, combined hearing
Decision made by a court to investigate and hear two cases at the same time because of their close connection with each other.

jouasse (f) * : kick* (from drugs)

jour (m) : day

  à ce ~ : to date

  à ~ : up to date

  ~ chômé : statutory day's holiday

  ~ civil : 24 hours

  ~ de congé : day off

  ~ de grâce : day of grace

  ~ de repos : rest day

  ~ férié : bank holiday

  ~ franc : clear day (midnight to midnight)

  ~ J * : day of reckoning, D-day

  ~ ouvrable : working day

  ~ s amendes : day fines
  Fine as an alternative to imprisonment, payable in daily instalments.

journal (m) : diary, day book

  ~ d'annonces légales : official notices newspaper
  *In each **département**, the prefect issues an annual order, specifying the newspapers published in his area in which the various notices prescribed by law may be inserted.*

  ~ de bord : captain's log, ship's log

  ~ Officiel (JO) : Official Journal
  The official French government publication in which all newly-passed laws and official notices are published.

judicature (f) : judiciary, the Bench

judiciaire : judicial, legal

  assistance ~ : legal aid

  casier ~ : criminal record, criminal records office

  débats ~s : hearing

  enquête ~ : judicial enquiry

  erreur ~ : miscarriage of justice

identité ~ : forensic science and identification service

nouvelles ~s : law reports

pièce ~ : exhibit

police ~ : criminal investigation department

poursuites ~ : legal proceedings

pouvoir ~ : power to judge and sentence, the courts

procédure ~ : rules of legal procedure

juge (m) : judge, magistrate

~ **de l'application des peines** : sentence review judge
High Court judge who supervises the serving of sentences, both custodial and non-custodial. He can grant parole, reductions in sentence, etc.

~ **délégué** : deputy to presiding judge

~ **de paix** : stipendiary magistrate, justice of the peace; (2) * rod*, shooter*, handgun

~ **départiteur** : arbitrating judge
One who rules when the bench is unable to agree on a verdict.

~ **de police** : stipendiary magistrate (sits alone)

~ **des enfants/mineurs** : juvenile court judge (sits alone)

~ **d'instance** : police court magistrate

~ **d'instruction** : examining magistrate, investigating judge
*Conducts the initial investigation into criminal matters, gathers the evidence (via **officiers de police judiciaire**) and refers the case to the appropriate court. He may order the temporary detention of suspects. In serious or delicate matters the enquiry is conducted by three magistrates.*

~ **informateur** : see *juge d'instruction*

~ **mandant** : authorising judge

petit ~ : see *juge d'instruction*

jugement (m) : judgement, decision

annuler un ~ : to quash, rescind a judgement

expédition du ~ : copy of the judgement

~ **conditionnel** : suspended judgement

     ~ **contradictoire** : judgement after trial

     ~ **criminel** : sentence

     ~ **de sursis** : adjournment

     ~ **en premier ressort** : judgement subject to appeal

     ~ **frappé d'appel** : judgement under appeal

     ~ **par défaut** : judgement by default

     ~ **pénal** : sentence

     ~ **sur frais** : award of costs

     mettre en ~ : to commit for trial

juger : to judge, to try

     ~ **en appel** : to hear an appeal

     ~ **un accusé** : to try a prisoner

juré (m) : juror

     expert ~ : sworn expert

     premier ~ : foreman of the jury

     traducteur ~ : sworn translator

juridiction (f) : court, jurisdiction, province

     ~ **correctionnelle** : see ~ *pénale*

     ~ **de droit commun** : court normally competent
         *In criminal matters these are the **tribunal de police**, the **tribunal correctionnel**, the **cour d'appel** and the **cour d'assises**.*

     ~ **d'exception** : special courts
         Court whose competence is determined by statute, such as the juvenile courts, courts martial, etc.

     ~ **judiciaire** : the ordinary courts
         *All those civil and criminal courts which are subject to the **cour de cassation** (cf. administrative courts).*

     ~ **pénale** : criminal jurisdiction
         *There are two elements of this: the **juridiction d'instruction** (preliminary enquiry) and the **juridiction de jugement** (trial).*

juridique : judicial, legal

     conseiller ~ : legal adviser

jurisprudence (f) : case law, precedents, stated caes
Decisions made by the courts as opposed to legislation and doctrine.

juriste (m) : lawyer (both practising and academic), jurist

jury (m) : jury

    dresser la liste du ~ : to empanel the jury

    ~ **d'examen** : examining board

    membre du ~ : juror

    verdict du ~ : verdict

juste : accurate, fair

justice (f) : justice, law, legal proceedings

    déni de ~ : miscarriage of justice

    ~ **de paix** : police court
        *Now known as the **tribunal d'instance**.*

    descente de ~ : visit of experts and/or officials to the scene

    en toute ~ : by rights

    gens de ~ : lower grade court officials

    palais de ~ : law courts

    poursuivre en ~ : to prosecute

    repris de ~ : habitual criminal, recidivist

    se faire ~ : (1) to commit suicide; (2) to take the law into one's own hands

    traduire en ~ : to prosecute

justifiable : justifiable, warrantable

justificative : justificatory

    pièce ~ : document in proof

justification (f) : justification, proof, vindication

justifier : to justify, to prove

    ~ **de ses mouvements** : to give a satisfactory account of one's movements

    ~ **de son identité** : to prove one's identity

juteux (m) * : warrant officer (corruption of **adjudant**)

K

képi (m) : kepi, cap
    *Recognised throughout the world as typifying French uniformed officials,
    the **képi** is no longer worn by the Police Nationale, who abandoned it in
    favour of a cap (**casquette**) of more orthodox style.   It is still worn,
    however, by the Gendarmerie.*

keuf (m) * : cop, copper

kick (m) : kickstart

kidnapper : to kidnap

kif (m) : cannabis, hashish

kiosquier (m) : news stand holder, news vendor

klaxon (m) : horn

klaxonner : to sound the horn

kleptomane (m) : kleptomaniac, compulsive thief

kleptomanie (f) : kleptomania

L

laboratoire (m) : laboratory

lacets (mpl) **(marchand de ˜)** : gendarme

lacrymogène (gaz ˜) : tear gas

lacune (f) : loophole

laissez–passer (m) : pass, permit, platform ticket

lame (f) : blade, knife

lamedus (mpl) * : hot goods*, stolen property

lamer : to knife, to stab

laminer * : to kill

lance–parfum (m) * : sub–machine gun

lance–roquette (m) : rocket launcher

lanterne (f) : lantern, lamp

    ˜ sourde : lamp with shutter to mask the beam

"La plume est serve, mais la parole est libre"
    Principle by virtue of which the public prosecutors are required to prepare <u>written</u> cases for the prosecution in accordance with instructions from their superiors but are free, at the hearing, to develop <u>verbally</u> various points which reflect their own opinions.

larcin (m) : petty theft, pilfering

lardu (m) * : (1) police station, cop–shop; (2) policeman

largue (f) * : prostitute, hooker

larron (m) : robber, thief

lavé * : (1) exhausted, knackered; (2) penniless, skint

    chéque ˜ : fraudulently altered cheque

laver : (1) to clear (of a charge, of suspicion); (2) to sell off cheaply

lavage (m) : laundering (of "dirty" money)

lecteur (m) **de carte à mémoire (lecan)** : smart card reader

légal : legal, statutory

> **disposition ~e** : statutory provision
>
> **domicile ~** : legal domicile
>
> **médecine ~e** : forensic medicine, medical jurisprudence
>
> **sans motif ~** : unlawfully

légaliser : to legalize, to authenticate, to certify

légalité (f) : legality

> **~ de la poursuite** : principle of prosecution
> *The public prosecutor is required, before bringing a matter before the courts, to ensure that all the elements of the crime are present (actus reas, mens rea, objective and mental elements, etc.).*
>
> **~ des délits et des peines** : legality of crime and punishment
> *The Penal Code provides that no penalty may be imposed for any offence unless it has been prescribed by law, prior to the commission of the offence.*

légion (f) : legion.
*A formation of Gendarmerie, consisting of several **groupements** and commanded by a colonel.*

législation (f) : legislation

législature (f) : parliament (the period between two elections)

légiste (m) : jurist

> **médecin- ~** : medical expert appointed by the court

légitimation (f) : submission of credentials

> **titre de ~** : identity papers

légitime : legitimate

> **enfant ~** : legitimate child
>
> **~ défense** : self-defence
> *Justification for violently resisting an unlawful and current assault on persons or property.*
>
> **propriétaire ~** : rightful owner

Léon (gros ~) : "Mr Big", top man in the criminal fraternity

léser : to wrong, to wound, to injure

> **~ les droits de quelqu'un** : to encroach upon someone's rights

partie lésée : the injured party

lésion (f) : injury, wrong

~ **corporelle** : bodily injury

lettre (f) : letter

au pied de la ~ : by the book, strictly according to the rules

levée (f) : raising, lifting, removal

~ **d'écrou** : release from prison

~ **des scellés** : removal of the seals
The scene of a crime and real evidence is usually sealed by a senior police officer or magistrate in order to preserve the evidence. It is a serious offence for an unauthorised person to break these wax seals.

~ **d'une interdiction** : removal of prohibition

lever : (1) to levy, to lift, to raise; (2) * to nick*, to pinch*, to steal; (3) * to hook a client (prostitute); (4) * to arrest, to nick*, to knock off

~ **la main** : to swear an oath

~ **la séance** : to close the meeting

~ **les scellés** : to break, to remove seals

~ **un impôt** : to levy a tax

leveur (m) * : thief

leveuse (f) * : prostitute

levier (m) : lever

~ **de frein** : brake lever

~ **d'embrayage** : clutch lever

liasse (f) : wad, bundle

libelle (m) : lampoon, libel

libellé (m) : wording, particulars

~ **d'une loi** : text of a law

libeller : to draw up, to word a document, to sign and date, to draft

libéral : liberal

> **les professions ˜es** : the liberal professions

libération (f): discharge, release

> **˜ conditionnelle, sous surveillance** : release of prisoner on licence, on parole.

> **˜ définitive** : final discharge of prisoner

> **˜ sous caution** : release on bail

> **mouvement de ˜ de la femme (MLF)** : womens' liberation movement

libérer : to release, to free, to liberate

liberté (f) : freedom, liberty, right

> **˜ civile** : civil liberty
> *Freedom to do everything which is not prohibited by law.*

> **˜ de décision** : freedom of decision
> *In principle, the public prosecutor is entirely free to decide whether or not to prosecute. He is required to follow instructions but, if he fails to do so, his superiors cannot act in his stead. By virtue of the adage "la plume est serve mais la parole est libre", the prosecutor may make an oral submission contrary to his instructions and contrary to the case he has submitted in writing.*

> **˜ de réunion** : right of assembly.
> *A permit is required if the meeting is to be in the streets.*

> **˜ provisoire** : provisional release from custody
> *A prisoner must be released provisionally five days after the initial examination unless the judge decides to issue a commital warrant against him.*

> **˜ sous caution** : release on bail

> **˜ surveillée** : supervision order, probation of a minor

> **peine privative de ˜** : custodial sentence

licence (f) : (1) licence; (2) university degree

licenciement (m) : dismissal, discharge

> **indemnité de ˜** : dismissal payment, redundancy payment

> **˜ abusif** : unfair dismissal

> **préavis de ˜** : period of notice

licencier : to discharge, to sack, to lay off (an employee)

licite : lawful, licit

lien (m) : tie, bond

> **~ conjugal** : bonds of matrimony

> **~ de parenté** : blood relationship

> **~ du sang** : near in blood

lieu (m) : place, locality, spot

> **au ~ et place de** : in lieu of

> **descente/transport sur les lieux** : visit of experts or officials to the scene of an occurrence.

> **~ de séjour** : place of abode

> **~ de stationnement** : parking place

> **~ du crime** : scene of the crime

> **~ public** : public place

lieutenance–générale (f) **de police** : general lieutenancy of police.
Post created in 1667 to organise and control the policing of Paris.

lieutenant (m) : lieutenant
Apart from being a military rank (and therefore one used in the Gendarmerie) it is familiarly used to designate an **officier de la paix.** *Historically, it was the title given to the officer in charge of a group of watchmen of the Paris Watch (ca. 1688).*

> **~ –général** : lord lieutenant, representative of the monarch
> *Title given to a senior official of the court who represented the monarch in the 17th and 18th centuries. As such he was responsible for law and order, especially the policing of the capital. Not to be confused with the identically–named military rank in English–speaking countries, the equivalent of which is a* **général de corps d'armée.**

ligoter : to tie up, to bind

limier (m) : (1) bloodhound; (2) detective, sleuth

limitation (f) : limitation, restriction

> **~ de vitesse** : speed limit

> **sans ~ de temps** : without time limit

limite (f) : limit, cut–off

> **cas ~** : borderline case

date ~ : deadline

~ **d'âge** : age limit

~ **du territoire** : border

~ **fatidique** : psychological barrier

vitesse ~ : maximum speed

linéaire (m) : gondola, island display unit (in supermarkets)

lingue (m) * : blade*, knife

lip (f) : wristwatch (named after a well-known make of watches)

liquidateur (m) : liquidator

liquide (m) : ready cash

liste (f) **électorale** : electoral roll

lit (m) : bed, marriage

enfant d'un autre ~ : step-child

enfant du second ~ : child of the second marriage

litige (m) : litigation, dispute at law

littéral : literal

interprétation ~**e** : strict construction

preuve ~**e** : documentary evidence

livre (m) book

~ **de comptabilité, de comptes** : account book

~ **d'écrou** : prison calendar

livrer : to deliver, to hand over

livret (m) : booklet

~ **de banque** : bank book, pass book

~ **de chèques** : cheque book

~ **de famille** : family book
Booklet issued to newly-weds in which details of the marriage and subsequent births, deaths, etc are recorded.

local (m) : premises, building

location (f) : renting, hiring

loche (m) * : cabbie, taxi-driver

logement (m) : lodgings, housing

    indemnité de ~ : lodging allowance, rent allowance

    ~ garni : furnished rooms

logiciel (m) : software

logisticien (m) : logistics expert

logistique (f) : logistics

    Direction de la ~ de la Police : National Police Logistics Department

loi (f) : statute, law, act of parliament
Usually refers to a specific statute, rather than law in general (le droit)

    appliquer la ~ : enforce the law

    hors-la- ~ : outlaw

    ~-cadre : enabling act
    Act in which parliament simply sets out the general principles and basic rules regarding a particular matter, leaving the government to take the detail steps by way of regulation.

    ~ d'ordre public : public policy
    Rule of law which provides that laws relating to public policy or morality cannot be negated by any private agreement.

    ~ impérative : mandatory rule of private law
    This overrides any private agreement or contract which is contrary to public policy or interests.

    ~ municipale : bye-law

    ~ plus douce : retroactive leniency
    The application of a less-severe criminal law to an offence committed prior to its being passed and which has not been definitively dealt with by the courts.

    ~ supplétive : supplementary law
    Rule of law which applies in the absence of any express intention to the contrary, or else is used to supplement an inadequately expressed agreement.

    passer en force de ~ : to become effective, enforceable

    tourner la ~ : to cheat, to get around the law

    transgresser la ~ : to break the law

violation de la ~ : breach of the law

loisible : permissible, optional

longe (f) * : year (of incarceration)

écoper de cinq ~s : to cop a five-year stretch

loulou (m) * : yobbo*, hooligan, vandal

louper : to botch, to bungle, to miss

loupiotte (f) : dim light, weak torch

lourdeur (m) * : burglar

lourdière (f) : caretaker, concierge

lorsque : where
This is the usual translation where this word appears in legal texts.

"lu et approuvé" : "read and approved"

lucratif : lucrative, profitable

dans un but ~ : for gain, for profit

lunette (f) **arrière** : rear window

lusophone : Portuguese-speaking

M

macadam (m) : pavement, sidewalk, footpath

    faire le ~ : to solicit for the purposes of prostitution

macaron (m) : (1) button-hole insignia worn by holders of decorations such as the **Légion d'honneur;** (2) disc on the windscreen of official cars belonging to important people, giving exemption from parking restrictions, etc.; (3) steering wheel

macchabée (m) * : stiff*, corpse

machination (f) plot, conspiracy

magasin (m) : shop, warehouse, store

    ~ de proximité : neighbourhood shop, corner shop

magistrat (m) : law officer, judge, magistrate, public prosecutor
In general, a functionary or officer who has a judicial, administrative or political power but, more usually, it refers to lawyers who are either appointed to preside over hearings or to act as prosecutors.

    ~ assis : judge, magistrate
        So called because they sit on the bench and dispense justice. The term includes **juges d'instruction**

    ~ debout : public prosecutor
        So called because they make their submissions standing on the floor of the court. They direct criminal investigations made by the police and gendarmerie, receive complaints of crime and supervise the implementation of court decisions.

    ~ du ministère publique : see **magistrat debout**

    ~ du parquet : see **magistrat debout**

    ~ du siège : see **magistrat assis**

    ~ instructeur : see **juge d'instruction**

magot (m) : hoard of money, savings

magouille (f) : suspect, doubtful or illegal activities

main (f) : hand

    ~ courante : log book, note book

    ~ -forte ; assistance, help, support (to or of authority)

mainlevée (f) : removal, withdrawal

---

mainmise (f) : seizure, distraint

maintien (m) **d'ordre** : maintenance of public order

maire (m) : mayor
> *The head of a **commune**, elected from amongst the members of the **conseil municipal**. Although an elected official, a French mayor serves for four years and performs the rôle of chief executive as well as chairman of the town council. In the larger towns it is a full-time job. The mayor is also a representative of the State, responsible for the registration of births, deaths and marriages and is, ex officio, an **officier de police judiciaire** and head of any municipal police force but he has no control over the National Police or Gendarmerie units stationed in his area.*

    ~-adjoint (m) : deputy mayor, assistant mayor

    ~ d'arrondissement (m) : district mayor
> *In the larger cities such as Paris, Lyons, Marseilles, there are mayors elected for and by the local districts (**arrondissements**). They have a minor function to play and are subordinate to the mayor for the city as a whole.*

mairie (f) : town hall, civic centre

maison (f) : house

    gens de ~ : domestic servants

    grande ~ * : police station

    ~ centrale : central prison (for long-term prisoners)

    ~ close : brothel

    ~ d'aliénés : mental institution

    ~ d'arrêt : prison for those on remand and those with only short sentences to serve

    ~ de correction : reformatory

    ~ d'éducation surveillée : reform school, borstal institution

    ~ de jeu : gaming house, casino

    ~ de plain-pied : bungalow

    ~ de retraite : retirement home, old folks' home

    ~ de santé : nursing home

    ~ de tolérance : licensed brothel (ceased in 1946)

    ~ de ville : town hall

~ **jumelée** : semi-detached house

maître (m) : master
Courtesy title given to members of the legal profession (except magistrates) and usually abridged to Me.

~ **de chien** : dog handler

~ **des requêtes** : legal adviser to the Conseil d'Etat

maître-nageur-sauveteur (MNS) (m) : life-saver

majeur : of full age

force ~**e** : act of God, force majeure

major (m) : senior warrant officer (gendarmerie and the other armed forces)
Identifiable by one broad and three narrow bars worn on the cuff, with similar bands around the kepi.

~**-général** : general in charge of military headquarters
      NOTE : unlike the British army, this is a post and not a rank.

majorité (f) : age of majority
The age at which a young person becomes an adult in the eyes of the law. For most purposes, including the criminal law, this is 18.

maladie (f) : sickness, illness

congé de ~ : sick leave

~ **professionnelle** : occupational, industrial disease

par suite de ~ : through illness

malfaiteur (m) : offender, criminal

association de ~**s** : conspiracy

mal famé : disreputable, notorious

malfrat (m) * : crook, criminal

malhonnête : dishonest, deceitful

malice (f) : malice.   **avec intention malicieuse** : with malice aforethought

malin (m) : crook, miscreant.   **petit** ~ : small time crook

maljugé (m) : miscarriage of justice (error of justice only)

maltraitance (f) : child abuse (within the family)

malveillance (f) : malevolence, ill-will, spite, foul play

malversation (f) : malpractice, fraudulent conversion

malverser : to convert fraudulently, to misappropriate

malvie (f) : poor quality of life

manchard (m) * : tramp, beggar

Manche (f) (La ~) : the English Channel

mandat (m) : warrant, authorisation

    décerner, lancer un ~ : to issue a warrant

       ~ d'amener : magistrate's warrant
          Warrant issued by the public prosecutor or examining magistrate
          instructing the police to bring before him, without delay, a person
          who is to be the subject of a preliminary hearing.

       ~ d'arrêt : arrest warrant, remand warrant, writ of capias
          Warrant issued by the court or an examining magistrate to the
          police to locate the person named therein (being the subject of an
          indictment or preliminary hearing) and take him to the remand
          prison named.

       ~ de comparution : summons
          Official notice sent by an examining magistrate to the subject of a
          preliminary hearing to attend before him at the date and time given.

       ~ de dépôt : committal warrant
          Warrant addressed to the governor of a prison ordering him to
          receive and hold the person named therein.

       ~ de perquisition : search warrant

    signifier un ~ : to execute a warrant

mandater : to commission, to authorise

mander : (1) to command, to summon; (2) to declare

mangaver : to beg

manif (f) : see **manifestation**

manifestation (f) : demonstration

manifestement : overtly

manigance (f) : underhand practice, hanky-panky*, jiggery-pokery*

mannequins (mpl) * : fuzz*, cops*, old Bill*, the police

manoeuvres (fpl) : scheming, working, handling

~ **abortives** : procuring an abortion

~ **frauduleuses** : fraudulent representation, cheating, swindling

manouche (m) : gipsy, romany

manque (m) : withdrawal symptoms

manquement (m) : lack, failure

maqué : working for a pimp

maquereau (m) : pimp, person living on immoral earnings

maquiller : to fake, to doctor

maraudage (m) : picking and eating fruit belonging to another, scrumping*

marauder : to ply for hire in the streets (taxi)

marchand (m) : merchant, trader, shopkeeper

~ **ambulant** : pedlar, hawker

~ **de bobards** : con-man, swindler

~ **de lacets** : gendarme

– **des quatre-saisons** : costermonger

~ **de viande** : white slave trader

~ **forain** : stall holder, market trader

marcheur (m) * : burglar, housebreaker

marcheuse (f) * : prostitute

maréchal des logis (m) : sergeant (Gendarmerie Auxiliaire)
Identifiable by a single broad inverted chevron on the epaulettes.

~ **-chef** : staff sergeant (Gendarmerie Nationale)
Identifiable by three inverted chevrons worn normally on the cuff

maréchaussée (f) : corps of marshals, marshalsea, mounted constabulary
*The forerunner of the **Gendarmerie**, formed around the XIII century and lasting until 1791 when it became the **Gendarmerie Nationale**.*

marie–jeanne (f) * : marijuana, cannabis

marijuana (f) : marijuana, cannabis

marlon (m) : pimp, person living on immoral earnings

margeo/marjo (m) : drop-out

marginal (m) : social deviant, person living on the fringe of society

marmite (f) * : prostitute

    grande ~ : top-security prison

marqué (m) : a month of imprisonment

    tirer trois ~s de ballon : to get sent down for three months

marron : (1) reddish brown;   (2) operating without the necessary qualifications

    yeux ~ : brown eyes

matériel (m) : equipment, supplies

matière (f) : basis, grounds of a charge, gravamen

matraque (f) : truncheon, baton, staff

    coup de ~ : inflated bill

matuche (m) * : cop*, old Bill*, police

mauvaise foi (f) : ill will, mala fides

mauvais traitement envers les animaux : ill-treatment of animals

mec (m) * : guy, bloke, fellow, chap

mécano (m) * : mechanic

médecin (m) : doctor, physician

    ~ légiste : forensic pathologist, doctor giving expert evidence to a court

    ~ sanitaire : medical officer of health

médecine (f) : medicine

    ~ légale : forensic medicine, medical jurisprudence

médicament (m) : medicine, medicament

méfiance (f) : suspicion, mistrust

mélécass (m) : brandy mixed with blackcurrant liqueur

mêler : to implicate, to involve

menace (f) : threat, intimidation, pressure
Expression of an intention to harm someone

    ~ et voies de fait : assault and battery

menacer : to threaten

mendicité (f) : begging

mendigot (m) * : tramp, beggar, vagrant

menottes (fpl) : handcuffs, handbolts

mention (f) **en marge** : marginal note
Note written in the margin of an official document in order to add to, correct or up-date it.

menu fretin (m) : small fry

mépris (m) : contempt, defiance

    au ~ de la loi : holding the law in contempt

merde (f) * : shit, cannabis

mesures (fpl) : measures, steps, arrangements

    ~ d'instruction : investigative measures
The steps taken to discover the author of a crime and to bring him to justice.

    ~ de sûreté : preventive measures
Non-penal sanctions imposed on persons showing criminal tendencies. These may consist of holding in a secure place, therapeutic treatment or re-education.

métier (m) : trade, profession, craft, occupation

mettre : to put, to lay, to set

    ~ à disposition : to make available, to bring before the courts

    ~ à exécution : to implement

    ~ au courant : to inform, to put in the picture

    ~ au point : to devise, to work out (a plan), to perfect (a product)

    ~ en pratique : to apply, to implement

    ~ en rapport : to put in touch

    se ~ en rapport : to get in touch

meublé (m) : furnished accommodation, digs*

    police des ~s : hotel check section
Police officers whose task it was to check details of hotel guests by way of the now obsolete registration card system

meule (f) * : bike, motorbike

meurtre (m) : murder, intentional homicide

meurtrier (m) : murderer, assassin

michetonner : to solicit for the purposes of prostitution

mignonnette (f) * : supposed dirty postcard
> *Sold outside Paris nightclubs to gullible tourists, these are often mere reproductions of well-known nude paintings to be found in the Louvre.*

milice (f) : militia

milicien (m) : auxiliary

     ~ **gendarme** : auxiliary gendarme (Belgium)

milieu (m) : background, environment, social class

     "le milieu" : the underworld

militaire (m) : soldier, gendarme

militaire : appertaining to the army, military

     à l'heure ~ : precisely, on the dot

minéralogique (plaque ~ **)** : number plate, registration plate

mineur (m) : minor, young person
> *In French law, a minor is one under the age of 18 years.*

     ~ **émancipé** : emancipated minor
> *A minor is automatically emancipated once he marries and may become emancipated by parental declaration, provided he is over 16 years.*

     tribunal des ~**s** : juvenile court

minima (appel à ~ **)** : appeal by prosecutor against an excessively light sentence

Ministère (m) : (1) ministry; (2) duty, function

     ~ **de la Défense** : Ministry of Defence
> *The ministry responsible for the armed forces and national defence. It includes the **Gendarmerie Nationale**, this being the senior branch of the army.*

     ~ **de la Justice** : Ministry of Justice, Lord Chancellor's Office

     ~ **de l'Intérieur** : Ministry of the Interior
> *Equivalent of the Home Office. The responsible body for the Police Nationale (but not the Gendarmerie Nationale).*

~ **public** : public prosecution
> *Exercised by those professional magistrates who are responsible, on behalf of society as a whole, to prosecute offenders against the criminal law. Independent of the judges on the Bench, they have their own hierarchy and may be removed from office where necessary. In minor cases brought before the lower courts, this function may be exercised by a* **commissaire de police.**

Ministre (m) : minister

~ **de la Défense** : The Defence Minister
> *(See* **Ministére de la Défense)**

~ **de l'Intérieur** : Minister of the Interior
> *Equivalent of the Home Secretary. Responsible for law and order and directly responsible for the* **Police Nationale.**

~ **d'Etat** : secretary of state (responsible for a major department of state)

minorité (f) **pénale** : child or young person (under 18)

minute (f) : original document (as opposed to mere copy)

minuteur (m) : timer (for explosive device, etc.)

mire (f) : sighting, aiming

point de ~ : aim, target

mise (f) : placing, putting

~ **à jour** : elucidation (of a mystery)

~ **à la retraite** : pensioning, superannuation

~ **à l'épreuve** : conditional discharge

~ **à pied** : sacking, firing, act of dismissing someone

~ **en accusation** : committal for trial (at assize court)

~ **en demeure** : formal notice to do, or refrain from doing, something

~ **en détention provisoire** : detained pending trial

~ **en fourrière** : impounding

~ **en garde** : warning, caution

~ **en l'air** * : (1) burglary, break-in; (2) confidence trick

~ **en liberté** : release, setting free a prisoner

~ **en liberté provisoire** : release on bail

    ~ **en marche** : starting (of engine, etc.)

    ~ **en mouvement (de l'action publique)** : initiation of criminal proceedings
        Usually represented by the opening of an **instruction.**

    ~ **en pratique** : carrying out, practical application

    ~ **en prévention** : held on suspicion, in custody on remand

    ~ **en route** : starting up, getting under way

    ~ **en vigueur** : putting into force, enforcing

    ~ **sous scellés** : affixing of official seals

mission (f) : mission, assignment, task, duty

missionner : to send on assignment

mitigation (f) **des peines** : mitigated penalty
*Substitution of a lighter sentence than that prescribed by law in the case
of certain offenders because of their age or sex.*

mitrailler : to machine-gun, to rake with gunfire

mitraillette (f) : sub-machine gun

mitrailleur (m) : machine gunner

    fusil-~ : Bren gun

    pistolet-~ : machine pistol

mitrailleuse (f) : machine gun

mob (f) * : moped (Mobylette)

mobilard (m) * : riot squad policeman (from **gendarmerie mobile**)

mobile (m) : (1) motive, grounds; (2) mobile

    gendarmerie ~ : gendarmerie emergency and riot division

modération (f) **de peine** : mitigation of penalty

modifier : to amend, to modify

moeurs (fpl) : morals, manners, mores

    brigade des ~ : vice squad

mondaine (brigade ~ **)** : vice squad

moniteur (m) : instructor

mono–canon (fusil de chasse ˜) : single–barrelled (shotgun)

monseigneur (f) : jemmy, crowbar

montagnard (m) : mountaineer

monte–en–l'air (m) : cat burglar

monter en grade : to be promoted

morale : moral

    personne ˜ : company, body corporate, legal entity, artificial person

moralité (f) : morality, morals, honesty

mordante (f) : (1) rasp, file; (2) hacksaw

mordants (mpl) : shears, scissors

mordicus : dogged, stubborn, unshakeable about something

mordu : fanatical, mad about something

morganer * : to grass*, to inform on

morgue (f) : (1) mortuary, morgue; (2) search room in a prison

morlingue (m) : purse, wallet

mort (f) : death

    arrêt de ˜ : death sentence

    peine de ˜ : death penalty (abolished 1981)

    ˜ subite : sudden death

    ˜ suspecte : suspicious death

mortel : fatal

motard (m) : biker*, especially a police motorcycle patrolman

moteur (m): engine, motor

    ˜ à deux–temps : two-stroke engine

motif (m) : ground, motive, cause, reason

    exposé des ˜s : preamble (to a Bill)

    ˜ d'un jugement : grounds of judgement

moto (f) : motorbike
*Abbreviation of **motocyclette***

motocyclette (f) : motorcycle

mouchard (m) : informer, police spy

mouche (f) : see **mouchard**

moukala (m) * : shooter*, handgun

moumoute (f) * : (1) sheepskin coat; (2) toupee, wig, rug*

mousqueton (m) : blunderbuss, cavalry rifle

mouton (m) * : grass*, snout*, informer,

mouvement (m) **de la libération de la femme (MLF)** : womens liberation movement,
"Womens' Lib."

moyenne surface (f) : small supermarket

moyens (mpl) : resources

moyeu (m) : hub

multirécidiviste (m&f) : persistent offender

municipal : municipal

   arrêté ~ : bye law

   conseil ~ : town council

   police ~ : borough police force
      *Locally appointed officers having fewer powers than the national
      police or gendarmerie. Mainly concerned with the enforcement of
      the town's bye laws, local traffic regulations and public health.*

munitions (fpl) : ammunition, munitions

mur (m) : pickpocket's accomplice

   faire le ~ : to "go over the wall", to escape

mûr : (1) ripe; (2) drunk

   âge ~ : middle age

muscler : to beef up, to strengthen

musique (f) * : (1) flattery; (2) pack of lies; (3) confidence trick; (4) blackmail

mutation (f) : transfer, posting

muter : to post, to station

mutilation (f) : wounding, grevious bodily harm

    ~ **volontaire** : self-inflicted wound

    ~ **des arbres** : destruction of trees and bushes

mutilé : disabled, maimed.   ~ **de guerre** : disabled ex-serviceman

mutiler : to mutilate, to maim, to disfigure

mutin : insubordinate, disobedient, unruly

mutin (m) : mutineer

mutiné (m) : mutineer

mutinement (m) : mutiny

mutiner : to incite to rebellion

se mutiner : to rise in revolt, to mutiny

mutinerie (f) : rebellion, mutiny

mutisme (m) : dumbness, muteness, refusal to speak

mystification (f) : hoax

N

naissance (f) : birth

>>**acte/extrait de ~** : birth certificate

>>**lieu de ~** : place of birth

narco (m) * : drug pedlar

narcocratie (f) : rule by drug traffickers, the hierarchy of drug barons

narcotique (m) : narcotic, drug

narcotraffiquant (m) : drugs dealer

nardu (m) * : police superintendent

naufrage (m) : shipwreck

naval : naval

>>**chantier ~** : shipyard, dockyard

navetteur (m) : commuter

navigation (f) : navigation, sailing, shipping

>>**~ aérienne** : air navigation

>>**~ fluviale** : transport by inland waterways

nécrops (m) * : post-mortem examination

néerlandophone : Dutch-speaking

négligence (f) : carelessness, negligence, neglect

>>**~ criminelle** : gross neglect

neige (f) * : snow*, cocaine

>>**blanc comme ~** : totally innocent

"Nemo censetur ignorare legem" : ignorance of the law is no excuse

nettoyage (m) * : hit*, contract killing

nice : simple

night (m) : nightclub

noctambus (m) : late-night bus

noir : black, unofficial

> **caisse ~e** : slush fund, bribery fund

> **chiffre ~** : dark figure, grey figure
> *The number of crimes not reported to the police and therefore not appearing in official statistics.*

> **marché ~** : black market

> **travail ~** : moonlighting

noire (f) * : raw opium

nom (m) : name

> **~ de baptême** : forename, Christian name

> **~ de famille** : surname

> **~ de jeune fille** : maiden name

> **~ supposé** : assumed, false, fictitious name

> **décliner ses ~s et qualités** : to state one's full name and status

nomade (m&f) : person of no fixed abode, vagrant, gipsy

nomenclature (f) : list, terminology

nominal : by name

> **appel ~** : roll call

nomination (f) : appointment

non–activité (f) : retirement (from active service)

non–assistance (f) **à personne en danger** : failure to aid a person in peril
Misdemeanour committed by a person who wilfully fails to render to a person in peril the aid which he needs and which it is possible to give without endangering the helper or a third party.

"non bis in idem" : "a person who has been tried for an offence cannot be tried again for the same offence"

non–comparution (f) : non-appearance

non–culpabilité (f) : lack of guilt, innocence

non–cumul (m) **des peines** : concurrence of penalties
Principle under which a person convicted of several offences punishable by imprisonment, not dealt with separately by a definitive conviction, may only receive the penalty applicable to the more serious of the offences.

non-dénonciation (f) **(de crime)** : misprision (of felony)

non-lieu (m) : no grounds for further action
Decision of an examining magistrate not to proceed with a case due to lack of evidence or on legal grounds.

non-obstacle (m) **à la commission d'infraction** : failure to prevent the commission of an offence

nonobstant : notwithstanding

non-recevable : inadmissible (evidence, etc.)

non-révocabilité (f) : irremovability

notaire (m) : solicitor, lawyer
Lawyer authorised to authenticate legal documents and to advise individuals.

notation (f) : marks, rating
Every civil servant, including police officers, are awarded marks each year in recognition of their efforts and on which promotion is largely based.

note (f) : note, memorandum

˜ d'audience : summary transcript of criminal trial (by the Clerk)

notifier : to notify

notoriété (f) : repute, notoriety

acte de ˜ : identity certificate (made by a magistrate before three witnesses)

de ˜ publique : matter of public knowledge

˜ de droit : proof by documentary evidence

˜ de fait : proof by evidence of witnesses

noyautage (m) : infiltration

noyauter : to infiltrate

noyer : to drown

˜ le poisson : to cloud the issue with irrelevancies

nubilité (f) : age of consent

nuire : to injure, to cause harm to

nuisance (f) : nuisance

nuit (f) : night (sunset to sunrise)
   Theft is regarded as being aggravated if committed by night.

   de ~ : on the night shift

nul : null, void, invalid

   ~ et non avenue : null and void

nullité (f) : nullity, invalidity

numéro (m) **de code secret** : personal identification number, PIN

O

obéissance (f) : obedience, submission

objecteur de conscience (m) : conscientious objector
A citizen who, on moral grounds or because of his beliefs, refuses to carry out his or her military obligations but without avoiding the legal consequences (as opposed to failure to join the colours or desertion). Since 1963 France has accepted conscientious objection by giving such persons exemption from military service provided he/she carries out certain civil tasks instead.

objet (m) : (1) object, thing; (2) subject, subject matter; (3) object, aim, purpose

bureau des ˜s trouvés : lost property office

cette réunion a pour ˜ : the purpose of this meeting is to ...

˜ d'un litige : subject of an action

˜ scellé : exhibit

sans ˜ : aimless, aimlessly

obligation (f) : requirement, obligation, liability

˜ militaire : liability for national service

obligatoire : compulsory, mandatory, obligatory

s'obliger (pour quelqu'un) : to undertake to stand surety (for someone)

obscène : obscene, lewd, smutty

publication ˜ : obscene publication

observateur (m) : observer

observer (les règlements) : to observe, to comply with (the regulations)

faire ˜ la loi : to enforce the law

obtempérer : to obey

˜ à une requête : to accede to a request

˜ à un ordre : to comply with an order

obtention (f) : obtaining, attainment, acquisition

occulte : secret, hidden, covert, clandestine

occupation (f) : occupation, employment, profession

    sans ~ : out of work

octroi (m) : municipal tax (on goods coming into certain towns)

oeilleton (m) : (1) spy hole in door; (2) eyepiece (of rifle sight, camera, etc.)

offense (f) : offence, transgression

    ~ à la cour : contempt of court

offenseur (m) : offender

office (m) : (1) office, function, duty; (2) bureau, office, board, official agency; (3) legal practice

    d' ~ : officially, as a matter of course, routinely, spontaneously

    ~ central pour la repression de la grande délinquance financière : serious fraud office

    ~ central pour la repression du trafic illicite des stupéfiants : national drugs intelligence unit

    mise à la retraite d'~ : compulsorily retired

    poursuite pénale d'~ : prosecution ex officio

officiel : official, formal

officiellement : officially

officier (m) : officer (civil and military)

    ~ de justice : law officer

    ~ de l'état civil : registrar, official in charge of the registers of births, deaths and marriages

    ~ de paix : assistant inspector (uniformed officer)

    ~ de paix principal : inspector (uniformed officer)

    ~ de police judiciaire (m) : officer of the criminal court
        *Officials who, under the authority of the public prosecutor, carry out the various missions connected with criminal investigations and implement the orders of the examining magistrates. The term includes (a) mayors and their assistants, (b) gendarmerie officers and senior NCOs, (c) police **commissaires** and **inspecteurs** and more senior police officers. They may only exercise their authority as an OPJ if they are actively employed on work directly connected to a criminal investigation and personally authorised by the public prosecutor for the area in which they work. They are assisted by* **agents de police judiciaire** *who have less wide-ranging powers.*

~ **de ministère public** : public prosecutor

~ **ministériel** : law official (notary, huissier, etc)
These have a monopoly of their functions and are appointed by the President of the Republic on the recommendation of their predecessor, to whom they pay a sum of money for his sponsorship.

~ **public** : public official
Title given to persons who have the authority to authenticate official documents, such as a mayor, a notary, a bailiff.

officieux, —euse : (1) officious (2) unofficial, semi-official (3) busybody

omission (f) d'assistance : see **non—assistance à personne en danger**

opération (f) : operation, mission

opiacé : containing opiates

opportunité (f) des poursuites : discretion of prosecution
*Authority given to the public prosecutors to decide not to prosecute despite the availability of sufficient evidence. This decision may be overturned in the event that the injured party lays a **plainte avec constitution de partie civile**.*

opposition (f) opposition

~ **à un chèque** : stopping a cheque

~ **à un jugement** : stay of execution

ordinaire (m) : two—star petrol

ordinateur (m) : computer

micro—~ : microcomputer

ordonnance (f) : (1) ordinance, order; (2) emergency legislation; (3) judgement made by a judge sitting alone, order made by a judge in chambers; (4) prescription (for medicines)

~ **de clôture** : case closing order (final decision of examining magistrate)

~ **de comparution** : summons to appear

~ **de mise en accusation** : arraignment

~ **de mise en détention** : detention order

~ **de mise en liberté** : order for release (possibly on bail)

~ **de non—informer** : formal refusal by an examining magistrate to open an investigation

~ **de non-lieu** : discharge order (no case to answer or prosecution other-
      wise precluded)

~ **de police** : regulations made by a Prefect of Police

~ **de prise de corps** : writ of capias

~ **de référé** : summary order, injunction

~ **de règlement** : case disposal order (final decision of examining
      magistrate)

~ **de renvoi** : committal for trial

~ **de transmission (de pièces)** : transfer order
      Order transferring the case to the Indictment Division of the Court
      of Appeal for decision as to whether to send the accused for trial
      at the Court of Assize.

~ **de soit communiqué** : notification order
      Order by the examining magistrate to pass the case file to the
      public prosecutor.

~ **de visite domiciliaire** : search warrant

~ **d'incarcération provisoire** : interim detention order

~ **pénale** : administrative conviction (in police court)
      Procedure whereby the magistrate determines the case on the
      strength of the written evidence only and in the absence of the
      accused. The latter then has 30 days to pay the fine or to lodge an
      objection, in which event the case is put back for a normal hearing.

ordonner : to order

ordre (m) : (1) order, command, warrant;   (2) hierarchy

délit contre l' ~ public : breach of the peace

~ **d'arrestation** : arrest warrant

~ **de comparution** : summons

~ **d'écrou** : committal order

~ **de juridiction** : the jurisdictions (judicial [civil/criminal], adminisative)

~ **de la loi** : in the service of the law
      Justification afforded to persons executing the law who would
      otherwise be criminally liable.

~ **de mise en liberté** : release from prison

~ **de mission** : duty instructions

~ **de service** : duty instructions

~ **du jour** : agenda, (parliamentary) timetable, order of the day

~ **public** : public order, law and order

loi d'~ public : see under *loi*

troubler l' ~ public : commit a breach of the peace, create a disturbance

organigramme (m) : organisation chart, flow-chart

organisation (f) : organisation

~ **judiciaire** : the French judiciary system

orientation (f) : trend, tendency

~ **professionnelle** : vocational guidance

os (m) : (1) bone; (2) hitch, unexpected problem; (3) ugly customer

avoir un ~ dans le fromage : enquiries have come to a halt

avoir dans l'~ : to have been duped

oseillé * : loaded*, filthy rich*

otage (m) : hostage

ouir : oyez, to hear (obsolete)

outil (m) : (1) tool, implement; (2) * knife, blade

déballer ses ~s * : (1) to expose oneself; (2) to confess

outrage (m) : insult, threat
The expression of insulting, threatening or harmful words calculated to diminish the authority of a person holding one of the public offices defined by law.

faire subir les derniers ~s : to rape a woman

~ **à agent** : insulting behaviour towards a policeman

~ **à magistrat** : contempt of court

~ **aux (bonnes) moeurs** : offence against public decency, obscene publication
To offend against public decency, by writing, drawing, discussion and all other means of expression.

~ **public à la pudeur** : indecent exposure

outre-mer : overseas

outrepasser : to go beyond, to exceed

    ~ ses pouvoirs : to exceed one's authority

ouvrage (m) : break*, burglary

ouvrier (m) : (1) worker, workman; (2) * burglar

    la classe ~e : the working class

    ~ agricole : farm worker

    ~ d'usine : factory worker

    ~ qualifié : skilled worker

    ~ spécialisé : semi-skilled worker

ouvrir : (1) to confess; (2) to open

    ~ une information : to commence a criminal investigation

P

paie (f) : wages, pay

paix (f) : peace

    gardien de la ~ : police constable

    troubler la ~ publique : to cause a breach of the peace

palais de justice : law courts

panache (m) **(faire ~)** : to take a fall (from horse, bike, etc.)

panaché (m) : shandy

pandore (m) * : cop, copper, policeman

panier (m) **à salade** : Black Maria, police van (for picking up prisoners)

panne (f) : breakdown

    ~ d'électricité : power cut, power failure

    ~ d'essence : breakdown through lack of fuel

    tomber en ~ : to break down

panneau (m) : sign(post)

pante (m) * : mug*, sucker*, dupe

pantruchard (m) : Parisian, native of Paris

paperasse (f) : red-tape, bureaucratic formalities

papiers (mpl) **(d'identité)** : (identity) papers

parasitage (m) : interference, atmospherics

parade (f) : (1) parade, guard mounting; (2) parry, riposte

    ~ juridique : legal answer

    ~ technologique : technological response

paraître : to appear.   **~ en justice** : to appear before a court

paragraphe (m) : sub-section

parapher (un document) : to initial (a document)

parc (m) : park, fleet, stock

> ~ **d'automobiles, de véhicules** : vehicle fleet

> ~ **immobilier** : housing/building stock

parcmètre (m) : parking meter

> ~ **individuel à fente** : smart-card parking meter
> *Parking meters operated by prepaid cards which the driver inserts in the slot. The meter deducts the sum corresponding to the period parked and returns the card for future use.*

parcours (m) : route, distance covered, course

pardon (m) : pardon, remission (of sentence)

pare-balles (m) : bullet proof

> **gilet** ~ : bullet-proof vest

> **verre** ~ : bullet-proof glass

pare-brise (m) : windscreen, windshield

pare-chocs (m) : bumper

parents (mpl) : (1) parents, mother and father; (2) kinfolk, relatives

pari (m) : bet, wager, stake

> ~ **mutuel** : totalisator system

> **taxe sur les** ~**s** : betting tax

Paris (Ville de) : (City of) Paris
The City of Paris is the geographical seat of two distinct territorial authorities - the **commune** *(borough) of Paris and the* **département** *(county) of Paris. Since 1977 each has been subject, in principle, to the usual laws relating to local authorities of this nature but with certain differences. In particular, the* **Conseil de Paris**, *presided over by the Mayor and responsible for the administration of the* **commune**, *also exercises the functions which, in other* **départements**, *devolve on the* **Conseil Général**. *The interests of the State are, as in other* **départements**, *looked after by a* **Préfet** *and, as in certain other large towns, there is also a special* **Préfet de Police**.

parlement (m) : parliament

parler-faux (m) : double-speak

parler-vrai (m) : straight talking

parloir (m) : council chamber

parlophone (m) : entry-phone

parquet (m) : public prosecution department, state counsel's office
So called because the members used to exercise their functions from the floor of the court, below the judge's dais.

parrain (m) : (1) godfather, sponsor; (2) * witness in court

parricide (m) : parricide
Killing one's father or mother, natural or adoptive, or a legitimate grand parent.

part (m) : new-born child

　célation de ~ : concealment of birth

　exposition d'un ~ : abandonment of new-born child

　suppression de ~ : concealment of birth

partenaire (m&f) : partner

parti (m) : decision, choice, course, advantage

　prendre un ~ : to make up one's mind

　prendre ~ : to take sides

　tirer ~ : to take advantage

participation (f) **criminelle** : see **complicité**

particulier : privately owned.　　　**voiture ~ière** : private car

particulier (m): individual, person.　**à titre ~** : in a private capacity

partie (f) : party (to a dispute)

　~ civile : civil party
　　Victim of a breach of the criminal law claiming damages through the criminal courts.

　~ lésée : the injured party

　" ~s ouies" : "having heard the parties", "in the light of the evidence"

pas-de-porte (m) : key-money

passage (m) passage

　~ à tabac : assault on a defenceless person

　~ clouté : pedestrian crossing
　　So-called because the crossing is defined by metal studs ("clous")

> ~ **piétons** : pedestrian crossing, zebra crossing

> ~ **sur un terrain semé** : allowing animals to trespass on arable land before the crop has been harvested

passe–partout (m) : skeleton key, pass key

passeport (m) : passport

passer : (1) to pass, to proceed;   (2) to smuggle

> **"je vais vous** ~ : "putting you through" (telephone)

> ~ **à l'ordre du jour** : to proceed with the day's business

> ~ **aux aveux** : to confess

> ~ **en force de loi** : to be lawful

> ~ **en jugement** : to stand trial

> ~ **une loi** : to pass a law

passible : liable to, likely to incur

> ~ **d'une amende** : liable to a fine

> **jugement** ~ **d'opposition** : judgement subject to a stay of execution

passionnel (crime ~ **)** : (crime) due to jealousy

pasto (m) * : dead-end street, cul–de–sac

patin (m) **(faire le** ~ **)** : to go shoplifting

patiner : to run away

patro (m) * : church–run youth club

patron (m) : (1) employer, boss, "guv'nor"; (2) pattern, model

patronyme (m) : family name, surname

patrouille (f) : patrol.   ~ **légere de sécurité** : general street patrol

patuche (f) * : market trader's licence

paume (f) * : deportation to the penal colony in French Guiana

paumer : to lose.   **se faire** ~ : to get arrested, to get nicked*

pauvre (m) : poor person, pauper

pavé (m) : pavement, paving stone, cobble

    brûler le ˜ * : to drive recklessly fast

    sur le ˜ : (1) out of work; (2) near destitute, penniless

paveton (m) : cobblestone

pavillon (m) : (1) flag, colours; (2) detached house

pavot (m) : poppy.   **˜ somnifère** : opium poppy

payer–prendre (m) : cash and carry

pays (m) : country, land

    ˜ d'asile (politique) : country of (political) asylum

    ˜ limitrophe : borderland

paysage (m) **(partir dans le ˜)** : to run off the road, to run out of road

péage (m) : toll, toll booth

    autoroute à ˜ : toll motorway

    barrière de ˜ : turnpike

    pont à ˜ : toll bridge

pébroque (m) * : (1) umbrella; (2) shaky alibi, cover job to conceal illegal activities

pêche (f) : fishing

péculat (m) : embezzlement of public funds, peculation

pécule (m) : savings, prisoner's earnings paid on discharge, gratuity

pédéraste (m), **pédé** (m) * : pederast, person who commits homosexual acts with young boys

pédigrée (m) * : "form", criminal record

pègre (f) : underworld, gangland

pégrer * : to arrest, to nick*, to knock off*

pégrillot (m) * : novice or small-time crook

peigne (m) * : crowbar, "jemmy"

peine (f) : penalty, sentence

    adoucissement, atténuation, réduction de la ˜ : mitigation of penalty aggravation de ~ : increase in penalty

commutation de ~ : commutation of penalty

conversion de ~ : change of penalty (mostly in mitigation)

cumul de ~s : accumulative sentence, concurrent sentences

~ accessoire : ancillary penalty
    *Additional penalty, such as the prohibition on exercising a partic-
    ular profession, automatically imposed following conviction for
    certain offences.*

~ afflictive : custodial sentence

~ -à-jouir * : suspect whose confession has to be dragged out of him

~ complémentaire : additional penalty (which must, or may, be imposed by
        the judge)

~ corporelle : see **peine afflictive**

~ correctionnelle : penalty for misdemeanour (over 2 months imprisonment
        or a fine over a certain amount)

~ criminelle : penalty for felony (imprisonment and/or loss of civil rights)

~ de mort : death sentence (abolished in 1981)

~ de police : punishment for summary offence (under 2 months
        imprisonment or small fine, confiscation of certain items, etc)

~ de simple police : summary sentence (up to two months imprisonment or
        small fine)

~ de substitution : alternative to imprisonment

~ fixe : fixed penalty

~ incompressible : irreducible sentence

~ infamante : deprivatory sentence (penalty involving loss of civil rights)

~ pécuniaire : fine

~ principale : principal penalty (as opposed to **peine accessoire**)

~ privative de droits : withdrawal of civic rights

~ privative de liberté : custodial sentence

~ restrictive de liberté : penalty restricting freedom

purger une ~ : to serve one's sentence

remise de la ~ : remission

sous les ~s de droit : under the penalties prescribed by law

sous ~ de : under penalty of, on pain of

subir sa ~ : to serve one's sentence

sursis à l'exécution de la ~ : suspended sentence

pékin (m) **(habillé en tenue de ~)** * : in civvies, out of uniform

pèlerines (fpl) * : "Old Bill", the police

peloton (m) : squad, section

~ de surveillance et d'intervention: special patrol squad
A special motorised squad of Gendarmerie whose task is to augment crime prevention patrols, especially at night.

~ mobile : mobile squad

~ motorisé : road traffic patrol section

pénal : criminal.   **code ~** : the criminal code, the criminal law

pendaison (f) : hanging

pendantes (fpl) : ear-rings

pendule (f) * : (1) one whose movements are as regular and predictable as clockwork; (2) parking meter; (3) taxi meter

pénitencier (m) : penitentiary, convict prison
Prison where one performs hard labour.

pension (f) : pension, allowance

être en ~ : to be a guest of the Government (in jail)

~ complète : full board and lodging

~ d'ancien combattant : ex-serviceman's pension

~ de guerre : war pension

~ de retraite : retirement pension

~ de vieillesse : old-age pension

~ d'invalidité : disability allowance

~ militaire : retired pay

~ pour cause de limite d'âge : superannuation

pensionner : to pension off

percuter : to hit, to collide with

percuteur (m) : hammer, firing pin

perdreau (m) * : plain-clothes police officer
*In its plural form (**perdreaux**), there seems to be no distinction between plain-clothes and uniformed police officers.*

péremption (f) : time limitation

    dévolu per ~ : lapsed

    ~ d'instance : extinction of an action (where no steps have been taken within the prescribed time)

péremptoire : peremptory, categorical, conclusive

    délai ~ : strict time limit

    preuve ~ : conclusive evidence

perfectionnement (m) : improvement

    stage de ~ : advanced training course

perfecto (m) : black blouson jacket

péri-informatique (f) : computer peripherals

périph. (m) * : boulevard périphérique

périmer : to lapse, to become out of date

péripatéticienne (f) : prostitute

permanence (f) : in operation round the clock

    de ~ : on duty, on call

    ~ d'un commissariat de police : police station open at all times

permis (m) : licence, permit

    ~ de chasse : game, shooting licence

    ~ de conduire : driving licence
        *Driving licences may be suspended, either as an administrative measure by the **Préfet** where a driver is guilty of a serious offence against the road traffic laws, or by the courts as an additional penalty for certain offences. They may also be suspended as an alternative to a short term of imprisonment. Only the courts may order permanent disqualification.*

~ **de pêche** : angling permit

~ **de port d'armes** : licence to carry firearms

~ **de séjour** : residential permit (required by foreigners)

~ **d'établissement** : permission to reside permanently

~ **de travail** : work permit (required by foreigners)

permission (f) : leave, permission

~ **de sortir** : release of prisoner on licence
Permission granted to a prisoner to leave a place of custody for a given period of time in order that he might prepare himself for eventual return to society and to working, to maintain family ties or to carry out an undertaking which demands his presence.

~ **de voirie** : authority to have exclusive use of part of the highway

permutation (f) : exchange of posts

perpétrer : to perpetrate

perpétuité (f) : perpetuity

travaux forcés à ~ : penal servitude for life

perquisition (f) : search of a person's home to seek evidence

mandat de ~ : search warrant

perroquet (m) * : drink consisting of *pastis* and *sirop de menthe*

personnalité (f) **des peines** : principal under which only the person committing an offence may be penalised

personne (f) : person

~ **morale** : artificial person, body corporate
A body, such as a limited company, deemed to be a person and permitted to go to law, to be sued, etc.

~ **physique** : natural person

tierce ~ : third person, third party

personnel (m) : personnel, staff

délégué (syndical) du ~ : shop steward

~ **de bureau** : office staff

~ **d'encadrement** : executives

~ **dirigeant** : management

personnellement (responsable) : personally (liable, responsible)

perspectives (fpl) : prospects

perturber : to disturb

perversion (f) : perversion

pervertir : to pervert, to corrupt

pétard (m) : (1) firecracker; (2) pistol

petit juge : see *juge d'instruction*

petite (f) : little girl, little one

    mettre en ~ : (1) to steal petty items; (2) to salt away

    prendre une ~ : to take a one-gramme fix of heroin

pétrole (m) * : "hooch", illicitly distilled liquor

pétroleur (m) : fire raiser, agitator

pese/peze (m) * : "brass", "loot", cash

phare (m) : headlamp

pharmacodépendant (m) : drug-dependent

photocopie (f) : photocopy, photostat

photographier (se faire ~ **)** : to get oneself noticed, to be spotted

piano (m) * : fingerprint, "dab"

    passer au piano : to have one's fingerprints taken

picouse (f) * : "jab", injection

pie (voiture ~ **)** : Panda car, police patrol car

pièce (f) : (1) piece, unit, fragment; (2) document, documentary evidence

    ~ **à conviction** : exhibit

    ~ **à l'appui** : proof in support of a case

    ~ **communiquée** : discovered document

    ~ **de la procédure** : case paper

    ~ **d'identité** : identity paper

~ **en instance** : document pertaining to the case

~ **fausse** : forged document

~ **jointe** : enclosure

~ **judiciaire** : document in a case

~ **justificative** : document in proof

pied (m) : foot, basis

    être mis à ~ : to be temporarily suspended

    ~ **–de–biche** : crowbar

piège (m) : trap

pieton (m) : pedestrian, foot passenger

pige (f) * : year (in the sense of a prison sentence)

piger : to "cop" a sentence, to get sentenced to a term of imprisonment

pigeon (m) * : "sucker", dupe

pile : precisely, exactly

    s'arrêter ~ : to stop dead, to come to an abrupt halt

piller : to loot

pilonner : to beg, to solicit alms

pince–monseigneur (f) : jemmy, crowbar

pincer : to arrest, to nick*, to knock off*

pincettes (fpl) : handcuffs

pin's (m) : lapel badge

pipelet (m), **pipelette** (f) : concierge, caretaker

pipette (f) **(vol à la** ~ **)** : theft of petrol by siphoning it from parked cars

piquet (m) guard.   ~ **d'honneur** : guard of honour

piqûre (f) : injection

piratage (m) : hijacking, skyjacking

pirate (m) **informatique** : computer hacker

piraterie (f) : (1) piracy at sea; (2) pirating films, videos, etc.

   ~ aérienne : hijacking, skyjacking
      Crime committed by any person on board an aircraft in flight who
      uses violence or threats in order to take over control of the plane.

piscine (f) * : HQ of the French Secret Services

piste (f) : trail, track

pister : to shadow, to watch, to keep track of

pistolet (m) : pistol

   ~ automatique : automatic pistol

   ~ d'abattage : humane killer

   ~ de signalisation : signal pistol, Verey pistol

   ~ lance–fusées : Verey pistol, signalling pistol, flare gun

   ~ –mitrailleur : machine-pistol

placard (m) : (1) prison; (2) sum paid by one pimp to another for the transfer
of a prostitute to his control

placarde (f) : (1) village square; (2) market trader's pitch; (3) hiding place

placer : to station, to place

plaider : to plead

plaidoirie (f) : counsel's speech

plaidoyer (m) : address to the court by the defence

plaignant (m) : plaintiff, complainant

se plaindre : to complain

plainte (f) : crime complaint
Document by means of which the injured party brings the facts of a crime
or offence committed against him to the notice of the public prosecutor,
either directly or through an intermediary (eg. the police or gendarmerie)

   ~ avec constitution de partie civile : crime complaint with claim for
      damages or compensation

   porter ~ : to report an offence to the police, to lay an information

plaisance (bateau de ~) : pleasure (boat)

planche (f) **(faire la ~)** : to lie low, to keep a low profile

planque (f) : (1) hiding place for precious objects; (2) savings, nest-egg; (3) hideout, hiding place; (4) plum job, cushy number

>**être en ~** : to be on observations, on a stake-out

planquer : to hide, to conceal

planter : to run off the road (motorist), to crashland (aircraft)

plaque (f) : plate

>**~ d'immatriculation** : see **plaque minéralogique**

>**~ minéralogique** : number plate
>*The number plate on a French car always includes the number of the **département** in which it is registered, from 01 to 95.*

platanisme (m) : tendency for drivers to crash into (plane) trees

plâtre (m) * : "loot", "brass", cash

plein : full, whole.   **de ~ droit** : by right, with good reason

plénitude (f) **de juridiction** : extent of competence
Procedural rule whereby the criminal courts are competent to decide on any defence raised by the offender (except those specifically listed in the code of criminal procedure).

pli (m) : cover, envelope

>**~ cacheté** : sealed letter, orders

>**~ neutre** : plain cover, plain envelope

>**sous ce ~** : herewith

>**sous ~ séparé** : under separate cover

plongeur (m) : diver, skindiver, frogman

plumer : to fleece, to rip-off

pneu (m) : tyre

poche (f) : pocket.   **~ -revolver** : hip pocket

poids (m) **lourd** : heavy goods vehicle (HGV)

poignard (m) : dagger

poignarder : to stab

poignée (f) **tournante** : twist grip

pointe (**heures de ~**) : peak periods, rush hours

pointé (rester ˜) : to be kept in police custody

poison (m) : poison

poisson (m) : pimp, procurer

faire une queue de ˜ : to cut in front of another vehicle after overtaking

noyer le ˜ : to cloud the issue with irrelevancies

poivrier (m) (vol au ˜) : "rolling" drunks, robbing persons under the influence

polar (m) : paperback detective novel

police (1) (f) : government, administration, organisation;
The judicial and material means used to ensure the tranquility, safety and health of citizens, and also the regulations made to this end.

˜ **administrative** : public order and safety
Those administrative actions by which the authorities intervene in the activities of individuals so that public tranquility is maintained. It is characterised by its essentially <u>preventive</u> role, (as opposed to **police judiciaire**, *the main objective of which is to investigate crimes and to bring offenders before the criminal courts).* **Police administrative** *includes the licensing of liquor, firearms and places of public resort, and road traffic law. Together with* **police judiciaire** *and* **police de renseignement** *it forms the basis of all police activity.*

˜ **de renseignement** : intelligence collation
The gathering of information of a social, economic and political nature is a function of the **Service des Renseignements Généraux** *of the national police. The object of this intelligence collation is to keep the government (via the local* **Préfet***) informed of current trends (possible strikes, public unrest, economic problems, etc.) so that it might take remedial measures.*

˜ **judiciaire** : criminal investigation
An essential rôle of the police is to investigate breaches of the criminal law in order to identify the offenders and to bring them to justice. In France the execution of these tasks is entrusted to certain persons who are designated agents or officers of the criminal courts. With the exception of cases where the investigator is in hot pursuit of the offender, all investigations must be carried out under the direction of the public prosecutor (or examining magistrate where authority has been delegated to this official), usually under the authority of a **commission rogatoire.** *Investigations are supervised by the* **Procureur Général** *and controlled by the courts. The stage of* **police judiciaire** *starts where the role of* **police administrative** *(prevention of crimes by surveillance, patrol, licensing, etc.) ends and finishes where the stage of the* **instruction** *begins.*

~ **scientifique** : forensic science; scenes of crime examination
The examination of the scene of a crime for real evidence such as fingerprints, hairs, blood, etc. and its laboratory examination.

police (2) (f) : police
*Those bodies and institutions ensuring the maintenance of public tranquility (**police administrative**) and the repression of breaches of the criminal law (**police judiciaire**).*

agent de ~ : police officer

commissaire de ~ : police superintendent (see under **commissaire**)

indicateur de ~ : police informer, informant

~ **communale** : city/borough police force (Belgium)
Belgium has nearly 600 autonomous city and borough police forces.

~ **de l'Air et des Frontières (PAF)** : Air and Border Police
*Branch of the **Police Nationale** responsible for policing sea and air ports and for immigration matters. In this respect it fulfils the roles performed in the U.K. by Special Branch and the Home Office Immigration Department. It is also responsible for the enforcement of air navigation law and the investigation of aircraft accidents.*

~ **de proximité** : community policing

~ **des garnis** : hotel control section

~ **des moeurs** : vice squad

~ **fluviale** : river police

~ **municipale** : municipal police
A locally-appointed police force, usually quite small and with limited powers, responsible to the mayor for the enforcement of local bye-laws and regulations such as car parking, markets, etc. In many ways similar to the traffic warden in England.

~ **Nationale** : the National Police Force
*With the **Gendarmerie Nationale,** one of the two main law-enforcement agencies in France. Formed in 1968 by the amalgamation of the former **Sûreté Nationale** and the **Préfecture de Police de Paris,** it is responsible for policing all towns with more than 10,000 inhabitants (**polices urbaines**) and for the provision of certain specialist services such as the CRS, the PAF, **Police Judiciaire, Renseignements Généraux, Surveillance du Territoire,** etc.*

~ **secours** : emergency response unit

~ **urbaine** : town police
*That section of the **Police Nationale** which polices an urban area (both uniform and plain clothes officers).*

voiture de ~ **secours** : emergency car, 999 car

police (3) ((f) : policy.

policier (m) : policeman.

policière (f) : policewoman

politique (f) : (1) policy; (2) politics

polluer : to pollute

polycopieuse (f) : duplicating machine

pompier (m) : fireman

pont-radio (m) : radio link

port (1) (m) : port, harbour

~ **aérien** : airport

~ **de guerre** : naval base

~ **de mer** : seaport

port (2) (m) : the act of carrying, wearing

permis d' ~ : licence to carry firearms

~ **d'armes** : carrying a weapon (without authority)

~ **et transport des armes** : possessing a firearm in a public place

~ **illégal du costume ressemblant à un uniforme** : wearing dress resembling an official uniform

~ **illégal d'uniforme (et décorations)** : illegal wearing of uniform (and decorations)
A misdemeanour where the uniform is that of, or similar to a gendarme, policeman or (in time of war) a military uniform or decoration. It is a summary offence in the case of certain other official uniforms (military, forest guards, rural constables, etc.). The offence also covers the dress worn by judges, lawyers, academics, etc.

port (3) (m) : cost of transport, carriage

porte (f) : door

porter plainte : to lay an information, to report an offence to the police

portes (fpl) **ouvertes** : open day

porte-à-porte (m) : door to door

porte-bagages (m) : luggage carrier

~ **d'assurance** : insurance policy

~ **en civil** : plainclothes policeman

portique (m) : metal-detecting gantry (at airport, etc.), signal gantry (on motorway)

portrait (m) **robot** : indentikit picture

poste (f) : the postal service

poste (m) : post, place, appointment, station

    ~ **de commandement** : command post

    ~ **de contrôle** : road check

    ~ **de police** : police office

    ~ **de radio** : radio, wireless set

    ~ **de sapeurs-pompiers** : fire station

    ~ **de surveillance** : covert observation point

    ~ **téléphonique** : telephone extension

poster : to post, to station

postulant : applicant for a post

postuler : to apply for

pot (m) **catalytique** : catalytic converter

pot (m) **d'échappement** : exhaust silencer

pot-de-vin (m) : bribe, inducement

potence (f) : gallows.   **gibier de** ~ : gallows-bird

poucettes (fpl) * : handcuffs, bracelets*

poulaga (m) * : cop, copper, policeman

    Maison ~ : cop-shop*, police station

poulaille (f) * : the law*, the fuzz*, the police

poule (f) : lady of easy virtue.   **la** ~ : the police

pouleman (m) **(la Maison** ~ **)** : (1) the law*, the fuzz*, the police; (2) cop-shop*, police station

poulet (m) * : cop, copper

pourboire (m) : gratuity, tip

"pour copie conforme" : "certified true copy"

pourparlers (mpl) : negotiations

poursuites (fpl) : proceedings, lawsuit

    commencer, engager, entamer, exercer, intenter des ˜ : to institute proceedings

    ˜ disciplinaires : disciplinary action

    ˜ du ministère public : prosecution

poursuivre (quelqu'un en justice) : to take proceedings against someone

pourvoi (m) : appeal (esp. to the **cour de cassation**)

se pourvoir : to lodge an appeal

    ˜ en cassation : to appeal to the Supreme Court

    ˜ en grâce : to petition for mercy

pousse-café (m) : drink of alcohol taken after meal to aid digestion

poussette (f) * : (1) hypodermic syringe; (2) fraudulently tipping scales

pouvoir (m) : power, authority

    abus de ˜ : misuse of authority

    commettre un excès de ˜ : to exceed one's powers

    ˜ de pleine juridiction : having full and unlimited power to try questions of law and of fact

    ˜ disciplinaire : disciplinary body

    ˜ discrétionnaire du président : full authority of presiding judge

    ˜ exécutif : the executive
        In France, this is the President and the Government. In the UK it is the Crown (the monarch plus the cabinet); in the USA the President alone represents the executive.

    ˜ judiciaire : the judiciary, the courts

    ˜ législatif : the legislative authority, parliament

    ˜ réglementaire : power to make regulations
        This power is held by the Prime Minister, the regulations being countersigned by the minister responsible for their application.

    vérification de ˜s : checking of credentials

préavis (m) : notice.   **˜ de congé** : notice of discharge

précaution (f) : precaution, caution. **mesures de** ~ : precautionary measures

précédent (m) : precedent (in law).   **créer un** ~ : to create a precedent

Préfectance (f) * : the **Préfecture de Police**

préfet : prefect, county commissioner
  *The government official who is responsible to the central government for the administration and public order within a **département**.*

  ~ **de Police** : prefect of police, commissioner of police
    In the largest French cities (Paris, Lyons, Marseilles, Lille, Bordeaux, Toulouse, Nice and Ajaccio), a Prefect of Police is appointed to head the police services in the city. As such, he is a senior civil servant rather than a career policeman and answers directly to the Minister for the Interior.

  ~ **de Région** : regional commissioner, regional prefect
    *Commissioner responsible for a region comprising several **départements**.*

Préfecture de Police (f) : Police Headquarters
  *The headquarters of the Paris Police which, since 1968, has formed part of the Police Nationale but still retains a large degree of autonomy. This title is now extended to include the offices of the other **Préfets de Police**.*

préjudice (m) : tort, damage, wrong, prejudice

  indemnité pour ~ **moral** : exemplary damages

  porter, faire ~ : to inflict injury, to cause a loss

  ~ **corporel** : bodily injury

  ~ **moral** : mental distress

  sans ~ : without prejudice

préjugé (m) : precedent (in law)

préjuger : to prejudice, to prejudge, to anticipate beforehand

prélèvement (m) : advance deduction, appropriation, sample, withdrawal

préliminaire : preliminary

préméditation (f) : premeditation

  avec ~ : deliberately, with malice aforethought

prendre : to take

  ~ **acte** : to take cognizance

  ~ **effet** : to take effect, to become effective

~ **en considération** : to take into account

~ **sur le fait** : to catch in the act, red-handed

preneur (m) **d'otages** : hostage taker, kidnapper

prénom (m) : forename, Christian name

(le) pré-nommé (m) : (the) aforesaid

préposé (m) : official, agent

prescription (f) : prescription, regulations, directions, barring by limitation

~ **de l'action publique** : limitation on procedings
*Prosecution is barred unless proceedings are taken within the
prescribed time (10 years for felonies, 3 years for misdemeanours
and 1 year for summary offences).*

~ **de la peine** : limitation on imposition of penalty
*Where an offender has not served his sentence within the periods
prescribed by law (20 years for felonies, 5 years for misdemeanours
and 2 years for summary offences) the sentence will lapse.*

prescrire : to prescribe, to render invalid by prescription, to bar by statute of
limitations

prescrit : prescribed

chèque ~ : out-of-date cheque

dans les délais ~**s** : within the required time

présélection (f) : lane arrow (road marking)

présent :   present, current.   **par les** ~**es** : hereby

président : chairman, president

~ **de la cour** : the presiding judge

~ **du conseil d'administration** : chairman of the Board of Directors

présider : to chair, to preside over (meetings, etc)

présomption (f) : presumption

dans le doute la ~ **est en faveur de l'accusé** : benefit of the doubt must
be given to the accused

~ **absolue, de droit, juridique, légale** : legal presumption

~ **de décès** : presumption of death

~ **de fait** : presumption of fact

    ~ **d'innocence** : presumption of innocence

    ~ **irréfragable** : irrebuttable presumption

    preuve par ~ : circumstantial evidence

prestation (f) : provision, benefit, service

    ~ **de caractère social** : social benefits

    ~ **de serment** : taking the oath

    ~ **de sûretés** : standing bail

    ~ **familiale** : family allowance

    ~ **maladie** : sickness benefit

présumer : to presume, to deem

    il est à ~ **que** : the presumption is that

    le meurtrier présumé : the alleged murderer

prétendre : to claim, to allege

prétention (f) : claim

prêteur (m) **sur gages** : pawnbroker

prétoire (m) : floor of the court

preuve (f) : evidence, proof

    charge de la ~ : burden of proof

    commencement de la ~ ; prima facie evidence

    ~ **à charge** : evidence for the prosecution

    ~ **à décharge** : evidence for the defence

    ~ **authentique** : duly certified documentary evidence

    ~ **concluante** : conclusive evidence

    ~ **contraire** : evidence to the contrary

    ~ **de culpabilité** : evidence as to guilt

    ~ **directe** : direct evidence

    ~ **indirecte** : circumstantial evidence

    ~ **irrecevable** : inadmissible evidence

~ **libératoire** : peremptory proof

~ **littérale** : documentary evidence

~ **par commune renommée** : common knowledge

~ **par oui-dire** : hearsay

~ **patente** : proof positive

~ **recevable** : admissible evidence

~ **testimoniale** : evidence by witness

prévance (f) * : remand in custody

prévarication (f) : prevarication, maladministration of justice

prévenir : to forestall, to inform, to warn, to give notice, to charge

prévention (f) : prevention, forestalling

    détention préventive : detention on suspicion, detention awaiting trial

    en état de ~ : in custody, committed for trial

    mise en ~ : charge, indictment, committal for trial

    ~ **de la criminalité** : crime prevention

    ~ **routière** : road safety

prévenu (m) : defendant, prisoner, accused (in indictable cases heard by the **tribunaux d'instance** and **tribunaux de grande instance**)

prévision (f) : forecast, estimate, expectation

prévisionnel : estimated

prévoir : to anticipate, to forecast, to provide for

prévôt (m) : provost

prévôte (m) : provost, provost marshal
*(1) Historically, the title given to various civil and royal judicial officers such as the Grand Prévôt de France, the head of the municipal administration of Paris. (2) An officer of the **Gendarmerie** responsible for military discipline abroad.*

prévoté (f) : military police establishment

prime (f) : premium; allowance; bonus

    ~ **d'ancienneté** : seniority allowance

~ **d'assurance** : insurance premium

~ **de licenciement** : redundancy payment, severance pay

~ **de logement** : rent allowance

primitif (texte) : original (text)

primordial : primary, overriding, original

principal : principal, main, chief

auteur ~ d'un crime : principal in the first degree

prioritaire : prior, taking precedence

priorité (f) : priority

~ **à droit** : give way to vehicles from the right

prise (f) : (1) taking up, capture; (2)   fix* (of drugs)

ordonnance de ~ de corps : writ of capias

~ **d'armes** : parade under arms

~ **de corps** : arrest

~ **d'otage** : taking of hostage
Holding a person against his will in order (1) to prepare or facilitate the commission of a criminal offence, (2) to aid the escape of the offenders, or (3) for the purposes of carrying out an order or condition (eg. ransom).

~ **d'un voleur** : capture of a thief

prison (f) : prison, jail, gaol

prisonnier (m) : prisoner

~ **de droit commun** : prisoner convicted under ordinary criminal law (as opposed to one sentenced for political offences or by a special court)

se constituer ~ : to give oneself up, to surrender

privation (f) : deprivation

privé : private, personal.   **es ~ nom** : in his own name

probabilité (f) : probability, likelihood, expectation (of life)

probant : convincing, cogent

document en forme ~e : duly certified document

argument ~ : conclusive, cogent argument

probation (f) : probation.   **comité de** ~ : probation committee

problème (m) : problem, issue

procéder : to proceed

~ **au criminel** : to institute proceedings in the criminal courts

~ **à une enquête** : to set up an enquiry

procédure (f) : (court) procedure
The rules under which the courts dispense justice in the name of the State.

acte de ~ : writ, process, summons

~ **de renseignements judiciaire** : judicial enquiry procedure
Procedure under which initial enquiries are made with a view to the issue of a commission rogatoire and the opening of a full investigation.

~ **accélérée** : expeditious procedure

~ **accusatoire** : accusatorial procedure
System in most common law countries whereby parties and their representatives have primary responsibility for finding and presenting the evidence. The judge does not investigate the facts. This system does not generally apply in France where the inquisitorial procedure is the norm.

~ **inquisitoire** : inquisitorial procedure
The system normally applicable in France, under which the judge searches for the facts, listens to witnesses, examines documents and orders that evidence be taken, after which he investigates further if he deems it necessary. In practice, the system has similarities with the accusatorial procedure in that the evidence must be contradictoire, or given in the presence or knowledge of both parties.

~ **normale** : normal hearing (cf. **procédure simplifiée** and **amende forfaitaire**)

~ **pénale** : criminal procedure

~ **simplifiée** : simplified procedure (eg. **ordonnance pénale**).

~ **sommaire** : summary procedure

procès (m) : trial

procès-verbal (m) : official report, minutes, record

procureur général (m) : senior public prosecutor (at the court of appeal)

procureur de la République (m) : public prosecutor
*Responsible for prosecuting cases at the Courts of Grande Instance (=
Crown Courts)*

profane (m) : layman

profile (m) **de pneu** : tyre tread pattern

programme (m) **(d'ordinateur)** : (computer) program

prohibé : prohibited

projecteur (m) : headlamp

projet (m) : project, scheme, plan, draft

~ **de loi** : bill (draft law presented to parliament by the prime minister)

promotion (f) : (1) promotion; (2) graduation, the class which passes out in a
particular year

promulguer (une loi) : to promulgate (a law)

prononcé (m) **(du jugement)** : delivery of verdict

prononcer : to pronounce

~ **une peine** : to impose a penalty

~ **une sentence** : to sentence

se ~ **sur** : to come to a decision on

proposition (f) **de loi** : private member's bill
*Draft law presented to parliament by a deputé or senateur. (cf projet de
loi).*

proscription (f) : proscription, banishment, outlawry

prostitution (f) : prostitution

~ **clandestine** : unlawful prostitution

~ **réglementée** : tolerated prostitution (in approved brothels, etc)

protecteur (m) : protector, pimp

protection (f) : protection, safety

~ **civile** : civil defence, public safety.

~ **rapprochée** : close/personal protection (by bodyguard), minding

protéger : to protect, to shelter

protester : to protest, to assert, to plead

prouver : to prove

provenance (f) : origin, source, provenance

provision (f) : provision, funds, reserve

    chèque sans ~ : worthless cheque, bouncing cheque

    insuffisance de ~ : insufficient funds (to meet cheque, etc)

    verser des ~s : to pay a deposit

provisoire : provisional, temporary, acting

    en liberté ~ : on bail

    être en liberté ~ : to be out on bail

    sentence ~ : provisional sentence

provocation (f) : provocation, instigation

    excuse absolutoire de ~ : plea of provocation entailing acquittal

    excuse atténuante de ~ : pleading provocation as extenuating circumstance

    ~ au crime : incitement to commit felony

provocateur (agent ~) : inciter, instigator

provoquer : to cause, to incite, to induce

proxénétisme (m) : living on immoral earnings, pimping, procuring for immoral purposes

prudence (f) : caution, care

prune (f) * : (1) bullet, slug; (2) blow, punch; (3) "ticket" for motoring offence;

pruneau (m) * : bullet, slug (usually from a handgun)

psychotrope (m) : mood-affecting drug, stimulants and depressants, "uppers and downers"

pub (f) : publicity, the advertising industry

public (–ique) : public, open (meeting, etc.)

    agent de la force ~ : police officer, gendarme

    audience ~ : open court

    droit ~ : public law

      emploi ~ : public office

      fille ~ : prostitute

      fonds ~ : public funds

      force ~ : police and gendarmerie

      ministère ~ : public prosecutor

      ordre ~ : public order

      rumeur ~ : hearsay

      service ~ : public utility

      travaux ~s : public works

publication (f) : publication

      ~ **des condamnations** : publication of sentence
        Sanction added to a principal penalty, consisting of publishing the
        court's decision by means of a poster or a notice in the press.
        This is imposed as a defamatory penalty and should not be confused
        with the general availability of details of sentences from the office
        of the clerk of the court.

publicité (f) : publicity

      ~ **des débats** : the hearing of cases in open court

      ~ **du jugement de condamnation pénale** : availability of details of sentences
        In principle, any person may obtain from the office of the clerk of
        the court, details of any judgement made in that court, even if he
        is not involved.

pudeur (f) : sense of decency, modesty

      attentat à la ~ : sexual offence, indecent assault

      outrage public à la ~ : indecent exposure

puissance (f) : power, force, authority

punir : to punish

punissable : punishable

punition (f) : punishment

      ~ **corporelle** : restraint

      ~ **disciplinaire** : disciplinary punishment

pupille (f) : ward.   ~ **de l'état** : child in care

---

pur (m) **(un ~)** * : a "regular guy", one who can be trusted (by other criminals)

purger : to purge, to clean, to clear

> ~ **l'accusation** : to submit the indictment to the jury

> ~ **la condamnation, une peine** : to serve one's sentence

> ~ **la contumace** : to surrender to law after being sentenced in one's absence

> ~ **une peine** : to serve a sentence

> **se ~ d'une accusation** : to prove one's innocence

putain (f) : prostitute

pute (f) * : see **putain**

Q

quadritube : four-barrelled (gun)

quai (m) des Orfèvres : Headquarters of the Paris **Police Judiciaire**

qualification (f) : legal definition

    ~ judiciaire : acceptance by the court
        Document by means of which the judge confirms that the facts agree
        with the legal text concerned.

    ~ légale : statutory definition
        Document by means of which the legislator defines the elements of
        an offence.

qualifié : (1) qualified, skilled; (2) aggravated

    acte ~ de crime : action amounting to a felony

    crime ~ : aggravated felony

    le service ~ : the competent service

qualité (f) : quality, qualification, capacity, class

    agir en ~ de ... : to act in one's capacity as a ...

    avoir ~ pour agir : to be qualified, entitled to act, to have authority to act

    ~ substantielle d'un crime : essence of a crime

    ~s d'un jugement : record of proceedings before judgement

quarantaine (f) : quarantine

quart (m) * :   "cop-shop", police station

    faire le ~ : to go soliciting for prostitution

    ~ d'oeil : police superintendent

quartier (m) quarter, area, district

    ~ de semi-liberté : semi-custodial wing

    ~-général : headquarters

quasi-collision (f) : near miss (air navigation)

quasi-délit (m) : technical offence

quatre-quatre (m) : four wheel drive vehicle

querellé : contested

question (f) : question, point at issue

      en ~ : at issue

    ~ de droit, de fait : issue of law, of fact

    ~ préjudicielle : matter outside the competence of the court

    ~ subsidiaire : supplementary question

    ~ tendancieuse : leading question

queue (f) : tail, queue

    faire une ~ de poisson : to cut in front of another vehicle after having overtaken

    laisser une ~ : to leave without paying (restaurant, etc.)

qui de droit : to whom it may concern

quidam (m) : person, name unknown

quincaillerie (f) * : (1) loose change, small value coins; (2) gongs*, medals; (3) expensive jewellery; (4) computer hardware

quitte (être ~) : to have paid one's debt to society, to have served one's sentence and be going straight

R.

rabatteur (m) : tout, barker

rabattre : to come back, to return

> ~ **un défaut** : to cancel a sentence passed *in absentia*

> **se** ~ : (1) to swerve back to the correct side of the road to avoid oncoming traffic; (2) to return to one's old haunts

raboter : to nick*, to pinch*, to steal from someone

rabouin (m) : gipsy

raccroc (m) **(faire le** ~ **)** : to tout (especially for purposes of prostitution)

raccrochage (m) ; accosting

racket (m) : protection racket

racketter : to conduct a (protection) racket

racketteur (m) : racketeer

raclée (f) * : thrashing, beating

raclette (f) **(coup de** ~ **)** : successful police raid

racolage (m) : soliciting for the purposes of prostitution

racoler : to solicit

radariser : to "clock" speeding vehicle by radar

radeuse (f) * : prostitute

radiation (f) : deletion, striking out

> ~ **du tableau d'avancement** : deletion from the promotions list

radier : to delete, to erase

rafale (f) : burst of gunfire, hail of bullets

raffut (m) : noise, din, hullabaloo

rafle (f) : surprise raid (by police or by criminals), smash and grab raid

rage (f) : (1) rabies;   (2) rage, anger

ragoter : to gather street gossip where other leads have fizzled out

raison (f) : reason, motive, ground

    ~ **probante** : evidence

ralentisseur (m) : speed ramp, "sleeping policeman"

râleur (m) : persistent complainer

rallonge (f) : (1) rise, increase in salary; (2) extended leave; (3) extension of prison sentence following the uncovering of further offences; (4) knife

rallye (m) : (1) car rally; (2) exclusive dance for the young of "good family"

ramasser (se faire ~) : (1) to get arrested; (2) to get a severe reprimand;

ramastique (f) : confidence trick, scam, sting
Usually consists of selling a worthless item of jewellery to a passer-by, dropped by accomplice A, picked up by B and highly praised by C, posing as an expert.

rambours (mpl) : information

rampe (f) : light bar
The combined "Police" sign and flashing blue lamps mounted on the roof of a police car.

se rancarder : to make enquiries

rançon (f) : ransom

rang (m) : rank, status.   **par ~ d'ancienneté** : in order of seniority

raper : to scrape

rapine (f) : robbery, rapine, pillage

rapport (m) : report, statement, account

    ~ **de police** : police report

    ~ **d'expertise** : report by court-appointed expert/consultant

    ~ **juridique** : report as to legal position

rapporter : (1) to bring back, to restore; (2) to relate, to refer; (3) to revoke, to rescind

rapt (m) : forcible abduction, kidnapping

rassemblement (m) **illicite** : unlawful assembly

râtelage (m) : theft of hay left in meadows after hay-making

ratiboiser : to nick*, to pinch*, to steal

raticide (m) : rat killer

ratier (m) : inmate, prisoner

ratière (f) * : nick*, clink*, jail

ratifier : to confirm, to ratify

ratissage (m) : sweep, dragnet

ratisser : to nick*, to pinch*, to steal

rature (f) : erasure

ravisseur (m) : kidnapper

rayon (m) : ray, radius, scope, territory

      chef de ~ : head of department

      ~ d'action : scope of activity

réactif : quick to react, sensitive to trends

réactualiser : to update, to revise

réagir : to react

réassignation (f) : fresh summons

rébellion (f) : rebellion, revolt

      faire ~ à la justice : to resist authority, resist the law, contempt of court

rebichoter : to identify a suspect

rebiffe (f) * : vengeance, revenge, reprisal

récapitulation (f) : recapitulation, summary, résumé, summing up

recassage (m) : redeployment

recel (m) : handling stolen property

      ~ de malfaiteur : harbouring a criminal

receleur (m) : receiver of stolen property, fence

récépissé (m) : written acknowledgement of receipt of a complaint

réception (f) **de femmes de débauche** : harbouring prostitutes

recevabilité (f) : admissibility

recevable : admissible.   **preuve ~** : admissible evidence

recevoir : to receive, to get

    fin de non-~ : plea in bar

    ~ une déposition : to take someone's evidence

recherche (f) : pursuit, quest, search, research

    frais de ~ : research costs

    ~ criminelle : criminal investigation

    ~ de police : police investigation

    ~ des preuves : investigation, enquiry

    ~ opérationnelle : operational research

    ~ scientifique : scientific research

    sous-direction de ~ s criminelles : serious crimes squad (Paris CID)

récidive (f) : recidivism,
The commission of an offence after having been convicted for a previous offence. The condition of a person who has been so previously convicted. (Grounds for enhancing the penalty for the subsequent offence)

récidiviste (f) : recidivist, previous offender *(see récidivisme above)*

réclamation (f) : complaint, objection, protest, request, claim, demand
This term is used to describe the demand made by the prosecutor for a particular sentence to be imposed.

    ~ en dommages-intérêts : claim for damages

réclamer : to claim, to complain

    ~ contre une décision : to appeal against a decision

réclame (f) : advertisement, advertising

reclassement (m) : regrading, rehabilitation

réclusion (f) : imprisonment for five to twenty years for felony
This punishment replaced sentences to hard labour, often served in a penal colony overseas.

    ~ à temps : fixed term sentence

    ~ perpétuelle, à perpétuité : imprisonment for life

récolement (m) : verification

    ~ des dépositions : reading their depositions to witnesses récolter : (1) to harvest, to gather in; (2)* to "cop", to get, to receive

recomparaître : to appear again

récompense (f) : compensation

reconnaissance (f) : recognizance

reconnaître : to recognize, to acknowledge

    se ~ coupable : to admit one's guilt

reconstitution (f) : reconstruction (of a crime)

recourir : to resort, to have recourse

    ~ à la violence : to resort to violence

recours (m) : recourse, resort, resource, appeal

    ~ en cassation : appeal on points of law

    ~ en grâce : petition for reprieve

    ~ en révision : application for retrial

    ~ irrecevable : inadmissible claim

    ~ pour excès de pouvoir : application for judicial review of an administrative action

recouvrement (m) des amendes : enforcement of fines

recrutement (m) : recruitment

recruter : to recruit

rectifieur (m) * : hit-man, hired muscle, "heavy"

recto (m) : face.   ~ -verso : printed on both sides, double-sided

récupération (f) de métaux : scrap metal merchant's yard

récupérer * : to nick*, to pinch*, to steal

récusation (f) : challenge, objection (to judge, juror, etc.)

    ~ de témoin : exception to a witness

recyclage (m) (cours de ~) : refresher course, retraining

recycleur (m) : laundering agent (for drug money)

rédaction (f) : drawing up, composing (a report, etc.)

rédiger : to draw up, to compose, to draft (a document, etc.)

redresser : (1) to rectify, to redress, to right; (2) to spot, to identify

réduction (f) : reduction; elimination

    ~ **d'ancienneté d'echelon** : loss of seniority

    ~ **de peine** : mitigation of penalty

réfection (f) : repair

référé (m) : summary jurisdiction and procedure in matters of special urgency

    juger en ~ : to hear a case in chambers

réformer : to reform, to amend, to discharge (soldiers, etc.)

    ~ **un jugement** : to reverse a decision (by appeal court)

refourguer : to sell stolen goods

refus (m) : refusal

    ~ **d'assistance à personne en danger** : failure to assist a person in peril

    ~ **d'assistance contre une infraction** : failure to prevent a crime or misdemeanour against the person
      Where a person who is able, by his immediate action, without risk to himself or another, to prevent the commission of a crime or misdemeanour against the person, wilfully fails to do so.

    ~ **de déférer à une réquisition** : refusal to respond to a call for assistance
      Offence committed by a military commander who fails to answer to a legally-made requision for military aid (in the case of civil disorder).

    ~ **de dénoncer** : failure to report a crime

    ~ **de témoigner** : refusal to give evidence

    ~ **de vente** : refusal to sell, to provide a service
      Where a trader or other professional refuses to meet a customer's demand for a product or service which he is capable of providing. This is an offence against the criminal law but there are a number of legitimate excuses and justifications which may be invoked, in particular the customer's lack of good faith or the unusual nature of the requirement.

    ~ **d'informer** : refusal to open an investigation
      *The examining magistrate may issue an **ordonnance de refus d'informer** if it appears to him that, according to the terms of the **réquisitoire**, no criminal offence has been committed, or that the matter cannot be prosecuted.*

~ **d'obéissance** : insubordination

~ **d'obtempérer** : refusal to comply with a lawful instruction

réfuter : to rebut

regardateur (m) : village constable in pre-Revolutionary France

régime (m) : (1) form of government or administration; (2) system, scheme

~ **pénitentiaire** : penal system

région (f) : region
*(1) The 1982 Decentralisation Act provided for a new strata of local government; the region. Each region comprises a number of **départements**. Day-to-day administation is entrusted to a regional council and the central government is represented by a **Préfet**. The functions of a region are to draw up regional structure plans, to promote economic development (including tourism) and to train manpower (further education and apprenticeships). (2) A formation of several **Légions** of Gendarmerie, commanded by a General.*

régistre (m) : register, record

~ **d'écrou** : prison calendar

~ **du commerce et des sociétés** : commercial and company register

~ **du personnel** : staff register

~ **électoral** : electoral register
*Register in which are recorded the names of the authorised electors for a **commune** and which is signed by them.*

règle (f) : rule, law, principle

règlement (m) : (1) settlement (of account, dispute); (2) payment (of debt)

~ **de compte** : "settlement of account", revenge killing

règlements (mpl) : regulations, statutory instruments
*The term covers all statutory instruments, including **décrets, arrêtés, ordonnances** and **circulaires**.*

~ **administratifs** : bye-laws

~ **de police** : police regulations (made by the Prefect of Police)

~ **des juges** : referral of a case to a competent lower court by a higher one

~ **intérieurs** : general orders, standing orders

régul * : see **régulier**.   ~ **-régul** : by the book, according to the rules

régulier : in order, correct, on the level, straight

réhabilitation (f) : spending of a conviction

reins (mpl) : kidneys

rejeter : to disallow, to reject, to dismiss, to throw out

relâcher : to release

   ~ **un prisonnier** : to release a prisoner

   ~ **sous caution** : to release on bail

relais (m) : relay, shift

relarguer * : to release from prison

relaxe (f) : acquittal of a prisoner by a court other than an assize court

relégation (f) : transportation for life

relevé (m) : statement, return

relevée (f) : afternoon

relèvement (m) : dispensation
   Right of a judge to dispense with all or part of the consequences associated with a conviction.

relever (d'un tribunal) : to fall within the competence (of a court)

relief (m) **d'appel** : extension of the time allowed for lodging an appeal

remettre : to deliver, to hand over, to remit

   ~ **à une date ultérieure** : to postpone, to adjourn

   ~ **une affaire** : to adjourn, to remand a case

remise (f) : remission (of penalty, etc.)

remorque (f) : trailer.   **semi-** ~ : articulated vehicle

remplacer : to deputize (for someone)

remplir : to fill, to fill in, to meet

rémunération (f) : payment, reward, consideration

rencard (m) : appointment, date*

se rencarder : to make enquiries

rencards (mpl) : information

rendez-moi (m) **(vol au ~)** : to "ring the changes"
> *Fraud perpetrated by a customer who offers a large-denomination bank
> note to the cashier, gets his change and, by sleight-of-hand, also gets the
> note back.*

rendre : to give, to render, to pay back, to return

> **~ compte** : to report

> **~ la justice** : to dispense justice

> **~ témoignage** : to bear witness, to give evidence, to testify

> **~ un verdict** : to return a verdict

rendez-vous (m) : appointment, meeting

rênes (fpl) : reins

renifle (f) * : (1) the police, "old Bill"; (2) sniff of cocaine

renommée (f) : renown, repute.   **commune ~** : common report, hearsay

renoncer : to renounce, to waive, to disclaim

renseignements (mpl) : information, intelligence

> **~ Généraux (Service des ~)** : Intelligence Service
> *Branch of the **Police Nationale** responsible for collating intelligence
> of a political, social and economic nature on behalf of the
> government. Maintains files on all major enterprises, public and
> political figures and various organisations, mainly on a regional
> basis. Not generally involved in the collation of criminal
> intelligence. (Has no equivalent in Great Britain although some of
> its functions may be carried out by Special Branch or the
> Intelligence Service. (See **police de renseignement**).*

rente (f) : annuity, pension, private income, allowance

renvoi (m) : transfer to another court, referral, adjournement

> **~ d'un employé** : dismissal of an employee

renvoyer : (1) to refer to the party concerned or to the competent authority;
(2) to discharge; (3) to postpone, to adjourn

réparation (f) : reparation, redress

> **~ civile** : compensation

> **~ de dommages** : damages

> **~ légale** : legal redress

réparer : to repair, to rectify

repassage (m) : con trick, swindle

repentir (m) : repentance, remorse

> ~ **actif** : expiation
> > *Where an offender makes amends for his action, insofar as he is able. Such reparation does not affect his guilt but may be regarded as attenuating circumstances when sentencing.*

> **se ~** : to repent, to feel remorse

repérer : (1) to identify; (2) to keep an eye on, to watch closely

répertoire (m) : index, table, catalogue

> ~ **d'adresses** : directory

> ~ **de jurisprudence** : summary of leading cases and decisions

répit (m) : respite.   **jours de ~** : days of grace

réplique (f) : re-examination, response

répondant (m) **(pour quelqu'un)** : security, surety (for someone)

répondre : to answer, to reply, to guarantee

> ~ **aux conditions** : to meet the requirements

réponse (f) : reply, response, plea

reporter : to report to, to serve under

reporting (m) : report

repose-pied (m) : footrest

repousser : to throw out, to reject, to rebut

répréhensible : objectionable, reprehensible

représentant (m) : representative, agent.   ~ **légale** : legal representative

répressif : repressive.   **loi ~** : criminal law

réprimande (f) : censure, caution

repris (m) **de justice** : habitual criminal, persistent offender

reproduction (f) : publication

réputation (f) : reputation, repute

réputé : regarded as

requérir : to ask for, to claim

> ~ **aide et assistance** : to demand assistance
>
> ~ **la force publique** : to call out the public order forces (police, gendarmerie) in the event of public disorder or riot
>
> ~ **l'application de la loi** : to claim the enforcement of law

requête (f) : request, suit, petition

réquisition (f) : submission by the prosecution made during the investigation

réquisitoire (m) : (1) details of the charge; (2) prosecutor's address to the court; (3) certain applications concerning the conduct of an investigation

> ~ **définitif** : final charge(s)
> *Document written by the public prosecutor after the stage of examination, recording what action he intends to take in the matter. This decision is conveyed orally to the court.*
>
> ~ **introductif** : draft charge(s)
> *Document by means of which the public prosecutor brings a criminal matter to the attention of the examining magistrate, thereby obviating the **citation directe***
>
> ~ **supplétif** : additional charge(s)
> *Supplementary document usually prepared at the request of the examining magistrate enabling him to investigate matters not covered by the **réquisitoire définitif** and disclosed during the examination.*

réseau (m) : network, system

réserve (f) : reservation, reserve

> **sans** ~ : unreservedly, unconditionally
>
> **sous** ~ : without prejudice

réserver : to reserve, to book (a seat, etc.)

réservoir (m) **d'essence** : fuel tank, petrol tank

résidence (f) : residence

> ~ **effective** : actual residence
>
> ~ **habituelle** : customary residence
>
> ~ **principale** : main residence
>
> ~ **secondaire** : secondary residence

resilier : to annul, to cancel, to terminate

résine (f) (**~ de cannabis**): (cannabis) resin

responsabilité (f) : responsibility, liability

~ **civile** : civil liability

~ **collective** : collective responsibility, joint and several liability
*Rules of incrimination applicable to a person, by virtue of his
membership of a group, for the illegal activities of that group. The
principle of individuality of penalties bars the application of
collective responsibility.*

~ **pénale** : criminal responsibility
*Obligation to answer for illegal acts by undergoing the penalty
prescribed by law. In particular, this term is used in regard to
certain persons by virtue of their position (eg. doctors) or the
manner in which they are involved in the offence (eg. instigator)*

~ **pénale pour autrui** : responsibility for the criminal actions of others
*Rules of incrimination applicable to a person by virtue of his
connection with another who has taken part in a crime. The
principle of individuality of penalties bars the application of this
type of responsibility.*

responsable (m) : official, person in charge, supervisor

ressort (m) : (1) competence, scope, province, jurisdiction; (2) spring

jugement en dernier ~ : judgement not subject to appeal

jugement en premier ~ : judgement subject to appeal

~ **hélécoïdal** : coil spring

ressortissant (m) : national (of a country), citizen, subject

~ **étranger** : alien

rester * : to "hang out", to live somewhere

restitution (f) : restitution
*The return of stolen property and property subject to the charge to its
rightful owners.*

résumé (m) : summary.   ~ **des débats** : summing up

rétablir (l'ordre public) : to restore (public order)

rétamé : blind drunk

retapissage (m) : identity parade

retapisser : to identify, to recognise someone

rétention : detention (of illegal immigrants)

retenu (m) : detainee

retourner : to grass*, to inform on someone

rétracter : to retract, to withdraw, to revoke

retrait (m) : cancellation, withdrawal

> ~ **d'une plainte** : withdrawal of a complaint

> ~ **d'un permis** : cancellation of a licence

> ~ **du permis de conduire** : disqualification from driving

retraite (f) : retirement

> **mise à la** ~ **d'office** : compulsorily retired

> **pension de** ~ : retirement pension

> **pension de** ~ **militaire** : retired pay

> **régime de** ~ : superannuation plan

> **retenue pour** ~ : superannuation contribution

> ~ **anticipée** : early retirement

retraité (m) : retired person

rétroactivité "in mitius" (f) : application of a less-severe law to acts committed prior to its promulgation and not yet definitively dealt with

rétrogradation (f) : demotion

rétroviseur (m) : rear-view mirror

réunion (f) : meeting, coming together.　　~ **publique** : public meeting

(se) réunir : to meet

révision (f) : review, revision, inspection, appeal

> **conseil de** ~ : military appeal court

> **pourvoi en** ~ : application for retrial

révocation (f) : (1) dismissal;　(2) rescinding

> ~ **avec suspension des droits à pension** : dismissal with loss of pension rights

> ~ **d'un décret** : revocation of an edict

> ~ **d'un sursis** : repeal of suspension

rhum (m) : rum

rhume (m) : cold, coryza

riboustin (m) * : "shooter", handgun

ricaine (f) * : large American car

rideau (m) **(tomber en ~)** : to break down in a motor vehicle

ridère : "flash", smart, elegant

rien-du-tout (m) : scoundrel, ne'er-do-well

rififi (m) * : violence, rough-stuff

rigolo (m) : (1) fly-by-night, unreliable person; (2) "shooter", handgun; (3) jemmy, crowbar

rigoustin (m) * : "shooter", handgun

ring (m) : ring-road

riper : to nick*, to pinch*, to steal

ripou (m) : bent cop*, corrupt policeman

rixe (f) : brawl, scuffle, affray

robot (m) **(portrait ~)** : photofit picture

rôdailler : to loiter (with intent)

rôder : to prowl

rôdeur (m) : prowler

rôdeuse (f) : street walker, prostitute

rodeur (m) : prowler

rogatoire : see **commission rogatoire**

rogomme (m) : strong liquor (usually of the moonshine variety)

rôle (m) : court list

ronde (f) : patrol

Roquette (f) **(prison de la ~)** : women's prison in Paris

rosser : to beat up, to give someone a good hiding

rossignol (m) : picklock, skeleton key

roublard : crafty, cunning

rouchie (f) * : (1) kept woman, mistress; (2) low-class prostitute

roue (f) : wheel.   ~ **de secours** : spare wheel

roulement (m) : shift system

rouler : to "con", to swindle, to cheat

rouleur (m) : driver, road-user

roulotte (f) : caravan.   **vol à la** ~ : stealing from cars, autotheft

roulottier (m) : (1) one who steals from cars; (2) car thief

roupane (f) : policeman's cape

rouspéter : to complain, to grumble

rousse (f) * : "Old Bill", the cops, the "fuzz"

roussin (m) * : policeman, cop, detective;   "grass", informant

roustir * : (1) to "con", to swindle, to cheat; (2) to nick*, to steal

route (f) : road, route, highway

> **code de la** ~ : road traffic law
> *It should be noted that this has the force of law, unlike the*
> *Highway Code which is merely advisory.*

> **frais de** ~ : travelling expenses

routier (m) : long-distance lorry driver

> **vieux** ~ : "old hand", someone skilled through long experience

routier : appertaining to the roads

> **relais** ~ : commercial hotel
> *Reasonably priced hotels and restaurants originally aimed at truck*
> *drivers but now available to the general travelling public.*

> **transport** ~ : road transport

ruban (m) : road, highway

RUBIS : radio network used by the Gendarmerie

rumeur (f) **publique** : hearsay, common knowledge

rupture (f) **de ban** : breach of deportation order

rural : rural.   **code** ~ : the laws relating country property and activities

S

sabot (m) **d'Anvers** : wheelclamp, Denver boot

sabotage (m) : malicious damage, sabotage

sabre (m) : sabre, sword

saccagé : ransacked, pillaged, ravaged

saccagne (f) * : knife, blade

sain : healthy, sound

    ~ **d'esprit** : compos mentis, of sound mind

    ~ **et sauf** : safe and sound

saisie (f) execution, attachment, distraint

saisine (f) **directe** : summary jurisdiction
    System created in 1981 whereby the public prosecutor could bring minor matters before the court with the minimum of delay. Replaced in 1983 by **comparution immédiate.**

saisir : to catch, to seize, to grasp, to refer, to involve

    ~ **la justice** : to go to law

    ~ **un tribunal d'une affaire** : to refer a matter to a court

salle (f) : room, hall

    ~ **d'audience** : court room

    ~ **de commande** : control room

    ~ **opérationnelle** : operations room

salubrité (f) **publique** : public health

sanction (f) : (1) approbation, assent; (2) sanction, penalty

    ~ **disciplinaire** : disciplinary punishment

    ~ **légale** : legal sanction

    ~ **pécuniaire** : fine

    ~ **pénale** : penalty, sentence

sans domicile fixe : of no fixed abode

sans-papiers (m) : person without means of identification

Santaga/Santoche (f) * : the **prison de la Santé** in Paris

sape (m) * : see **sapement**

sapement (m) : "stretch", prison sentence

saper : to send down, to sentence

sapeur–pompier (m) : fireman, firefighter
*The Paris fire brigade is controlled by the **Préfet de Police de Paris.***

SAPHIR : one of the Gendarmerie's radio networks

sardine (f) : familiar term for a **galon**

sataner : to hit violently, to pummel

saucisson (m) : difficult case to solve

saucissoner : to arrest, to nick*
The implication here is that the prisoner is shackled or restrained in some way.

sauret (m) : pimp, procureur

sauter : to arrest, to nick*, to knock off*

sauvage : wild.　　　　**grève** ˜ : wildcat strike

sauvegarder : to safeguard, to protect

sauvette (f) (**vendre à la** ˜) : street trading without a licence

savoir–faire (m) : ability.　　　　˜ **technique** : know–how

sbire (m) * : (1) copper, policeman; (2) "minder" (bodyguard to a major criminal)

scalp (m) * : arrest, prisoner, "collar"

schnaps (m) * : strong liquor

schnouf (f) * : "coke". cocaine

schtar(d)/schtibe/schtilibem (m) * : clink*, nick*, prison

sceau (m) : seal
Stamp held by a public official, the imprint of which serves to authenticate a legal instrument or to seal an object.

　　le Garde des ˜**x** : the Minister of Justice, = the Lord Chancellor

scellé (m) : imprint of official seal, sealed
Strip of paper or material affixed by sealing wax bearing a magistrate's seal to the door of a room or an item of furniture in order to prevent it from being opened or removed without authority.

bris de ~s : breaking of seals

scènes (fpl) **(faire des ~)** : to pick a quarrel

sciemment : knowingly

sciences (fpl) **criminelles** : criminal sciences, criminal justice studies
This general term includes criminal law and procedure, criminology, crime prevention, forensic science, penology, etc.

scion (m) * : knife, blade

scolarisable : of school age

scooter (m) : (motor) scooter

score (m) * : "stretch", prison sentence

scotch (m) : (1) whisky; (2) transparent adhesive tape

scribouiller : to scribble

scrogneuneu (m) : "dinosaur", "die-hard", one who fails to keep up with the times

séchoir (m) * : "cooler", punishment cell

secouée (f) * : "rocket", telling-off, reprimand

secouer : (1) to nick*, to pinch*, to steal; (2) to severely reprimand someone

secourir : to help, to aid, to relieve

secourisme (m) : first aid

secours (m) : help, aid

premier ~ : first aid

voiture de police ~ : emergency response car

secret (m) : secret, solitary confinement

~ professionnel : professional secrecy
Obligation imposed on certain persons not to disclose matters which come to their notice in the course of their professional activities. Failure to maintain secrecy is punishable under the criminal law.

secrétaire (m&f) : secretary

~ d'Etat : junior minister
Unlike the system which appertains in the UK, a secrétaire d'Etat ranks below a minister.

~ de mairie : town clerk

    ~ général (de ministère) : permanent secretary

    ~ particulier : private secretary, confidential clerk, personal assistant

secrétariat (m) : administration department, general office

    ~-Général pour l'administration de la Police : regional police administration and supplies service

secrétariat-greffe : court and public prosecutor's office

section (f) : section, branch

    ~ opérationnelle et spécialisée : joint crime branch
        *A mixed uniform/plain clothes unit, forming part of the **Corps Urbain** in the larger divisions. It is responsible for initial attendance at scenes of crimes and making immediate enquiries.*

sécurité (f) : security, safety

    ~ générale : general divisional personnel
        The function of these officers is to patrol the streets, control road traffic and generally keep order.

    ~ publique : public safety

    ~ routière : road safety

sédition (f) : sedition, mutiny

séduction (f) : seduction, enticement, subornation (of witnesses)

    rapt par ~ : abduction with consent

séjour (m) : stay, sojourn

    durée de ~ : period of stay

    interdiction de ~ : banishment from a prescribed area

    ~ habituel : permanent address

sélecteur (m) **de vitesses** : gear change lever

selle (f) : saddle.   **~ biplace** : dual-seat (motorcycle)

semer : to shake off, to give a follower the slip

semi (m) : see **semi-remorque**

semi-liberté (f) : temporary release on parole, ticket-of-leave
System whereby a prisoner may be released to exercise a professional activity, receive education, vocational training or medical treatment outside the prison. The prisoner returns to the prison for the rest of the time.

semi-remorque (f) : articulated goods vehicle

sénéchal (m) : seneschal, majordomo, steward, grandee

sens (m) : direction, sense

> **au ~ de l'article ..** : within the meaning assigned by (section ..)

sensible : sensitive

sentence (f) : sentence, judgement

> **prononcer une ~** : to pass a sentence
>
> **~ capitale, de mort** : death sentence
>
> **~ criminelle** : sentence, penalty
>
> **~ par défaut** : sentence in absence

sentier (m) : sweatshop system (mainly in immigrant districts of large towns)

séquestration (f) : sequestration, detention, arrest

> **~ arbitraire** : unlawful arrest, false imprisonment

sérail (m) **(passage en ~)** : "gang-bang", collective rape

serbillon (m) **(envoyer le ~)** : to warn someone, to tip someone off

sergent (m) : servant, steward, constable
*The title given to the early French police officials. Over the years they took titles such as **sergent de Châtelet, sergent de justice** and **sergent à la douzaine.** Originally they were employed by an ecclesiastical or secular noble from whom they received delegated authority.*

> **~ de ville** : police constable
> *Predecessor (up to 1870) of the **gardien de la paix.***

série (f) : series

> **~ noire** : detective novel
> *A famous collection of paperback novels published by Gallimard which has given its name to any book of this type.*

seringue (f) : (1) syringe; (2) firearm

serment (m) : oath

> **déclaration sous ~** : sworn statement, affidavit
>
> **faux ~** : perjury (in a civil case)
> *This offence is punishable in the criminal courts.*
>
> **prêter ~** : to take an oath

refus de ~ : refusal to be sworn
Punishable as refusal to give evidence.

serré * : "strapped for cash", short of money

serrure (f) : lock

serrurier (m) : (1) locksmith; (2) metal worker

service (m) : duty, service, department

agent de ~ : duty officer

local de ~ : operational police station

règlement de ~ : standing orders

~ actif : on the active list

~ armé : armed forces

~ commandé : on duty

~ d'aide médicale urgente (SAMU) : emergency paramedic ambulance
service

~ de la Cooperation Technique Internationale de la Police : Police
International Technical Aid Service
*The department of the National Police which provides aid and
assistance with police training for such countries as wish it
(usually third world countries and former French colonies)*

~ de la voirie : highways department

~ de protection et de sécurité du Métro. : Underground (Tube) police

~ des Voyages Officiels : Official Transport Service
*The department of the National Police responsible for arranging and
protecting the movements of officials and VIPs*

~ d'ordre : stewards (at a meeting, etc. to keep order)

~ extraordinaire : secondment

~ mobile d'urgence et de réanimation (SMUR) : emergency resuscitation
ambulance service

~ national : national service, conscription
*All adult males have to perform national service in one of the armed
forces, on an overseas aid programme, in the police, gendarmerie
or similar organisation. Persons performing their national service
in the police or gendarmerie are known as "auxiliaries".*

~ **ordinaire** : normal (permanent) duties

~ **public** : public utility

~ **Régionale de la Police Judiciaire (SRPJ)** : Regional Crime Squad

~**s extérieurs (sous-direction des ~)** : territorial CID service
> *That branch of the Paris CID responsible for territorial CID units.*

~**s généraux (sous-direction des ~)** : general CID support services
> *The police service responsible for scenes of crime, forensic science laboratories, etc. in Paris.*

~ **sociale** : welfare department

service (f) centrale : headquarters, central service

~ **automobile** : central motor pool
> *Responsible for providing the Police Nationale with the necessary vehicles and the maintenance of these.*

~ **de la Police de l'Air et des Frontières (PAF)** : Headquarters of the Air and Border Police

~ **des Compagnies Républicaines de Sécurité** : Headquarters of the CRS

~ **des Polices Urbaines** : headquarters of the Town Police Service
> *One of the central services of the National Police, it is responsible for providing the policing in all towns with populations of 10,000 or more (smaller towns and villages are usually covered by detachments of Gendarmerie).*

serviette (f) : (1) table napkin; (2) briefcase

coup de ~ : police raid

servietter : (1) to arrest, to nick*, to knock off*; (2) to make a swoop, to organise a police raid

session (f) : session, sitting

set (m) : kit

~ **aggression sexuelle** : rape investigation kit
> *A set of equipment, instruments and instructions for the taking of forensic evidence in cases of sexual assault.*

seuil (m) : lower limit, threshold

sévices (mpl) : cruelty, ill-treatment

sevrage (m) : weaning.   **symptômes de ~** : withdrawal symptoms

shooté : drugged

shooter : to mainline, to inject drugs

shooteuse (f) * : hypodermic syringe

siège (m) : bench, seat

    jugement rendu sur le ~ : judgement delivered without retiring

    le ~ du tribunal est fait : the court has reached a decision

    magistrat du ~ : judge

    ~ principal : head office

    ~ social : registered office (of a company)

siéger : to sit (as a judge)

sieur (m) : mister

sigle (m) : acronym

signalement (m) : description (of a person), particulars (of a vehicle)

signalétique (fiche ~) : descriptive form

signe (m) : sign

    faire un ~ : to give a sign

    ~s distinctifs : special peculiarities

signification (f) : service (of summons, writ), notification

    acte de ~ : writ, process

    ~ à domicile : service at place of abode

    ~ à personne : personal service

    ~ de jugement : notification of judgement

    ~ ordinaire : service by post or leaving at last known address

    ~ par avis public : notification by poster, notice in the press, etc.

signifier : to serve

silencieux (m) : gun fitted with a silencer

simulé : bogus, sham

sinistre (m) : disaster, catastrophe

sinistré : damaged, wrecked

sinistré (m) : victim of a disaster

site (m) : site

situation (f) : (1) situation, state, condition; (2) location, site

    rapport de ~ : statement, survey

    ~ de famille : family status

    ~ de fin de mois : monthly return

    ~ de fortune : financial standing

    ~ géographique : location

    ~ juridique : legal status

    ~ personnelle : personal data or history

    ~ sociale : social status

slalom (m) : sudden lane changing, to weave in and out of traffic

smicard (m) * : low-wage earner, one who only receives the SMIC

sniff (m) : snort (of drugs)

sniffeur (m) : cocaine user

social : social

    assistance ~e : social security

    assistante ~e : social worker

    nom ~, raison ~ : name, style of firm

    siège ~ : registered office

société (f) : company, firm

    ~ anonyme (SA) : public limited company

    ~ à responsabilité limitée (SARL) : (private) limited liability company

    ~ en commandite : partnership

    ~ fantôme : bogus company

    ~ sans but lucratif : non-profit making organisation

soit–communiqué (ordonnance de ~) : notification of result of an investigation
*Document by means of which the examining magistrate forwards a case file
to the public prosecutor in order for him to determine what charges
should be preferred against an alleged offender.*

solaires (fpl) : sunglasses, "shades"

solde (f) : military pay

    officier en demi– ~ : officer on half pay

    ~ de non–activité : unemployment benefit

    ~s et indemnités : ordinary pay and allowances

solidairement : jointly and severally

solidarité (f) pénale : joint and several liability for the civil consequences of
criminal acts

solliciter : to ask for, to request

sommaire (m) : summary, contents

sommation (f) : summons, notice, order

    faire les trois ~s légales : to read the Riot Act

    ~ à comparaître : summons to appear

sommeil (m) (marchand de ~) * : keeper of a low–class hotel

sommier (m) : register

    ~ judiciaire : criminal record, criminal records office, CRO

sonne (f) * : "old Bill", "the law", the police
*This derogatory term implies the strong–arm methods allegedly used by
the police.*

sonner : to "bash", to beat up

sophistication (f) : adulteration of foodstuffs or wine

sorgue (f) : night (after dark)

sorlingue (m) * : knife, blade

soudoyer : to bribe, to nobble

soufflant (m) * : "shooter", handgun

souffler * : to nick*, to pinch*, to steal

soulever * : to "lift", to pinch*, to steal

soupçon (m) : suspicion

soupe (f) **(se mettre à la ~)** : to take stimulants

sourdine (f) * : secret police

souricière (f) : police trap

sous : under, below, within (time)

> ~ **clef** : under lock and key

> ~ **le nom de** : known as, alias, AKA

> ~ **inculpation de** : on a charge of

> ~ **peine de** : on pain of

sous–commission (f) : sub-committee

sous–direction (f) : sub-directorate, service, department

> ~ **de la logistique** : logistics department
> *Branch of the Gendarmerie responsible for testing major items of equipment such as boats, helicopters, etc.*

> ~ **des affaires économiques et financières** : fraud squad

sous–dit (m) : below-mentioned, undermentioned

sous–mac (m) : brothel keeper

sous–officier (m) : non-commissioned officer, NCO

> ~ **d'élite** : senior NCO (Belgian Gendarmerie)

sous–ordre (m) : subordinate

sous–préfet : under-prefect
*The representative of the central government in an **arrondissement**. He answers to the **Préfet** for the **département** and is generally responsible for, amongst other things, public order and tranquility in his area.*

sous–virage (m) : understeer

soussigné (m) : undersigned

soustraire : to abstract, to take away, to withdraw

> **se ~ à la justice** : to abscond

soutache (f) : (military) braid

souteneur (m) : pimp, person living on immoral earnings

soutier (m) : baggage handler

spectacle (m) : entertainment

spoiler (m) : spoiler (automobile)

sporter : to exercise, to work out

squattage (m) : squat (unauthorised occupation of premises)

stage (m) : course of instruction, probationary period

stagiaire (m) : trainee

stand (m) : stand, stall

    ~ **de tir** : shooting range

standardiste (m&f) : switchboard operator

station (f) : station

    ~ **de travail** : work station

    ~ **touristique** : holiday resort

    ~-**service** : service station, filling station

stationnement (m) : parking.   " ~ **interdit**" : "no parking"

statuer : to decree, to enact, to ordain, to rule

    ~ **à nouveau** : to review a judgement

    ~ **au fond** : to decide a case on its merits

    ~ **en premier ressort** : to pronounce judgement open to appeal

    ~ **sur un appel** : to dispose of an appeal

statut (m) : statute, ordinance, articles, rule, regulation, status

    ~ **juridique** : legal position

    ~ **légal** : legal status

    ~ **local** : bye-law

    ~ **personnel** : personal status

stellionat (m) : obtaining property by deception, fraud
Selling or mortgaging an item to more than one person or selling an item which one does not own.

stick (m) * : "joint", "reefer", cannabis cigarette

stimulant (m) : stimulant, "upper"

stop (m) : (1) stoplight (on motor vehicle); (2) hitch-hiking

stoppeur (m) : hitch-hiker

strict : stringent

studio (m) : bed-sitter, bed-sit, one-room flat

stupéfiants (mpl) : narcotics, dangerous drugs

      trafic en ~ : drug trafficking

      usage de ~ : use of drugs

stups (mpl) * : (1) narcotics; (2) the drugs squad (**Brigade des stupéfiants**)

subalterne : subordinate, secondary

      officier ~ : subaltern (captain or below)

subdélégation (f) : sub-delegation
*The transfer of delegated authority to a third party; for example, where authority is delegated to a **juge d'instruction** under an international letter of request, he/she may sub-delegate this authority to the investigating police officer.*

subornation (f) : subornation of perjury

      ~ des témoins : tampering with, intimidation or bribery of witnesses

      ~ d'un juré : embracery

subrogation (f) : delegation (of powers, etc.)

subsistance (f) : subsistence

substance (f) : substance, matter

      ~ nuisible : harmful substance

      ~ abortive : substances used to procure an abortion

substitut (m) : deputy (esp. deputy public prosecutor)

subtile : subtle

subtiliser : (1) to nick*, to pinch*, to steal; (2) to hide

subvenir : to supply, to provide for, to support someone

      ~ aux frais : to defray expenses

subversif : subversive

succédané (m) : substitute, ersatz

succession (f) : inheritance

sucrer : (1) to nick*, to pinch*, to steal; (2) to beat up, to assault

suicide (m) : suicide, felo de se.   **assistance au ~** : aiding a suicide

suite (f) : continuation

> **comme ~ à** : with reference to

> **donner ~ à** : to give effect to

> **par la ~** : hereafter, subsequently

suivette (f) : steward (on demonstration)

sujet (m) subject, object.   **au ~ de** : with regard to, re, in re, concerning

sujétion (f) : subjection, constraint

super (m):see **supercarburant**

supercarburant (m) : four-star petrol

supercherie (f) : fraud
Fraud usually consisting of substituting an imitation (eg. a fake painting) for the real item.

supérieur : higher, upper, senior

> **école nationale ~e de la Police** : Police Staff College

> **enseignement ~** : higher education

super-mouchard (m) : super-grass

suppléant (m) : deputy, temporary replacement, locum tenens

supposition (f) : presenting something as genuine

> **~ d'enfant** : passing off a child as belonging to another, in order to deceive

> **~ de nom** : giving a false name

> **~ de personne:** personation

> **~ de pièce** : presenting a forged document

suppression (f) : (1) suppression; (2) removal, abolition, destruction

> **~ de part** : concealment of birth

sûr : safe, sure, reliable

surdélinquance (f) : excessive criminality

surdose (f) : overdose

sûreté (f) safety, security

> **période de ~** : basic sentence
>> *Period during which a prisoner may not be released on parole or obtain a commutation of sentence.*
>
> **~ Nationale** : national police force (obsolete)
>> *The **Sûreté Nationale** was amalgamated with the Paris **Préfecture de Police** in 1968 to form the **Police Nationale***
>
> **~ publique** : public safety
>
> **~ urbaine** : town CID detachment
>> *The detective unit at a police station. Like their uniformed colleagues, its members are part of the National Police and work under the orders of the **commissaire** appointed to head the police in that town (or **arrondissement** in the case of Paris)*

surin (m) : knife, blade

surineur (m) * : knife-carrying villain

surmultiplié (m) (**vitesse ~**) : overdrive

surnom/surnombre (m) : nickname

surnuméraire (m&f) : supernumary

surprenante (f) : illegal and rigged lottery

surprendre : to surprise

> **~ quelqu'un en flagrant délit** : to catch someone red-handed, in the act

sursalaire (m) : bonus, extra pay

surseoir : to stay, to postpone, to suspend

sursis (m) : delay, stay, postponement

> **peine avec ~** : suspended sentence
>> *The suspension of sentence (imprisonment, fine, etc) may be unconditional (**sursis simple**) or subject to the performance of some form of community service (**sursis assorti de l'obligation d'accomplir un travail d'intérêt général**) or to a form of probation (**sursis avec mise à l'épreuve**).*

surveillance (f) : supervision, surveillance, superintendence, patrol

> **direction de la ~ du territoire (DST)** : police counter-espionage service
> *Branch of the Nationale Police responsible for counter-espionage*
> *work. It has no direct equivalent in Great Britain, combining some*
> *of the activities of MI5 and the police Special Branch.*

> **~ de la voie publique** : street patrol

> **~ nocturne** : night patrol

surveillant (m) **(rondier)** : (patrolling) watchman, guard

survirage (m) : oversteer

survivant (m) : survivor

susnommé (m) : aforenamed, above named

suspendre : to suspend, to adjourn

suspect (m) : suspect
A suspect is known as such during the police investigation until the first
*examination by the **juge d'instruction** when he becomes the **inculpé**.*

suspension (f) : suspension, interruption
(1) An interruption of the period after which proceedings are statute
barred. (2) Suspension from office, from duty (disciplinary measure).

> **~ de l'exécution des peines** : suspension of penalty (where there are
> serious medical, professional or social grounds)

suspicion (f) suspicion

> **être en ~** : to be suspected

> **~ légitime** : suspicion that a fair trial will not be given

syndic (m) : agent, representative, proxy

syndicat (m) : trade union, trade association
An association of persons exercising the same profession or performing
similar tasks with a view to defending their economic and professional
*interests. (See also **union**, **féderation syndicale** and **confédération***
***syndicale**).*

> **~ communal** : joint venture between local authorities
> *A voluntary economic grouping of a number of **communes** in order*
> *to meet the cost of major capital items such as electricity/water*
> *supplies, sewage, school buses, etc.*

SYDONI (système de documentation nationale informatisée) : legal data bank

système (m) : system, method, set, network.   **cravate ~** : clip-on tie

T

tabassage (m) * : "third degree", alleged ill-treatment by police

tabasser : to beat up, to assault

table (f) : table

    se mettre à ~ : to turn informer, to grass*

    ~ d'écoute : telephone tap

    ~ ronde : round table discussions

tableau (m) : board, list, table, schedule, panel

    ~ d'avancement : list of persons due for promotion

    ~ des traitements : salary scale

tac (m) * : taxi, cab

tâche (f) : task, job, work

tacot (m) * : boneshaker, old jalopy

taf (m) * : "cut", share of ill-gotten gains

talc (m) * : "snow", "coke", cocaine

tapage (m) : (1) uproar, din, clamour, commotion;   (2) scandal

    ~ nocturne : breach of the peace by night

tape–cul (m) * : (1) boneshaker, old jalopy; (2) rubbish, balderdash

    faire du ~ : to go horse-riding

taper : (1) to tap, to hit;   (2) to type

    ~ aux fafs : to ask for identity documents

    ~ le 180 km/h : to top 100 mph easily

tapin (m) : (1) prostitute, hooker;   (2) soliciting for prostitution

tapinage (m) : soliciting for the purposes of prostitution

tapineuse (f) : prostitute

tapis (m) * : seedy drinking establishment, low dive

tapissage (m) : identification of a suspect

tapisser : to identify, to recognise a person

tarde (f) : night, night-time

tartarin (m) : hunter, participant in a shoot
Derived from the name of the hero of a series of novels by Alphonse Daudet.

tateuse (f) * : skeleton key, pick-lock

tatoué (m) * : "heavy", tough, muscleman

tatouille (f) * : (1) hiding, thrashing; (2) dressing-down, reprimand

taule (f) * : nick*, clink*, jail

    grande ~ : police headquarters in a major city

taulière (f) : (1) "Madam", brothel keeper; (2) proprietress of a low class hotel or restaurant

taxe (f) : (1) fixed price (for certain foodstuffs, etc.), fixed rate of wages (2) tax (payable by the beneficiary for services rendered by the authorities)

    ~ **d'aéroport** : airport tax

    ~ **de habitation** : rates

    ~ **de séjour** : tourism tax (payable by persons staying in certain holiday resorts)

    ~ **de voirie** : road fund tax

    ~ **d'utilisation** : rates (esp. for public utilities)

    ~ **postale** : postage

    ~ **sur la valeur ajoutée (TVA)** : value added tax, VAT

taxi (m) * : (1) any mode of transport (plane, car, etc.); (2) prostitute; (3) go-between, intermediary

télécarte (f) : phonecard

télécommande (f) : remote control

télématique (f) : information technology

    fraude ~ : computer fraud

    ~ **bancaire** : videobanking

téléobjectif (m) : telephoto lens

télépéage (m) : teletoll
System which enables motorists to pay motorway tolls without stopping, by means of a smart card located behind the windscreen.

téléphone (m) : telephone.   ~ **arabe** : grapevine

télescoper : to smash up, to concertina (vehicles)

télétype (m) : teleprinter

télex (m) : telex (machine or message)

témoignage (m) : evidence (by a witness)

    faux ~ : false testimony, perjury

    recueillir des ~**s** : to gather evidence from witnesses

témoigner : to testify, to bear witness

    refus de ~ : non-attendance of duly-called witness

témoin (m) : witness
An individual who has been invited to make a statement at a hearing as to facts about which he has personal knowledge after having been duly sworn to tell the truth. Persons who are not competent to give evidence may nevertheless be heard, unsworn.

    déposer comme ~ : to depose, to give evidence

    subornation de ~ : subornation of perjury

    ~ **à charge** : witness for the prosecution

    ~ **à décharge** : witness for the defence

    ~ **défaillant** : defaulting witness

    ~ **de fait** : material witness

    ~ **direct** : direct witness

    ~ **oculaire** : eye-witness

    ~ **réticent** : reluctant witness

temps (m) (**tirer son** ~) : to serve one's sentence

tendancieuse (**question** ~) : leading question

tentative (f) : attempt
Action leading to the commission of an offence in which execution is commenced and not interrupted voluntarily.

tenue (f) : uniform, dress.   ~ **de combat** : riot gear

terminal (m) : terminal

terminé : out (end of radio transmission)

terrain (m) : land, ground

terreur (m) * : enforcer, frightener, "heavy"

territoire (m) : territory

> ~ **d'Outre Mer (TOM)** : overseas territory
> *Dependancies which do not merit being classed as a **département**. These include New Caledonia, Wallis & Futuna, St Pierre & Miquelon.*

terrorisme (m) : terrorism

terroriste (m&f) : terrorist

testament (m) : will

texte (m) : text.   ~ **législatif** : enactment

tiercé (m) : forecast (laying a bet on three horses in one race)

tierce (f) : (1) third person, third party; (2) small gang of criminals

tiers (m) : third person, third party

> ~ **-monde** : third-world

tigiste (m&f) : worker on a TIG (*travaux d'intérêt général*) scheme

timbre (m) : stamp

> **droit de** ~ : stamp duty
>
> **papier timbré** : stamped legal paper
>
> ~ **amende** : penalty stamp
> *One means of paying a fixed penalty ticket.*

tir (m) : shooting.   **champ de** ~ : firing range

tire-bouchon (m) : police road patrol charged with clearing traffic hold-ups

tirer : (1) to draw; (2) to fire (weapon); (3) to nick*, to pinch*, to steal

> ~ **au sort** : to draw lots
>
> ~ **un cheque** : to make out a cheque

tireur (m) : (1) drawer (of cheque, etc.); (2) rifleman; (3) pick-pocket

> ~ **d'élite** : marksman, sniper, sharpshooter

titre (m) : official title, status, diploma, certificate, qualification

    à bon ~ : fairly, rightly

    à ~ **de** : by way of, as a, by virtue of

    à ~ **d'office** : ex officio

    à ~ **de précaution** : just in case

    à ~ **indicatif** : as a guide, for guidance

    destruction de ~ : destruction of official documents
        It is an offence to burn or destroy in any manner any of the
        prescribed documents, registers, minutes, bill of exchange, etc.

    preuve par ~ : documentary evidence

    ~ **d'identité** : identity documents (identity card, passport, etc.)

    ~ **restaurant** : luncheon voucher

titulaire (m&f) : holder, bearer, occupant

toc * : (1) fake, sham, paste; (2) dangerously violent, psycopathic

tocasse (f) * : low-class prostitute

tôlard (m) : jail-bird, recidivist

tôle (f) : nick*, clink*, jail

tolérance (f) **de la prostitution** : living on immoral earnings

tôlerie (f) : sheet metal work, bodywork (of car)

tôlière (f) : (1) "Madam", brothel keeper; (2) proprietress of a low class hotel
tomber * : (1) to get arrested, to get nicked*; (2) to get sentenced

tombereau (m) * : "old heap", motor car

tombeur (m) * : "heavy", enforcer

tondre : (1) to shear, to mow, to clip; (2) * to "fleece", to "rook"

tonneau (m) **(faire un** ~ **)** : to roll a car (through 360°)
    This term has its origins in the "victory roll" performed by airmen.

torchon (m) **(coup de** ~ **)** : police raid

toucher : to cash (a cheque), to receive (a salary)

touilleur (m) * : shady dealer, an "Arthur Daley"

Tour (m) **(La ~ de l'Horloge)** : headquarters of the Paris CID
*This is the former **Conciergerie** prison at 36 quai des Orfèvres, Paris.*

Touring Club de France (m) : motoring organisation (similar to AA or RAC)

tourlousine (f) * : (1) blow, slap, punch, kick; (2) thrashing, good hiding

tournailler : to loiter about (not necessarily for criminal purposes)

tournante (f) : key (often where used for unlawful purposes)

tournicoter : to loiter about (not necessarily for criminal purposes)

tourniquet * (m) : court martial

Tout-Paris (m) : the Parisian smart set, French society

tout-terrain (m) : mountain bike

toxico/toxicomane (m) : drug addict

toxicomanie (f) : drug addiction

traboule (f) : labyrinth of alleyways in Lyons

trace (f) : track, imprint .   **~ de pas** : footprint

tracteur (m) : tractor

   ~ antibarricade : barricade-removing truck

   ~ routier : tractor, towing unit (of articulated vehicle)

traducteur (m) : translator .   **~ assermenté** : sworn translator

traduire : to translate, to interpret, to express

   ~ quelqu'un en justice : to sue, to prosecute, to indict, to arraign someone

trafic (m) : traffic

   ~ aérien : air transport

   ~ clandestin : black market

   ~ d'armes : arms smuggling

   ~ d'êtres humains : white slave traffic

   ~ de stupéfiants : drug traffic

   ~ frontalier : traffic across borders

   ~ routier : road transport

trafiquer : (1) to smuggle, to deal; (2) to adulterate (wine); (3) to "soup-up" a motor car

trahison (f) : treason, betrayal

train (m) **(filer le ~ à quelqu'un)** : to follow someone, to tail someone closely

trainée (f) * : loose woman, prostitute

traintrain (m) : routine.   ~ **quotidien** : the daily grind

traitement (m) : salary

     échelle des ~s : salary scale

     échelon de ~ : salary grade

     mauvais ~ : ill-usage

     retenue sur le ~ : docking of pay

trancher (une question) : to settle (a matter)

transaction (f) : composition, agreed settlement terms

transfèrement (m) : transfer of prisoner from one place to another

    ~ **cellulaire** : transfer of prisoner by police/prison van

transfrontalier : cross-border

transgresser : to transgress, to contravene, to break, to infringe (the law, etc)

transit (m) : transit
The movement of goods across a State without being cleared by customs on entry or exit.

    ~ **international routier (TIR)** : see **transport sous douane**

transitaire (f) : freight forwarder, haulage contractor

transmission (f) : radio transmission

transport (m) : transport, conveyance

   ~ **routier** : road transport

   ~ **sous douane** : conveyance of uncleared goods in sealed containers or vehicles
Tax arrangement whereby goods may be carried across a country in order to convey them to a customs warehouse or customs clearing centre within that country without having to complete the customs clearance formalities at the point of entry into the country. This system has become necessary as a result of the growth of international movements, especially by road. The TIR is one version of this.

transporter : to transport, to convey

traquer : to track down, to hunt down

travail (m) : work, labour

    accident de ~ : industrial accident

    faire un petit ~ : to go on a job, to commit burglary

    ~ à mi-temps : part-time work

    ~ d'intérêt général : community service
        Punishment which may be imposed instead of a custodial sentence,
        consisting of carrying out specified work of benefit to the
        community for a period of up to 18 months. The offender must
        agree to be so sentenced.

    ~ en équipe : team work

travaux (mpl) : work(s)

    opposition aux ~ publics : obstructing public works

    ~ d'entretien : maintenance work

    ~ forcés : hard labour (abolished in 1939)

    ~ publics : public works, civil engineering

travelo (m) * : transvestite

travesti (m) : (1) transvestite; (2) travesty

trébuchet (m) : (1) bird trap; (2) small balance for weighing gold, drugs, etc.

trempe (f) : thrashing, good hiding

tremper : to be involved, to be implicated

trésor (m) : treasure trove, found property

    ~ public : Treasury (branch of the Ministry of Finance)

tribunal (m) : court, tribunal

    gazette des tribunaux : law reports

    greffier du ~ : clerk of the court

    salle du ~ : courtroom

    ~ aux armées : court martial (outside France)

~ **correctionnel** : criminal court
    *A court of grande instance, it hears cases involving misdemeanours
    and appeals from the magistrates' courts. Normally presided over
    by three judges but a solitary judge may hear minor cases.*

~ **de grande instance** : = Crown court/High court
    *Second-tier court, dealing with both criminal and civil cases which
    are too serious for hearing in the tribunaux d'instance. In the
    Chambre correctionnelle (criminal court) the court tries délits
    (misdemeanours).*

~ **de police** : magistrates court, police court
    *A tribunal d'instance, this is the lowest level of criminal court and
    deals with contraventions (summary offences).*

~ **d'exception** : special court

~ **d'instance** : district court
    *The lowest level of court, hearing both simple civil cases (= County
    Court) and summary offences under the criminal and administrative
    law (= magistrates' court). When dealing with criminal matters it is
    sometimes referred to as the tribunal de police.*

~ **permanent des forces armées** : court martial (for offences committed in
    peacetime; in use up until 1982)

~ **pour enfants** : juvenile court

~ **répressif** : criminal court (as opposed to civil court)

~ **territorial des forces armées** : court martial
    *Court set up in time of war to judge offences committed by
    servicemen or enemy agents and offences against state security.*

tricard (m) * : ex-prisoner who is subject to an **interdiction de séjour**

tricoche (f) : enquiries carried out by policemen on behalf of private individuals
    *Often carried out during working hours, such misuse of police authority
    is naturally unlawful.*

tricocheur (m) : policeman who undertakes private jobs, using his official status

tricorps (m) : three-box bodied car (as opposed to a two-box hatchback)

trictrac (m) * : "fiddle", shady deal

trifouiller : to rummage, to search

trimardeur (m) : tramp, vagrant, nomadic worker

trimardeuse (f) * : prostitute

tripatouillage (m) : (1) tampering, unwarranted intervention; (2) fiddling,
    cooking the books

tripes (fpl) * : entrails, guts

    réaction des ~ : gut-feeling, knee-jerk reaction

tripot (m) : (1) gambling den; (2) bawdy house

tripotage (m) **des comptes** : cooking the books, tampering with the records

tripoter : to interfere with sexually, to indulge in gross indecency

triquard (m) : ex-prisoner who is subject to an **interdiction de séjour**

trique (f) * : (1) cosh, truncheon; (2) slang for **interdiction de séjour**

trombinoscope (m) : mug-shot

tromperie (f) : deception, fraud, deceit, cheating (relating to goods)

trottoir (m) : pavement, sidewalk

    faire le ~ : to solicit for prostitution, to walk the streets

trou (m) * : clink*, nick*, prison

trouble (m) : confusion, disorder, perturbation, breach of the peace

troubler : to disturb

trouvés (**objets ~**) : found property

truand (m) : criminal, crook.   **~-indic** : crook informer

truc (m) : gimmick, trick

truquer des comptes : to doctor accounts

tuer : to kill

tueur à gages (m) : hired killer, hit man

turpitude (f) : turpitude, depravity, baseness

tutelle (f) : guardianship, tutelage

    ~ pénale : ticket of leave
        This temporary (up to 10 years) restriction may be imposed on habitual criminals on the completion of their sentence, performed either in a special probation hostel or externally under the supervision of a probation officer.

tuyeau (m) : tip, clue

    ~ d'échappement : exhaust pipe

U

unanime : unanimous

uniforme (f) : uniform.   **port illégal d'~** : unlawful wearing of a uniform

union (f) : association of trades unions
*A local association of several **syndicats** which cover different trades.*

unité (f) : unit, formation

   ~ aérienne : air unit (Gendarmerie)

   ~ cynophile : dog section

   ~ d'autoroute : motorway patrol unit

   ~ de Coordination de la Lutte anti-terroriste : counter-terrorism unit

   ~ de police de la route : road traffic patrol unit

   ~ de recherche, assistance, intervention et dissuasion : unit formed to mount counter-terrorist operations

   ~ de recherches judiciaires : criminal investigation unit (Gendarmerie)

   ~ de roulement : relief
     A section of foot patrol officers, usually working shifts.

   ~ d'intervention : immediate response unit, special patrol group

   ~ fluviale : river patrol unit

   ~ montée : mounted branch

   ~ motocycliste : motor cycle section

   ~ spécialisée de montagne : alpine unit, mountain rescue unit

   ~ de surveillance et de recherches : crime investigation unit

   ~ territoriale : operational section, territorial division

université (f) : university

urbain : urban

   corps ~ : uniformed town police
     *A section of the National Police formed of those officers who have been posted to a particular town to perform normal patrol duties there. With the **sûreté urbaine**, it forms the **police urbaine**.*

urbanisme (m) : town planning

urgence (f) : emergency, urgency

> **mesures d'~** : emergency measures

usage (m) : (1) custom and practice;   (2) use, employment

> **article d'~ courant** : item of everyday use

> **à ~ personnel** : for personal use

> **~ de faux** : production of a forged instrument

> **~ indu** : illicit practice

> **~s locaux** : local customs

usure (f) : (1) usury, imposition of excessive interest; (2) wear and tear
Usury is a misdemeanour where the rate of interest exceeds that specified by law.

usurier (m) : loan shark

usurpation (f) **(d'identité, etc.)** : usurpation (of identity, etc.)

utile : useful, relevant

utilitaire (véhicule ~) : commercial vehicle

utilité (f) : utility, useful purpose, usefulness

> **expropriation pour cause d'~ publique** : expropriation for a public purpose, compulsory purchase

> **reconnaissance d'~ publique** : official recognition of an institution as serving the public interest

V

vacance (f) : vacancy.   ~ **accidentelle** : casual vacancy

vacances (fpl) : holidays, leave

vacations (fpl) : (1) lawyers' fees; (2) court vacation, recess

vache (f) * : copper, policeman, fuzz*
   *The term originated in German occupied Alsace-Lorraine after the 1870 war
   where unrest was focussed on the German military police, the **Wache**.*

vagabond (m) : vagabond, tramp
   *Persons of no fixed abode or means of support, having no profession or
   job who may, on these grounds alone, be punished by the courts or, with
   their consent, taken into care by the social services.*

vaguer : to frisk, to rifle through someone's pockets

vagabondage (m) : vagrancy.   ~ **spécial** : living on immoral earnings

valise (f) **diplomatique** : diplomatic bag

vandale (m&f) : vandal, one who commits criminal damage

vandalisme (m) : vandalism, criminal damage

vaporisateur (m) * : machine gun

varloper : to drift about casually gathering information

vedette (f) : motor boat, power boat, launch

véhicule (m) : vehicle

   ~ **d'intervention** : rapid response vehicle, emergency car

   ~ **tous usages** : general purpose vehicle

veilleur (m) **de nuit** : nightwatchman

vélo (m) bicycle.   ~ **tout-terrain** : mountain bike

vélomoteur (m) : lightweight motorcycle (50 to 125 cc)

vendange (f) * : haul, loot, proceeds of crime

vendre : to "shop" someone, to inform on someone

vendu (m) * : double-crosser, traitor to the cause

vent (m) : wind

vente (f) : sale

    salle de ~ : saleroom, auction room

    ~ à la boule de neige : snowball selling
        The offering of goods for sale to the public by encouraging potential buyers to believe that the goods will be obtained free or at an advantageous price and subjecting the sale to the placing of vouchers or coupons with third parties or the obtaining of subscriptions or membership fees. This practice is contrary to the criminal law.

    ~ à perte : sale at less than cost price
        The selling of goods at a price less than the cost price, reduced by discounts on invoices, increased by VAT and, where appropriate, the cost of transport. Apart from certain exceptions, this practice is a criminal offence.

    ~ au déballage : clearance sale, sale by deception, sale of "distressed" goods
        The sale of new goods which appear to be used or otherwise exceptional, preceded or accompanied by advertising.

    ~ au détail : retail trade

    ~ aux enchères : auction sale

    ~ en gros : wholesale trade

    ~ forcée : sale by delivering unsolicited goods on sale or return

    ~ par correspondance : sale by mail order

    ~ publique : sale by public auction

ventouse (f) * : motor car which appears to have been abandoned

verbalisateur (m) : official who took down particulars (of motoring offence, etc.)

verbalisation (f) : taking down offender's details

verbaliser : to report (with a view to prosecution)

verdict (m) : verdict, finding of the jury

    ~ d'acquittement : verdict of not guilty

    ~ de culpabilité : guilty verdict

verdine (f) : (1) snag, hitch occurring during an enquiry; (2) gypsy caravan (the type of vehicle which would not pass any police inspection; (3) cock-up*, mix-up

véreux : shady, dishonest, untrustworthy

verge (f) : baton (symbol of authority)

vérification (f) : verification, checking, inspection

~ **des comptes** : auditing of accounts

~ **d'identité** : personal identification
Enquiry carried out by an **officier de police judiciaire** *as to the identity of person who is unable or unwilling to provide proof of his identify when he is checked. It involves the detention of the person concerned at the scene of the check or at a police station.*

vérifier : to check, to verify

vérité (f) : truth

verrou (m) : bolt, bar.   **sous les ~s** : in safe custody, locked up

versement (m) : payment, remittance

~ **global** : lump sum

~ **partiel** : instalment

verser : to pay, to deposit.   ~ **une caution** : to put down a deposit

verso (m) : back, reverse (of a sheet), overleaf

verte (f) : risqué story, dirty joke

vertu (f) : (1) courage, valour; (2) virtue; (3) quality, property (of something)

en ~ **de** : by virtue of, pursuant to, under, whereby

vétéiste (m&f) : mountain bike rider

véto (m) : veterinary surgeon

veuf (m) : widower

veuve (f): widow

vévé (f) : Volkswagen car, VW

viande (f) * :   carcass, human body

marchand de ~ : white-slaver, procurer of prostitutes

~ **froide** : "stiff", corpse

viander : to get oneself killed (in an accident, etc.)

vice (m) : (1) vice, depravity, corruption; (2) fault, defect, blemish

~ **caché** : latent defect

~ **de forme** : vice of form, faulty drafting

vicelard (m) : "dirty old man", salacious character

victime (f) : victim, casualty

videur (m) : "bouncer", doorman

vie (f) : life, living

    assurance sur la ~ : life assurance

    à ~ : for life

    coût de la ~ : cost of living

    gagner sa ~ : to earn one's living

    niveau de ~ : standard of living

    qualité de ~ : quality of life

    ~ **privée** : personal privacy

vieillard (m) : old person

vieillesse (f) : old age

    assurance ~ : old age insurance

    pension ~ : old age pension

vif (m) : alive, living person

vigie (f) : look-out

vignette (f) : licence, permit, certificate

    ~ **automobile** : vehicle excise licence
    A document affixed to the inside of a vehicle's windscreen, similar to a vehicle excise licence and serving a similar purpose.

    ~ **d'assurance** : insurance certificate

vigueur (f) : vigour, strength

    entrer en ~ : to come into force, into effect, into operation

    en ~ : in force (law, regulation, etc)

    mettre en ~ : to put into effect

    mettre une loi en ~ : to enforce a law

villa (f) : detached house

ville (f) : town.   **~ nouvelle** : new town

villégiature (f) : holiday resort.   **être en ~** : to be in prison

vingt-deux! : "look out!", "run for it!", "scram!"

viol (m) : rape
> *Act of sexual penetration of any kind committed against another person,*
> *by threats, force or surprise. The vulnerability of the victim (pregnancy,*
> *illness, infirmity, mental deficiency, etc.) or where the victim is under 15*
> *years of age, the use of weapons, the relationship of the offender to the*
> *victim, etc. are all aggravating circumstances. Fellato will constitute rape*
> *where there is penetration against the will of the victim.*

   ~ collectif : gang rape

violation (f) : violation, breach, trespass

   ~ de domicile : criminal trespass
   > *Misdemeanour committed by an administrative or judicial official, a*
   > *police officer or an officer or representative of the military or*
   > *gendarmerie who enters the home of another against his will. The*
   > *offence may also be committed by a private individual but only if*
   > *entry is effected by subterfuge, threats, violence or force.*

   ~ de la loi : breach of the law

   ~ de la paix publique : breach of the peace

   ~ de propriété : trespass (on land)

violence (f) : violence, force or intimidation, duress

   ~ et voies de fait : battery
   > *An assault not necessarily amounting to a blow; eg. pushing*
   > *someone, spitting in their face, knocking them over.*

violer : to violate, to transgress, to rape

violeur (m) : rapist, violator

violon (m) * : police cells

virer : to make a U-turn

viron (m) : short trip

vis (f) **(serrer la ~ à quelqu'un)** : to put the screws on someone, to subject
   someone to considerable pressure

visa (m) : authentication by signature or initials, endorsement

visée (f) : sight (of rifle, etc.)

   lunette de ~ : telescopic sight

~ **laser** : laser sight

~ **télescopique** : telescopic sight

visite (f) : visit

~ **de personnes** : body search

~ **des lieux** : see **descente sur les lieux**

~ **domiciliaire** : search of house

~ **médicale** : medical examination

vitesse (f) : speed.   **excès de** ~ : exceeding the speed limit

vitriol (m) : (1) vitriol, sulphuric acid; (2) strong liquor (usually moonshine)

vivre : to live

apprendre à ~ **à quelqu'un** : to teach someone a lesson, to put someone in his place

~ **à la colle** : to cohabit

voie (f) : highway, track, way

~ **administrative, hiérarchique** : official channels

~ **de recours** : avenue of appeal

~ **d'exécution** : means of execution (of decrees, judgements, etc.)

~ **en rocade** : inter-suburban route

~ **ferroviaire** : railway track

~ **pénale** : prosecution

~ **privée** : private road

~ **publique** : public highway

~s **de fait** : act of violence, assault and battery

~s **et moyens** : ways and means

voirie (f) : the highways

police de la ~ : traffic police, highway patrol

service de la ~ : highways, roads department

voiture (f) : car, vehicle, carriage

    être rangé des ~s : to have retired from a life of crime, to have gone straight

    ~ cellulaire : police van, "Black Maria"

    ~ décapotable : convertible

    ~ de sport : sports car, roadster

    ~ de sport GT : GT car

    ~ de tourisme : saloon car

    ~ pie : "black and white" car, Panda car, patrol car

voiturier (m) : carter, carrier.   **~ public** : common carrier

voix (f) : voice, vote

vol (m) : theft

    receleur d'un ~ : receiver, fence

    ~ aggravé : aggravated theft

    ~ à l'américaine : confidence trick

    ~ à l'arraché : handbag snatching, mugging

    ~ à la roulotte : theft from motor vehicle

    ~ à la tâche : theft from the person
        Theft committed by purposely spilling food or drink over a diner's clothes and then stealing from him in the ensuing confusion.

    ~ à la tire : pick-pocketing

    ~ à l'entôlage : "rolling" a client, robbery by a prostitute

    ~ à l'étalage : shoplifting

    ~ à la fourchette : theft from the person
        Picking pockets by using two fingers to extract the item

    ~ à main armée : armed robbery

    ~ avec effraction : burglary

    ~ avec violence : robbery

    ~ dans une voiture : theft from a vehicle

    ~ de grand chemin : highway robbery

~ **de l'encerclement** : theft by mobbing
Usually committed by gangs of children who seize hold of the victim and, in the process, steal his or her wallet or handbag, etc.

~ **de l'imperméable, du manteau** : pickpocketing, using a coat to conceal the action

~ **d'oeuvres et objets d'art** : art theft

~ **d'une voiture** : theft of a car, auto theft

~ **d'usage** : unauthorised use of an item (eg. taking and driving away a motor vehicle)

~ **par domestique** : larceny servant

~ **qualifié** : aggravated theft

~ **salarié** : embezzlement, larceny servant

~ **simple** : minor theft, petty larceny

volaille (f) * : (1) police, fuzz*; (2) prostitute

volant (m) : (1) steering wheel; (2) leaf (of a cheque book, etc)

branche du ~ : steering wheel spoke

Volante (la Brigade ~ **)** : the Flying Squad

voler : to steal, to rob

volet (m) : shutter

voleur (m) : thief

volière (f) : brothel, "cat-house"

volontaire (m) : volunteer

~ **de l'aide technique** : person performing voluntary aid overseas (as alternative to military service)

~ **du service national en entreprise** : person employed by a commercial firm as an alternative to military service

volontairement : wilfully, voluntarily

volonté (f) : will, intention

voter : to vote
A right in France and the UK but an obligation in some countries such as Belgium and Luxembourg where failure to vote without good reason is punishable by a fine.

~ **par procuration** : to vote by proxy
> *This possibility is open to French citizens who are absent from the area in which they are registered for electoral purposes for reasons of work (armed forces, ex patriates,) or live in another area (including French citizens abroad), or who are unable to attend the polling station for reasons of ill-health, etc. Proxy authorisations are obtained from a judge, a police or gendarmerie station or the French Consulate in other countries. Postal votes were possible until 1975 but have now been discontinued because of the abuses and fraud to which this system was open.*

voyage (m) : journey, voyage, travel

agence de ~ : travel agency

chèque de ~ : traveller's cheque

étre en ~ : to be in prison

frais de ~ : travelling expenses

gens de ~ : circus folk

service des ~**s officiels** : VIP transport and security service
> *Department of the National Police responsible for arranging the transport and safety of important persons.*

voyeur (m) : peeping tom, voyeur, salacious ogler

voyou (m) : thug, lout, yob*

vrai : true, veritable

pour de ~ : "for real", in earnest, for good, once and for all

un ~ **de** ~ : tough nut, hard man

vrille (f) * : dyke*, lesbian

vu : with reference to

vu (m) (**d'un arrêt**) : the preamble (to a decree)

vu que : whereas

vurdon (f) : gypsy caravan (the type of vehicle which would not pass any police inspection)

Z

zigouiller : to bump off, to kill

zinc (m) : bar (in a café)
So called because most bar tops used to be covered with a sheet of zinc.

zone (f) : region, area, zone, district

    la ~ * : the slums

   ~ bleue : restricted parking zone

   ~ d'aménagement concerté : mixed (public/private) housing development

   ~ d'aménagement différé : area for future development

   ~ industrielle : industrial estate, business park

   ~ piétonnière : pedestrian precinct

SIGLES

A.P.J.	Agent de Police Judiciaire
A.P.R.	Agent Privé de Recherches
A.P.S.	Autorisation Provisoire de Séjour
A.R.	Ambulance de Réanimation
B.A.C.	Brigade Anti-Criminalité
B.A.J.	Bureau d'Aide Judiciaire
B.A.S.	Bureau d'Aide Sociale
B.C.F.	Bureau des Chemins de Fer
B.C.N.	Bureau Central National (Interpol)
B.C.R.	Bureau Central de Recherches (Belgium)
B.E.M.S.G.	Brevet d'Etudes Militaires Supérieures de la Gendarmerie
B.I.J.	Bulletin d'Information Judiciaire
B.Mo.	Brigade Motorisée
B.P.A.	Bureau de la Police Aeronautique
B.R.	Brigade des Recherches
B.S.P.P.	Brigade des Sapeurs Pompiers
B.T.	Brigade Territoriale
B.T.C.	Bureau du Travail Clandestin
B.T.G.	Brevet Technique de la Gendarmerie
B.T.P.	Bâtiment et Travaux Publics
C.A.G.	Certificat d'Aptitude à la Gendarmerie
C.A.P.	Certificat d'Aptitude Professionnelle
C.A.P.U.	Centre d'Application des Personnels en Uniforme
C.C.P.	Compte Courant Postal
C.D.P.	Centre de Documentation et de Pédagogie
C.D.S.P.	Corps Départemental de Sapeurs Pompiers
C.E.D.I.J.	Centre d'Informatique Juridique
C.E.G.E.T.I.	Centre Electronique de Gestion et de Traitement de l'information
C.E.J.	Certificat d'Etudes Judiciaires
CELEX	Computerised law data bank (European Commission)
C.E.R.P.N.	Centre d'Etudes et de Recherche de la Police Nationale
C.E.S.G.	Centre d'Enseignement Supérieur de la Gendarmerie
C.F.M.C.	Centre de Formation des Maîtres de Chien
C.F.O.R.	Centre de Formation des Opérateurs Radiotélégraphistes
C.F.P.	Centre de Formation de la Police
C.F.P.A.	Centre de Formation Professionnelle d'Avocats
C.F.T.T.	Centre de Formation des Techniciens des Transmissions
C.G.I.	Code Général des Impôts
C.I.G.A.	Centre d'Instruction des Gendarmes Auxiliaires
C.I.J.	Cour Internationale de Justice
C.I.P.A.	Centre d'Information et de Prévention de l'Automobile
C.M.P.N.	Club Motocycliste de la Police Nationale
C.N.E.P.S.	Centre National d'Education Physique et Sportive
C.N.I.S.A.G.	Centre National d'Instruction en Ski et à l'Alpinisme de la Gendarmerie
C.N.P.C.E.	Centre National de Préparation aux Concours et Examens
C.N.S.	Centre National des Sports
C.N.T.P.	Centre National de Tir de la Police
C.O.D.I.S	Centre Opérationnel de la Direction de la Sécurité Civile
C.O.S.	Commandant des Opérations de Secours
C.P.	Code Pénal
C.P.P.	Code de Procédure Pénale
C.R.A.	Centre de Rétention Administrative

C.R.D.	Capsule Représentative des Droits
CRIDON	Centres de Recherche, d'Information et de Documentation Notariale
C.R.S.	Compagnie Républicaine de Sécurité
C.R.S.	Centre de Recrutement at de Sélection des Forces Armées (Belgium)
C.S.G.	Cotisation Sociale Généralisée
C.T.G.N.	Centre Technique de la Gendarmerie Nationale
C.T.R.	Conseillers Techniques Régionaux (sport/firearms instruction)
D.A.T.	Diplôme d'Aptitude Technique
D.C.	Direction Centrale
D.C.P.T.	Direction Centrale de la Police Territoriale
D.C.S.P.	Direction Centrale de la Sécurité Publique
D.D.P.U.	Direction Départemental des Police Urbaines
D.D.S.I.S.	Direction Départemental des Services d'Incendie et de Secours
D.E.A.	Diplôme d'Etudes Approfondies
D.E.S.	Diplôme d'Etudes Supérieures
D.E.S.G.	Diplôme d'Etudes Supérieures de la Gendarmerie
D.E.S.S.	Diplôme d'Etudes Supérieures Spécialisés
D.E.U.G.	Diplôme d'Etudes Universitaires Générales
D.G.G.N.	Direction Générale de la Gendarmerie Nationale
D.G.P.N.	Direction Générale de la Police Nationale
D.L.	Décret-loi
D.M.	Décision Ministérielle
D.M.D.	Délégué Militaire Départemental
D.O.M.	Département d'Outre-Mer
D.O.T.	Défense Opérationnelle du Territoire
D.P.M.	Direction de la Population et des Migrations
D.Q.S.G.	Diplôme de Qualification Supérieure de la Gendarmerie
D.R.R.F.	Délégation Régionale au Recrutement et à la Formation
D.S.T.	Direction de la Surveillance du Territoire
E.G.M.	Escadron de Gendarmerie Mobile
E.M.	Etat-Major
E.N.A.	Ecole Nationale d'Administration
E.N.A.D.E.P.	Ecole Nationale de Droit et de Procédure
E.N.A.P.	Ecole Nationale d'Administration Pénétentiaire
E.N.D.	Ecole Nationale des Douanes
E.N.M.	Ecole Nationale de la Magistrature
E.N.P.	Ecole Nationale de Police
E.N.S.P.	Ecole Nationale Supérieure de Police
E.O.G.N.	Ecole des Officiers de la Gendarmerie Nationale
E.S.I.P.	Ecole Supérieure des Inspecteurs de Police
E.S.O.G.	Ecole des Sous-officiers de Gendarmerie
E.S.O.P.	Ecole Supérieure des Officiers de Paix
F.F.A.	Forces Françaises en Allemagne
F.M.U.	Formation Motocycliste Urbaine
F.P.R.	Fichier des Personnes Recherchées
F.R.C.	Fichier des Recherches Criminelles
F.S.P.F.	Fédération Sportive de la Police Française
F.V.V.	Fichier de Véhicules Volés
G.A.	Gendarme Auxiliare
G.D.	Gendarmerie Départementale
G.B.G.M.	Groupement Blindé de Gendarmerie Mobile
G.I.G.N.	Groupement d'Intervention de la Gendarmerie Nationale
G.I.P.N.	Groupement d'Intervention de la Police Nationale
G.I.T.	Groupement d'Instruction des Télécommunications
G.M.	Gendarmerie Mobile

G.N.	Gendarmerie Nationale
G.R.	(Chemin de) Grande Randonée
G.R.B.	Groupe de Répression de Banditisme
G.R.V.P.	Groupe de Répression de la Voie Publique
G.S.I.G.N.	Groupement de Sécurité et d'Intervention de la Gendarmerie Nationale
H.L.M.	Habitation à Loyer Modéré
I.G.A.M.E.	Inspecteur Général de l'Administration en Mission Extraordinaire
I.G.P.N.	Inspection Générale de la Police Nationale
I.G.S.	Inspection Générale des Services
I.H.E.S.I.	Institut des Hautes Etudes de la Sécurité Intérieure
I.M.L.	Institut Médico-Légal
I.N.A.	Individu Non-admis
I.N.C.A.	Institut National des Cadres Administratifs
I.N.F.P.N.	Institut National de Formation de la Police Nationale
I.N.S.E.E.	Institut National de la Statistique et des Etudes Economiques
I.R.	Impôt sur le Revenu
I.R.A.	Institut Régional d'Administration
J.A.P.	Juge de l'Application des Peines
J.I.	Juge d'Instruction
J.O.	Journal Officiel
JURINPI	Computerised law data bank
JURIS-DATA	Computerised law data bank
LEXIS	Computerised law data bank
L.P.C.	Laboratoire Photographique Central
M.d.L.C.	Maréchal de Logis-chef
M.L.F.	Mouvement de Libération de la Femme (Women's Lib.)
M.N.S.	Maître-Nageur-Sauveteur
M.O.	Maintien d'Ordre
M.O.	Modus Operandi
O.C.R.G.D.F.	Office Central de Répression de la Grande Délinquance Financière
O.C.R.T.I.S.	Office Central pour la Répression du Trafic Illicite des Stupéfiants
O.M.I.	Office des Migrations Internationales
O.M.O.	Observation en Milieu Ouvert
O.N.I.	Office National d'Immigration
O.N.L.	Ordonnance de Non-Lieu
O.P.	Ouvrier Professionnel
O.P.J.	Officier de Police Judiciaire
O.R.S.E.C.	Organisation des Secours
O.S.	Ouvrier Spécialisé
O.T.A.N	N.A.T.O.
P.A.F.	Police de l'Air et des Frontières
P.C.	Poste de Commandement
P.D.G.	Président Directeur Général
P.G.H.M.	Peloton de Gendarmerie de Haute Montagne
P.G.S.M.	Peloton de Gendarmerie de Surveillance en Montagne
P.I.A.F.	Parcmètre Individuel à Fente
P.J.	Police Judiciaire
P.N.	Police Nationale
P.M.E.	Petites & Moyennes Entreprises
P. et T.	Postes et Télécommunications
P.S.	Police Secours
P.S.I.G.	Peloton de Surveillance et d'Intervention de la Gendarmerie
P.U.	Police Urbaine
P.V.	Procès Verbal

P.V.D.	Pays en Voie de Développement
R.A.I.D.	Service de Recherche, Assistance, Intervention et de Dissuasion
R.A.T.P.	Régie Autonome des Transports Parisiens
R.D.	Route Départementale
R.D.A.	République Démocratique Allemande (G.D.R.)
R.E.R.	Réseau Express Régional
R.F.A.	République Fédérale Allemande (F.G.R.)
R.G.	Renseignements Généraux
R.N.I.S.	Réseau Numérique à Intégration des Services
R.U.B.I.S.	(Data transmission network)
S.A.	Société Anonyme
S.A.M.U.	Service d'Aide Médicale Urgente
S.A.M.U.	Service d'Assistance Médicale d'Urgence
S.A.P.H.I.R.	(Data transmission network)
S.A.R.L.	Société à Responsabilité Limitée
S.A.S.	Set Agression Sexuelle
S.A.T.I.	Service Archives et Traitement de l'Information
S.C.	Service Central
S.C.A.	Service Central Automobile
S.C.E.D.	Service Central d'Etude de la Délinquance
S.C.P.A.F.	Service Central de la Police de l'Air et des Frontiéres
S.C.P.U.	Service Central de la Police Urbaine
S.C.R.G.	Service Central des Renseignements Généraux
S.C.T.I.P.	Service de Cooperation Technique Internationale de Police
S.D.C.T.	Sous-Direction de la Circulation Transfrontière
S.D.E.C.E.	Service de Documentation Extérieure et de Contre-Espionnage
S.D.F.	Sans Domicile Fixe
S.F.P.M.	Stage de formation des personnels motocyclistes
S.G.A.P.	Secrétariat Général pour l'Administration de la Police
S.M.I.G.	Salaire Minimum Interprofessionnel garanti
S.M.U.R.	Service Mobile d'Urgence et de Réanimation
S.N.C.F.	Société Nationale des Chemins de Fer Français
S.O.S.	Section Opérationnelle et Spécialisée
S.R.P.J.	Service Régionale de Police Judiciaire
S.T.I.	Service des Transmissions du Ministère de l'Intérieur
S.T.I.C.	Système de Traitement de l'Information Criminelle
S.Y.D.O.N.I.	Système de Documentation Notariale Informatique
T.C.F.	Touring Club de France
T.G.I.	Tribunal de Grande Instance
T.I.R.	Transit International Routier
T.O.M.	Territoire d'Outre-Mer
T.T.	Immatriculation des Véhicules en Transit Temporaire
U.C.L.A.T.	Unité de Coordination de la Lutte Anti-Terroriste
U.R.J.	Unité de Recherche Judiciaire (Gendarmerie)
U.R.S.S.	(U.S.S.R.)
V.A.T.	Violence, Attentats et le Terrorisme
V.L.C.	Véhicule Léger de Commandement
V.P.C.	Véhicule - Poste de Commandement
V.S.A.B.	Véhicule de Secours aux Asphyxiés et aux Blessés
V.T.T.	Vélo Tout-Terrain
V.T.U.	Véhicule Tous Usages